POLICE TRAUMA

POLICE TRAUMA

Psychological Aftermath of Civilian Combat

Edited by

JOHN M. VIOLANTI, Ph.D.

Department of Criminal Justice
Rochester Institute of Technology
Rochester, New York
Department of Social and Preventive Medicine
School of Medicine and Biomedical Sciences
State University of New York at Buffalo

and

DOUGLAS PATON, Ph.D., C. PSYCHOL.

School of Psychology
Massey University
Palmerston North
New Zealand

CHARLES C THOMAS • PUBLISHER, LTD.
Springfield • Illinois • U.S.A.

Published and Distributed Throughout the World by

CHARLES C THOMAS • PUBLISHER, LTD.
2600 South First Street
Springfield, Illinois 62794-9265

© *1999 by* CHARLES C THOMAS • PUBLISHER, LTD.

ISBN 0-398-06954-9 (cloth)
ISBN 0-398-06955-7 (paper)

Library of Congress Catalog Card Number: 99-17948

With THOMAS BOOKS *careful attention is given to all details of manufacturing
and design. It is the Publisher's desire to present books that are satisfactory as to their
physical qualities and artistic possibilities and appropriate for their particular use.*
THOMAS BOOKS *will be true to those laws of quality that assure a good name
and good will.*

Printed in the United States of America
SM-R-3

Library of Congress Cataloging in Publication Data

Police trauma : psychological aftermath of civilian combat / edited by
   John M. Violanti and Douglas Paton.
      p.   cm.
   Includes bibliographical references and index.
   ISBN 0-398-06954-9 (cloth). -- ISBN 0-398-06955-7 (pbk.)
   1. Police--Assaults against--United States. 2. Police psychology--United
States. 3. Violent crimes--United States. 4. Police--community relations-
-United States. I. Violanti, John M. II. Paton, Douglas.
HV8143.P638   1999
364.15'0883632--dc21   99-17948
                                                    CIP

CONTRIBUTORS

Cedric Alexander, Psy.D

Dr. Alexander is with the Department of Psychiatry at the University of Rochester, NY Medical Center. A clinical member of the American Association for Marriage and Family Therapy, Dr. Alexander specializes in family therapy and behavioral medicine, focusing on the utilization of the biopsychosocial model in health care systems in his practice and teaching of medical residents. He also facilitates male groups for recovery and addiction psychiatry. As a 12-year veteran of the Metro-Dade County, Florida Police Department, he has presented lectures on police trauma, stress, and burnout.

Ingrid. V.E. Carlier, Psy.D, Ph.D.

Dr Ingrid V.E. Carlier is a clinical and social psychologist. Since 1991 she has headed the Psychotrauma Section, Department of Psychiatry, Academic Medical Center of the University of Amsterdam. She leads the diagnostics and treatment of traumatized clients, and the research on prevention and treatment of posttraumatic stress disorders.

Yael Danieli, Ph.D.

Yael Danieli is a clinical psychologist in private practice in New York City; traumatologist, victimologist; Cofounder and Director, Group Project for Holocaust Survivors and their Children; Cofounder, past-President and United Nations Representative of the International Society for Traumatic Stress Studies, former UN Representative, World Federation for Mental Health. Integrates treatment, care, worldwide study, extensive publishing, teaching/training, expert consulting, and advocacy for the rights of victims/survivors of crime and abuse of power. Editor, "International Responses to Traumatic Stress. . . " and The Universal Declaration of Human Rights: Fifty Years and Beyond" (both published for and on behalf of the United Nations), and "International Handbook of Multigenerational Legacies of Trauma".

Christine Dunning, Ph.D.

Chris Dunning is a Professor and Chair of the Department of Governmental Affairs at the University of Wisconsin-Milwaukee. She received her Ph.D. in Criminal Justice/Social Science from Michigan State University with a joint major in Public Administration and Organizational Sociology. In addition, she attended Marquette University Law School. Dr. Dunning formerly served as Associate Director-Police at the Des Moines, Iowa Criminal Justice Center and as Director of In-Service Police Training for south-eastern Wisconsin Police Academy located at Milwaukee Area Technical College. She has published extensively on police stress and trauma, disaster stress management, and in numerous areas of police administration. A three term Board Member and former Vice-President of the International Society for Traumatic Stress Studies, she has consulted with officials responsible for mitigation in a large number of catastrophic events internationally.

Liisa Eränen, Ph.D. Cand.

Liisa Eränen is a social psychologist. She is a founding board member of European Society for Traumatic Stress Studies and has published several articles and book chapters on trauma and disaster psychology. Since 1985, she has worked as a researcher for the Ministry of Interior and as a researcher and assistant professor at University of Helsinki, Department of Social Psychology where she created a new research tradition through her empirical research studies in trauma psychology. With Clay Foreman, and in cooperation with the Finnish Ministry of Interior, she initiated and supervised the research project on UN civilian police duty. Recently, she was appointed to be the (first female) Head of Social Services in the Finnish Navy.

Charles Figley, Ph.D.

Charles Figley is a psychologist, traumatologist, and professor in the Florida State University School of Social Work and Directs the FSU Traumatology Institute. The Institute sponsors the Green Cross Project which hires police officers on their off time to provide assistance to traumatized people. He has lectured at the FBI Academy and contributed to their publications on trauma recovery and stress management. He is founder of the International Society for Traumatic Stress Studies and winner of its 1994 Pioneer Award. He is founding editor of three refereed, scholarly journals and three professional book series.

Ross Flett, Ph.D.

Ross Flett is a Senior Lecturer in Psychology at Massey University where he has been located since 1990. Prior to that he was a Lecturer in Psychology at Otago University, a Research Officer in the Alcohol Research Unit at Auckland Medical school, and a Research Officer in the Department of Behavioral Science at Otago University Medical school. His research interests and activity span a number of areas including: occupational stress in a range of contexts (human service providers, police, rural/farming communities), predictors of health service utilization in New Zealand Vietnam veterans, and the experience of trauma. His teaching interests are mainly in the area of research methods at undergraduate and graduate level.

Rhona Flin, Ph.D.

Professor Rhona Flin is a Chartered Psychologist specializing in the application of psychology to safety and emergency management. She is Professor of Applied

Psychology at Aberdeen University, where she leads a team of psychologists working with the energy industry, civil aviation and the emergency services. They are currently working on projects funded by the HSE, the nuclear industry, the offshore oil industry, onshore power generation and an EC study on pilots' nontechnical skills. She is a Visiting Fellow at the UK Fire Service College, has been involved with the ACPO MODACE course at the Police Staff College, Bramshill, and lectures on the Inspectors' Course at the Scottish Police College. Her most recent books are *Sitting in the Hot Seat* (Wiley, 1996) and *Decision Making Under Stress* (coedited, Avebury, 1997).

Clay Foreman, M.A.

Clay Foreman is a clinical psychologist and an Instructor at Napa College. As a trauma counselor and family therapist, he has extensive experience with police and emergency workers, and their families. He was an early member of the International Society for Traumatic Stress Studies and former Vice President of the International Association of Trauma Counselors. He has extensive experience of working with police from different countries and a thorough understanding of typical police working conditions in various countries. During his stay in UNPROFOR he conducted the on-duty interviews of the participants in the UN civilian police and met and researched the work of CIVPOL with officers from 16 countries.

Merle Friedman, Ph.D.

Merle Friedman is at the Department of Psychology, University of the Witwatersrand Johannesburg, South Africa. Dr Friedman holds a Ph.D. from the University of the Witwatersrand , Johannesburg, South Africa and is a part time faculty member of the psychology department at the University of the Witwatersrand. She also runs a consulting company, Psych-Action, consulting to organizations primarily on issues of stress and traumatic stress. She is currently working with the South African Police Service through Business Against Crime to upgrade the training and care of police in South Africa. She is one of the founders of the African Society of Traumatic Stress Studies

Heidi Kopel, M.A.

Heidi Kopell holds a BA Honors in Psychology from the University of the Witwatersrand, as well as a MA (Research, Psychology) from the Rand Afrikaans University both in Johannesburg, South Africa. Her research dissertations for both of these degrees investigated levels of PTSD in two different specialist units of the South African Police Service. She is currently completing her MA in Clinical Psychology at Macquarie University in Sydney, Australia and is involved in critical incident stress debriefing for a private organization.

Robert Loo, Ph.D.

Robert Loo is currently Professor of Human Resource Management and Organizational Studies in the Faculty of Management at the University of

Lethbridge, Alberta, Canada. Dr. Loo started his professional career as an infantry officer in the Canadian army in the 1960s with NATO and UN service. He has changed careers several times since then with management positions in the high-tech industry and the federal government before joining the University of Lethbridge in 1989. Dr. Loo has a long-standing interest in occupational stress, but he first addressed police suicide when he joined the Royal Canadian Mounted Police Headquarters in 1982 as their first Chief Psychologist. Dr. Loo has published extensively in the occupational stress field and continues to have a special concern for those who serve and protect—police officers.

Nigel Long, Ph.D.

Nigel Long is Professor and Head of the Department of Psychology at Massey University, New Zealand. He is Editor of the *New Zealand Journal of Psychology* and has edited a book and has published many book chapters and papers in the area of posttraumatic stress disorder. His main research interest is in the area of psychological trauma and he is undertaking a national investigation into the prevalence of trauma and patterns of health and mental health utilization in the community and researching multiple trauma in police and tertiary students. He is a consultant to a number of government departments and has received many external grants.

Malcolm MacLeod, Ph.D.

Malcolm MacLeod is a lecturer in social and forensic psychology in the School of Psychology at the University of St. Andrews, Scotland. He has published widely in the field of eyewitness testimony, person identification and criminal victimization. His current research focuses on the social cognition mechanisms by which people adjust to, and recover from, victimization episodes, illness, and other traumatic events.

Peter Mastin

Peter B. Mastin retired from the Bureau of Alcohol, Tobacco, and Firearms in 1998 after 31 years of service. Among his numerous positions in ATF, he was the Special Agent in Charge in St. Paul, Minnesota and New Orleans, Louisiana, the Ombudsman for ATF, and most recently the Chief of the ATF National Academy in Glyco, Georgia. Mr. Mastin was the Deputy Incident Commander of the Waco Raid. He also assisted in the development, implementation, and coordination of ATF's Critical Incident Peer Support program and the Substance Abuse Peer Support program.

Margaret Mitchell, Ph.D.

Margaret Mitchell is Director of Research at the Police Research Unit, Glasgow Caledonian University. She has worked with police services for ten years studying the impact of the Lockerbie Disaster of 1988, and completing work for the Scottish Office and the Home Office on various aspects of critical incidents in the occupational setting. She is currently commissioned by the Health and Safety Executive (UK) on a project Managing Trauma in the Police Service.

Douglas Paton, Ph.D., C.Psychol.

Douglas Paton is an Associate Professor at Massey University, New Zealand and an Honorary Senior Lecturer at St. Andrews University, Scotland. He is a foundation member of the Australasian Society for Traumatic Stress Studies and the founding editor of the *Australasian Journal of Disaster and Trauma Studies.* He is currently involved in a longitudinal study of occupational and traumatic stress in New Zealand police officers.

George T. Patterson, Ph.D.

George T. Patterson is an assistant professor at New York University Ehrenkranz School of Social Work. He previously taught a variety of courses in criminal justice, sociology, and social work. Dr. Patterson has 12 years experience with military and paramilitary personnel. He has conducted extensive research on stress and coping among police, lectured on the topics and is presently writing articles and a book on police coping.

Joseph M. Rothberg, Ph.D.

Joseph M. Rothberg is an Adjunct Associate Professor of Psychiatry at the Uniformed Services University of the Health Sciences, Bethesda, Maryland, and Scientist Emeritus at the Walter Reed Army Institute of Research, Washington, D.C. The major emphasis of his preretirement work with the Department of Defense concerned military drug use, deployment stress, and the epidemiology of suicide in the military. He is currently involved with program evaluation and is working on the application of a public health approach to suicide prevention in the military.

Eugene Schmuckler, Ph.D.

Eugene Schmuckler is Coordinator of Behavioral Sciences/Management at the Georgia Public Safety Training Center. He received his B.S. degree from Brooklyn College in psychology, and his M.A. and Ph.D. degrees from Louisiana State University in industrial/organizational psychology. Dr. Schmuckler is a member of the International Society for Traumatic Stress Studies and the Association of Traumatic Stress Specialists (ATSS). He has served on the board of directors of ATSS and was editor of the association's newsletter, *Trauma Lines.* Dr. Schmuckler is a diplomate in police psychology and is a certified trauma specialist.

Leigh M. Smith, M.Sc.

Leigh M. Smith is Head of the School of Psychology at Curtin University of Technology in Perth Western Australia. His main research foci are the development and application of research techniques and data analyses in applied settings, measurement theory and the construction of psychological response scales. He is interested in psychological well-being in work, and in particular the relation between organizational practices and the mental health of workers.

Roger M. Solomon, Ph.D.

Roger M. Solomon is a clinical psychologist and Director of Critical Incident Recovery Resources in Amherst, New York. He provides trauma recovery services, training programs, and critical incident peer support workshops. He is on the Senior Faculty of the Eye Movement Desensitization and Reprocessing (EMDR) Institute and on the faculty of International Critical Incident Stress Foundation. He is a consultant with the critical incident programs of the Bureau of Alcohol, Tobacco, and Firearms; the Federal Bureau of Investigation; the Department of Justice; and the trauma programs of other agencies; and provides services following major critical incidents and training programs. He was formally the Department Psychologist with the Washington State Patrol.

Christine Stephens, Ph.D.

Christine Stephens is a lecturer in research methods in psychology at Massey University, New Zealand. Her research interests are in organizational and health psychology. She is currently involved in an ongoing program of research with the New Zealand Police. This project includes inquiry into the psychological effects of traumatic experiences suffered by police officers at work. A particular focus of Dr Stephens' work has been the variables that contribute to resilience and recovery from trauma.

John M. Violanti, Ph.D.

John M. Violanti is an Associate Professor of Criminal Justice at RIT, Rochester, New York, and a Clinical Assistant Professor at the University of Buffalo, New York School of Medicine and Biomedical Sciences. Dr. Violanti has authored many publications on police suicide, traumatic stress, and police survivors. He has been an author and coauthor of three previous books on police retirement, suicide and trauma. Dr. Violanti is a retired twenty-three year veteran of the New York State Police.

Mary Beth Williams, Ph.D., LCSW, CTS

Mary Beth Williams is in private practice in Warrentown, Virginia. She is the author, coauthor, and editor of numerous publications about trauma. Dr. Williams is a Board member of the International Society of Traumatic Stress Studies (ISTSS) and the Association of Traumatic Stress Specialists. She is a consultant to the Finnish Academy of Police Psychologists. Dr. Williams has also been a school social worker for the Falls Church, Virginia City School System for over two decades.

Kathleen M. Wright, Ph.D.

Kathleen M. Wright is a Research Psychologist in the Division of Neuropsychiatry at the Walter Reed Army Institute for Research in Washington, D.C., and Adjunct

Assistant Professor of Psychiatry at the Uniformed Services University of the Health Sciences, Bethesda, Maryland. Her major research interests concern individual, group, and organizational responses to trauma and disaster, to include posttraumatic stress responses and Gulf War Illness. She is currently serving as the Research Director for the Congressional Commission on Military Training and Gender-Related Issues.

PREFACE

The police fight a different kind of war. It does not take place on the battlefield of a foreign land, but instead on the streets of their nation. The enemy is the police officer's own civilian population: those who engage in crime, social indignity, and inhumane treatment of others. The result for the police officer is both physical and psychological battering, occasionally culminating in the officer sacrificing his or her life to protect others.

This book focuses on the psychological impact of police civilian combat. During a police career, the men and women of our police agencies are exposed to distressing events that go far beyond the experience of the ordinary citizen. There is an increased need today to help police officers deal with these traumatic experiences. As police work becomes increasingly complex, this need will grow. Mental health and other professionals need to be made aware of the conditions and precipitants and trauma stress among the police. A goal of this book is to provide such important information.

Our perspective in this book is based on the idea that trauma stress does not necessarily occur within the vacuum of the individual. Instead, trauma is a product of the rather complex interaction of person, place, situation, support mechanisms, and interventions. To effectively communicate this to the reader, we included some new conceptual and methodological considerations, essays on special cases and groups in policing, and innovative ideas on recovery and treatment of trauma. Our hope is that this information will be used to prevent or minimize trauma stress in police officers and, if this is not possible, that it be used to help in establishing improved support and therapeutic measures for police officers.

John M. Violanti
Douglas Paton

CONTENTS

Page

Preface   xiii

Chapter

Introduction

1. POLICE TRAUMA: PSYCHOLOGICAL IMPACT OF
     CIVILIAN COMBAT   5
   John M. Violanti
   Introduction   5
   The Goals and Content of This Book   5
     Section I.: Conceptual and Methodological Issues   6
     Section II: Special Police Groups   7
     Section III: Recovery and Treatment   8
   References   9

Section I: Conceptual and Methodological Issues

2. ASSESSMENT, CONCEPTUAL AND METHODOLOGICAL
     ISSUES IN RESEARCHING TRAUMATIC STRESS
     IN POLICE OFFICERS   13
   Douglas Paton and Leigh Smith
   Introduction   13
   Risk Populations   13
   Assessing Duty-related Psychological Trauma   14
     The Content of Work-Trauma Assessment   15
       Traumatic Stressors   15
       Symptoms of Work-Related Trauma Exposure   17
       Vulnerability: Individual and demographic differences   17
   Environment: Reactivity and Recovery Influence   18
   Longitudinal Analysis   19
   Conclusion   20
   References   21

3. POLICE OFFICERS AND VIOLENT CRIME: SOCIAL
   PSYCHOLOGICAL PERSPECTIVES ON IMPACT
   AND RECOVERY   25
   Malcolm D. MacLeod and Douglas Paton
   Introduction   25
   The Social Cognition of Victimization and Recovery   26
      Attributions and Recovery in Victims   26
      Counterfactual Thinking   30
      Perceived Avoidability and Outcome Expectancies   30
      Helper Stereotype   31
   The Social Context of Impact and Recovery   32
   Conclusion   33
   References   34
4. POLICE COMPASSION FATIGUE (PCF): THEORY, RESEARCH,
   ASSESSMENT, TREATMENT, AND PREVENTION   37
   Charles R. Figley
   Introduction   37
   A Review of the Literature   38
   Stress in Law Enforcement   39
      Common Symptoms   39
      Socialization Influences   41
      Police Role Influences   42
      Conjoint Police Officer Marriages   42
   Contrasts Between Secondary Traumatic Stress and Other Concepts   43
      Burnout versus Secondary Traumatic Stress (Compassion
         Stress/Fatigue)   43
      Secondary Traumatization   44
   A Model of Police Compassion Fatigue (PCF)   45
   Do Something!   46
   Institutional Policies and Procedures   46
   Five Fundamental Principles   46
      Awareness of the Risks and Costs of Police Work on Officers
         and Their Families   46
      Commitment to Lower the Risks and Costs   47
      Adequate Applicant Screening for Resilience and Awareness   47
      Adequate Policies and Procedures to Educate and Protect Workers   47
      Work Group Attitudes and Action Plans   47
         The 3:1 Ratio Rule   47
         CISD/M Plans and Actions   48
         Humor and Other Stress Reduction Methods   48
         Low Tolerance of Substance Abuse   48
         Facilitation of Coworker Health and Self Care   48

Individual Actions 49
    Letting Go of Work 49
    Strategies for Gaining a Sense of Achievement 49
    Strategies for Acquiring Adequate Rest and Relaxation 50
    The Perfect Stress Reduction Methods 50
Counseling Assistance for Compassion Fatigue and Family Burnout 50
    Phase ONE: Specifying the goals of treatment 50
    Phase TWO: Telling the story 50
    Phase THREE: Reconsidering the story through insight 50
    Phase FOUR: Developing a healing theory 51
References 51

5. POLICE PSYCHOLOGICAL BURNOUT AND TRAUMA 54
Cedric Alexander
Introduction 54
Conceptualization of Police Burnout 54
Why Police Officers Burn Out 56
Organizational Characteristics 56
    Lack of Social and Administrative Support 57
    Rotating Shifts 58
    Lack of Participation in Decision Making 59
    Career development 59
Race and Gender 60
Personal Reflections: Police Burnout, Stress and Trauma 61
References 63

6. VULNERABILITY TO PSYCHOLOGICAL DISORDER:
    PREVIOUS TRAUMA IN POLICE RECRUITS 65
Christine Stephens, Nigel Long and Ross Flett
Introduction 65
Traumatic Stress and Early Retirement 65
More Traumatic Stress Is Related to Higher Symptoms 67
Traumatic Experiences of Police Recruits 69
Conclusions 74
References 74

7. CHRONIC EXPOSURE TO RISK AND TRAUMA: ADDICTION
    AND SEPARATION ISSUES IN POLICE OFFICERS 78
Douglas Paton, John Violanti, and Eugene Schmuckler
Introduction 78
Dependence and Acute Traumatic Experiences 78
Behavioral Addiction and Police Work 80
Stress Reactions and Separation 82
Family Issues 84
Conclusions 85
References 85

8.   TRAUMA IN POLICE WORK: A PSYCHOSOCIAL MODEL   88
     John Violanti
     Introduction   88
     The Police Role and Trauma: A Model   88
        Assimilation Into the Police Role   88
           Individual Assimilation   89
           Social Assimilation   89
        Coping Efficacy and the Acquired Police Role   90
           Constrictive Inflexibility   90
           Diminished Use of Other Social Roles   91
           The Police Role and Relationships   91
     Discussion   92
     Suggestions for Intervention   93
     References   93

                  Section II: Special Police Populations

9.   EFFECTS OF EXPOSURE TO VIOLENCE IN SOUTH
     AFRICAN POLICE   99
     Heidi Kopel and Merle Friedman
     Introduction   99
     Methods   103
        Subjects   103
        Procedure   104
           Demographic Information   104
           Stressor Scale   105
           Impact of Event Scale   105
     Results   105
     Discussion   107
     References   110

10. THE EMOTIONAL AFTERMATH OF THE WACO RAID:
     FIVE YEARS REVISITED   113
     Roger M. Solomon and Peter Mastin
     Introduction   113
     Primary Reason   114
        The Existence of a Critical Incident Program   115
           Program Utilization   116
        Concerned Leadership   116
        Peer Support   117
        Reinforcement of Group Cohesion and Support   117
        An Opportunity to Mourn   118
     Multifaceted Intervention   118

	Immediate Availability of Peer Support and Psychological Services	118
	Psychological Services upon Returning Home	119
	The Availability of Specialized Psychological Services	120
	Access to the Facts	120
	Alleviating Agents of Blame	120
	An Opportunity to Remember	121
	Support from the Law Enforcement Community and Concerned Citizens	121
	Learning from It	121
	Conclusion	122
	References	123
11.	INCIDENT RESPONSE AND RECOVERY MANAGEMENT	124
	Douglas Paton, Rhona Flin, and John Violanti	
	Introduction	124
	Incident-Related Stress for Commanders	124
	Incident Command and Control	127
	Planning for Major Emergencies and Disasters	128
	Operational Systems and Structures	128
	Coordination and Team Work	129
	Communication and Information	131
	Stress and Decision Making	131
	Incident Command Training	132
	Recovery Management	135
	Management Style	135
	Returning to Work	135
	Conclusion	136
	References	136
12.	DEATH ON DUTY: POLICE SURVIVOR TRAUMA	139
	John M. Violanti	
	Introduction	139
	Impact on Police Survivors	140
	The National Police Survivor Study	141
	Psychological Impact on Police Spouse Survivors	143
	Symptoms of Psychological Distress	143
	Posttraumatic Stress Disorder	144
	Grief Responses	145
	Ways of Coping	146
	Self-Esteem	146
	Physical Health	147
	Survivors and Responses to the Death	148
	Death Notification	148
	Support After the Death	148

Police Agency Survey Responses 148
    Death Notification and Follow-up 149
Impact of Death on the Department 150
Intervention 150
    Group Level Intervention 151
    Death Notification 152
    Supporting the Family During the Ordeal 152
    Follow-up with the Police Family 153
    Individual Treatment Issues 153
        Police Coworkers 155
Conclusion 155
References 156

13. IMPACT OF DUTY-RELATED DEATH ON OFFICERS
    CHILDREN: CONCEPTS OF DEATH, TRAUMA
    REACTIONS, AND TREATMENT 159
Mary Beth Williams
Introduction 159
A Child's View of Death 160
    The Preschool Child 161
    Elementary-Age Children 162
    Preteen and Adolescent 163
Reactions and Symptomatology 164
    Elementary-Age Children 165
    Preadolescents and Adolescents 166
Healing Strategies and Techniques 167
School Interventions 170
Final Considerations 171
References 172

14. INTERGENERATIONAL LEGACIES OF TRAUMA IN
    POLICE FAMILIES 175
Yael Danieli
Introduction 175
Trauma and the Continuity of the Self 175
The Intergenerational Context 176
Vulnerability and/or Resilience? 177
Legacies of Trauma to the Family 179
A Legacy Change? 181
Suicide and Trauma 183
Some Concluding Remarks 183
References 184

15. TRAUMA OF WORLD POLICING: PEACEKEEPING DUTIES 189
Clay Foreman and Liisa Eränen
Introduction 189
Trauma Membrane 190
Survivor Groups as Systems 190
United Nations Military Operations 191
   Dynamics of Interpersonal Violence 192
CIVPOL Context 192
   Cross-cultural Issues 193
   No Weapons 193
   Driving on Patrol 194
   Living Environment 194
   Corruption 195
   Planning for Catastrophe 195
Human Rights Abuse and Other Crimes 196
   Criminal Activity 196
Psychological reactions 197
Conclusion 198
References 199

Section III: Recovery and Treatment

16. TRAUMA PREVENTION IN THE LINE OF DUTY 203
Joseph M. Rothberg and Kathleen Wright
Introduction 203
Army Training for Trauma 204
Disasters, Traumatic Events and Mass Casualties 205
Disaster on Green Ramp 206
   Process in Action 206
Primary Prevention 207
   Training Prior to the Event 207
   Command Consultation 208
Secondary Prevention 209
   Critical Incident Stress Debriefing 209
   Outreach to Soldiers 209
   Outreach to Staff 210
   Outreach to Families 211
   Outreach to Community 211
Tertiary Prevention 212
   Army After-Action Report Process 212
Research Opportunities 213
Conclusion 213
References 213

17.   COPING EFFECTIVENESS AND OCCUPATIONAL
      STRESS IN POLICE OFFICERS   214
      George T. Patterson
      Introduction   214
      A Review of the Literature   215
      Stressful Occupational Events Among the Police   215
      Coping Among Police Officers   216
      The Present Study   217
          Hypotheses   217
          Methods   217
          Sample   217
          Procedures   218
          Measures   218
              Stress   218
              Secondary Appraisal   218
              Coping   219
              Psychological Distress   219
          Strategy of Analysis   220
      Results   220
      Conclusion   223
      References   224
18.   FINDING MEANING IN POLICE TRAUMAS   227
      Ingrid V.E. Carlier
      Introduction   227
      Trauma Experienced by Police Officers   227
      Consequences of Police Traumas   229
      Constructing Meaning in the Treatment of Police Officers
          with PTSD   230
          Frame of Reference for the Symptoms   231
          Working Through Emotions Hitherto Avoided   232
          Existential Questions and Insights   234
          Personal Growth   234
          Acceptance and Farewell Ritual   235
      Conclusion   236
      References   239
19.   POLICE SUICIDE: THE ULTIMATE STRESS REACTION   241
      Robert Loo
      Introduction   241
      Issues in Addressing Police Suicide Rates   241
          Public Image   241
          Suicide Data and Misclassification   242
          Calculating Suicide Rates   242

National Differences and Cultural Change 243
Women and Visible Minorities 243
A Typology of Police Suicide 244
Prevention and Postvention 245
    Prevention 245
    Prevention Measures 245
        Recruit Selection Criteria 247
        Stress Management Training 247
        Stress Inoculation Training 247
        Supervisor Training 247
        Identify and Track High-Risk Officers 248
        Psychological Assessments for Special Duties 248
        Critical Incidents 248
        Psychological Services 248
        Drug Abuse and Life-Styles 249
        Suicide Hotlines 249
        Peer Support Programs 249
        Spousal Support Program 250
        Preretirement Counseling 250
    Postvention 250
        Psychological Autopsies 250
        Survivor Supports 251
        Intervention Evaluation 251
Closing Comments 251
References 252

20. A CURRENT VIEW FROM THE UK ON POST INCIDENT
    CARE: "DEBRIEFING," "DEFUSING" AND JUST TALKING
    ABOUT IT 255
    Margaret Mitchell
    Introduction 255
    Critical Incident Debriefing in the United Kingdom 257
    The CIDB Model 258
        The Facts 258
        The Feelings 258
        The Future 259
    The Process in the UK 259
    The Current Survey of UK Forces 260
    New Research on Social Support Amongst Police Officers 263
    References 267

21. POST-INTERVENTION STRATEGIES TO REDUCE POLICE
       TRAUMA: A PARADIGM SHIFT   269
     Chris Dunning
     Introduction   269
     History of Debriefing in Law Enforcement for Work-Related
       Mental Injuries   269
     Debriefing for Police Stress or PTSD?   270
     Police Traumatic Duty Assignment and Pathology   271
     Traumatic Exposure and Posttraumatic Growth   272
     Paradigm Shift: Debriefing Orientation from Pathogenic to
       Salutogenic   276
     The Salutogenic Debrief   278
     Conclusion   285
     References   286

Conclusion

22. TRAUMA STRESS IN POLICING: ISSUES FOR
       FUTURE CONSIDERATION   293
     Douglas Paton and John M. Violanti
     Introduction   293
     Police Work and Combat   293
     Managing Occupational and Traumatic Stressors   294
     Organizational, Social and Community Issues   294
     A Lifespan Perspective   295
     Pathology Versus Resilience   295
     Conclusion   297
     References   297
Appendix   299
Compassion Satisfaction/Fatigue Self-Test for Helpers   301
Author Index   307
Subject Index   315

POLICE TRAUMA

INTRODUCTION

Chapter 1

POLICE TRAUMA: PSYCHOLOGICAL IMPACT OF CIVILIAN COMBAT

JOHN M. VIOLANTI

INTRODUCTION

The title of this book is drawn from the similarity between military combat and civilian police work that led Williams (1987) to describe police officers as being involved in peacetime combat: "for cops, the war never ends . . . they are out there 24 hours a day, 7 days a week to protect and serve, to fight the criminal . . . our peacetime enemy. The police officer is expected to be combat-ready at all times while remaining normal and socially adaptive when away from the job. The psychological toll for many is great, unexpected, and not well understood" (p. 267).

While police officers are not in military combat, they experience similar conditions: a continual sense of danger from an unknown enemy; witnessing violence and death; depersonalization of emotion; and lack of public support exert harmful psychological and social consequences, including increased risk of suicide, substance abuse, and disrupted family life (Farberow, Kang, & Bullman, 1990; Laufer, Gallops, & Frey-Wouters, 1984). However, while the Vietnam veteran was at war for a minimum of nine months, police officers alternate between the violence of the street (e.g., shootings, witnessing death and mutilation, dealing with abused children) and the normalcy of civilian life on a daily basis (Violanti, 1996). Just like their Vietnam veteran counterparts, traumatic stress, and even PTSD, can be a reality for officers dealing with civilian combat.

THE GOALS AND CONTENT OF THIS BOOK

This book is about the psychological impact of what we choose to call "police civilian combat." We have gathered contributions from professionals who work with police officers, and in some cases, those who are or have been police officers, to provide the reader with different perspectives on policing. These contributions define what we currently know, what we need to find out, and provide a resource for those who manage stress and trauma in policing. Chapters are grouped into three sections: conceptual and methodological issues, special police groups, and recovery and treatment.

Section I: Conceptual and Methodological Issues

Understanding and managing psychological trauma in policing requires a sound conceptual and methodological base. In Chapter 2, Paton and Smith discuss the construct of duty-related traumatic stress and its implications for assessment. They discuss police stress phenomena within a hazard-risk management model. This affords opportunities to examine both positive and negative outcomes, and to appreciate how psychological processes interact with environmental and organizational factors to affect risk status.

Social cognitive theories have proved beneficial in promoting understanding of victimization processes. In Chapter 3, MacLeod and Paton explore the use of constructs such as perceived control, likelihood of event recurrence, and counterfactual thinking to understand police officers' experience of criminal victimization from repeatedly witnessing violent criminal episodes and/or the emotional costs incurred in supporting victims of violence. They discuss how this perspective helps understand the effectiveness of police agencies and attitudes towards victims and the criminal justice system.

Figley introduces his model of "police compassion fatigue" in Chapter 4. This model suggests that if police officers are empathic, have sufficient concern for others, and are exposed to traumatized people on a continuous basis, they may develop a debilitating psychological fatigue. Figley suggests methods to help officers deal with compassion fatigue and provides a measure for this concept.

Alexander, in Chapter 5, discusses job burnout and its implications for well-being and for precipitating the onset of trauma. He focuses on the role organizational stressors (e.g., administrative support, involvement in decision making) in this context. The last section of the chapter discusses burnout and trauma in policing from the author's (a former police officer) perspective.

In Chapter 6, Stephens, Long, and Flett discuss the impact of previous life trauma for those entering police work. Police recruits who have already suffered traumatic stress are, following exposure to subsequent distressing experiences, at increased risk of mental health problems and more likely to retire from police service early. This is a double loss: of psychological health for the officer, and of a highly trained officer to the department. This theme is continued in Chapter 7 with Paton, Violanti, and Schmuckler's discussion of the long-term implications and after-effects of repetitive exposure to high risk and duty-related traumatic incidents. Here they explore its implications for behavioral addiction and separation from active police duties.

Section I ends with Violanti proposing a model describing the relationship between psychological trauma, coping, and the police role. This model suggests that, through occupational socialization, the police role comes to serve as a primary coping resource for officers exposed to traumatic events. Reliance on the rigidly defined police role can limit cognitive style in solving problems and the use of other more flexible life roles in coping with trauma and, in turn, increase the risk of PTSD.

Section II: Special Police Groups

Section II focuses on special police groups and commences, in Chapter 9, with Kopel and Friedman's case study of trauma in South African police. This study was undertaken to establish whether the conditions under which South African police operate resulted in a particular type of traumatic symptom constellation. They confirmed that exposure to violence is predictive of intrusive symptoms. Symptoms of intrusion were correlated with those of avoidance, providing tentative support for avoidance being a defensive response to intrusive phenomena which are direct effects of exposure to violence.

In Chapter 10, Solomon and Mastin (a former ATF Agent) give an inside view of psychological trauma at the Waco, Texas incident. While being the worst tragedy in the Bureau of Alcohol, Tobacco, and Firearms history, the fact there has been only one medical retirement among agents involved points to the resiliency and strength of the agents. They also discuss how organizational activities (e.g., critical incident program, leadership, peer support) contributed to emotional recovery.

While much has been written about the impact of critical incidents on line police officers, police incident commanders have been surprisingly neglected. Paton, Flin, and Violanti redress this imbalance in Chapter 11 and discuss response and recovery management issues from an incident command perspective.

In Chapter 12, Violanti discusses the psychological impact on survivors of police duty-related death. While the loss of a police officer to a community is serious, the sudden and often violent death of a loved one is emotionally devastating to family, friends, and other officers. For them, such deaths are a reminder of the dangers that officers face each day. Violanti provides measures of psychological symptomatology, trauma, and the impact of support factors on police spouse survivors.

Children of law enforcement officers who have died in duty-related deaths can experience mental health problems as a direct result of their loss and from exposure to the distress of others, including the remaining parent. In Chapter 13, Williams describes how loss under these circumstances can be more intense compared with death from natural causes. In addition, she discusses how sociolegal proceedings can precipitate or exacerbate reactions, and how the death can challenge their sense of control and disturb their sense of historical continuity and ability to plan for the future.

In Chapter 14, Danieli examines intergenerational aspects of trauma in law enforcement families. Following a brief presentation of her intergenerational framework, Danieli's describes how trauma can reverberate within the officer's family in both an historical and contemporary sense. She draws comparisons between Nazi Holocaust survivors, World War II and Vietnam veterans, and police officers to illustrate the policy, selection, training, preventive, and therapeutic implications of using an intergenerational approach.

The difficult task of "world policing" is the topic of Chapter 15 by Foreman and Eränen. Peacekeeping forces throughout the world are often exposed to atrocities and trauma in the very countries they seek to protect and bring peace. Foreman and Eränen provide a firsthand discussion of police work in this context.

Section III: Recovery and Treatment

Coping with, and recovering from, the impact of trauma has long been the concern of survivors, researchers, and mental health professionals. The final section discusses these issues in relation to police personnel.

Rothberg and Wright, in Chapter 16, discuss a public health approach to trauma for police based on a military model. This is justified on the grounds of organizational similarities (hierarchical organization, leadership style) and by the exposure of their personnel to uniquely stressful environments, including violence, injury, and death. Their model contains three elements: primary prevention addresses the preparations and training prior to the event, secondary prevention focuses on the participants in the event(s) during or shortly afterwards, and tertiary prevention considers how to limit the long-term effects and better prepare for, and manage, future events.

Patterson, in Chapter 17, attributes the success of recovery from stressful police events to effective coping. Using a transactional model, he describes how interaction between a stressful event, appraisal and coping affect well-being following exposure. The manner in which social factors (e.g., gender and race) influence exposure to, and response to, stressful events is also discussed.

In Chapter 18, Carlier discusses how finding meaning in traumatic events can aid police officers in recovery from trauma. She describes a professional therapeutic intervention that emphasizes finding meaning in traumatic experiences as a basis for facilitating officers' acceptance and adaptation.

Loo examines the complex issue of police suicide in Chapter 19. He emphasizes suicide prevention and discusses a variety of acceptable, practical, and cost-effective measures. Even with effective preventive measures, suicide will likely still occur as a rare event; therefore, several key postvention measures are discussed to help survivors and to help departments improve their suicide prevention effectiveness. This discussion provides police departments and individual officers with an armory of preventive measures readily available to minimize such needless loss of life.

In Chapter 20, Mitchell reviews the origins, development, and current status of interventions, primarily Critical Incident Debriefing, developed to assist police officers in the United Kingdom after a traumatic incident. She argues that the practical necessity for having some form of intervention in place may well have prevented a comprehensive evaluation of them.

In Chapter 21, Dunning discusses the current controversy surrounding debriefing. She contends that current debriefing methods have their roots in the theoretical orientation of learned helplessness based on a pathogenic model. As an alternative, she proposes that interventions be based on a Wellness or Salutogenic paradigm that incorporates research and theory on hardiness, resiliency, and learned resourcefulness.

As we stated at the beginning, it is the psychological impact of police civilian combat that concerns us in this book. In our conclusion, we will review the issues raised by authors throughout the book and identify future directions for the conceptualization, assessment, intervention, and effective treatment of psychological trauma in policing. The men and women who serve in law enforcement worldwide deserve no less.

REFERENCES

Farberow, N. L.; Kang, H. K., & Bullman, T. A.: Combat experience and postservice psychosocial status as predictors of suicide in Vietnam veterans. *Journal of Nervous and Mental Disease, 178*: 32-37, 1990.

Laufer, R.; Gallops, M. S., & Frey-Wouters, E.: War stress and trauma: The Vietnam veteran experience. *Journal of Health and Social Behavior, 25*: 6585, 1984.

Violanti, J. M.: Trauma stress and police work. In D. Paton & J. M. Violanti, *Traumatic stress in critical occupations: Recognition, consequences, & treatment.* Springfield, IL., Charles C. Thomas, 1996.

Williams, C.: Peacetime combat: Treating and preventing delayed stress reactions in police officers. In T. Williams (Ed.) *Post-traumatic stress disorders: A handbook for clinicians.* Cincinnati, Ohio, Disabled American Veterans, 1987.

SECTION I

CONCEPTUAL AND
METHODOLOGICAL ISSUES

Chapter 2

ASSESSMENT, CONCEPTUAL AND METHODOLOGICAL ISSUES IN RESEARCHING TRAUMATIC STRESS IN POLICE OFFICERS

DOUGLAS PATON & LEIGH SMITH

INTRODUCTION

As this book demonstrates, stress and traumatic stress in police officers are subject to considerable academic and professional scrutiny. In this chapter, we explore the construct, duty-related traumatic stress, and its implications for assessment instruments and strategies. We must also bear in mind that, when discussing the "police organization," we are describing the integrated role of several groups. Considering the similarities and differences between these groups is where this discussion commences.

RISK POPULATIONS

If theoretical models, and the assessment instruments they generate, are to be adequately tested, care must be taken to ensure that the samples upon which evaluation takes place are representative of all possible risk populations. Failure to do so may result in a loss of cross-population/cultural validity and reduce their assessment and/or diagnostic effectiveness. This activity also determines normative data requirements.

Police organizations are highly cohesive communities. Consequently, the impact of a traumatic event can spread out to affect individuals on the basis of their physical or psychological association ("ripple effect") with an event or those affected, and extend risk status to others. While several groups (officers, dispatchers, families) could thus be affected, differences between them (e.g., group identity, nature of involvement) means that they cannot be regarded in a uniform manner. Salient differences in group and

13

individual vulnerability must be identified and used to inform the development of assessment, support and preparatory strategies (Smith & Paton, 1997). Intergroup differences may be valuable in other respects.

There are two ways that reactions to traumatic stress can be studied in relation to groups. Existing groups such as occupational groups (police, fire fighters) or those based on type of traumatic event (road accidents), can be compared and contrasted. These groups represent appropriate foci both for determining norms and, by contrasting patterns of symptomatology, for isolating factors that affect reactions (Smith & Paton, 1997). Groups can also be formed on the basis of officers' reactions to events. Groups defined in this manner represent an appropriate means of exploring individual differences in reactivity. For example, can police be divided into subgroups on the basis of their reactions to murder victims?

There are many techniques, collectively known as cluster analysis, for separating individuals into groups based upon their scores on a set of measures. This technique, when extended to the effects of trauma, would operate on the assumption that groups could be defined on the basis of disposition and response patterns. Some preliminary work along these lines by the authors (Paton, Cacioppe, & Smith, 1992) demonstrated that emergency and human service workers can be classified into a limited number of groups on the basis of their responses to stress and symptom measures. Despite the crudeness of the measures, the results indicated that the method can be useful in planning training programs for police officers.

ASSESSING DUTY-RELATED PSYCHOLOGICAL TRAUMA

The quality of the research and intervention strategy is a function of the conceptual validity of the construct under scrutiny and the availability of instruments with known and sound psychometric properties (Paton & Smith, 1996; Smith & Paton, 1997). Having access to such instruments will be essential to the task of defining the status of officers with respect to the salient variables known to influence traumatic reactivity, assessing the impact of acute traumatic episodes, and monitoring changes in psychological status resulting from cumulative exposure to stressful events.

One issue that deserves further consideration is the question of how differences between groups should be represented. A developing theme in the methodological literature on change has been concerned with the form it may take (Golembiewski, Billingsley, & Yeager, 1976; Millsap & Hartog, 1988; Magnusson & Bergman, 1990; Collins & Horn, 1991). Golembiewski et al. (1976) proposed three types of change: alpha, beta, and gamma. From the perspective of a structural measurement model an alpha change occurs when an increase or a decrease in the score from a multi-item scale directly reflects a corresponding change in the latent construct. A beta change occurs where an increase or decrease in the score signals a recalibration of the scale by respondents. When the structural relations of the items to the latent construct(s) alter, a gamma change has occurred.

It would seem appropriate to extend this typology of change to differences between groups, based on occupation or experience, in respect of traumatic stress measurement devices. Thus groups may differ quantitatively (alpha difference), in anchoring the scale (beta difference), or qualitatively (gamma difference). It follows from this conception of the response patterns of groups to multi-item scales that n*ot only differences in magnitude of responses are important, but also the manner in which groups structure the item set in relation to the latent constructs* (Byrne, 1991; Smith & Paton, 1997; Viet & Ware, 1983). Basically, we interpret this as implying a need for a more searching analysis of both the nature of the latent construct under investigation and the manner in which it is assessed.

Instruments used to assess any psychological construct are used on the assumption that there is a degree of stability in the psychological constructs (e.g., duty- related traumatic stress) being assessed. The assumption that the underlying construct is robust and manifests itself in the same way in all those affected provides a consistent platform for intervention planning, design, administration, and evaluation (Paton & Smith, 1996). However, this assumption may not always be justified (Byrne, 1991; Smith & Paton, 1997; Viet & Ware, 1983). Smith and Paton's (1997) structural reanalysis of Impact of Event Scale data revealed that traumatic reactivity reflected the interaction between a traumatic event, nationality, and organizational and professional membership, suggesting that assessment and intervention procedures, in addition to variables such as stressors, symptoms, and individual differences, must also include organizational characteristics.

The Content of Work-Trauma Assessment

Traumatic Stressors

Establishing the nature and intensity of traumatic stressors plays a central role in understanding the traumatic stress process (Peterson, Prout & Schwarz, 1991) and constitutes a central element in the assessment process. Stressor assessment is best served by focusing on the event characteristics that transcend officers' operational schemata and to their being perceived as stressors (Hartsough & Myers, 1985; Green, Wilson & Lindy, 1985; Janoff-Bulman, 1992; Paton, 1994) rather than the events themselves (e.g., road traffic accidents, hostages situations). However, the assessment process must proceed beyond simply identifying these characteristics.

Police officers' awareness of the risks faced, their role in protecting the public, and their training for this role makes it possible to anticipate both positive and negative responses to traumatic events (Moran & Colless, 1995). It would thus be prudent to conceptualize operational demands (e.g., equipment failure, assault, communication problems, leadership issues, exposure to noxious stimuli) as hazards which influence, rather than prescribe, the risk status of those exposed to them. Once potential hazards are identified, the next step is to determine how, under what conditions, and to what extent, they affect the risk status of officers. Differentiating between hazards and risk provides a more appropriate conceptual framework for researching traumatic impact, particularly in regard to identifying precursors of positive and negative outcomes. The adoption of this framework is useful in other respects.

While identifying hazards is relatively straightforward, defining their implications for safety is more complex. Officers' perceptions of hazards, and the risks they pose, will change over time as a result of, for example, training, experience, new safety equipment. Additional complexity is introduced by the fact that officers' perceptions of hazard and risk reduction strategies (e.g., training). As a consequence, these can generate unintended secondary consequences and, ironically, may increase, rather than decrease, risk status and behavior. Consequently, objective analyses of hazard and risk must be supplemented with a social evaluation which identifies the meaning attributed to hazards by officers and its implications for perceived vulnerability and acceptance of risk.

For example, risk homeostasis (e.g., Adams, 1995) describes the operation of a mental model of the relative balance between risk and safety. Its operation results in a perceived increase in extrinsic or intrinsic safety manifesting itself as an increase in the level of risk behavior undertaken and an artificial reduction in the perception of risk attributable to a hazard. Beliefs about risk are also influenced by the complex system of beliefs and values which constitute the organizational "culture." The existence of a "macho" culture that encourages risky behavior can affect exposure to hazards, risk perception, and subsequent psychological well-being.

Essentially this means that risk, risk assessment, and generalized notions of safety are social and psychological products, not absolutes. This state of affairs reflects the role of the social system and the ideological premises inherent within police organizations that determine perceptions of risk and the manner in which officers respond to hazards. It should not be assumed that implementing safety devices and training programs, and promoting awareness of their existence, will automatically have the desired effect. Careful monitoring of behavior and educating staff in the correct use of procedures, and the limitations of safety devices, are also required. Assessment instruments and procedures will thus be required to cover hazard, risk, and social assessment.

When officers are exposed to a risky or traumatic situation, they will experience a reaction. It is to a discussion of the outcomes associated with exposure to traumatic stressors that we now turn.

Symptoms of Work-Related Trauma Exposure

The quality of symptom measures will be a function of the structural integrity, validity, and reliability of the instruments applied and the availability of normative data that can be used as a basis for gauging relative impact (Smith & Paton, 1997). Smith and Paton's analysis suggested that the latent construct (duty-related traumatic stress), and consequently, its symptomatic correlates, are worthy of more rigorous analysis.

High levels of job demand and chronic exposure to traumatic events will elevate baseline levels of stress and traumatic stress symptomatology in duty-related populations to a level exceeding those prevailing within the general population, necessitating the development of group specific norms for police officers (Paton & Smith, 1996). Without appropriate baseline data, it would be difficult to quantify the impact of a given event or series of events. Induction norms (status when first recruited) and norms for experienced officers would also be required to assess changes in mental health resulting from the operational and traumatic demands of police work and to assess the effectiveness of intervention measures (e.g., training, debriefing).

In addition, work will need to be done to develop measures capable of discriminating between officers who have been adversely affected and those who have not, and to detect positive outcomes (e.g., Tedeschi & Calhoun, 1996). More objective appraisal of individual outcome, and researching the factors contributing to positive outcomes, could provide information to assist selection and training, the development of organizational response strategies, and contribute to the evolution of more representative models of traumatic reactivity. Similarly, measures will need to be developed with discriminant validity such that those who may be affected by future events can be distinguished from those who may not be affected.

Vulnerability: Individual and Demographic Differences

The often pronounced differences in reactivity amongst those involved in a traumatic incident has heightened awareness of the role of individual determinants of reactivity. For example, Lyons (1991) and Scotti et al. (1995) identified several demographic, personal, and personality factors with a potential to play a mediating role in this content. These included perceived meaning, behavioral self-blame, hardiness, physiological reactivity, socioeconomic status, experience of child abuse, social skills deficits leading to problems obtaining and utilizing social support, hypervigilance of threat-relevant cues, inadequate problem-solving behavior, domestic violence, and drug and alcohol abuse. Peterson et al.(1991) identified coping strategies as important determinants of outcomes.

From the point of view of preventing or minimizing reactivity, several strategies could be envisaged. One involves using vulnerability factors for preselection and screening out individuals deemed to be at risk (Lyons, 1991; Tehrani, 1995). Screening could also be used, postevent, to identify vulnerable officers, prioritizing them for support and monitoring. However, more research is needed to articulate the nature of risk factors and coping strategies and their relationship to trauma impact and recovery (Green & Solomon, 1995; Janik, 1992; Scotti et al., 1995).

ENVIRONMENT: REACTIVITY AND RECOVERY INFLUENCE

There is a growing body of evidence to suggest that, for duty-related populations, the organizational environment plays a direct role in the causation of traumatic stress reactions (Smith & Paton, 1997). Organizational factors are particularly relevant when dealing with duty-related psychological trauma because the work environment defines the context within which both traumatic experiences and recovery occur.

Prevailing organizational practices, including leadership style, managerial attitudes to stress, prevailing levels of social support, and the level of overt organizational concern for staff well-being influence the intensity and duration of impact and the rate of recovery (Alexander & Wells, 1991; Doepal, 1991; Hart, Wearing & Headey, 1995; Paton, 1994; Thompson, 1993, Violanti, 1996) and increase absenteeism, turnover, performance decline, and treatment and compensation costs (Bonifacio, 1991; Doepal, 1991; Thompson, 1993).

Acknowledging that officers face repeated exposure to traumatic events, and that their reactions reflect the interaction between events, personal and environmental factors (whose influence develops and changes over time) means that duty-related traumatic stress phenomena are best conceptualized and studied over time.

LONGITUDINAL ANALYSIS

The fact that the key variables discussed in this paper will interact in a dynamic and discontinuous fashion throughout the career of a police officer renders the typical snapshot approach to the study of duty-related traumatic stress particularly inadequate. Rather, a longitudinal approach is required. Adopting such an approach has a number of implications for research and assessment processes.

Assessment techniques, and the methodology employed, should be capable of coping with the complexities of analyzing change-data. Multiwave, longitudinal designs are appropriate for research and modeling the processes associated with the development of traumatic stress reactions and the recovery processes at individual and organizational levels, and how these change over time (Paton & Smith, 1996). A longitudinal framework is also better suited to anticipating support requirements, for mapping these to the needs of personnel, and for evaluating intervention.

Designing research to assess change presents special problems. Two features of such research require particular attention. The design of true experiments is virtually precluded on ethical grounds and the measures used do not have high reliabilities. Thus the research designs will almost always be quasi-experimental (Cook & Campbell, 1979) or "natural experiments" and the analysis of change-scores and must cope with regression effects (Cohen & Cohen, 1983) and other technical problems. Methodologists and measurement theorists have made considerable progress in developing longitudinal designs and data analysis techniques (Hagenaars, 1990; Collins & Horn, 1991; Magnusson & Bergman, 1990; Magnusson et al., 1991; van Eye, 1990). These advances enhance the ability of researchers to untangle the complex web of interacting factors that affect the development of psychological responses over the duration of critical events and their after-effects.

While the difference in scores on measures used to evaluate change between two points in time is an intuitively appealing index of change , the use of raw change-scores is not generally recommended. If the true scores of all cases change to the same degree the difference-scores will have low reliability. If, however, the rate of change among individuals varies then difference-scores will give unbiased estimates of individual change that have reliabilities less than their component scores (Burr & Nesselroade, 1990). The generally low reliability of these difference-scores provides a misleading basis for assessing correlates of change (Francis et al., 1991).

When individuals are observed on more than one occasion changes in measures may occur as a result of events in the intervening period, or may be the result of unreliable aspects of the measures. Changes in self-ratings may also occur because respondents have formed different relations to, or perceptions of, the items they rate. Researchers therefore need to assess whether changes in measures across time reflect real change, and if they do what type of change they reflect. Schaubroeck and Green (1989) used a confirmatory factor analysis model, augmented by means profiles, to analyze change in a manner that separates shifts in perspective (beta, gamma change) from changes in factor means across time (alpha change). In order to assess these forms of change through the use of covariance structure analysis (including confirmatory factor analysis) it is necessary to use measures based on multiple indicators. The use of single-indicator measures and single-group, pretest -posttest designs cannot answer questions about change. A variety of techniques is now available for the analysis of longitudinal data: examining stability and change (Pitts, West & Tein, 1997), and survival rates (Velicer, Martin & Collins, 1996). The problem of modeling change over time with multiwave categorical data has also been extensively addressed in Hagenaars's (1990) book on log-linear panel, trend, and cohort analysis.

In addition to the technical problems associated with analyzing change data, the investigation of change processes has necessitated the development of research designs that control for confounding effects and threats to the validity of inferences drawn from research. Simple comparisons across time of group members designed to investigate change are vulnerable to validity threats that render them nugatory. However, designs such as the Solomon four-group design (Braver & Braver, 1988) can overcome some of the threats to validity of the simple pretest-posttest design. Moreover, Willett (1989) has argued that more than two waves of data must be collected for effective measurement of change. Willett concluded that the reliability of change measurement can be considerably improved by the addition of more observation times.

A further problem in researching processes that extend over time is that not all relevant events occur or peak simultaneously (Cohen, 1991). Thus, studies involving only two observation points gamble that observations are made when their relations are optimal. In general, this is unlikely. It is better to collect data on more than two occasions, with one or more groups being followed through a sequence of events. When more than one group is used, they can be studied in parallel (e.g., comparison designs), or as lagged cohorts. The latter represents a superior method for studying the etiology of traumatic stress in police populations.

CONCLUSION

Duty-related traumatic stress should be conceptualized differently from traumatic stress phenomena studied in individuals and in nonpolice populations. Repetitive exposure, their role in safeguarding the public, their expectations and training, opportunities to utilize their experience when responding to traumatic events, and the interactive role of event, dispositional and organizational factors in the development of duty-related traumatic reactions render this population unique.

For police populations, conceptualizing stress phenomena within a hazard-risk management framework affords opportunities to examine processes leading to both positive and negative outcomes, and is better suited to appreciating how psychological processes interact with environmental factors to affect risk status. For symptomatic assessment, group specific "point-of-entry" and "operational" norms are required and intergroup differences require examination of the structural integrity, validity, and reliability of instruments. Assessment instruments are also required for individual and organizational factors. We recommend the development of measurement devices based upon properly explicated measurement models and using such measures to study cultural, individual, occupational, and group similarities and differences in order to reveal the dynamics of traumatic reactivity and to provide more specific baseline data.

At a methodological level, the nature and unpredictability of traumatic stress phenomena, and the necessity of dealing with changes in individual responses, present several analytical challenges. The use of multiwave designs for such research and for modeling the processes associated with reactivity is recommended. Finally, we advocate the use of designs that can cope with the complexities of analyzing change-data, instead of relying upon simple pretest-posttest designs and treating the data at face value.

While we recognize that the nature of the subject under study may render adherence to these recommendations difficult in some circumstances, a greater understanding of methodological and assessment problems will allow researchers and practitioners to make more informed judgements regarding the quality of the information used to develop and test theories and interventions.

REFERENCES

Adams, J.: *Risk*. London, UCL Press, 1995.

Alexander, D. A., & Wells, A.: Reactions of police officers to body handling after a major disaster: A before and after comparison. *British Journal of Psychiatry, 159*: 517–555, 1991.

Bonifacio, P.: *The psychological effects of police work: A psychodynamic approach*. New York, Plenum, 1991.

Braver, M. C. W., & Braver, S. L.: Statistical treatment of the Solomon four-group design: A meta-analytic approach. *Psychological Bulletin, 104*: 150-154, 1988.

Burr, J., & Nesselroade, J. R.: Change measurement. In A. von Eye (Ed.). *Statistical Methods in Longitudinal Research: Principles and Structuring Change, Vol. 1.* New York, Academic Press, 1990.

Byrne, B. M.: The Maslach Burnout Inventory: Validating factorial structure and invariance across intermediate, secondary and university educators. *Multivariate Behavioral Research, 26*: 583–605, 1991.

Cohen, P.: A source of bias in longitudinal investigations of change. In L. M. Collins & J. L. Horn (Eds.), *Best methods for the analysis of change: Recent advances, unanswered questions, future directions.* Washington, DC: American Psychological Association, 1991.

Cohen, J., & Cohen, P.: *Applied multiple regression/correlation analysis for the behavioral sciences.* Hillsdale, NJ, Lawrence Erlbaum, 1983.

Cook, T. D., & Campbell, D. T.: *Quasi-experimentation: Design and analysis for field settings.* Chicago, Rand McNally, 1979.

Collins, L. M., & Horn, J. L. (Eds.).: *Best methods for the analysis of change: Recent advances, unanswered questions, future directions.* Washington, DC., American Psychological Association, 1991.

Doepel, D.: Crisis management: The psychological dimension. *Industrial Crisis Quarterly, 5*: 177-188, 1991.

Francis, D. J.; Fletcher, J. M.; Stuebing, K. K.; Davidson, K. C., & Thompson, N. M.: Analysis of change: Modeling individual growth. *Journal of Consulting and Clinical Psychology, 59*: 27-37, 1991.

Green, B. L., & Solomon, S. D.: The mental health impact of natural and technological disasters. In J. R. Freedy & S. E. Hobfoll (Eds.), *Traumatic stress: From theory to practice.* New York, Plenum, 1995.

Golembiewski, R. T.; Billingsly, K., & Yeager, S.: Measuring change and persistence in human affairs: Types of change generated by OD designs. *Journal of Applied Behavioral Science, 12*: 133-157, 1976.

Green, B. L.; Wilson, & Lindy, J. D.: Conceptualizing post-traumatic stress disorder: A psychosocial framework. In C. R. Figley (Ed.) *Trauma and its wake: The study and treatment of post-traumatic stress disorder.* New York, Brunner/Mazel, 1985.

Hagenaars J. A.: *Categorical longitudinal data: Log-linear panel, trend and cohort analysis.* Newbury Park, CA, Sage, 1990.

Hart, P. M.; Wearing, A. J., & Headey, B.: Police stress and well-being: Integrating personality, coping and daily work experiences. *Journal of Occupational and Organizational Psychology, 68*: 133–156, 1995.

Hartsough, D. M., & Myers, D. G.: *Disaster Work and Mental Health: Prevention and control of stress among workers.* Rockville, MD, U.S. Department of Health and Human Services, No. (ADM) 85–1422, 1985.

Janik, J.: Addressing cognitive defenses in critical incident stress. *Journal of Traumatic Stress, 5:* 497–503, 1992.

Janoff-Bulman, R.: *Shattered assumptions.* New York, The Free Press, 1992.

Lyons, J. A.: Strategies for assessing the potential for positive readjustment following trauma. *Journal of Traumatic Stress, 4:* 93-112, 1991.

Magnusson, D., & Bergman, L. R. (Eds.): *Data quality in longitudinal research.* Cambridge, MA, Cambridge University Press, 1990.

Magnusson, D.; Bergman, L. R; Rudinger, G., & Torestad, B: *Problems and methods in longitudinal research: Stability and change.* Cambridge, MA, Cambridge University Press, 1991.

Millsap, R. E., & Hartog, S. B.: Alpha, beta and gamma change in evaluation research: A structural equation approach. *Journal of Applied Psychology, 73*: 574-584, 1988.

Moran, C., & Colless, E.: Positive reactions following emergency and disaster responses. *Disaster Prevention and Management, 4*: 55–61, 1995.

Paton, D.: Disaster Relief Work: An assessment of training effectiveness. *Journal of Traumatic Stress, 7*: 275–288, 1994.

Paton, D., & Smith, L. M.: Assessment of work-related psychological trauma: Methodological issues and implications for organizational strategies. In D. Paton, & J. M. Violanti (Eds.), *Traumatic stress in critical occupations: Recognition, consequences and treatment.* Springfield, IL., Charles C Thomas, 1996.

Paton, D.; Cacioppe, R., & Smith, L. M.: *Critical Incident Stress in the West Australian Fire Brigade.* Perth, Western Australia, 1992.

Peterson, K. C.; Prout M. F., & Schwarz, R. A.: *Post-traumatic stress disorder: A clinicians guide.* New York, Plenum, 1991.

Pitts, S. C.; West, S. G., and Tein, J. U.: Longitudinal measurement models in evaluation research: Examining stability and change. *Evaluation and Program Planning, 19*: 333-350, 1996.

Scotti, J. R.; Beach, B. K.; Northrop, L. M. E.; Rode, C. A., & Forsyth, J. P.: The psychological impact of accidental injury. In J. R. Freedy & S. E. Hobfoll (Eds.), *Traumatic stress: From theory to practice.* New York, Plenum, 1995.

Schaubrock, J., & Green, S. G.: Confirmatory factor analytic procedures for assessing change during organizational entry. *Journal of Applied Psychology, 74*: 892-900, 1989.

Smith, L. M., & Paton, D. (1997) A structural re-assessment of the Impact of Event Scale: The influence of occupational and cultural contexts. In G. Habermann (Ed.), *Looking back, moving forward: Fifty years of New Zealand psychology.* Wellington, New Zealand Psychological Society.

Tedeschi, R. G., & Calhoun, L. G.: The posttraumatic growth inventory: Measuring the positive legacy of trauma. *Journal of Traumatic Stress, 9*: 455-471, 1996.

Tehrani, N.: An integrated response to trauma in three Post Office businesses. *Work & Stress, 9*: 380-393, 1995.

Thompson, J.: Psychological impact of body recovery duties. *Journal of the Royal Society of Medicine, 86*: 628–629, 1993.

van Eye, A. (Ed.): *Statistical methods in longitudinal research: Vol 1. Principles and structuring change.* New York, Academic Press, 1990.

Willett, J. B.: Some results on reliability for the longitudinal measurement of change: Implications for the design of individual growth. *Educational and Psychological Measurement, 49*: 587-602, 1989.

Velicer, W. F.; Martin, R. A., & Collins, L. M.: Section III. Methods for analyzing longitudinal relapse data: Latent transition analysis for longitudinal data. *Addiction, 19*: (Supplement), S197-S209, 1996.

Viet, C. T., & Ware, J. E.: The structure of psychological distress and well-being in general populations. *Journal of Consulting and Clinical Psychology, 51*: 730-742, 1983.

Violanti, J.: Trauma stress and police work. In D. Paton, & J. Violanti (Eds.), *Traumatic stress in critical occupations: Recognition, consequences and treatment.* Springfield, IL., Charles C Thomas, 1996.

Chapter 3

POLICE OFFICERS AND VIOLENT CRIME: SOCIAL PSYCHOLOGICAL PERSPECTIVES ON IMPACT AND RECOVERY

MALCOLM D. MACLEOD & DOUGLAS PATON

INTRODUCTION

Social cognitive theories have proved beneficial in promoting understanding of victimization processes in several groups (Janoff-Bulman, 1992; Edward & MacLeod, 1996; Frazier, 1990; Meyer & Taylor, 1986). This chapter explores the use of this body of theory with police officers in relation to the implications of criminal victimization. Issues such as perceived control, perceived likelihood of event recurrence, and perceived avoidability are particularly salient for police officers whose professional status can expose them to primary and secondary victimization repeatedly. Models of traumatic reactivity, and interventions developed for its management, have precluded several areas of social-cognitive theory. In the absence of a comprehensive theoretical base, interventions may be inconsistent with the actual psychological mechanisms underlying reactivity, muting their effectiveness.

Police officers can be the targets of physical violence and have to contend with the stress associated with witnessing violent criminal episodes and/or the emotional costs incurred in supporting victims of violence. Such victimization can also affect the efficiency and effectiveness of police agencies and the criminal justice system (Violanti, 1996). It is thus important to understand how each experience affects officers' attitudes and behavior and its implications for how they prepare for and deal with subsequent events, including interaction with victims and the systems (e.g., criminal justice) established to manage the societal implications of criminal victimization.

THE SOCIAL COGNITION
OF VICTIMIZATION AND RECOVERY

Experiencing criminal violence, directly or indirectly, elicits a variety of reactions, ranging from anger and frustration to symptoms of psychological trauma (MacLeod, Carson, & Prescott, 1996). These reactions, in turn, affect the ability of those affected to cope and adjust to such experience (see e.g., Frazier, 1990; Winkel, Denkers & Vrij, 1994). The effects of criminal victimization often extend beyond those directly involved and affect family members, close friends, and colleagues (e.g., Amick-McMullen, Kilpatrick & Resnick, 1991; Kahler & MacLeod, 1996).

The cognitive processing associated with recovery involves organizing or working through event-related ideation and memories, which are themselves emotionally challenging (Horowitz, 1993), to reconcile their emotionally-charged and discordant content with schemata capable of assimilating and understanding them and facilitating normal performance (e.g., Janoff-Bulman, 1992). Threats to psychological integrity can heighten the subjective experience of loss of control and result in the process of reestablishing control becoming more difficult (Eränen & Liebkind, 1993). However, if opportunities to impose meaning on the experience are afforded the individual, perceived control can be enhanced and well-being safeguarded (Janoff-Bulman, 1992; Paton, 1994). Perceived control, therefore, has an important role to play in understanding professional responses to traumatic events. In addition, concepts of control, attributions regarding causation, and avoidability may have more general applicability in facilitating our understanding of response to criminal victimization or traumatic events.

Attributions and Recovery in Victims

Janoff-Bulman's influential work (1992) indicates that self-blame attributions, in particular behavioral self-blame attributions, are related to better adjustment (see also Winkel et al., 1994). By blaming the cause of the negative event on some aspect of one's behavior, one can reassert control over future events. If one identifies the cause as being due to some aspect of modifiable behavior then one can re-assert control over the likelihood of it happening in the future by changing one's behavior. Allied to this notion is Tennen and Affleck's (1991) model which suggests that other-blame is dysfunctional and that there are particular circumstances under which people are more likely to blame another person for a negative event having occurred. Other-blame attributions are more likely to be made when another person is present during the event, when that person is in a position of authority, and when the outcome is severe.

In control terms, other-blame can be considered dysfunctional because one ascribes blame to factors beyond one's control (i.e., to someone or something else). Additionally, Timko and Janoff-Bulman (1985) found that other-blame was associated with lower levels of self-esteem, presumably because it also implies that one had been unable to prevent the situation having occurred which, in turn, undermines beliefs about one's abilities and perceptions of invulnerability. This is consistent with the observation that participating in formal recovery interventions (e.g., debriefings) may threaten perceived control and, because receiving and/or seeking help may be interpreted as unfavorable information about one's own abilities, threaten recipients' self-esteem (Coyne, Ellard & Smith, 1990; Shalev, 1994), and increase vulnerability. Additionally, Tennen and Affleck (1991) argue that the act of blaming someone else restricts the range of available adaptive coping strategies and hinder adaptation (Silver & Wortman, 1980). In short, blaming others should impair rather than maintain self-esteem.

Although the notion of perceived control over future negative events (and therefore prevention of similar events in the future) has been influential in shaping research in this field, its link with behavioral self-blame remains at odds with therapeutic approaches that actively discourage self-blame among victims. Similarly, it is possible to speculate that justice procedures which seek to apportion blame will encourage the externalization of blame and hinder adaptation. Clearly, it is important to determine which approach is likely to have the greatest therapeutic effect. If Janoff-Bulman's view is vindicated, then any attempt to eliminate self-blame attributions may prove detrimental.

Some studies, however, have indicated that self-blame attributions (behavioral and characterological) may hinder adjustment (see Edward & MacLeod, 1996; Frazier, 1990; Meyer & Taylor, 1986). This is consistent with what could be predicted on the basis of Abramson, Seligman, and Teasdale's (1978) reformulated model of learned helplessness where external attributions for bad outcomes should actually buffer self-esteem and facilitate recovery. Self-esteem will be substantially lowered by blaming oneself for the negative event. Clearly, there is a need to go beyond the issue of cause and the ascription of blame when considering the most appropriate basis for support intervention, particularly when one considers the possible reasons for this confusion in the literature.

First, there is the failure to draw a distinction between low- and high-control events. Although self-blame for low-control events may be associated with poor recovery, self-blame attributions for high-control events may help oneself to regain control over one's life. Even in incidents where future avoidance is not an issue (police officers cannot predict or choose the events they will be involved with), being able to interpret the (original) incident as avoidable, and therefore controllable, may actually help some people to maintain the belief in a world where negative events are not seen as indiscriminate and unpredictable (Davis & Lehman, 1995).

Perceived control, however, may function independently from attributions of blame. Perceived control can be focused in three ways: on past events; on the effects of the event (i.e., present control); and on future events. Consistent with Frazier and Schauben's (1994) model, one would expect that police officers who typically focus on past and present control are more likely to show poorer recovery from stress and trauma than those who focus on future events. Similarly, those who perceive a high level of control over past events and a low level of control over future events will tend to show poorer recovery than those who perceive a low level of control over past events and a high level of control over future events. Enhancing perceived control over future events in this way can promote adaptation (Alexander & Wells, 1991; Duckworth, 1986).

Strategies that assist police officers to reinterpret past experience to identify ways of enhancing future performance and a coping style that focuses on reappraising events in terms of personal and professional growth may be effective in this context. Self-blame, if accompanied by a process which focuses on extending capability to manage high-risk situations, would be adaptive in this context. However, his goal is often inconsistent with the mode of operation of the criminal justice system (Violanti, 1996). Managing these complex and contradictory demands is an issue deserving of further attention.

Although perceived control appears to be central to understanding the relationship between how we think about an event and recovery from associated stress and trauma, Edward and MacLeod (1996) point out that the evidence put forward by Frazier and Schauben (1994) to support their model is actually concerned with perceived likelihood of the event recurring rather than perceived control over future events per se. This point may be particularly important for understanding recovery from stress in police officers. In low control incidents (such as those likely to be experienced by the police), perceived likelihood of recurrence may be an important factor in the recovery process.

Additional support for this idea comes from a recent study by Carson and MacLeod (in press), who found that perceived intention on the part of the offender was linked to perceived likelihood of recurrence. The greater the perception of intention, the greater the perceived likelihood of recurrence, and the greater the associated psychological distress. In contrast, where an incident was perceived to be due to bad luck or chance, victims were less likely to expect a recurrence and reported lower levels of distress. Direct extrapolation of this issue to police officers would suggest that perceived control over future traumatic incidents may play only a limited role in the recovery process for those who have experienced low control incidents. However, a crucial difference between primary and secondary (e.g., law enforcement) victims lies with the fact that the latter possess professional expectations regarding future capability, and, indeed, train in a context defined by these expectations. There is a need to examine the role of professional expectations and perceived control over future incidents, but the issue does not end here.

Further questions have been raised about the importance of perceived control in recent work by Carver (1997) which indicates that the measurement of perceived control (i.e., locus of control) has typically been confounded with outcome probability–specifically expectancies about future events. This is consistent with Carver and Scheier's (1990, 1994) earlier argument that the expectations we have about an event occurring at some point in the future are perhaps more important to our understanding of the underlying processes involved in recovery than are perceptions of personal control.

Second, there is the issue of outcome severity. If the consequences of the negative event are relatively low, then loss of self-esteem through blaming oneself is likely to be negligible. On the other hand, where outcome severity is high self-blame may increase feelings of vulnerability and lower self-esteem. This seems to be borne out by the findings in the literature which suggest that for relatively minor outcomes behavioral self-blame is adaptive while for serious outcomes both behavioral and characterological self-blame tend to be related to poor recovery.

Thus, the parallel drawn by Winkel et al. (1994) between victims of house theft and stranger rape (based on the anonymous and invasive nature of both crimes) would appear to be spurious. In addition, it denies both the qualitative differences in the victimization experience and the outcome severity (actual and perceived) for these victims. We need to be cautious, therefore, where assumptions are being made about the nature of an event and its likely effects on police officers–especially where those assumptions are based on one dimension such as control. It is far too simplistic to expect to devise an appropriate and effective therapeutic strategy for complex and varied traumatic events on the basis of a unitary dimension. Clearly, we are not saying that perceived control should no longer be considered as an important mediating factor in recovery. Rather, it needs to be considered in conjunction with other potentially important factors such as outcome severity plus recent advances in the field of social psychological theory such as counterfactual thinking, perceived avoidability, and outcome expectancies.

Counterfactual Thinking

Counterfactual thinking (mentally undoing an event so that the outcome is envisaged differently and, most often, for the better) appears to be significantly related to recovery. One possibility is that undoing an event may represent an attempt by people to gain some control over an apparently uncontrollable event. However, where future control is unlikely, counterfactual thinking may contribute to poorer recovery. In a recent study of people who had lost a family member in a vehicle accident (because the driver was drunk or driving too fast), those who currently reported making counterfactuals showed higher levels of distress than did those who did not engage in counterfactual thinking or those who said they had done so only in the past (Davis et al., 1995). A significant relationship was also found between frequency of undoing the event in the past month and current level of distress. This relationship held even when other factors such as rumination had been partialled out. Interestingly, when counterfactual thinking was partialled out, no relationship between rumination and reported distress was found. Even if police officers do not engage in counterfactual thinking themselves, exposure to media reporting and judicial inquiry and interpretation regarding how an incident could have been managed differently could increase the likelihood of their engaging in this kind of activity, influencing recovery, patterns of adaptation, and future expectancies.

Perceived Avoidability and Outcome Expectancies

A related line of enquiry has suggested that blaming oneself for the cause of the incident may be less important for recovery than whether one believes one could have avoided it in the first place (Davis et al., 1996). If one perceives that one's own actions leading up to the event were mutable, it is more likely that one will perceive the outcome as having been avoidable and therefore assign greater responsibility and blame to oneself for the incident having occurred. Although some studies have indicated that perceptions of avoidability are associated with higher levels of negative effect such as guilt and depression (Davis et al., 1995; Frazier, 1990), other research would indicate that perceptions of avoidability may be adaptive in that it confers a sense of control over future events or their avoidance (Boninger, Gleicher & Strathman, 1994). Such processes could be important in events involving, for example, riots, hostage-taking situations, shootings, police chases, and sieges, where officers could perceive themselves as influencing the development of the situation and would have opportunities to review their actions prior to the culmination or termination of an incident.

Helper Stereotype

Another construct that assists understanding why self-blame may be counterproductive is a professional belief in being powerful, resourceful, and able to deal with any eventuality: the "helper stereotype" (Short, 1979). This belief is inculcated into police officers' psyche through socialization into a highly cohesive profession and is reinforced through the successful performance of their role in the majority of the operational situations they encounter. Over time, officers accumulate experience of violence and the control or management of violence and, consequently, develop expectations with regard to their ability to manage or cope with violent episodes.

While these expectations may provide an appropriate preparatory basis for some violent episodes, more extreme events (c.f. dealing with a drunken brawl versus the carnage encountered following the Lockerbie disaster) may render this stereotype less applicable as a basis for evaluating performance. Nevertheless, police officers approach potentially hazardous and threatening tasks with high performance expectations. If these expectations are not realized, feelings of inadequacy and performance guilt are generated, and psychological health threatened (Duckworth, 1986).

In many traumatic contexts situational (rather than personal or professional) constraints can prevent or limit action. However, the helper stereotype can lead to the perception of these constraints being subordinated, with causal attributions about performance failure being internalized. This tendency results in these failed enactments subsequently becoming prominent aspects of the postevent ideation of those involved (Wilson, 1989). With respect to the relationship between self-blame and recovery, it is difficult to reappraise an experience in terms of how to change behavior to deal with future events when the expectation is that the behavior should have been there in the first place. These problems may be compounded through interaction with societal processes (e.g., the criminal justice system, the media) which focus attention, post hoc, on their possible preventability (e.g., identifying the perpetrator as high risk prior to the Dunblane massacre). Lengthy proceedings which focus on attributing responsibility, whether accurately or otherwise, will inhibit or hinder adaptation and recovery.

Further, feelings of performance guilt and self-blame may lead to social withdrawal and decreased use of social support (Joseph, Yule, Williams, & Andrews, 1993) because failure is seen as emanating from the self. If particularly pronounced, it can result in individuals deciding to leave police work (Duckworth, 1986). However, it is worth considering that this pattern of interaction reflects a cultural process and may confound the operation of the social psychological mechanisms that mediate recovery. This has clear implications for operational management.

The influence of the helper stereotype needs to be managed under circumstances where it is impossible to realize performance expectations. For example, following the Bradford football stadium fire, Duckworth (1986) concluded that police officers benefited in this respect by senior officers emphasizing the situational constraints on performance and by reminding them that they did the best that they could under the circumstances.

Clearly, there is much to be done to untangle the complexities of the relationship between control and traumatic reactivity and recovery management. Moreover, these issues have not been addressed in the process of developing support resources (e.g., psychological debriefing) and systems for police officers.

THE SOCIAL CONTEXT OF IMPACT AND RECOVERY

Given that recovery from trauma can be facilitated by discussing emotional reactions in a socially supportive context (Pennebaker, 1992), it will be affected by personal and social factors that hinder disclosure, including avoidance. Common avoidance factors in police groups include refraining from talking about the trauma and attempting to suppress memories of the event (Mann & Neece, 1990; Pogrebin & Poole, 1991).

Trying not to think about the trauma may actually have the opposite effect to that which might be expected. Recent research has indicated that ruminations about a traumatic event not only occur because of the trauma itself but as a result of trying not to think about the event or its implications (Gold & Wegner, 1995). Trying to suppress a traumatic memory may lead to a search for the very thing that the person is trying to forget. Wegner (1994), for example, has demonstrated that suppressed thoughts are not only difficult to keep out of mind but when people are asked to think about a target thought after initially trying to suppress that thought, they are more likely to think about the suppressed thought than people who never suppressed the thought in the first place.

The act of trying to suppress traumatic memories, therefore, may actually result in hyperaccessibility, leading to repeated and uncontrollable intrusions of unwanted thoughts and ideas. As Gold and Wegner point out, the harder we try to push away unwanted thoughts, the more likely we are to think about them. Clearly, recovery will be facilitated by reviewing memories and working through them within a socially supportive environment. However, the social context need not always function supportively.

Group cohesion can complicate recovery in other ways. Exposure to an intense experience can result in the acquisition of a social identity defined by the experience of a traumatic event. This may lead to alienation from the members of an otherwise salient group (e.g., police colleagues who were not involved), resulting in a loss of support social and hindering adaptation and readjustment.

Ironically, group support sessions may compound recovery problems. Participating in group sessions (e.g., debriefing), can result in a merging of identities, strengthening of in-group bonds between participants to form a new sense of collective identity, and the transmission of negative reactions (Gump & Kulik, 1997; Shalev, 1994), hindering rather than facilitating recovery. The group dynamics stimulated by involvement in a traumatic incident can generate other consequences.

When a violent episode is especially destructive and eliminates a sense of control and/or the opportunity to act, it may be difficult for an officer to find the positive characteristics in the group necessary to maintain a positive group identity. Under these circumstances, a breakdown of support networks may occur and a negative group social identity can develop (Shalev, 1994). Where positive differentiating features are lacking, individuals dissociate themselves from the group, reducing their opportunities to engage in emotional disclosure. If this perception extends beyond the period of the event, the quality of support available and therefore opportunities to discuss the development of future capabilities (even amongst those who were involved) may be poor or nonexistent.

Thus the coping strategies of individuals who are protecting themselves, or those of the group in response to other work demands, may stifle the responses necessary to promote the recovery from adverse reactions to trauma and make it more difficult to discuss strategies for enhancing control over future events.

CONCLUSION

While social cognitive theories have not been applied extensively to understanding traumatic reactivity and recovery in police populations, there exists good grounds for assuming their utility in this context. Self-blame (characterological and behavioral) attributions, perceived control, and perceived likelihood of event recurrence are constructs that appear capable of providing additional avenues for exploring the complexity and dynamics of reactivity and recovery from the stress and trauma associated with criminal victimization in police officers.

The theoretical frameworks discussed here can assist the development of recovery interventions and contribute to understanding how environmental factors (e.g., police organizations, family systems, and criminal justice systems and procedures) affect patterns of adaptation, well-being, and the risk status of police officers. From this brief discussion, it is clear that the relationship between social-cognitive factors and trauma and stress recovery is complex and more systematic research of these relationships is called for. Work of this nature will contribute to policy initiatives concerned with the development of training, support and organizational systems that reconcile humanistic, legal and organizational goals in a manner that assists adaptation to the effects of criminal violence, disasters, and other traumatic events.

REFERENCES

Abramson, L. Y.; Seligman, M. E. P., & Teasdale, J. D.: Learned helplessness in humans: Critique and reformulation. *Journal of Abnormal Psychology, 87*: 49-74, 1978.

Alexander, D. A., & Wells, A.: Reactions of police officers to body handling after a major disaster: A before and after comparison. *British Journal of Psychiatry, 159*: 517-555, 1991.

Amick-McMullen, A.; Kilpatrick, D. G.,& Resnick, H. S.: Homicides as a risk factor for PTSD among surviving family members. *Behavior Modification, 15*: 545 - 559, 1991.

Boninger, D. S.; Gleicher, F., & Strathman, A.: Counterfactual thinking: From what might have been to what may be. *Journal of Personality and Social Psychology, 67*: 297-307, 1994.

Carson, L., & MacLeod, M. D.: Explanations about crime and psychological distress in ethnic minority and white victims of crime: A qualitative exploration. *Journal of Community and Applied Social Psychology*, in press.

Carver, C. S.: The internal-external scale confounds internal locus of control with expectancies of positive outcomes. *Personality and Social Psychology Bulletin, 23*: 580-585, 1997.

Carver, C. S., & Scheier, M. F.: Principles of self-regulation: Action and emotion. In E. T. Higgins & R. M. Sorrentino (Eds.), *Handbook of motivation and cognition: Foundations of social behavior* (Vol. 2). New York, Guilford.

Carver, C. S., & Scheier, M. F.: Optimism and health-related cognition: What variables actually matter? *Psychology & Health, 9*: 191-195, 1994.

Coyne, J. C.; Ellard, J. H., & Smith, D. A. F.: Social support, interdependence, and the dilemmas of helping. In B. R. Sarason, I. G. Sarason & C. R. Pierce (Eds.), *Social Support: An Interactional View.* New York: Wiley, 1990.

Davis, C. G., & Lehman, D. R.: Counterfactual thinking and coping with traumatic life events. In N. J. Roese & J. M. Olson (Eds.), *What might have been: The social psychology of counterfactual thinking.* Hillsdale, NJ, Lawrence Erlbaum, 1995.

Davis, C. G.; Lehman, D. R.; Silver, R. C.; Wortman, C. M., & Ellard, J. H.: Self-blame following a traumatic event: The role of perceived avoidability. *Personality and Social Psychology Bulletin, 22*: 557-567, 1996.

Davis, C. G.; Lehman, D. R.; Wortman, C. M.; Silver, R. C., & Thomson, S. C.: The undoing of traumatic events. *Personality and Social Psychology Bulletin, 21*: 109-124, 1995.

Duckworth, D.: Psychological problems arising from disaster work. *Stress Medicine, 2*: 315-323, 1986.

Edward, K. E., & MacLeod, M. D.: *Blame, beliefs and recovery: An examination of factors affecting victim recovery from sexual and non-sexual crimes.* Paper presented at the VI European Conference on Psychology & Law, Siena, 1996.

Eränen, L., & Liebkind, K.: Coping with disaster: The helping behavior of communities and individuals. In J. P. Wilson & B. Raphael (Eds.), *International Handbook of Traumatic Stress Syndromes.* New York, Plenum, 1993.

Frazier, P. A.: Victim attributions and post-rape trauma. *Journal of Personality and Social Psychology, 59*: 298-304, 1990.

Frazier, P. A., & Schauben, L.: Causal attributions and recovery from rape and other stressful life events. *Journal of Social and Clinical Psychology, 13*: 1-14, 1994.

Gold, D. B., & Wegner, D. M.: Origins of ruminative thought: Trauma, incompleteness, nondisclosure, and suppression. *Journal of Applied Social Psychology, 25*: 1245-1261, 1995.

Gump, B. B., & Kulik, J. A.: Stress, affiliation, and emotional contagion. *Journal of Personality and Social Psychology, 72*: 305-319, 1997.

Horowitz, M. J.: Stress-response syndromes: a review of posttraumatic stress and adjustment disorders. In J. P. Wilson & B. Raphael (Eds.), *International Handbook of Traumatic Stress Syndromes.* New York, Plenum, 1993.

Janoff-Bulman, R.: *Shattered Assumptions: Toward a New Psychology of Trauma.* New York, The Free Press, 1992.

Joseph, P.; Yule, W.; Williams, R., & Andrews, B.: Crisis support in the aftermath of disaster: A longitudinal perspective. *British Journal of Clinical Psychology, 32*: 177-185, 1993.

Kahler, A. S., & MacLeod, M. D.: *Blame, revenge and the bereavement process.* Paper presented at the XXVI International Congress of Psychology, Ottawa, 1996.

MacLeod, M. D.; Carson, L., & Prescott, R. G. W.: *Listening to victims: Victimization episodes and the criminal justice system in Scotland.* Edinburgh, HMSO, 1996.

Mann, J. P., & Neece, J.: Workers, compensation for law enforcement related to post traumatic stress disorder. *Behavioral Sciences and the Law, 8*: 447-456, 1990.

Meyer, C. B., & Taylor, S. E.: Adjustment to rape. *Journal of Personality and Social Psychology, 50*: 1226-1234, 1986.

Paton, D.: Disaster relief work: An assessment of training effectiveness. *Journal of Traumatic Stress, 7*: 275-288, 1994.

Pennebaker, J. W.: Inhibition as the linchpin of health. In H. S. Friedman (Ed.), *Hostility, coping and health.* Washington, American Psychological Association, 1992.

Pogrebin, M. R., & Poole, E. D.: Police and tragic events: The management of emotions. *Journal of Criminal Justice, 19*: 395-403, 1991.

Shalev, A. Y.: Debriefing following traumatic exposure. In R. J. Ursano, B. G. McCaughey & C. S. Fullerton (Eds.), *Individual and community responses to trauma & disaster.* Cambridge, Cambridge University Press, 1994.

Short, P.: Victims and helpers. In R. L. Heathcote & B. G. Tong (Eds.), *Natural hazards in Australia.* Canberra, Australian Academy of Science, 1979.

Silver, R., & Wortman, C.: Coping with undesirable life events. In J. Garber & M. Seligmam (Eds.), *Human helplessness.* New York, Academic Press, 1980.

Tennen, I. I., & Affleck, G.: Blaming others for threatening events. *Psychological Bulletin, 108*: 209-232, 1991.

Timko, C., & Janoff-Bulman, R.: Attribution, vulnerability and psychological adjustment: The case of breast cancer. *Health Psychology, 4*: 521-546, 1985.

Violanti, J.: Trauma stress and police work. In Paton, D. & Violanti, J. (Eds.), *Traumatic stress in critical occupations: Recognition, consequences and treatment.* Springfield, IL., Charles C. Thomas, 1996.

Wegner, D. M.: *White Bears and Other Unwanted Thoughts.* New York, Guilford, 1994.

Wilson, J. P.: *Trauma, transformation, and healing: An integrated approach to theory, research, and post-traumatic therapy.* New York, Brunner/Mazell, 1989.

Winkel, F. W.; Denkers, A., & Vrij: The effects of attributions on crime victims' psychological readjustment. *Genetic, Social and General Psychology Monographs, 120*: 147-168, 1994.

Chapter 4

POLICE COMPASSION FATIGUE (PCF): THEORY, RESEARCH, ASSESSMENT, TREATMENT, AND PREVENTION

CHARLES R. FIGLEY

Sometimes I think that no one notices and no one cares. Then when they care they hate us.
–Officer Frank Kelly, a 30-year veteran police detective in Chicago area

Although I did not admit it to anyone–my partner, my wife–I kept dreaming of the little kid's eyes.
—"Sgt. Bob" after-effects of an emergency rescue

INTRODUCTION

Cops often talk about burnout from dealing with paper work, dumb rules, and inept supervisors. Yet there is another form of burnout that affects law enforcement. It involves caring so much about community members hurt by criminals that police officers, develop, over time, a kind of stress called compassion fatigue. Lack of appreciation from the public is not really what affects Officer Kelly. What affects him is the loss of his partner three years ago. What affects him is a 60-year-old grandmother screaming at him for killing her "baby." Officer Kelly knows that her son was a crack addict and had gotten away with murder, yet he walked every time because of cracks in the system. What affects Officer Kelly is knowing that the criminal justice system is criminal and without justice. These are the common stressors of modern policing and I choose to call it "Compassion Fatigue." It describes officers burned out because of their work's emotional toll. The term was first used by a journalist and health reporter, Beverly Joinson (Joinson, 1985). She described the effects of trauma work on nurses and described the problem as less a psychiatric disorder and more a type of burnout resulting in rather insensitive patient care. It is and it is not.

Police Compassion Fatigue (PCF), in the case of Officer Kelly, is not fill-
ing out reports accurately, being insensitive to the public in handling duties
(e.g., being rude), endangering lives, and being dangerous to oneself and
one's family. The model designed to account for the development and mitigation of PCF draws on the Compassion Fatigue Model (Figley, 1995). A
copy of the Police Compassion Fatigue (PCF) Self Test can be found at the
end of this book (Appendix I). Completing such a self-administered test in
the privacy of the officer's home (maybe asking one's spouse to help fill it
out) will give him or her some feedback, help him or her slow down, bring
some joy back into life, find some good things that can replace the bad; get
help if you can't do it yourself.

In this chapter, I will first focus on helping police officers to understand
the health risks of not confronting and dealing with the demons of the work
that cause chronic stress. My hope is that at least some officers may be
inspired to change their habits and live out a career. The second section will
discuss research literature and theories that suggest that work stressors leave
lasting impressions. The more the traumatic experience the more the
impact. We also discuss the similarities and differences between burnout,
police compassion fatigue (PCF), and the Freudian notion of countertransference. The third section brings everything together, in a model of Police
Compassion Fatigue that begins with one's ability to empathize, and predicts
the circumstances under which police officers develop and maintain compassion fatigue to the detriment of themselves, their families, and their duties
as police officers. The final section is the "DO SOMETHING!" section. It
describes what other cops have done to get over PCF.

A REVIEW OF THE LITERATURE

Among the trends in modern policing affecting large numbers of
American police is community policing, increasing contact between police
agencies and the communities they serve. A recent report entitled
"Organizational Issues in Community Policing," published by the National
Institute of Justice Solicitation (1997), noted: "Shifts and changes in the landscape of criminal behavior and criminal enterprise challenge the ability of
community-oriented policing agencies to respond and adapt. Perhaps more
importantly, community-oriented policing poses a very real challenge to the
integrity of the police organization. This paper focuses on the impact of
community-oriented policing on the organization, structure, operations, and
procedures of the police agency." These views challenge long-held assumptions about appropriate command and supervisory structure; methods of
evaluation; paths of promotion; the need for diversity in a police agency; and
the management of time, space (geography), and staffing.

Many police agencies have significantly altered the functions of police officers operational units by shifting to community-oriented policing. Increasingly, police and communities recognize the importance of citizens to address crime and disorder. More and more, police agencies are assessing the advantage of redesigning organizational structures and administrative processes to allow officers appropriate levels of discretion and flexibility in their complex community environments. Persistent problems of policing, such as the unwarranted use of force and the issue of police integrity, take on a new significance in departments where community policing has brought officers in closer partnership with (and sharper scrutiny by) the community they serve. At the same time, police officers endure not only traumatic but chronic stress over more than a decade. They are more likely to develop PTSD and are as much as 150 times more likely to suffer from one or more medical maladies (Boscarino, 1997). Consequently, we, as members of the community in which these officers work, must be far more diligent in caring for them.

STRESS IN LAW ENFORCEMENT

Police officers do not share stressful information about their job because they believe that it would upset their family/spouse. They are right. However, there are unintended and unwanted consequences in not telling. By understanding the phenomenon of Secondary Traumatic Stress(STS) and Secondary Traumatic Stress Disorder (STSD) we can both manage and prevent it much more effectively. Increasing the quality of police officer disclosure to their spouses reduces work-related stress, increases morale, and enhances the marital bond. This is illustrated in the case in Figure 4.1.

Common Symptoms

Recently, Maslach and Leiter (1998) suggested that modern workforces experience job burnout in epidemic proportions and departments like those in which Officer Kelly work are in large part responsible. Yet, for Officer Kelley and his wife, the job stress leading to compassion fatigue, though similar, takes on much greater importance than regular burnout. In other words, the pressures caused by organizational structure and culture pales in comparison to the traumatic consequences of work leading to compassion fatigue. A review of the burnout literature suggests that the symptomatic reactions of those with duty-related (work-induced) PTSD or Compassion Fatigue embrace those symptoms described in Table 4.1.

Figure 4.1. A Composite Case Example of Compassion Fatigue.

Sam Kelley is a former narcotics officer released from service due to a dramatic series of incidents that resulted in the death of his partner. A well-known drug dealer in the community killed his partner. Officer Kelley had been a member of the Department for 20 years. Yet, most of the stress he experienced from the numerous critical incidents was felt following retirement. His wife, Cassie, experienced all of the stress her husband felt including the themes of the nightmares: Helplessness. They have a 2-year-old daughter, Sarah Sue.

This police couple sought help at the Florida State University Traumatology Institute's weekly clinic for traumatized people with "stress problems." They were concerned about the husband's behavior becoming a threat to his family. The wife describes an incident in which the husband suddenly behaved like he was being called to go on a drug enforcement mission. He thought that he had heard his beeper go off (though his wife told him at the time that his beeper is turned off and is a drawer). Appearing to be in a trance, the officer hurriedly began to put on his gear in preparation. The wife immediately went to the garage, hid his weapon, unplugged the garage door opener (so that he would take their old, second car), and other actions. Through a special routine of assurances and distractions, the wife gradually convinced her husband that he needed to come back to bed. The next morning the officer did not remember the situation except for vague scenes. This happened at least five times in the last three years since retirement.

The counselor trained in traumatology would recognize that the officer was suffering from Compassion Fatigue caused by incidents involving his partner's death. The client reenacted the various incidents and searched, though rather haphazardly, for peace of mind. The counselor suggested that the couple participate in a new type of therapy called Eye Movement Desensitization and Reprocessing (EMDR). The therapy is designed to uncover critical information that will enable the client to replace the current feelings of frustration, rage, anger, the urge to protect, the feelings of incompetence with more realistic perspectives. The Traumatologist suggested that the EMDR session be videotaped so that the client would be able to watch it with his wife and discuss it together in the safety and support of their family and home. The tape will be the target of future sessions. Eventually the client, with the help of his wife, will answer five fundamental questions: (1) What incidents happened that resulted in my partner's death? (2) Why did it have to happen? (3) Why did the client and other officers act as they did at the time of and after the death? (4) What if something like this happens again to you—what will you do? Their story is discussed at the end of this chapter.

Reiss (1970) was one of the first to note the secondary effects of police work on the friends and family of officers. Depue (1981) found that police family life included considerable stress, due, in part, to police work involving shift work, the need for confidentiality, danger, public apathy/hostility, isolation, and boredom. Niederhoffer (1978) suggested that the law enforcement profession is more a way of life than just a job and that conflicts between the officer and the spouse and children can be traced to this.

Table 4.1. Examples of compassion fatigue burnout symptoms.

Cognitive	Emotional	Behavioral	Spiritual	Personal Relations	Physical/ Somatic	Work Performance
Lowered concentration	Powerlessness	Impatient	Questioning the meaning	Withdrawal	Shock	Low morale
Decreased self-esteem	Anxiety	Irritable	of life	Decreased interest in	Sweating	Low motivation
Apathy	Guilt	Withdrawn	Loss of	intimacy	Rapid heartbeat	Avoiding tasks
Rigidity	Anger/rage	Moody	purpose	or sex	Breathing	Obsession about details
Disorientation	Survivor guilt	Regression	Lack of self-	Mistrust	difficulties	Apathy
Perfectionism	Shutdown	Sleep disturbance	satisfaction	Isolation from others	Aches and pains	Negativity
Minimization	Numbness	Nightmares	Pervasive hopelessness	Over protection	Dizziness	Lack of appreciation
Preoccupation with trauma	Fear	Appetite changes	Anger at God	as a parent	Increased number and	Detachment
Thoughts of self-harm or	Helplessness	Hyper-vigilance	Questioning of prior religious	Projection of anger or blame	intensity of medical	Poor work comm.
harm to others	Sadness	Elevated startle	beliefs	Intolerance	maladies	Staff conflicts
	Depression	response	Loss of faith in a higher	Loneliness	Other somatic complaints	Absenteeism
	Emotional roller coaster	Accident proneness	power	Increased interpersonal	Impaired immune	Exhaustion Irritability
	Depleted	Greater	Greater skepticism	conflicts	system	Withdrawal from colleagues
	Overly sensitive	Losing things	about religion			

Madamba (1986) found a significant relationship between the stress of police work and marital satisfaction when police cultural variables were controlled, demonstrating the connection in the minds of the officers surveyed.

More recently, Borum and Philpot (1993) noted three major categories of influences in the work of law enforcement personnel that can influence family relationships. These influences are from the law enforcement agency, from peer/socialization influences, and from the police officer's role generally. Agency influences on police family relationships include the time and energy required of the job, as well as the unpredictability of various assignments. Rarely is police work a 9 to 5 job. Those promoted are most often those who attended more to the requirements of their job than to their marriage or children.

Socialization Influences

Socialization influences on police family relationships include the inevitable changes that take place for officers, in contrast to their spouse. As with any new employee who joins a closely-knit, interdependent company, police officers are drawn toward one another for support, protection, and encouragement. This form of comradeship is critical because of the special nature of the work. Also, there is a perceived lack of support by the public. Many studies have noted that values and attitudes change during and following initial police officer training (see Chapter 8). The characteristics of a person who values control, rigidity, dominance, competition, autonomy, rationality, and rules contrast and clash with the characteristics of a loving, sensitive, responsive spouse. When marriage begins with a certain set of expectations and behaviors and the rigors of a career force change in these expectations, resentment toward the career in inevitable. As one wife suggested, when considering the changes in her husband after becoming an officer: "His outlook on things has changed, his views, his opinions, his personality. He's changed, and we're not changing together. And that frightens me a lot" (Borum & Philpot, 1993, p.124).

Police Role Influences

Police role influences on police family relationships include the constant shifting between the role of peacemaker/law enforcer and the role of a loving, sensitive, and responsible spouse and parent. Indeed, few careers require so much of the professional for so long, for so little money with a social status whose competencies are so at variance with those of a loving spouse and parent. Borum and Philpot (1993) note that because of these various influences connected with work, police families must contend with an uncommon set of stressors: structural problems, police attitudes, job-related problems, social-interpersonal problems, and problematic behaviors (e.g., substance abuse, verbal and physical abuse).

There are also special stressors on children of police officers. Children report that they are treated differently by peers and adults who are aware that either parent is a police officer. Children report the pressure to "be good" and not get in trouble. For to do so would not only reflect poorly on themselves, but seemingly more important, it would embarrass the family and the police profession. This is especially true for the children of senior officers. Moreover, it is more newsworthy if an officer's child gets in trouble, compared to any other child.

Conjoint Police Officer Marriages

When both partners are in law enforcement, the police family can avoid some of these stressors, but others may be amplified. For example, conjoint police officer marriages could combine the needs for both a police partner and a marital partner. They more immediately understand each other's pressures changing attitudes and values, as noted above. However, disadvantages include the inability to separate work from home, coworker interference, disruptions, and meddling in marital affairs. Perhaps more important, is the difficulty of shift work (Borum & Philpot, 1993). There is growing evidence that job-related burnout and family readjustment problems may be far more troublesome for officers than job-related problems. There are considerable advantages for police officers who are part of a family system since the system is an important resource. The challenge is attending to the needs of the family system, recognizing how it is affected by police work, and preventing and eliminating unwanted consequences.

CONTRASTS BETWEEN SECONDARY TRAUMATIC STRESS AND OTHER CONCEPTS

Police Compassion Fatigue is the latest in an evolving concept known in the field of Traumatology as secondary traumatic stress (Figley, 1982, 1983, 1985, 1989). It has also been called vicarious traumatization (McCann & Pearlman, 1989); secondary survivor (Remer & Elliott, 1988a; 1988b); "emotional contagion," defined as an affective process in which "an individual observing another person experiences emotional responses parallel to that person's actual or anticipated emotions" (Miller, Stiff & Ellis, 1988, p. 254); rape-related family crisis (Erickson, 1989; White & Rollins, 1981); "proximity" effects on female partners of war veterans (Verbosky & Ryan, 1988); generational effects of trauma (McCubbin, Dahl, Lester, & Ross, 1977); and the need for family "detoxification" from war-related traumatic stress (Rosenheck & Thomson, 1986). Finally, some view difficulties with client problems as one of simple countertransference (Maroda, 1991). This view, however, is encased in an elaborate theoretical context that is difficult to measure. Typically this phenomenon is associated with the "cost of caring" (Figley, 1982) for others in emotional pain.

Burnout versus Secondary Traumatic Stress (Compassion Stress/Fatigue)

Some view the problems faced by workers with job stress as simply burnout (see Chapter 5). In contrast to burnout, which emerges gradually and is a result of emotional exhaustion, Secondary Traumatic Stress (STS) can emerge suddenly and without warning. In addition, Figley (1995) noted that with Secondary Traumatic Stress, in contrast to burnout, there is a sense of helplessness and confusion. Also, there is a sense of isolation from supporters, symptoms are often disconnected from real causes, and yet there is a faster rate of recovery from symptoms. STS may be defined as the natural consequent behaviors and emotions resulting from knowledge about a traumatizing event experienced by a significant other. It is the stress resulting from helping or wanting to help a traumatized person. A model that emerges from these two perspectives suggests that families affected by major life events can, in the process of living with or providing direct assistance to traumatized family members, experience secondary traumatic stress themselves (Figley, 1983).

Secondary Traumatization

Close family members who come in contact with a traumatized person may experience considerable emotional upset and may, over time, become indirect "victims" of the traumatic event, experiencing secondary traumatization (Figley, 1982) or traumatic stress. Numerous studies have confirmed the existence of this phenomenon among spouses and children of Holocaust survivors (Davidson, 1980; Freyberg, 1980), war veterans (Kulka et al., 1990; Maloney, 1988; Rosenheck & Nathan, 1985; Solomon et al., 1996; Waysman et al., 1995), and therapists of trauma clients (McCann & Pearlman, 1990). Recently, Figley and Kleber (1995) suggested that secondary traumatic stress (STS) is an important frontier for scholars concerned with accurately accounting for the long-term effects of traumatic events and, given the evidence, STS should be incorporated into the documentation of PTSD diagnostic evaluations.

More recently, Figley (1997a), in a collection of articles by experts in secondary traumatic stress in families, declared that family burnout is the best concept to describe this phenomenon in that context. Thus, police wife Cassie Kelly has family burnout from dealing with her husband's mental problems caused by his work as a police officer.

In summary, we learned about compassion fatigue through research on interpersonal relationships, from studying the systemic effects of trauma in families to the effects of working with traumatized people and traumatizing work situations. These include, but are not limited to, 911 operators, law enforcement officers, firefighters, military personnel, emergency medical technicians, the clergy, and those who counsel the traumatized. A model of family burnout was recently presented (Figley, 1997b). Below is a model devoted exclusively to the compassion fatigue experience by police officers like Officer Sam Kelley.

A MODEL OF POLICE COMPASSION FATIGUE (PCF)

A model is an arrangement of critical factors acting together over time to account for an effect. The effect in this case is both compassion stress and compassion fatigue (Figure 4.2). The model is derived from the generic compassion fatigue model (Figley, 1995) and suggests that if you are empathic, have sufficient concern, and expose yourself to traumatized people, you will give the right compassionate, empathic response as needed in police work.

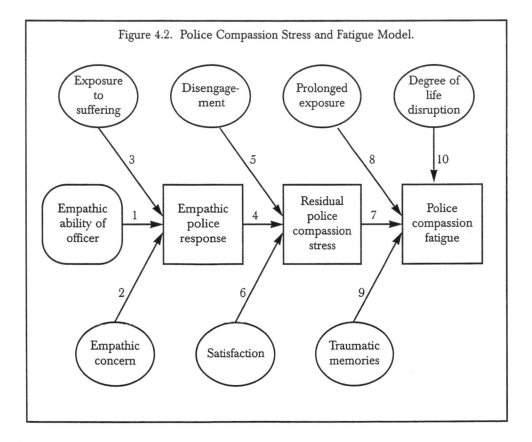

Figure 4.2. Police Compassion Stress and Fatigue Model.

However, the model also suggests the existence of residual stress from being compassionate and empathic that, if left without attention, may developed into a debilitating condition called compassion fatigue. To reduce this residual distress, the police officer either must get their mind off the work, to let it go from their attention or convince themselves that they have done all they can do. If their efforts are insufficient to eliminate compassion stress, there is a build-up of distressing, unprocessed memories and sensations that requires discharging. With sufficient, prolonged exposure to duty-related stressors of all sorts, this will lead to compassion fatigue eventually. Moreover, if there are unprocessed traumatic memories from one's personal life that have not been dealt with and desensitized, this could lead more quickly to police compassion fatigue. Even minor life changes may be enough to tip the scale toward this debilitation. Therefore, the model suggests at least 10 intervention points for lowering a police officers compassion-related distress and fatigue. These are discussed in the next section.

DO SOMETHING!

In this section, I report on what other officers have done to get over Police Compassion Fatigue. A copy of the PCF Self-Assessment Test can be found in the Appendix. It should be useful in police departments concerned about the health of their officers.

Strategies for Prevention

Maslach and Leiter (1998) suggest that policies and procedures should take into account all that causes distress and takes it away. They argue for a work-sensitive approach that insures employees personal needs are considered in providing health care, vacation and leave policies, strategies for mental health promotion, and other effective strategies. They are the latest in a series of experts on burnout that promote a more friendly and sensitive workplace. Unfortunately, Maslach and Leiter did not know about the secret world of law enforcement. Other chapters in this volume will discuss the special culture of police departments and police work. For the purposes of this chapter, we offer the following suggestions to departments managing law enforcement services.

INSTITUTIONAL POLICIES AND PROCEDURES

Five Fundamental Principles

Awareness of the Risks and Costs of Police Work on Officers and Their Families

Recognize that good officers hurt sometimes, and good families hurt with them and somehow enable them to return to work in better spirits.

Commitment to Lower the Risks and Costs

There is a constant source of support of the troops in showing that the department is attempting to lower the risks of police compassion fatigue and family burnout. Moreover, when officers and families are affected, the depart dispatches the best help possible to help them recover as quickly as possible.

Adequate Applicant Screening for Resilience and Awareness

Those most at risk are those officers and families without resiliency. Moreover, those who thrive in this work are especially aware of its effect on them as an officer and as a family. As a result, corrective actions are implemented promptly, and there is greater acceptance of duty-related stress and the need to take action to deal with it.

Adequate Policies and Procedures to Educate and Protect Workers

Every Academy class, every rookie orientation, every postincident debriefing should include information about critical incident stress, police compassion fatigue, and police family burnout. There should be sufficient education and effective and informed procedures for handling stress and its cumulative effects.

Work Group Attitudes and Action Plans

When considering the work group, including partners on patrol, officers should also be knowledgeable about, and effective in, handling critical incident stress, compassion fatigue, and family burnout. There appears to be five axioms in operation in this area:

1. The 3:1 Ratio Rule

For every three hours of discussing a case that is traumatic, there should be one hour devoted to personal processing. This may take the form of non-work conversation over a beer off duty, it may be a formal postincident debriefing, it may be humor regarding the nature of the work, or other activities that result in attention to the self.

2. *CISD/M Plans and Actions*

Critical Incident Stress Debriefings and Stress Management are now part of every modern police department in most developed countries. The theory is that if officers are able to discuss freely with fellow officers or others experiencing the event with them, they will avoid the predictable acute stress and more troubling posttraumatic stress disorder or compassion fatigue. Each team should have at least one well-trained person trained in debriefing and defusing methods. Ideally, everyone would be trained and would work with any other group that needs their help.

3. *Humor and Other Stress Reduction Methods*

Gallows humor is common throughout the world among work groups dealing with stressful work. Humor plays a major role in reducing stress because it causes a release of endorphins in the brain. This hormone is associated with the class pleasure response and frequently overrides fear, depression, and inaction. In sufficient dosages, it even enhances the immune system thus keeping us healthier. Work groups should recognize those activities that result in a reduction of stress and do it more frequently. Most often, however, it is necessary for the group to adopt additional methods such as team sports, card playing, going to sporting events, and, if acceptable, forms of prayer or other spiritual and meditative activities that lower stress levels.

4. *Low Tolerance of Substance Abuse*

"Friends don't let friends who drink drive." Fellow officers should recognize that abuse of any substances is no substitute for more effective stress reduction methods. Team members need to speak up, take chances, and be honest with fellow officer.

5. *Facilitation of Coworker Health and Self Care*

Team members should be like siblings and promote health, healthy living, and self-care. This takes many forms including serving as a role model to younger officers.

INDIVIDUAL ACTIONS

In addition to action by departments and teams to prevent compassion fatigue and their causes, each individual officers should take action on their own behalf.

Letting Go of Work

Consistent with the PCF Model, officers need effective strategies for disengaging from the work. Many officer's lives are shaped by police work. It can be all consuming. Yet, to safeguard themselves from potential career-killing stress, boundaries should be erected. "Leave the station at the station and the ranch at the ranch." Officers may need help from their family to act on this. Some officers at a recent workshop shared their strategies:

> "When I get in my car and say to myself: this is my car and not the squad car." By doing so he recalls the facts that he is not being paid now, there will be plenty of bad guys when he returns to work.
> "The photo does it." Another takes out or imagines that he takes out and looks at a photo of his family. It reminds him of what is important in life and to not dirty his home with the trash from work.
> "It's the family stupid" is a statement one officer says to herself to remind her of her priorities.

Strategies for Gaining a Sense of Achievement

Another major factor in reducing compassion stress, especially at the end of the work day, is acquiring a sense of achievement. Officers can accomplish this by establishing achievable standards of work performance. If setbacks happen, officers can view their work in a larger context than a single incident. Allowing and welcoming support from others is also important. Colleagues offer reassurance, not just to be nice, but in return for similar reassurances when they need it. A recent workshop produced these strategies that help reduce compassion stress and retain a sense of job satisfaction:

> "I say 'I am only one person' to remind myself or others that it takes many people many days to achieve a difficult goal. "
> "My instincts are to be very self critical and get stuck there." I force myself to go to my file with copies of my achievements and commendations. It's made me cry at times the relief it's brought me."
> "I put my self in the hands of Jesus." I ask for direction and relax until that happens. Most often it's the next day at work.

Strategies for Acquiring Adequate Rest and Relaxation

Getting a solid night's deep sleep, regular exercise, good nutrition, and adequate time off to enjoy life is important. Yet many officers and their families believe they have insufficient time. They need to develop a schedule that includes these activities. Much time is wasted on strategies for lowering stress when these measures increase our tolerance for it.

The Perfect Stress Reduction Methods

Everyone must find the methods that work for them. One method discovered at Florida State University is available on the world wide web at the Green Cross Projects web site at www.fsu.edu~greencross.

COUNSELING ASSISTANCE FOR COMPASSION FATIGUE AND FAMILY BURNOUT

In "Helping Traumatized Families" (Figley, 1989) I share a procedure for helping families cope with traumatic stress. It was the best we could do at the time. Now, there is a better way. The Police Family Treatment Program includes three separate counseling approaches that are effective individually but even more powerful together.

Phase ONE: Specifying the Goals of Treatment

This includes identifying all of the thoughts, feelings, and sensations family members feel now and their dreams of replacing them with certain other more functional and acceptable thoughts, feelings, and sensations.

Phase TWO: Telling the Story

Here a spouse talks to the mate about an especially traumatic event. The spouse must not say or do anything that will sway the partner to tell the story as fully as needed with special attention to the thoughts and feelings and sensations at the time.

Phase THREE: Reconsidering the Story

Reconsidering the story through insight into new information that may lead to a new assessment of the circumstances.

Phase FOUR: Developing a Healing Theory

Developing a healing theory that answers the four questions noted above. Along the way the counselor helps the family through the various phases and insures that their listening follows the rules and that they reach an end point, the elimination of distress and the emergence of their healing theory.

This chapter ends with Officer Kelly and Cassie Kelly healing theory. They were able to work out their life crisis that threatened their marriage and career. Together they shared their healing theory:

> My partner was killed and my wife and I are were affected so much because we cared. He was affected more than she because it was his partner and he was there when he died. He felt ashamed, angry, vengeful, and felt hate for the perpetrator and everyone and thing connected with him. But that was part of caring for someone so much and the same reason when she reacted to my distress. Once we figured out what was happening, we sought help because we did not want our marriage to fail us now. We now know that this work takes a toll and we are better able to handle as a family. If something like this happens again we know we can depend on each other. Also, we know that we can be a resource to other officers and police families affected by the stress of police work.

REFERENCES

Alexander, D. A.: The impact of police work on police officers' spouses and families. In J. T. Reese & E. Scrivner (Eds.), *Law enforcement families: Issues and answers.* Washington DC, U.S. Department of Justice, 1994.

Bibbins, V. E.: The quality of family and marital life of police personnel. In J. T. Reese & H. A. Goldstein (Eds.), *Psychological services for law enforcement.* Washington, DC, US Government Printing Office, 1986.

Borum, R., & Philpot, C.: Therapy with law enforcement couples: Clinical management of the "high-risk lifestyle." *American Journal of Family Therapy, 21*: 122-135, 1993.

Boscarino, J. A.: Diseases among men 20 years after exposure to severe stress: Implications for clinical research and medical care. *Psychosomatic Medicine, 59*: 1121-1131, 1997.

Erickson, C. A.: Rape and the family. In C. R. Figley (Ed.), *Treating traumatized families.* New York, Brunner/Mazel, 1989.

Figley, C. R. (Ed.): *Stress disorders among vietnam veterans.* New York, Brunner/Mazel, 1978.

Figley, C. R. (Ed.): *Strangers at home: Vietnam veterans since the war.* New York, Praeger, 1980.

Figley, C.: *Traumatization and comfort: Close relationships may be hazardous to your health.* Keynote Conference Presentation. Families and close relationships: Individuals in social interaction, Texas Tech University, Lubbock, TX, February, 1982.

Figley, C. R.: Catastrophes: An overview of family reactions. In C. R. Figley & H. I. McCubbin (Eds.), *Stress and the family: Volume 2. Coping with catastrophe.* New York, Brunner/Mazel, 1983.

Figley, C. R.: The family as victim: Mental health implications. *Psychiatry, 6:* 283-291, 1985.

Figley, C. R: Post-traumatic stress: The role of the family and social support systems. In C. R. Figley (Ed.), *Trauma and its wake: Volume 2. Post-traumatic stress disorder: Theory, research, and treatment.* New York, Brunner/Mazel, 1986.

Figley, C. R.: *Helping traumatized families.* San Francisco, Jossey-Bass, 1989.

Figley, C. R.: *Secondary traumatic stress disorder conceptualization.* Paper presented at the International Society for Traumatic Stress Studies, Washington, D.C., October, 1991.

Figley, C. R: Post-traumatic stress disorder, Part II: Relationship with various traumatic events. *Violence Update, 2:* 1-11, 1992a.

Figley, C. R.: *Secondary traumatic stress and disorder: Theory, research, and treatment.* Paper presented at the First World Meeting of the International Society for Traumatic Stress Studies, Amsterdam, June, 1992b.

Figley, C. R. (Ed.): *Compassion fatigue: Secondary traumatic stress disorder from treating the traumatized.* New York, Brunner/Mazel, 1995.

Figley, C. R., & Kleber, R. J.: Beyond the "victim": Secondary traumatic stress. In R. J. Kleber, C. R. Figley, & B. P. R. Gersons (Eds.), *Beyond trauma: Cultural and societal dynamics.* New York, Plenum, 1995.

Figley, C. R. (Ed.): *Burnout in families: The systemic costs of caring.* Boca Raton, FL, CRC Press, 1997a.

Figley, C. R.: Burnout as a systemic traumatic stress: A model for helping traumatized family members. In C. R. Figley (Ed.), *Burnout in families: The systemic costs of caring.* Boca Raton, FL, CRC Press, 1997b.

Freyberg, J. T.: Difficulties in separation-individuation as experienced by offspring of Nazi Holocaust survivors. *American Journal of Orthopsychiatry, 50:* 87-95, 1980.

Joinson, C. (1992). Coping with compassion fatigue. *Nursing, 22:* 116-122, 1992.

Kulka, R. A.; Schlenger, W. E.; Fairbank, J. A.; Hough, R. L.; Jordan, B.K.; Marmar, C. R.; Weis, D. S., with Gradey, D. A.: *Trauma and the Vietnam war generation: Report of findings from the National Vietnam Veterans Readjustment Study.* New York, Brunner/Mazel, 1990.

Madamba, H. J.: The relation between stress and marital relationships in police officers. In J. T. Reese & H. A. Goldstein (Eds). *Psychological services for law enforcement.* Washington, DC, US Government Printing Office,.1986.

Maloney, L. J.: Post-traumatic stresses of women partners of Vietnam veterans. *Smith College Studies in Social Work, 58:* 122-143, 1988.

Maroda, K.: *The power of countertransference.* New York, Guilford, 1991.

Maslach, C., & Leiter, M.P.: *The truth about burnout.* San Francisco, Jossey-Bass, 1997.

McCubbin, H. I.; Dahl, B. B.; Lester, G. R., & Ross, B.: The POW and his children: Evidence for the origin of second generational effects of captivity. *International Journal of Sociology of the Family, 7*: 25-36, 1977.

McCann, I. L., & Pearlman, L. A.: Vicarious traumatization: A framework for understanding the psychological effects of working with victims. *Journal of Traumatic Stress, 3*: 131-149, 1990.

Means, M. S: Family therapy issues in law enforcement families. In J. T. Reese & H. A. Goldstein (Eds). *Psychological Services for Law Enforcement.* Washington, DC., US Government Printing Office, 1986.

Miller, K.; Stiff, J., & Ellis, B.: Communication and empathy as precursors to burnout among human service workers. *Communication Monographs, 55*: 336-341, 1988.

Reese, J. T., & Goldstein, H. A.: *Psychological Services for Law Enforcement.* Washington, D. C.: U.S. Government Printing Office, 1986.

Reiss, A. J.: The dimensions of police loyalty. *American Behavior and Science, 13*: 693-704, 1970.

Remer, R., & Elliot, J.: Characteristics of secondary victims of sexual assault. *International Journal of Family Psychiatry, 9*: 373-387, 1988a.

Remer, R., & Elliott, J. E.: Management of secondary victims of sexual assault. *International Journal of Family Psychiatry, 9*: 389-401, 1988b

Rosenheck, R., & Nathan, P.: Secondary traumatization in the children of Vietnam veterans with PTSD. *Hospital and Community Psychiatry, 36*: 538-539, 1985.

Rosenheck, R., & Thomson, J.: 'Detoxification' of Vietnam war trauma: A combined family-individual approach. *Family Process, 25*: 559-570, 1986.

Solomon, Z.; Waysman, J.; Avitzur, E., & Enoch, D.: Psychiatric symptomatology among wives of soldiers following combat stress reaction: The role of the social network and marital relations. *Anxiety Research, 4*: 213-223, 1991.

Solomon, Z.; Waysman, M.; Levy, G.; Fried, B.; Mikulincer, M.; Benbenishty, R.; Florian, V., & Bleich, A. (1992). From front line to home front: A study of secondary traumatization. *Family Process, 31*: 289-302, 1992.

Verbosky, S. J., & Ryan, D. A.: Female partners of Vietnam veterans: Stress by proximity. *Issues in Mental Health Nursing, 9*: 95-104, 1988.

White, P. N., & Rollins, J. C.: Rape: A family crisis. *Family Relations, 30*: 103-109, 1981.

Wilson, J. P., & Raphael, B. (Ed.): *International handbook of traumatic stress syndromes.* New York, Plenum, 1993.

Chapter 5

POLICE PSYCHOLOGICAL
BURNOUT AND TRAUMA

Cedric Alexander

INTRODUCTION

The first section of this chapter reviews some correlates of police burnout. Stressors such as danger are often assumed to be the primary causes of police stress. However, organizational stressors, lack of social and administrative support levels, limited participation in decision making, shift work, and career development are mentioned more often by police officers as their primary source of stress. Additionally, job burnout and stress can heighten vulnerability for traumatic stress reactions among police officers. The last section of the chapter brings together burnout and trauma through the author's (a former police officer) personal view of trauma in policing.

CONCEPTUALIZATION OF POLICE BURNOUT

Burnout has been associated with psychological stress and has been defined in a variety of ways. Maslach (1982) defined burnout as a syndrome of emotional exhaustion, depersonalization and reduced personal accomplishment that can occur among individuals who do "people" work of some kind. It is a response to the chronic emotional strain of dealing extensively with human beings, particularly when they are troubled or having problems. Thus, burnout can be considered one type of job stress. Although it has some of the same deleterious effects as other stress responses, burnout is unique in that the stress arises from the social interaction between helper and recipient. A pattern of emotional overload and subsequent emotional exhaustion is at the heart of the burnout syndrome. A person gets over involved emotionally, overextends, and feels overwhelmed by the emotional demands imposed by other people (Maslach, 1982).

54

Pines, Aronson, and Kafry (1981) stated that burnout is the result of constant or repeated emotional pressures associated with an intense involvement with people over a long period of time. Pines and Aronson (1988) described burnout as a state of physical, emotional, and mental exhaustion caused by long-term involvement in situations that are emotionally demanding. The emotional demands are often caused by a combination of very high expectations, which often cannot be realized, and chronic situational stresses.

Pines and Aronson (1988) argued that burnout tends to afflict people who enter professions highly motivated and idealistic, expecting work to give life meaning. It is particularly hazardous in occupations in which professionals tend to experience work as a kind of calling. Burnout is the expression of the painful realization that they have failed to make the world a better place, to help those in need, or to have a real impact on the organization. They perceive that all efforts were for nothing, that they no longer have the energy it takes to do what they promised themselves, and that they have nothing left to give.

Symptoms of burnout usually encompass three clusters of symptoms. First, exhaustion (intellectual, emotional, or physical) and lack of enthusiasm; second, depersonalization and emotional detachment, and lastly, reduced personal accomplishment, helplessness, and low selfesteem (Maslach, 1982). In its extreme form, burnout represents a breaking point beyond which the ability to cope with the environment is severely hampered.

Farber (1983) noted that burnout is characterized by physical depletion, feelings of helplessness and hopelessness, emotional drain, disillusionment, development of a negative self-concept, and negative attitudes towards work, life, and other people. Farber further observed that burnedout professionals may become cynical towards clients, blaming clients for creating difficulties or labeling clients in derogatory or diagnostic terms. Burned-out professionals are often absent or late to work more often than nonburned-out colleagues. In addition, burned-out professionals become noticeably less idealistic and more rigid, while performance at work deteriorates markedly and fantasies about leaving, or actual plans to leave the profession are formulated. Furthermore, the frustration attendant on the phenomena of burnout may lead to emotional stress, which can manifest as anxiety, irritability, sadness, or lowered selfesteem. Psychosomatic problems occur such as insomnia, ulcers, headaches, backaches, fatigue, high blood pressure, as well as increased marital and family conflicts may also present.

Farber (1983) contended that, despite the general unanimity of opinion regarding certain characteristics of burnout, determining whether a worker is burnedout or not is not easy. Burnout does seem to lend itself to such clear dichotomies, in part because burnout is a process, not an event. Nor is the process identical in each person. Burnout is a subtle pattern of symptoms, behaviors, and attitudes that are unique to each person, with no single factor capable of readily being singled out as a precursor to burnout (Farber, 1983). Contributing factors include the individual's personality, work environment stress levels, the individual's perception of stress, and family pressures.

Similarly, Freudenberger and Richelson (1980) described burnout as a state of fatigue or frustration brought about by devotion to a cause, way of life, or relationship that failed to produce the expected rewards. They noted that the seeds of burnout are contained in the assumption that the real world will be in harmony with one's idealistic dreams. In general, burnout can be conceptualized as a function of the stresses engendered by individual, work-related, or societal factors. It is in the interaction of these factors that the seeds of future burnout are likely to be sown. While initially highly motivated to "protect and serve," such idealistic expectations can be ground down by the reality of police work and the organizational, societal, and inherent stressors encountered over several years of police work. These stressors can thwart or constrain an officer's efforts to live up to the beliefs and expectations that are embodied in the "protect and serve" ethic. Consequently, an important starting point in understanding burnout in police officers involves identifying the demands that erode these expectations.

WHY POLICE OFFICERS BURN OUT

Police work has often been cited as a stressful profession (Eisenberg, 1975; Kroes, 1985; Reese, 1986; Violanti, 1985). Organizational and inherent police stressors emerge as the two major categories of job stressors mentioned by officers (Violanti & Aron, 1993). Inherent stressors refer to events generally occurring in police work that have the potential to be psychologically or physically harmful to officers, such as danger, violence, and crime. Many researchers have posited that organizational stressors affect officers more strongly than inherent stressors, and it is on the former that this discussion will concentrate.

ORGANIZATIONAL CHARACTERISTICS

Blau (1994) stated that the organizational structure of law enforcement agencies predisposes supervisors and managers to be somewhat insensitive to the stresses suffered by line officers. Because most ranking officers have come up through the ranks, the tendency is to assume that whatever these officers experienced, other law enforcement officers should be willing and able to tolerate. Ayres (1990) studied management practices and organizational characteristics in a variety of law enforcement settings. He concluded that a number of management practices created stress among police officers, including autocratic, quasimilitaristic models of management, hierarchical structure, lack of employee input into policy and decision making, lack of administrative support, adverse working schedule (shift work), and unfair discipline, performance evaluation, and promotion practices.

Violanti and Aron (1993) stated that organizational stressors refer to those events stemming from police administrations that are bothersome to members of the organization. Lack of social support, rotating shifts, lack of participation in decision making and career development have been found to be stressors among police officers. These factors intervene between an officers' belief in their role of protecting and serving and the opportunities they have to realize the expectations inherent within this ethos. As a consequence, their belief in their ability to help is eroded and the seeds of burnout are sown.

Lack of Social and Administrative Support

Social support is a critical moderating variable in burnout (Cohen & Willis, 1985). Social support is typically defined as action and/or information that leads a person to feel cared for, esteemed, and valued (Cobb, 1976). Social support is often viewed as a buffer between a stressor and the experience of stress outcome, because it bolsters the perceived ability to deal with imposed demands and prevents a situation from being appraised as highly stressful (Cohen & Willis, 1985).

Police officers frequently report that police administration often does not adequately support them. Kroes, Margolis, and Hurrell (1974) found the chief organizational stressor reported by Cincinnati police officers to be the department's administration. Officers reported being troubled by offensive policies, lack of participation in decision making, adverse work schedules, and lack of administrative support. Lack of organizational support was particularly evident in serious incidents involving the use of firearms. Terry (1981) commented that perceptions of the lack of administrative support among line officers were directed largely toward administrative policy. Kroes and Gould (1979) reported that most officers who viewed police administration as a problem felt that lack of support was the major source of difficulty. Consequently, over time, officers experience a progressive loss in their belief in being able to make a difference to the organization (Pines & Aronson, 1988), and continually having to contend with these obstacles eventually leaves them with nothing left to give.

Hurrell (1986) stated that burning out in policing is not entirely a function of job danger but also of administrative practices. Hurrell commented that only minimal work can be done to restructure the job of policing in such a way as to prevent the negative effects of such stressors as emotionally intensive interpersonal situations, boring routine patrols, or the numerous other stressful tasks inherent in law enforcement. It is possible, however, to eliminate or change some of the many organizational policies and practices found to be stressful for police officers.

Rotating Shifts

Rotating shifts are common in most police organizations and have been found to be a major source of distress for officers in their work and personal lives (Davidson & Veno, 1980; Kroes & Hurrell, 1975; Kroes, Margolis, & Hurrell, 1974). According to Hurrell (1986), rotating shift work was adopted by police departments on the assumption that it would both ensure adequate numbers of officers on each shift and prevent corruption. The validity of this assumption is clearly open to question. Penn and Bootzin (1990) stated that problems due to shift work such as fatigue at work, industrial accidents, and sleep disturbances have been well documented.

Penn and Bootzin (1990) argued that the stress of shift work is seen in health problems such as weight gain, gastrointestinal and musculoskeletal disturbances, cardiovascular irregularities, psychosomatic disorders, increased length of illness, and psychological problems. Penn and Bootzin suggested that shift work may lead some workers to abuse substances such as nicotine, caffeine, and other drugs in an attempt to regulate alertness and sleep. Major disturbances in social and family life result from shift work. It is also likely that shift workers have difficulty finding time for spouses and children, have fewer friends, and often are less able to engage in social and leisure activities.

According to Hurrell (1986), rotating shift work not only affects family life and health, but also job performance. Moreover, these problems may be exacerbated by the necessity of making irregular and lengthy court appearances at times when the officer would normally not be on duty (Hurrell, 1986). Occupational stress studies shows that shift changes can affect eating patterns sleep patterns, lifestyle, domestic patterns, and psychological and physiological health. Hurrell also stated that eating and drinking behavior of night-shift workers differed significantly from the day-shift workers. Night-shift workers ate fewer meals, had poorer appetites, and were less satisfied with eating habits than day-shift workers. Perhaps it can be argued that, over time, shift work, which limits opportunities to participate in social and family life, gradually results in disengagement from society officers serve. This, coupled with the physical depletion associated with shift work, will further fuel the experience of being burned out.

Lack of Participation in Decision Making

Absence of opportunities for participation in decision making is another frequently reported organizational stressor reported by line officers (Davidson & Veno, 1980; Hurrell, Pate & Kliesmet 1982.) Lack of input in decisions that affect job function is not only a common stressor, but a potent one as well. In a study of 1500 workers conducted by Margolis, Kroes, and Quinn (1974), lack of opportunities for participation were associated with poor physical health, depressed mood, low selfesteem, low job and life satisfaction, intention to leave the job, absenteeism, and escapist drinking.

Some two decades ago, Reiser (1976) argued that the trend towards participation in decision making, problem identification and solving, and performance evaluation in private industry should be mirrored in police organizations. Reiser further contended that if an officer's participation in decision making increases, communication between the officer, fellow officers, and superiors is also likely to increase. Among other benefits, the officer begins to feel less isolated from the work environment, and that they will have greater access to social support and more opportunities to avail themselves of these benefits. Increased involvement will also heighten officers' sense of "making a difference" and help reverse the sense of being thwarted in realizing their ideals that contribute to the experience of burnout.

Career Development

Eisenberg (1975) noted that the vast majority of police officers start and end careers as patrol officers. Opportunities for promotion to higher ranks are limited, as are specialized assignments within the patrol officer rank. Eisenberg commented that recognition and compensation for work well done are limited, adding to the officer's sense of frustration.

The increasingly precarious economic status of municipalities over the past ten years has clearly potentiated some of the aforementioned stressors. Freezes on promotions and salaries, for example, increase an officer's already high sense of frustration. Difficult economic times have served to exacerbate the powerful stressor of job insecurity. Job loss today for many officers is a real possibility. The effects of the fear of job loss on officers are diverse and far reaching, affecting somatic, and psychological health, job-related attitudes, and various behavioral manifestations of stress (Hurrell, Pate & Kliesmet,1982).

Burke (1989) cited research that suggests that police officers with 6-15 years of service reported a more negative work setting, greater experienced stress, greater psychological burnout, greater work alienation, greater work-family conflict, and more sick time taken. As these officers continue to age in rank, it becomes a significant challenge to manage, motivate, and supervise them. Burke argued that several factors that first appeared in the 1980s contribute to the problem. First, police departments are not growing as rapidly as during the '60s and '70s. Second, police departments have low attrition rates. Individuals who join police departments do so at 25 years of age (approximately), and remain with their first employing force throughout their careers. Many police officers believe that their police skills are not transferable to other kinds of work. Finally, police officers' salaries have significantly improved, therefore police officers believe they could not make as much money in other kinds of work, given their level of education and skills.

These factors operate to lock police officers into the job of policing (McGinnis, 1985). McGinnis suggested that it will be increasingly common for a police officer to remain in this position throughout his or her career. Career realities unfortunately collide with what McDonald (1983) termed an almost obsessive sentiment that apparently pervades police organizations: the feeling that status is almost exclusively attained through promotion. McDonald (1983) identified some features, unique to police organizations, which may exaggerate the link between promotion and a feeling of self-worth. These features include uncertainty and ambiguity in the police role which highlights issues such as the role of tangible promotion in confirming effectiveness as a police officer, the commonly deserved denigration of the patrol function, and the use of promotion as reward.

RACE AND GENDER

In addition to the stressors caused by performing the role of police officer, certain officers may face additional demands from other intrinsic life factors, such as their race or gender. While a detailed discussion of the implications of gender and racial issues is beyond the scope of this chapter, it must be acknowledged that certain groups of police officer must potentially deal with more and/or different stressors than others. Nevertheless, little academic attention has been paid to the stressors with which these officers must cope. While a few general remarks can be made regarding burnout in women officers, even less is known about the stress faced by non-Caucasian officers.

In his review of burnout literature, Whitehead (1989) stated that views regarding the importance of gender in relation to burnout were mixed, but concluded that the leading burnout theoreticians favored the hypothesis that gender is not an important correlate of job burnout. He argued that, based on the evidence he reviewed, the problems of women officers are the problems of male officers.

However, Pines, Aronson, and Kafry (1981) found that while the level of burnout in professional women was only slightly higher than that of their male counterparts, they were four times more likely to be at the most extreme level of burnout. Pines et al. (1981) observed that women felt they had less freedom, autonomy, and influence in their work as well as less variety, less challenge, and a less positive work environment.

In addition to the stresses of the job, female police officers may have to contend with the additional stresses caused by being women in a traditionally male occupation. Their ability and/or femininity may be called in question by others and even themselves . They may find themselves facing discrimination or harassment from coworkers and from the department's organization. For women and those officers from nonwhite backgrounds, intrinsic and organizational stressors combine together in a convoluted manner. The supposedly noninherent factor of discrimination is all too often deeply entrenched in police departments, exacerbating other job stressors, and contributing to the sense of emotional exhaustion and frustration characteristic of burnout.

Nonwhite officers are not immune to racial discrimination simply because they are police officers. In addition to their having to contend with the intrinsic stresses of being a police officer, and the organizational stressors associated with their job, officers who are members of ethnic/racial minorities must deal with the stressors acquired from their racial background and, possibly, problems relating to cultural differences in coping and support practices. They may even have to deal with stressors stemming from their perceived allegiance to the establishment or authority instead of being "loyal" to their ethnic group. Racism exists within the workplace as well as in the larger community in which the nonwhite officer must work. Little attention has been paid to this area and no adequate study has been made, making this a prime area for further research in the field.

PERSONAL REFLECTIONS:
POLICE BURNOUT, STRESS AND TRAUMA

Organizational and inherent stress and burnout have an integral role to play in regard to the experience and management of traumatic incidents. Police officers today must function in an automated and technical society that is, in itself, extremely stressful. Police officers are not immune from these demands and these will interact with their work experience to further complicate the stress management process. In addition, the wider society can, itself, be a prominent source of stress. Societal attitudes and practices can contribute to the experience of burnout in several ways. For example, police officers consistently view the criminal justice system as lenient and unwilling to impose sanctions against those that violate the law. Furthermore, police officers continue to perceive themselves as not being socially supported or understood by the agencies in which they are employed and the communities in which they serve. Officers are increasingly likely to see their efforts undermined and being unable to make the world a better place. Being thwarted in their ability to fulfill the expectations attributed to the "protect and serve" ethos, will fuel officers' sense of being burned out.

From my own invaluable experience as a police officer, traumatic events during the course of my career certainly impacted upon how I view the world, and resulted in marked differences between my perceptions and those of the general population, and colleagues in the mental health profession. Fundamental concepts such a being nonjudgmental, empathetic, and having unconditional regard, are basic to relationships between police officers during critical moments. However, this compassionate experience by police officers over time may not be applied to the communities in which they serve as stress and burnout finds their way into the routine day-to-day police experience and erode the motivation to live up to their ideals, and this problem will be compounded by the kinds of organizational experience described above.

My training as a psychologist and family therapist over the past 8 years suggests to me that my own evolution from civilian to police officer to a mental health clinician has had its own challenges. This experience has shaped how I once viewed the world after sixteen years as a police officer. Most of the time today in clinical training consists of working with police officers in the Rochester community who themselves experience trauma on a daily basis. Oftentimes, the direct correlation of their traumatic experiences and presenting problems in therapy is overlooked. I contend that ongoing trauma, as we understand it by definition, influences and imposes unusual conditions upon our personal and professional self. At times these connections can be made, but at other time these experiences go unaccounted for and adversely affect our daily function.

The DSM-IV defines trauma as "any person who has experienced, witnessed, or was confronted with an event or events that involved actual or threatened death or serious injury or a threat to the physical integrity of self or others" (American Psychiatric Association, 1994). As I reflect on this description, I am immediately overwhelmed with a flood of emotional feelings that finds their etiology in my police career. Police officers, by virtue of the nature of the work they perform, result in regular and repetitive exposure to events that the average citizen only reads about. As innocent members of our society attempt to flee an area that is potentially threatening to their physical and mental integrity, police officers quickly expose themselves to the danger oftentimes suffering repeated damage to every aspect to their mental and physical well-being. When these events become insurmountable, regardless of the availability of social support to buffer the traumatic event, a police officer will probably in some uncharacteristic way over time develop distressed emotions and maladaptive negative behaviors that may subsequently hinder any continued interpersonal growth and normative development.

REFERENCES

American Psychiatric Association: *Diagnostic and Statistical Manual of Mental Disorders.* Washington, DC, American Psychiatric Press, 1994.

Ayres, R.: *Preventing law enforcement stress: The organization's role.* Alexandria, VA, The National Sheriff's Association, 1990.

Blau, T. H.: *Psychological service for law enforcement,* New York, John Wiley, 1994.

Burke, R. J.: Career stages, satisfaction, and well-being among police officers. *Psychological Reports, 65*: 3-12, 1989.

Cobb, S.: Social support as a moderator of life stress. *Psychosomatic Medicine, 38*: 300-314, 1976.

Cohen, S., & Willis, T. A.: Stress, social support, and the buffering hypothesis. *Psychological Bulletin, 98*: 310-357, 1985.

Davidson, M. J., & Veno, A.: Stress and the policeman. In C. L. Cooper & J. Marshal (Eds.), *White collar and professional stress.* London, Wiley, 1980.

Eisenberg, T.: Job stress and the police officer: Identifying stress reduction techniques. In W. H. Kroes & J. J. Hurrell, Jr. (Eds.), *Job stress and the police officer.* HEW Publ. 76-187, Washington, DC., US Government Printing Office, 1975.

Farber, B. A.: *Stress and burnout in human service professions.* Elmsford, N., Pergamon, 1983.

Freudenberger, H. J., & Richelson, G.: *Burnout: The high cost of high achievement.* Garden City, NY, Anchor, 1980.

Hurrell, J. J. Jr.; Pate, A., & Kliesmet, R.: *Stress among police officers.* NTIS publ. 83195321, Washington, DC., National Technical Information Service, 1982.

Hurrell, J. T.: Some organizational stressors in police work and means for their amelioration. In J. T. Reese & H. A. Goldstein (Eds.), *Psychological services for law enforcement.* Washington, DC., US Government Printing Office, 1986.

Kroes, W .H.; Margolis, B. L., & Hurrell, J. J., Jr.: Job stress in policemen. *Journal of Police Science and Administration, 2*: 145-155, 1974.

Kroes, W. H., & Hurrell, J. J. Jr. (Eds.): *Job Stress and the police officer.* HEW Publ. 76-187, Washington, DC., US Government Printing Office, 1975.

Kroes, W. H., & Gould, S.: Stress in policemen. *Police Stress, 1*: 9-10, 1979.

Kroes, W. H.: *Society's victim: The police officer.* Springfield, IL, Charles C. Thomas, 1985.

Margolis, B.; Kroes, W. H., & Quinn, R.: Job stress: An unlisted occupational hazard. *Journal of Occupational Medicine, 16*: 659-661, 1974.

Maslach, C., with Zimbardo, P. G.: *Burnout: The cost of caring.* Englewood Cliffs, NJ, Prentice-Hall, 1982.

McDonald, V. N.: Ideology and its impact: Personal and organizational legitimacy. In J. P. Dowling & V. N. McDonald (Eds.), *The social realities of policing: Essays and legitimation theory.* Canadian Police College, 1983.

McGinnis, J. H.: Career development in municipal policing: Part II. *Canadian Police College Journal, 9*: 254-294, 1985.

Penn, P., & Bootzin, R.: *Behavioral techniques and enhancing alertness in shift work.* Tucson, AZ, University of Arizona Press, 1990.

Pines, A., Aronson, E., & Kafry, D.: *Burnout.* New York, The Free Press, 1981.

Pines, A., & Aronson, E.: *Career burnout: Causes and cures.* New York, The Free Press, 1988.

Reese, J. T.: Policing the violent society: The American experience. *Stress Medicine, 2*: 233-240, 1986.

Reiser, M.: Distress and adaptation in police work. *The Police Chief, 43*: 24-27, 1976.

Terry, W. C.: Police stress: The empirical evidence. *Journal of Police Science and Administration, 9*: 61-72, 1981.

Violanti, J. M.: The police stress process. *Journal of Police Science and Administration, 13*: 106-110, 1985.

Violanti, J. M., & Aron, F.: Sources of police stress, job attitudes, and psychological distress. *Psychological Reports, 72*: 899-904, 1993.

Whitehead, J. T.: *Burnout in probation and corrections.* New York, Preager, 1989.

Chapter 6

VULNERABILITY TO PSYCHOLOGICAL DISORDER: PREVIOUS TRAUMA IN POLICE RECRUITS

Christine Stephens, Nigel Long & Ross Flett

INTRODUCTION

Police recruits who have already suffered traumatic stress are at increased risk for subsequent health deficits and psychological disorder. In this chapter, we consider the suggestion that these individuals are more likely to retire from police service early. This is at least a double loss: of psychological health for the individual, and of a highly trained officer to the organization. In considering the deleterious effects of early traumatic stress, we argue that increased exposure to distressing experiences breaks down, rather than strengthens, coping abilities. This is supported by evidence, from both police and community groups, that multiple traumatic experiences, the experience of childhood trauma, and previous experiences of violence, are related to increased symptoms of posttraumatic stress disorder (PTSD).

In this chapter, a study of the traumatic experiences of police recruits in New Zealand is described and the data is compared with the reports of other community groups. Our findings suggest that police work attracts many individuals with prior traumatic experiences, particularly violent experience. There is also preliminary evidence that police officers who enter the service with higher levels of traumatic experience are among the first to leave. To conclude, we consider the implications of this evidence for the selection of police recruits and for the development of work place interventions to assist early career police officers cope with traumatic stress.

TRAUMATIC STRESS AND EARLY RETIREMENT

Many police departments are faced with the problem of recruiting and retaining sufficient numbers (Slater & Reiser, 1988) and much research has been directed into examining some of the reasons for the low retention of staff (Violanti, 1996a). This research has mainly focussed on the negative aspects of policing, for example, traumatic job stressors (Violanti & Aron, 1995) and organizational stressors (Anson & Bloom, 1988), as well as a range of individual factors such as well-being, personality, and coping (Hart, Wearing & Headley, 1995).

Some researchers suggest that the organizational, rather than the traumatic job stressors, are more important determinants of psychological health. However, many police officers exhibit posttraumatic stress disorder (PTSD) and these symptoms are extremely unlikely to originate solely from organizational stressors (Violanti, 1996a). Furthermore, there is good evidence which shows that the residual effects of traumatic stress are present during retirement when the effects of organizational stressors are minimal (Violanti, 1996b). While not discounting the effects of organizational stressors on workers, it is also important to take account of the health toll of trauma.

The problem of turnover has become a focus of concern for the New Zealand Police, in which a survey of early retirements from 1985 to 1990 (Miller, 1996) showed that psychological factors were the predominant reason for leaving (69.2%). Forty-three percent of the sample reported trauma as a factor in their applications to disengage and 17 percent were diagnosed by health professionals as exhibiting specific symptoms of posttraumatic reactions. When police officers in New Zealand were surveyed, 12 percent were classified as PTSD cases (Stephens & Miller, in press). These figures are comparable with United States samples, where it has been estimated that 12 to 35 percent of police officers suffer PTSD with various levels of psychological disabilities. PTSD has been ranked the fifth most common, overall referral problem presented to police psychologists (Mann & Neece, 1990). PTSD symptoms have also been linked to other psychological problems such as depression and alcoholism (Long, Chamberlain, & Vincent, 1992), to significantly increased physical complaints (Stephens & Long, 1997), and to more days off work (Kessler & Frank, 1997).

There is much evidence to support the deleterious effects of traumatic stress on police officers working (and postworking) lives. Given that traumatic stress is one potentially debilitating aspect of police work, then a secondary concern is the level of exposure to such stress that a police officer may encounter in his or her life, both before and after joining a police organization.

MORE TRAUMATIC STRESS IS RELATED
TO HIGHER SYMPTOMS

It is often assumed that emergency workers are hardier than most and that experience with traumatic incidents increases the ability to withstand the effects of subsequent exposure. The opposing view is that coping abilities break down with increased exposure to pain, death, or suffering and consequently individuals may become psychologically and physically debilitated (Moran & Britton, 1994). Recent studies of the effects of traumatic stress, in a variety of populations and situations, support this second view from three broad aspects. First, there is increasing evidence to support the notion that the number of traumatic events that an individual has experienced is related to the severity of their posttraumatic stress symptoms. Second, there is a body of work that explores the effects of childhood trauma on subsequent symptoms. Third, there are studies to show that severe exposure to some types of traumatic experience predisposes individuals to PTSD following later experiences. Work in these three areas will be described below.

Several studies (e.g., Follette, Polusny, Bechtle, & Naugle, 1996; Norris, 1992) demonstrate that the greater the exposure to traumatic experiences, the more likely a person is to demonstrate psychological symptoms such as PTSD. Also, where PTSD symptoms are delayed or in remission, psychiatric symptomatology may be reactivated by similar traumatic events (Long, Chamberlain & Vincent, 1994).

When Goenjian et al. (1994) examined the traumatic stress reactions of 202 adults exposed to political violence or an earthquake in Armenia, they found that, although the symptom profiles for those who had suffered each type of event were similar, the highest rates of PTSD symptoms were among those who had suffered both earthquake and violence. Horowitz, Weine, and Jekel (1995) found that among 79 urban adolescent girls, increased numbers of types of violent events were positively correlated with PTSD symptoms. Scott (1996) studied 87 females and 81 males from both clinical and nonclinical samples to assess their experiences of childhood abuse and community violence in relation to their PTSD symptoms. She concluded that PTSD is especially likely to be a sequel of interpersonal violence in those who had experienced more than one type of trauma. In a more general survey of a community sample of 440 American college students, Vrana and Lauterbach (1994) found that the highest rates of PTSD symptoms were among those who had suffered multiple traumas. These findings also apply to the experiences of police officers. A study of 527 working police officers in New Zealand (Stephens & Miller, 1998) showed that the number of different traumatic events, whether experienced on duty as a police officer or while off duty, was positively correlated with the intensity of PTSD symptoms and that repeated experience of the same type of event predicted higher PTSD scores.

Williams (1993) offers a theoretical explanation of the effects of additional traumatic experiences. If individuals have not successfully resolved previous trauma, they may "stair-step," according to William's model, to more pathological reactions to the new event. Police officers, owing to the nature of their work, are among groups at risk for these stair-stepping effects of stress exposure. A study by Moran and Britton (1994) lends further support to William's theory. A survey of 210 volunteer emergency workers demonstrated no association between individual personality characteristics and the severity or length of their reactions to traumatic experience. However, a greater number of incidents attended and more years of service, predicted a longer and more severe stress reaction. There is clear support for the cumulative effects on symptomatology of increasing numbers of traumatic experiences, and these findings have important implications for organizations in which employees are likely to suffer periodic or chronic exposure to traumatic events.

In addition to the evidence for the psychological effects of multiple trauma in adulthood, there are indications that stressful events that occur early in life have ongoing effects. For example, childhood sexual abuse has often been associated with enduring psychological dysfunction, such as depression and self-destructive behavior, in adulthood. A recent study (Boudewyn & Liem, 1995) involving 438 US college students, supported these findings in females and extended them to include males. Stallard and Law (1993) claim that the symptoms of PTSD and other psychological effects have not been generally recognized in children and an awareness of the ongoing effects of childhood trauma is relatively recent. Studies have indicated the likelihood of adult revictimization following childhood sexual abuse (Scott, 1996) and there is some evidence relating prior childhood abuse to the development of PTSD following the experience of domestic or community violence (Astin, Ogland-Hand, Coleman, & Foy, 1995; Breslau & Davis, 1992). Davidson, Hughes, Blazer, and George (1991) conducted a large-scale community survey in the US. Interviews of 2985 participants, at two times, supported the view that individuals who develop PTSD have frequently suffered adverse events during childhood such as parental separation, or sexual abuse.

A third aspect of traumatic experience that may predispose individuals to subsequent disorder is the severity of exposure to particular types of events. Research on battered women (Kemp, Green, Hovanitz & Rawlings, 1995), urban adolescents (Berton & Stabb, 1996), and combat veterans (Kulka et al., 1991) reveal that PTSD symptoms are positively correlated with the severity of exposure to violence. Scott (1996) found that civilian exposure to violent events such as being raped, physically assaulted, chased, or shot at was significantly related to PTSD severity, and even more strongly related in cases of previous childhood sexual abuse. Military combat may expose individuals to especially severe levels of violence and therefore to greater risk of later disorder. Helzer, Lee, Robins, and McEvoy (1987) surveyed 2493 US citizens in the general population. They found that the prevalence of PTSD symptoms was over three times higher in those who had been exposed to physical attack (as civilians or in combat) and twenty times higher in Vietnam war veterans who had been wounded. Studies of civilian populations (e.g., Long et al., 1992) have found higher percentages of PTSD cases among those who have served in combat. Among police officers who generally showed higher PTSD symptoms associated with higher numbers of traumatic experiences (Stephens & Miller, in press), members of the traffic safety branch who reported fewer traumas still had higher mean PTSD scores. A greater percentage of this group had experienced military combat and it is likely that this single important experience contributed to the elevated PTSD scores.

Hence, there is evidence that trauma experienced in childhood is an important predisposing factor for subsequent adult psychological disorder, particularly if followed by later traumatic experience and that, at any time of life, the experience of multiple trauma increases the likelihood of developing PTSD symptoms and the severity of those symptoms. Furthermore, exposure to severe violence, in experiences such as rape or military combat, has been demonstrated to predict severe PTSD symptoms, especially in persons who have experienced more than one type of trauma. Taken together, this evidence suggests that while both young and mature individuals recruited for police work may have already suffered one or more potentially traumatic experiences, these experiences will not have immured them against the sometimes distressing or horrifying aspects of police work. Rather, they place these individuals at increased risk for psychological disorder following trauma experienced as part of their later police duties.

TRAUMATIC EXPERIENCES OF POLICE RECRUITS

Two questions naturally follow a consideration of the effects of previous trauma on those whose work may expose them to horrifying events: what are the levels of traumatic experience reported by police recruits and how do these compare with other community groups? Paton (1996) has suggested the importance of baseline data for different occupational groups on which to base further research into the effects of occupational trauma. This section will describe a study (Buchanan, Stephens & Long, 1997) that was conducted to answer these questions and contribute to the development of such norms.

A convenience sample of 364 sworn police officers consisting of 187 recruits (from three different intake groups at the police college who had been there for times ranging from two weeks to three months) and 177 field staff who were on duty over the three days that the data was collected (at one city police station) completed a written questionnaire containing a traumatic stress schedule (Norris, 1990). The recruits were aged from 20 to 45 years, with the majority (96) in the 20 to 25 age group. The field officers were aged from 20 to 46 years, with the majority in the 26 to 45 age group (154). One hundred and five officers in the total sample were under 25 years and 13 were over 46. Length of police service was evenly spread across the sample of serving officers, from one to over 25 years. The percentage of participants reporting potentially traumatic events was 79.4 percent. Percentages of groups who reported any number of events were: 70.6 percent of recruits; 88.7 percent of field staff; 73.9 percent of male recruits; and 62.3 percent of female recruits.

The types of events included in the trauma schedule were: having something forcibly taken as in a robbery or mugging; a physical assault; a sexual assault; the tragic death (accident, murder or suicide) of a friend or relative; injury or loss because of fire, disaster, or environmental hazard; military combat; a motor vehicle accident causing injury; or some other shocking experience. In this sample 'other events' was often related to police work as the examples from field staff respondents in this category included such incidents as dealing with bodies, armed offenders, crowd control, and other specific police duties.

Table 6.1 shows the percentage of frequencies of each traumatic event as experienced by recruits compared to field staff. This data shows that

Table 6.1.
Percentage of lifetime frequencies of traumatic events for recruits and field staff (N = 364).

Event	Total % who reported this event	Percentage of Field Staff n=177	Percentage of Recruits n=187
Robbery	7.9	7.9	8.0
Assault	46.1	60.5	32.6
Sexual Assault	4.1	2.3	5.9
Tragic Death	28.5	31.0	26.3
Fire	9.3	12.4	6.4
Disaster	10.2	16.4	4.3
Hazard	9.9	14.1	5.8
Military Combat	0.3	0.6	0.0
Motor Accident	31.8	40.1	24.1
Other Event	29.2	41.2	17.6

although the field staff generally report higher lifetime incidence of traumatic events, the recruits report high percentages for some types of event also. The recruits and field staff were not significantly different in the numbers of lifetime events reported for four types of event: robbery, sexual assault, tragic death of somebody close, or loss or injury through fire. The significant differences between the lifetime frequencies of events reported by male and female recruits were more assaults by males and more sexual assaults by females. When events that occurred in the past year were considered, the recruits had higher numbers than field staff for one event: they reported significantly more experiences of motor vehicle accidents.

A comparison of the types of traumatic events reported by recruits, frontline staff, and other community groups indicates a high incidence of violent events for those joining the police. Although field staff generally reported a higher lifetime incidence of traumatic events, recruits (who were younger and had not been exposed to police duties) reported similarly high percentages for some types of incident. Of the specific types of event that were significantly different for recruits and older staff, assaults were very high for field staff and this was expected as this is a common type of incident in police work. However, the recruits also reported a very high percentage of assaults (33%). This percentage may be compared with the results from other surveys using the same instrument: Norris (1992) 15 percent (19% for a younger group) of a U.S. community sample; Eustace (1994) 15 percent of a New Zealand community group who had experienced a cyclone; or Long, McDonald and Flett (1996), 10 percent of a general New Zealand community sample. The differences between male and female recruits are also noteworthy. Men were more likely to have been assaulted and women were more likely to have suffered sexual assault (no male recruit reported sexual assault). The reporting of sexual assault by female recruits was particularly high (21%) compared to Norris (1992) 7 percent; Eustace (1994) 10 percent of the whole sample; or Long et al. (1996) 9 percent for adult sexual assault.

When comparing the numbers of events of these recruits with other community groups, the percentage of recruits who reported any number of events (71%) was high. In other studies using U.S. community samples, the prevalence levels for exposure to any traumatic event was between 39 and 82 percent (39 percent, Breslau, Davis, Andreski and Peterson, 1991; 43 percent, Giaconia et al., 1995; 56 percent, Kessler, Sonnega, Bromet, Hughes, and Nelson, 1995; 69 percent, Norris, 1992; 82 percent, Vrana and Lauterbach (1994). The results of community studies in New Zealand have also shown high percentages (75%, Eustace, 1994; 64%, Long et al., 1996). For more detailed comparisons between groups from the U.S., Table 6.2 shows the percentages of male and female recruits in the present study, and Table 6.3, the percentages of men and women in a large New Zealand community sample (Long et al., 1996), who reported experience of each event.

Police Trauma

Table 6.2.
Percentage of lifetime frequencies of traumatic events reported
by male and female recruits (N = 187).

Event	Total % reporting this event	Percentage of Females n=53	Percentage of Males n=134
Robbery	8.0	3.8	9.7
Assault	32.6	18.9	38.0
Sexual Assault	5.9	20.8	0.0
Tragic Death	26.3	28.3	25.4
Fire	6.4	7.5	6.0
Disaster	4.3	5.6	3.7
Hazard	5.8	11.3	3.7
Motor Accident	24.1	15.0	27.6
Other Event	17.4	11.3	20.2

Table 6.3.
Percentage of lifetime frequencies of traumatic events for a community
sample of New Zealand males and females (N = 1500).

Event	Total who reported this event		Percentage of Females n=964	Percentage of Males n=536
	n	%	%	%
Robbery	84	5.60	2.00	17.10
Assault	152	10.10	14.10	22.00
Childhood Sexual Assault	144	9.60	22.20	0.00
Sexual Assault	95	6.30	9.10	0.00
Tragic Death	375	25.00	33.30	22.00
Disaster	85	5.70	4.00	2.10
Hazard	101	6.70	3.00	7.30
Motor Accident	167	11.10	8.10	14.60
Other Event	189	13.20	14.70	10.70

Between these groups the noteworthy differences are those between the percentages of recruits (33%) and community members (10%) who reported having experienced physical assault, and those between recruits (24%) and community members (11%) who reported a motor vehicle accident. It is difficult to compare sexual assault as the larger sample was questioned specifically on childhood and adult sexual abuse. However, for all other types of events, the recruits tend to report higher percentages of events. These differences also apply across genders. For example, although males report more assaults than females in general, female recruits report more assaults (19%) than females in the community (14%). These differences are not necessarily due to age differences. When the community sample was examined, no differences were found across the age groups that correspond to the recruits' age groups, except in regard to motor vehicle accidents. In the community sample, 31 percent of males aged 26 to 30 years reported motor vehicle accidents and this corresponds to the higher rate of reporting for male recruits. This age difference did not apply to female members of the community sample, who had lower reporting rates than the female recruits in every age group.

Taken together, these comparisons suggest that any sample of young people is likely to have experienced traumatic stress. However, this sample of police recruits had experienced higher than usual levels of potentially traumatic events even before beginning police work. If individuals begin police work with high levels of traumatic stress, what problems may develop as they encounter police duties? This concern is a matter for further empirical investigation, although there are some suggestions from existing cross-sectional data, which will be briefly outlined here.

The percentage of frontline staff in Buchanan et al's. (1997) study, who reported one or more events (89%) may be compared with a similar sample of frontline New Zealand Police officers (Stephens & Miller, in press). Of these officers, 98 percent reported the experience of at least one event. However, only 41 percent reported having experienced any events before joining the police (71% for the Buchanan et al. recruits). Furthermore, there was a negative relationship between the number of events which were reported as occurring before and after these officers joined the police. In other words, the more events reported as having occurred since joining the police, the fewer events were reported before joining. One explanation is that the more trauma that officers experienced since joining the police, the less likely they were to remember earlier trauma, or the less important those experiences seemed over time. An alternative explanation that follows from the evidence reported above is that many of the officers who had higher numbers of traumatic experiences at the time of entry had already retired as unfit. Their earlier trauma had resulted in poorer long-term health. Hence, longer serving officers who remain in the police, report lower levels of previous trauma. As increasing numbers of such retirements are currently of concern to the New Zealand Police (Miller, 1996), this is an area that deserves closer investigation. Such conclusions from cross-sectional data remain equivocal until further longitudinal evidence is available.

CONCLUSIONS

These results have important implications for the selection and support offered to police recruits. Police officers may encounter high levels of duty-related trauma following previous exposure as children or as adults prior to their entering police work. Recent evidence suggests that previous traumatic exposure may not protect individuals from the adverse psychological effects of distressing events. Rather, those who have experienced trauma as children or adults are more likely to suffer from PTSD and other associated disorders, such as depression or physical symptoms, following later trauma.

Police work may attract those with unresolved traumatic stress. For these individuals, further exposure to stressful police duties is more likely to be harmful. Furthermore, current organizational interventions, including critical incident debriefing or peer support, are not designed to serve those with preexisting difficulties and deal with symptoms whose roots are in earlier traumatic experiences.

At present, the incidence of disengagement on psychological grounds is reason for concern. The suggestion that the prevalence of lifetime trauma in police recruits contributes to psychological problems, as they encounter the added stress of police duties, leads to concerns that officers who begin police duties with unresolved trauma, may be among the first to retire early from the police. The evidence to date justifies attention to the initial psychological fitness of current police recruits, and to the psychological services offered to early career police officers. This evidence also warrants further longitudinal investigation, which would take the level of traumatic experience and its effects on the subsequent career of young police officers into account.

REFERENCES

Anson, R. H., & Bloom, M. E.: Police stress in an occupational context. *Journal of Police Science and Administration, 16*: 229-235, 1988.

Astin, M. C.; Ogland-Hand, S. M.; Coleman, E., & Foy, D. W.: Posttraumatic stress disorder and childhood abuse in battered women: Comparisons with maritally distressed women. *Journal of Consulting and Clinical Psychology, 63*: 308-312, 1995.

Berton, M. W., & Stabb, S. D.: Exposure to violence and post-traumatic stress disorder in urban adolescents. *Adolescence, 31*: 489-498, 1996.

Boudewyn, A. C., & Liem, J. H.: Childhood sexual abuse as a precursor to depression and self-destructive behavior in adulthood. *Journal of Traumatic Stress, 8*: 445-459, 1995.

Breslau, N., & Davis, G. C.: Posttraumatic stress disorder in an urban population of young adults: Risk factors for chronicity. *American Journal of Psychiatry, 149*: 671-675, 1992.

Breslau, N.; Davis, G. C.; Andreski, P., & Peterson, E.: Traumatic events and post-traumatic stress disorder in an urban population of young adults. *Archives of General Psychiatry, 48*: 216-222, 1991.

Buchanan, G.; Stephens, C., & Long, N.: Traumatic events of new recruits and serving police. Manuscript submitted for publication. *Journal of Traumatic Stress.* 1997.

Davidson, J. R.; Hughes, D.; Blazer, D. G., & George, L. K.: Post-traumatic stress disorder in the community: An epidemiological study. *Psychological Medicine, 21*: 713-721, 1991.

Eustace, K. L.: *Cyclone Bola: A study of the psychological after-effects.* Unpublished manuscript, Massey University, Palmerston North, New Zealand, 1994.

Follette, V. M.; Polusny, M. A.; Bechtle, A. E.; & Naugle, A. E.: Cumulative trauma: The impact of child sexual abuse, adult sexual abuse and spouse abuse. *Journal of Traumatic Stress, 9*: 25-35, 1996.

Giaconia, R. M.; Reinherz, H. Z.; Silverman, A. B.; Bilge Pakiz, B. A.; Frost, A. K., & Cohen, E.: Traumas and posttraumatic stress disorder in a community population of older adolescents. *Journal of The American Academy of Child and Adolescent Psychiatry, 34*: 1369-1380, 1995.

Goenjian, A. K.; Najarian, L. M.; Pynoos, R. S.; Steinberg, A. M.; Petrosian, P.; Sterakyan, S., & Fairbanks, L. A.: Posttraumatic stress reactions after single and double trauma. *Acta Psychiatrica Scandinavica, 90*: 214-221, 1994.

Hart, P. M.; Wearing, A. J., & Headley, B.: Police stress and wellbeing: Integrating personality, coping and daily work experiences. *Journal of Occupational and Organizational Psychology, 68*: 133-156, 1995.

Helzer, J. E.; Lee, M. D.; Robins, N., & McEvoy, L.: Post-traumatic stress disorder in the general population. *The New England Journal of Medicine, 317*: 1630-1634, 1987.

Horowitz, K.; Weine, S., & Jekel, J.: PTSD symptoms in urban adolescent girls: Compounded community trauma. *Journal of the American Academy of Child and Adolescent Psychiatry, 34*: 1353-1361, 1995.

Kemp, A.; Green, B.; Hovanitz, C., & Rawlings, E. I.: Incidence and correlates of posttraumatic stress disorder in battered women: Shelter and community samples. *Journal of Interpersonal Violence, 10*: 43-55, 1995.

Kessler, R. C., & Frank, R. G.: The impact of psychiatric disorders on work loss. *Psychological Medicine, 27*: 861-873, 1997.

Kessler, R. C.; Sonnega, A.; Bromet, E.; Hughes, M., & Nelson, C. B.: Posttraumatic stress disorder in the national comorbidity survey. *Archives of General Psychiatry, 52*: 1048-1060, 1995.

Kulka, R. A.; Schlenger, W. E.; Fairbank, J. A.; Jordan, B. K.; Hough, R. L.; Marmar, C. R., & Weiss, D. S.: Assessment of posttraumatic stress disorder in the community: Prospects and pitfalls from recent studies of Vietnam veterans. *Psychological Assessment: A Journal of Consulting and Clinical Psychology, 3*: 547-560, 1991.

Long, N.; MacDonald, C., & Flett, R.: *Frequency and impact of different traumatic events: A New Zealand community study.* Poster presented at the 12th Annual Conference, International Society of Traumatic Stress Studies, San Francisco, 1996, November.

Long, N.; Chamberlain, K., & Vincent, C.: The health and mental health of New Zealand Vietnam war veterans with posttraumatic stress disorder. *The New Zealand Medical Journal, 105*: 417-419, 1992.

Long, N.; Chamberlain, K., & Vincent, C.: Effect of the Gulf war on the reactivation of adverse combat related memories in Vietnam Veterans. *Journal of Clinical Psychology, 50*: 138-143, 1994.

Mann, J. P., & Neece, J.: Workers' Compensation for Law Enforcement Related Post Traumatic Stress Disorder. *Behavioral Sciences and the Law, 8*: 447-456, 1990.

Miller, I.: *Demography and Attrition in the New Zealand Police 1985-95.* Unpublished report: Wellington, New Zealand Police National Headquarters, 1996.

Moran, C., & Britton, N. R.: Emergency work experience and reactions to traumatic incidents. *Journal of Traumatic Stress, 7*: 575-585, 1994.

Norris, F. H.: Screening for traumatic stress: A scale for use in the general population. *Journal of Applied Social Psychology, 20*: 408-418, 1990.

Norris, F. H.: Epidemiology of trauma: Frequency and impact of different potentially traumatic events on different demographic groups. *Journal of Consulting and Clinical Psychology, 60*: 409-418, 1992.

Paton, D.: Traumatic Stress in Critical Occupations. In D. Paton & J. M. Violanti (Eds.), *Traumatic stress in critical occupations: Recognition, consequences and treatment.* Springfield, IL, Charles C. Thomas, 1996.

Scott, S. T.: *Multiple traumatic experiences and the development of posttraumatic stress disorder.* Poster presented at the Annual Conference of the International Society for Traumatic Stress Studies, San Francisco, November 1996.

Slater, H. R., & Reiser, M.: A comparative study of factors influencing police recruitment. *Journal of Police Science and Administration, 16*: 168-176, 1988.

Stallard, P., & Law, F.: Screening and psychological debriefing of adolescent survivors of life-threatening events. *British Journal of Psychiatry, 163*: 660-665, 1993.

Stephens, C., & Long, N.: Post-traumatic stress disorder and physical health in New Zealand police officers. Manuscript submitted for publication. The *Journal of Psychosomatic Research,* 1998.

Stephens, C., & Miller, I. (in press). Traumatic experiences and post-traumatic stress disorder in the New Zealand Police. *Policing, 21*: 178-191, 1998.

Violanti, J. M.: Trauma stress and police work. In D. Paton & J. M. Violanti (Eds.), *Traumatic stress in critical occupations: Recognition, consequences and treatment.* Springfield, IL, Charles C. Thomas, 1996a.

Violanti, J. M.: Residuals of occupational trauma: Separation from police duties. In D. Paton & J. M. Violanti (Eds.), *Traumatic stress in critical occupations: Recognition, consequences and treatment.* Springfield, IL, Charles C. Thomas, 1996b.

Violanti, J. M., & Aron, F.: Ranking police stressors. *Psychological Reports, 75*: 824-826, 1995.

Vrana, S., & Lauterbach, D.: Prevalence of traumatic events and post-traumatic psychological symptoms in a nonclinical sample of college students. *Journal of Traumatic Stress, 7:* 289-302, 1994.

Williams, T.: Trauma in the workplace. In J. P. Wilson & B. Raphael (Eds.), *International handbook of traumatic stress syndromes.* New York, Plenum Press, 1993.

Chapter 7

CHRONIC EXPOSURE TO RISK AND TRAUMA: ADDICTION AND SEPARATION ISSUES IN POLICE OFFICERS

DOUGLAS PATON, JOHN VIOLANTI & EUGENE SCHMUCKLER

INTRODUCTION

This chapter will discuss the longer-term implications and after-effects of exposure to high risk and repetitive duty-related traumatic incidents in police work. It will explore the implications of acute and repetitive exposure to high-risk situations and traumatic events for dependence, behavioral addiction and separation from active police duties. Finally, the manner in which these experiences exercise an influence that extend into family life will be discussed.

DEPENDENCE AND ACUTE TRAUMATIC EXPERIENCES

Over involvement, and forms of dependent behavior, can occur following acute exposure as well more repetitive exposure to dangerous situations and traumatic incidents. We will commence our discussion by examining the implications of acute exposure. In acute situations, behavioral dependence can best be conceptualized with reference to the manner in which experience interacts with the officers' role expectations.

Raphael (1986) describes a form of dependent behavior that can arise when working in contexts characterized by substantial physical and/or time pressures, for example, in situations involving rescue. Officers perceive themselves, and their role, as essential for success resolution. There is always the risk that officers, particularly specialized police personnel, will suppress fear, ignore clues of danger, and continue on with a belief in indestructibility and request to be allowed to work on an assignment a little longer, take extraordinary risks in order to accomplish a mission, or otherwise try to "beat the odds."

Police officers not only like to do a good job, but they perceive that their role is to do a perfect job. They perform in an arena in which the stakes (life or death) are high. Without a doubt, they have a compelling need to do things just right. Recognizing that they can account for their own actions but not those of others, they will stick with a project to the end even thought they may be tired. In fact, as a result of trying to protect others, they can end up hurting themselves as well as those they are trying to protect. Acting to fulfill an intrinsic element of their belief system when faced with excessive demands can result in physical and psychological overinvolvement. At this point, their motivation and commitment, rather than their being a positive force for resolution, can lead to physical and psychological exhaustion and lessens response effectiveness.

A form of dependence reactions can also manifest itself during the postincident phase in the form of the "letdown" phenomenon (Hartsough & Myers, 1986). Traumatic events that have been perceived as rewarding can generate a sense of ambivalence about terminating their role. The postincident phase can involve a period of confusion and distress mixed with a sense of loss (of a situation which afforded opportunities for the exercise of professional skill at the highest possible level) as they attempt to work through and make sense of their feelings (and those of others). Both the "letdown" and "counterdisaster" phenomena emerge because the demands of an incident and officers' role expectations interact to encourage overinvolvement in the situation.

These phenomena raise both incident and operational management issues. It is important that nature and duration of involvement is carefully managed, that officers take adequate rest breaks and are given feedback on the quality of their effort and the implications of situational constraints on response effectiveness (Duckworth, 1986). The management of the letdown phase is more complicated, and involves those in senior management positions more directly (see Chapter 7).

The issues discussed above result in short-term changes that reflect psychological responses to acute exposure. However, police work rarely involves exposure to isolated traumatic events. Rather officers face an occupational reality defined by repetitive exposure to such events over the course of their career. It is to the implications of this "chronic" exposure that this chapter now turns.

BEHAVIORAL ADDICTION AND POLICE WORK

Police officers spend much of their careers preparing for the worst. As a result, officers can become occupationally and personally socialized into approaching situations with considerable caution and suspicion. This learned defensiveness towards life activities can become an obsession and a liability for officers (Williams, 1987; Gilmartin; 1986). This is not the only outcome that can follow such experiences. Repetitive encounters with risky or traumatic events can have other consequences. In this section, the behavioral and physiological implications of chronic exposure to traumatic events will be discussed.

Operational police work can demand rapid decision making, quick action, and specific task orientation. Police officers thus tend to be action-oriented, wanting to get things done, and seeking immediate results. Consequently, they may be easily bored and will seek out action when none is to be found in the immediate environment. Police officers, especially those in highly specialized activities (e.g., bomb squad, rescue divers), will not want to miss out on any of the action. Officers who enter specialized services tend to be risk takers. This is a natural adjunct to the traits of action orientation and the need to control others. They enjoy the euphoria of working against massive problems which others can only think about and the attendant exhilaration has both physical and psychological implications. The body is at a heightened state along with the pride and feelings of power, control and dominance. However, there is also a negative side to this.

Some officers become addicted to this excitement and cannot function effectively without it, both while serving and following separation from their professional role. Officers who experience long-term exposure to risk situations may become what Wilson (1980) refers to as "action junkies." This term implies that these officers are addicted to risk behavior.

Addiction to high-risk situations has been explored by several authors. Solursh (1988, 1989) argued that behavioral addiction occurs following multiple traumatic or high-risk experiences. This can stimulate mutually reinforcing excitatory states, subsequently reinforced by recurring and exciting recall of such experiences. Such "highs" are frequently followed by a depression or "downer" which borders on numbing (Kolb, 1984). These "risk" experiences appear to be highly reinforcing in the presence of a history of multiple exposures and seem to interact with other related excitatory experiences such as a compulsive need for the presence of readied weapons, reenacting threatening activities, seeking physical confrontation, and self-administered substance abuse patterns (Paton & Violanti, 1996).

Repetitive exposure to high-risk situations can also generate physiological consequences. For example, van der Kolk (1987) theorized that an endogenous opiod release could account for the calm upon reexposure to stress that is reported by many traumatized persons. van der Kolk (1988) went on to describe how the increased physiological arousal evident within traumatized persons decreases their ability to assess the nature of current challenges, and interferes with the resolution of the trauma. Gilmartin (1986) has argued that adrenaline addiction may be a result of learned behavior. Work experiences can create a learned perceptual set which alters the manner in which officers interact with the environment. Statements by officers that "police work gets into the blood" provide anecdotal support for this view. The interpretation of the environment as *always* dangerous may subsequently reprogram the reticular activating system, triggering a set of physiological consequences that are interpreted by the officer as a feeling of energization, rapid thought patterns, and a general "speeding up" of physical and cognitive reactions (Gilmartin, 1986).

Gilmartin adds that police work often leads officers to perceive even mundane activities not from a neutral physiological resting phase, but from a state of hypervigilance, scanning the environment for threats. Once a hypervigilant perceptual set becomes established and operating on a daily basis, officers alter their physiology without being exposed to any types of threatening events. Thus, officers may continuously be on a physiological "high" whether or not they are exposed to the stimuli normally associated with such levels of arousal. Chronically traumatized persons thus have difficulty in making calm and rational decisions and tend to rely on instant action rather than thought.

Kolb (1993) hypothesized that arousal of intense emotional response to traumatic events leads to hypersensitivity and impaired potential for habituation and relearning. Difficulty in rationally accepting and reviewing traumatic experiences may make it more difficult for those affected in this way to engage in coping behaviors which are essential for recovery.

Collectively, these authors are arguing that, as a result of chronic exposure, police officers face a progressive difficulty in rationally accepting and reviewing traumatic experiences. The difficulty that trauma addicted individuals have in reviewing their experiences (Kolb, 1993) may make it more difficult for those affected in this way to engage in appropriate recovery behaviors. An officer's history thus has implications for conceptualizing traumatic reactivity and for the nature, content, and timing of interventions designed to prevent or manage traumatic stress reactions and for training programs designed for stress inoculation. For example, an officer experiencing difficulty reviewing a traumatic experience could encounter problems participating in a group procedure such as a debriefing, lessening the effectiveness of this resource. Additionally, hypersensitivity and an increased tendency to process environmental stimuli as threatening (Gilmartin, 1986) may increase risk status following the wider exposure to traumatic experiences within a group setting. More research is needed into the nature of reactivity, and interventions should be developed and reviewed in a manner that reflects the development of this understanding.

STRESS REACTIONS AND SEPARATION

Police officers face the possibility of dealing with traumatic incidents over a period of twenty years or more. The psychological imprint of long-term exposure to often hazardous duties will not disappear simply by leaving police work. With a return to civilian life, the actual hazards associated with high-risk work may disappear, but officers may still carry with them into the separation/disengagement period the emotional baggage accumulated from years of traumatic work experiences.

The reality of this aspect of police psychology has been documented as the "residual stress hypothesis." This suggests that exposure to trauma leaves residual effects which are widespread, deep, and long-lasting (Figley, 1978; Kroll, Habenicht, & Mackenzie, 1989). Officers who leave police work, after possibly years of continual exposure to high-risk and traumatic situations, tend to be hypervigilant and generalize patterns of learned avoidance to stimuli resembling the trauma in their new environment (Hilberman, 1980; Solomon, 1992). As a result, they constrict their scope of activity, social ties, and civilian functioning and can develop a perception of the "civilian" environment as being inherently threatening and anxiety provoking. This is viewed as a detrimental pattern of residual trauma carried over into the new environment of the separated officer, making adaptation to civilian life more difficult.

The cumulative effect of exposure can extend risk status to those who may have (apparently) coped with the traumatic and administrative demands of their job. A significant factor here is the support officers provided for one another. The loss of the usual support resources following retirement or disengagement, and the corresponding loss of opportunities to share experiences, may compound problems. Police professionals often work within clearly-defined and psychologically influential subcultures defined by a sense of strong cohesion, a code of silence and secrecy, and dependence upon one another for survival (Paton & Violanti, 1996). Social interaction within cohesive groups can lessen the psychological discomfort resulting from traumatic exposure. Lindy, Grace, and Green (1981) described this "trauma membrane" effect, where a network of trusted, close persons served to protect traumatized persons from further distress. This cohesive work group provides support and assists in reducing psychological distress, since it provides environmental structure, leadership, companionship, and a source of motivation for recovery (Cohen & McKay, 1984; Green, 1993; Lin, Woelfel, & Light, 1985). While this may ameliorate stress during their working lives, this dependence may contribute to problems later on, particularly following separation.

It is not easy for police officers to leave this interpersonal web of protection. One of the major regrets of separated officers is that they no longer feel a part of the department. It is as if someone had removed an integral part of their personality. There is no longer a close-knit group of other police officers to provide needed support (Gilmartin, 1986). The absence of close ties can increase vulnerability to traumatic stress disorders (Ottenberg; 1987; Young & Erickson, 1988).

Thus, on separation from police duties, officers lose access to a very important coping resource. Officers can no longer depend on other officers, the police organization, and police benevolent groups, all of whom serve, within operational contexts, to reinforce a sense of understanding and recognition of their trauma (Williams, 1987). Finding relationships which substitute for the police subculture can be difficult. While on the job, they socialized predominantly with other officers. Some retirees become isolated from the community because they cannot find adequate substitutes. Officers become deficient in establishing new relationships with nonpolice factions. Many of them tend to cling to the vestiges of police work. They may, in the process, maintain links with former colleagues which no longer meet their needs. Or alternatively, they may move into other occupations (e.g., security work) in an attempt to fill what is missing in their lives.

This has implications both for traumatic stress assessment and management in operational contexts and for planning separation and retirement strategies. Officers separated from the force may benefit from intervention which reorients the officer's perceptual set into other roles. As a civilian, the officer must learn to adjust to a role which does not involve constant scanning for threats. This pattern has implications for the training and support given to officers and for separation/retirement planning within high-risk professions. Some officers may require intervention to assist them to learn new reactive patterns and to learn to once more appraise the environment as neutral in terms of threat to themselves. Retirement planning is increasingly being seen as an important component of the human resource portfolio in many organizations. Police organizations should embrace this concept and supplement existing separation procedures with strategies designed to, for example, facilitate the recognition and management of residual effects, assist reorientation to civilian life, and promote the development of social support systems that can be used to assist coping and adaptation.

FAMILY ISSUES

Involvement in, and possible dependence on, high-risk situations to maintain a sense of "well-being" has implications for others. For police officers' families, traumatic duty experiences, and the emotions that follow, can affect the quality of family life and disrupt emotional attachments between family members (Scaturo & Hayman, 1992; Wraith, 1994). According to Wraith (1994), family members can be affected by one or more of three related processes: transmission effects, repercussion effects, and induced effects. Transmission effects reflect alterations in family circumstances as a direct result of changes in an officers' emotional and behavioral state immediately following involvement in a specific traumatic event. Accordingly, and assuming reactions are adequately managed and resolved, they may have minimal deleterious effects on the family since the cause can be readily identified and changes directly attributed to a specific event (Wraith, 1994).

Repercussion and induced effects reflect repeated exposure to traumatic events. Wraith (1994) defines repercussion effects as those reactions generated within a family as a result of unresolved work stress issues being absorbed, over time, into an officers' personality. The ensuing behavioral, attitudinal and emotional changes can significantly alter family system functioning. The most serious changes to family functioning are wrought by induced effects. These reflect situations where repeated exposure to trauma and the unresolved issues emanating from such experiences may generate permanent, and often maladaptive, adaptations.

Repercussion and induced effects could generate significant long-term problems within family systems. Clearly, intervention needs to be extended to cover officers' families. Safeguarding against transmission effects could be accomplished through the development of training and support programs for family members (Paton & Kelso, 1991). Educational and support programs could be used to minimize the development of repercussion and induced effects. It is important to recognize the complex patterns of interrelationships that emerge between work, high-risk personnel, and their families. Interventions should be developed within a systems framework that accommodates these interrelationships. In other words, it is less appropriate to target groups separately. Rather, interventions should be comprehensive, integrated, and involve all significant groups and individuals.

The issues discussed here highlight how high-risk and traumatic exposure can occur over a prolonged period. As a consequence, it generates patterns of reactivity that can only be adequately conceptualized if they are viewed within a longitudinal framework (see Chapter 2). A longitudinal approach will be vital to the task of defining the changing patterns of relationship between the person, the job and their psychological status over the course of their career and to explore the relationship between repetitive exposure to traumatic or high-risk situations, stair-stepping of reactions, and behavioral addiction.

CONCLUSIONS

Exposure to high-risk work has both positive and negative implications for the well-being of police officers. This chapter described the long-term consequences of this exposure in terms of dependence, addiction, and family systems issues. Moreover, the effects of high-risk experiences do not automatically abate upon separation from specific incidents or from police work and may leave officers exposed to the residual effects of trauma. The absence of systematic longitudinal research in this area means that solutions, at this stage, must remain tentative. Exploring the nature and implications of this phenomenon will be facilitated by a recognition of its existence by police organizations. The pervasive and persistent nature of the effects of chronic exposure require that intervention be provided during the police career and this intervention should occur at organizational, managerial, and support levels.

REFERENCES

Cohen, S., & McKay G.: Social support, stress, and the buffering hypothesis: A theoretical analysis. In A. Baum, J. Singer, & S. Taylor (Eds.), *Handbook of psychology and health. Vol. IV.* Hillsdale, NJ., Erlbaum, 1984.

Duckworth, D.: Psychological problems arising from disaster work. *Stress Medicine, 2*: 315-323, 1986.

Figley, C. R.: Psychological adjustment among Vietnam veterans: An overview of the research. In C. R. Figley (Ed.), *Stress disorders among Vietnam veterans—Theory, research, and treatment.* New York, Brunner/Mazel, 1978.

Gilmartin, K. M. (1986) Hypervigilance: A learned perceptual set and its consequences on police stress. In J. T. Reese & H. A. Goldstein (Eds.), *Psychological services for law enforcement.* USGPO, 1986.

Green, B. L.: Identifying survivors at risk. In J. P. Wilson, & B. Raphael (Eds.), *International handbook of traumatic stress syndromes.* New York, Plenum, 1993.

Grigsby, J. P.: Combat rush: Phenomenology of central and autonomic arousal among war veterans with PTSD. *Psychotherapy, 28*: 354-363, 1991.

Hartsough, D. M., & Myers, D. G.: *Disaster work and mental health: Prevention and control of stress among workers.* Rockville, MD, U.S. Department of Health and Human Services, No. (ADM) 85 - 1422, 1985.

Hilberman, E.: The "wife-beater's" wife reconsidered. *American Journal of Psychiatry, 137*: 1336-1347, 1980.

Kolb, L. C.: The post-traumatic disorders of combat: A subgroup with conditioned emotional response. *Military Medicine, 149*: 237-243, 1984.

Kolb, L. C.: The psychobiology of PTSD: Perspectives and reflections of the past, present, and future. *Journal of Traumatic Stress, 6*: 293-304, 1993.

Kroll, J.; Habenicht, M., & Mackenzie, T.: Depression and post-traumatic stress disorder in southeast Asian refugees. *American Journal of Psychiatry, 146*: 1592-1597, 1989.

Lin, N.; Woelfel, M. W., & Light, S. C.: The buffering effect of social support subsequent to an important life event. *Journal of Health and Social Behavior 26*: 247-263, 1985.

Lindy, J. D.; Grace, M. C., & Green, B. L.: Survivors: Outreach to a reluctant population. *American Journal of Orthopsychiatry, 51*: 468-479, 1981.

Ottenberg, D. J.: Initiation of social support systems: A grass roots perspective. In E. Gottheil, K. A. Druley, S. Pashko, & S. P. Weinstein (Eds.), *Stress and addiction.* New York, Brunner Mazel, 1987.

Paton, D., & Kelso, B. A.: Disaster rescue work: The consequences for the family. *Counselling Psychology Quarterly, 4*: 217-223, 1991.

Paton, D., & Smith, L. M.: Assessment of Work-Related Psychological Trauma: Methodological issues and implications for organizational strategies. In D. Paton, & J. M. Violanti (Eds.), *Traumatic stress in critical occupations: Recognition, consequences and treatment.* Springfield, IL, Charles C. Thomas, 1996.

Paton, D., & Violanti, J.: *Traumatic stress in critical occupations: Recognition, consequences and intervention.* Springfield, IL, Charles C. Thomas, 1996.

Raphael, B.: *When Disaster Strikes.* London, Hutchinson, 1996.

Scaturo, D. J., & Hayman, P. M.: The impact of combat trauma across the family life cycle: Clinical observations. *Journal of Traumatic Stress, 5*: 273-288, 1992.

Solomon, Z. (1992) The "Koach" project for treatment of combat-related PTSD: Rationale, aims, and methodology. *Journal of Traumatic Stress, 5*: 175-193, 1992.

Solursh, L. P.: Combat addiction-PTSD re-explored. *Psychological Journal of the University of Ottawa, 13*: 17-20, 1988.

Solursh, L. P.: Combat addiction: Overview of implications in symptom maintenance and treatment planning. *Journal of Traumatic Stress, 2*: 451-462, 1989.

van der Kolk, B. A.: *Psychological trauma.* Washington, D.C.: American Psychiatric Press, 1987.

van der Kolk, B. A.: The trauma spectrum: The interaction of biological and social events in the genesis of the trauma response. *Journal of Traumatic Stress, 1*: 273-290, 1988.

Williams, C.: Peacetime combat: Treating and preventing delayed stress reactions in police officers. In T. Williams (Ed.), *Post-traumatic stress disorders: A handbook for clinicians.* Cincinnati, OH, Disabled American Veterans Association 1987.

Wilson, J. P.: Conflict, stress and growth: The effects of the Vietnam war on psychological development of Vietnam veterans. In C. R. Figley, & S. Leventman (Eds.), *Strangers at home: Vietnam veterans since the war.* New York: Praeger, 1980.

Wilson, J. Q.: *Varieties of police behavior.* Boston, MA, Harvard University Press, 1973.

Wraith, R.: The Impact of Major Events on Children. In, R. Watts & D. J. de la Horne (Eds.), *Coping with trauma.* Brisbane, Australian Academic Press, 1994.

Young, M. B., & Erickson, C. A.: Cultural impediments to recovery: PTSD in contemporary America. *Journal of Traumatic Stress, 1*: 431-443, 1988.

Chapter 8

TRAUMA IN POLICE WORK:
A PSYCHOSOCIAL MODEL

JOHN VIOLANTI

INTRODUCTION

Police officers vulnerability to posttraumatic stress (Carlier, Lamberts, & Gersons, 1997; Paton & Violanti, 1996) may reflect a lack of efficacious coping strategies employed by officers to deal with these events (Violanti, Marshall, & Howe, 1985; Patterson, 1998). In this chapter, I discuss how the police officer's role is used exclusively to cope with traumatic situations. The police role is defined here as a social coping resource, represented by interpersonal networks among other officers.

A common trait of the police role is the use of distinctive behavior patterns for problem resolution. Officers tend to assimilate a mode of dichotomized decision making–the situation is either "right or wrong"–with no discretionary middle ground (Blau, 1994). This type of occupationally-induced thought process may constrict consideration of alternatives for the amelioration of trauma. Dependence on the police role as a primary life role may also discourage officers from using other more flexible roles as resources to deal with trauma (Thoits, 1986).

THE POLICE ROLE AND TRAUMA: A MODEL

Assimilation into the Police Role

Entry into policing involves a process of abrupt resocialization. A first step in that process is assimilation into the police role (Violanti, 1997) as the rookie officer adapts to a new work role. This occurs interactively at individual and social levels (Harris, 1973). The acquisition process is very strong in initial police training and continues to dominate officers' lives throughout their career.

Figure 8.1. Police Psychological Trauma: A Proposed Model.

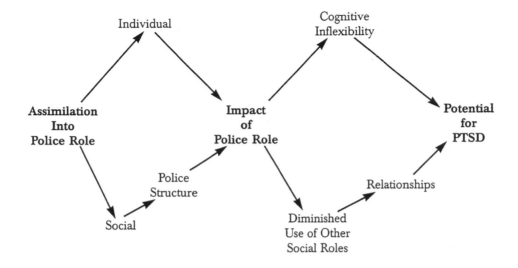

Individual Assimilation

Socialization into the police role begins early in police training and attachment to this role increases throughout their training (Paton & Violanti, 1996). A part of this process involves attempting to instill a sense of emotional invulnerability in officers (Violanti, 1990). Officers may adapt to excitement and danger (see Chapter 7) and became detached from any role unrelated to police work.

Social Assimilation

Social factors also perpetuate reliance by officers on the police role as a coping resource. The police culture exerts considerable influence on officers and often demands adherence to the police role (Whisenand, 1989). In response to outside influence, police organizations adjust by organizational design, controlling the officers to maintain an image of the police role (Violanti, 1981). The police organization is distinguished from other organizations by the *intensity* (using a powerful mix of militaristic and bureaucratic control methods) with which it restricts officers into their work role (Violanti, 1981). The typical police organization "compounds the felony" against officers in terms of control; they are coerced to behave in a manner consistent with the police role in a continuously changing environment and are punished when they do not conform (Gross, 1973).

Proscription of role by the police organization constricts officers into rigid behavior patterns, and decreases their propensity to assume other roles (Kirshman, 1983). One result of such constriction is "false personalization" (Harris, 1973), a facade of behavior that forces officers to act out roles contrary to true identities and feelings. Officers who employ false personalization may forsake true psychological self-representations and adopt role standards prescribed by the police organization (Kirshman, 1983).

The informal police structure also pressurizes officers to conform to the police role. This close-knit subculture prescribes a theme of solidarity among officers designed to help them deal with a perceived rejection from society (Neiderhoffer, 1967; Burbeck & Furnham, 1985). However, formal and informal police cultures are often at odds with each other (Kelling, Wycoff, & Pate, 1979; Hunt, McCadden & Mordaunt, 1983). As a result, the informal police culture may set up its own role requirements with strong pressure to conform. The foremost requirement is loyalty; an officer never "rats" on another officer, and the code of secrecy remains very influential (Brown, 1981).

Coping Efficacy and the Acquired Police Role

The second part of this model suggests that once officers acquire the police role, dependence on this role as a coping resource may affect trauma symptomatology. the cognitive and social inflexibility associated with the police role may hinder efficacious coping and thus precipitate risk factors associated with traumatic stress.

Constrictive Inflexibility

Officers socialized into the police role incorporate an array of predispositions and behaviors into their personality (Skolnick, 1972; Leftkowitz, 1975; Lester et al., 1980; Bonafacio, 1991). A prominent feature of this personality cluster is a cynical notion of reality (Niederhoffer, 1967; Regoli & Poole, 1979). Officers are by no means existentialists. Their view of reality as "black and white" is common (Skolnick, 1972).

Schniedman (1986) suggested that adjustment to stress involves being able to view frustrating life events as existential dichotomies rather than black and white situations. Police officers' view of themselves as problem solvers precludes their searching for meaning in work events. While conducive to good police work, this does not lend itself well to managing stress (Stratton, 1984). Thus, dependency on the police role as a primary coping resource constricts cognitive flexibility and leads officers to forsake other social roles which may be useful in coping with traumatic events.

Diminished Use of Other Social Roles

Attributes of the police role may affect the representational cognitive structure of officers which defines the self as having purpose and meaning in the social environment. When meaning is lost, role restriction results in officers' becoming isolated and increases their vulnerability following exposure to traumatic incidents (Turner & Roszell, 1994). Thoits (1983; 1986) found that psychological symptomatology varies inversely with the number of role identities possessed. Thoits (1986) argued that individuals conceptualize the cognitive self as a set of social "identities" that refer to assigned positions in the social structure accepted by the individual. Thus, the *more* social identities a person has, the *less* potential that person will have for psychological trauma. Similarly, Linville (1987) concluded that symptomatology may be influenced by differences in the complexity of self-representations. Identity role complexity thus appears to protect the self from being overwhelmed by psychological trauma.

Gecas and Seff (1990) found a significant relationship between the importance attached to roles and self-esteem at work and home. Stryker and Serpe (1982) hypothesized that individuals tend to organize role identities in relation to the social environment, placing such identities in a "salience hierarchy": the more salient the role, the greater the impact of a traumatic event. Consistent with these views, the present model suggests that utilization of the police role as a primary self-representation may discourage utilization of other life roles to cope with trauma. As a consequence, officers may deal with trauma almost exclusively from the standpoint of their work role.

The Police Role and Relationships

Reliance on the police role may impair interpersonal relationships for the traumatized officer. The police role calls for depersonalization—interpersonal relationships, on the other hand, call for human emotion (Violanti, Marshall & Howe, 1985). Police officers learn to not let emotion affect their work. When off-duty, however, they have difficulty turning their emotions back on. They remain stuck in prescribed "tough guy" roles that are seen as necessary for their effective performance as police officer (Reiser, 1974; Madamba, 1986). As a result, the personal relationships of police officers are not *personal* at all; they are more like a transaction on the street (Stratton, 1975).

Depersonalized interaction may impair supportive group relationships important for trauma amelioration (Green, 1993). Lindy, Grace, and Green (1981) described this function as the "trauma membrane" effect, where a network of trusted, close persons protects the traumatized person from further distress. Strong, cohesive social networks, particularly with others with similar characteristics, helps ameliorate distress (Boman, 1979; Kazak, 1991; Lin, Woelfel, & Light, 1985). Thus, social role constriction may increase vulnerability to traumatic stress and restrict opportunities for growth and adaptation that might otherwise be afforded by access to a variety of salient social roles.

Exposure to trauma without adequate coping resources increase stress vulnerability. As police officers encounter trauma through their career, they tax available coping resources to the maximum. Unfortunately, as the present model posits, officers strongly assimilated to the police role may lack important coping resources such as mental flexibility, other life roles, and supportive relationships (Turvey, 1996).

DISCUSSION

The present model suggests that assimilation of officers into the police role restricts cognitive flexibility and the use of other life roles, thus impairing their ability to deal with psychological trauma. As a result, the potential for PTSD amongst police officers exposed to traumatic incidents may increase. This model does not imply causality, nor is it intended to explain variance in PTSD rates among police officers. Certainly, police officers are differentially affected psychologically or by job exposure, status, rank, or length of service. The police role may be only a part of a complex interaction involving the individual, police organization, relationships within the police structure, and society.

While there exists substantial support for this model, the use of multiple roles to ameliorate trauma has been challenged. Gerson (1976), Kelling and Pate, 1975, and Repetti, Matthews, and Waldron (1989) theorized that multiple roles increase rather than decrease traumatic symptoms because individuals may encounter role conflict, ambiguity, or overload and have difficulty managing the demands of multiple roles. However, Marks (1977) hypothesized that human adaptability means that role strain will not always result from occupying multiple roles. The present model characterizes the role of police officer as a state of behavior rather than a work function. Thus, our model maintains that there is no multiplicity associated with the role of police officer, behavioral considerations are primary, and tasks and functions are secondary. Clearly, there still exists a need for more conceptual and methodological examination of this issue.

A second question concerns the causal relationship between roles and psychological symptomatology. The multiple role hypothesis posits that occupying multiple social roles positively affects psychological well-being, although it is possible that a preexisting selection process is operative. Incoming officers with higher levels of psychological well-being may be resistant to cognitive constriction and more willing to become involved in other life roles (Thoits, 1983; Verbugge, 1983).

Suggestions for Intervention

The selection process is an important tool in reducing the incidence of trauma among officers. Hiatt (1986) concluded that some applicants are unsuited for the pressures of police work and are more vulnerable to psychological problems. In 1990, 51 percent of police agencies in the United States did not use psychological screening in selection (Strawbridge & Strawbridge, 1990). Personality profiles of candidates can provide reliable evidence of psychopathology and personality traits that may affect susceptibility to trauma and can be used to assist selection (Blau, 1994; Neal, 1986). It may also be beneficial to test police officers at various times throughout their career. Meredith (1984) administered the MMPI to officers with several years on the job and found that they reported more somatic symptoms, anxiety, and alcohol vulnerability. These are important predictors of depression and suicide in police officers (Hyatt & Hargrave, 1988).

Other interventions worthy of consideration include stress management programs and salutogenic briefings after traumatic incidents. Restructuring the importance of the police role is also advocated. New officers should be made aware that the role police officer is important, but that it is not the only role in their lives. Recruits might be encouraged through sensitivity training to actively participate in family activities and establish friendships outside of policing. The narrow view of the police as "friend" and everyone else as "foe" should be strongly discouraged. With the advent of community policing in America, the police now have a great opportunity to enforce the law by working with the community in many roles (Manning, 1989).

Other suggestions for intervention can be found throughout this book. It is difficult to disentangle complex associations among individual traits, social situations, and occupational exposure as they relate to traumatic stress in police officers. Future research would must focus on this problem and reduce its incidence and prevalence.

REFERENCES

Blau T. H.: *Psychological services for law enforcement.* New York, Wiley, 1994.
Boman, B.: Behavioral observations on the Granville train disaster and the significance of stress for psychiatry. *Social Science and Medicine, 13A:* 463-471, 1979.

Bonafacio, P. *The psychological effects of police work.* New York, Plenum, 1991.

Brown, M. K.: *Working the street: Police discretion and the dilemmas of reform.* New York, Russell Sage, 1981.

Burbeck, E., & Furham, A.: Police officer selection: A critical review of the literature. *Journal of Police Science and Administration, 13*: 58-69, 1985.

Carlier, I. V.; Lamberts, R. D., & Gersons, B. P.: Risk factors for posttraumatic stress symptomatology in police officers: A prospective analysis. *Journal of Nervous & Mental Disease, 185*: 498-506, 1997.

Gecas, V., & Seff, M. A.: Social class and self-esteem: Psychological centrality, compensation, and the relative effects of work and home. *Social Psychological Quarterly, 53*: 165-173, 1990.

Gerson, E. M.: On quality of life. *American Sociological Review, 41*: 793-806, 1976.

Gilmartin, K. M.: Hypervigilance: A learned perceptual set and its consequences on police stress. In J. T. Reese & H. A.Goldstein, (Eds.), *Psychological services for law enforcement.* Washington, DC., US Government Printing Office, 1986.

Gilmartin, K. M.:. The brotherhood of biochemistry: Its implications for a police career. In H. E. Russel & A. Beigal (Eds.), *Understanding human behavior for effective police work.* New York, Basic Books, 1990.

Green, B. L.: Identifying survivors at risk. In J .P. Wilson & B. Rapheal (Eds.), *International handbook of traumatic stress syndromes.* New York, Plenum, 1993.

Gross, E.: Work, organization, and stress. In S. Levine & N. A. Scotch (Eds.), *Social stress.* Chicago, Aldine, 1973.

Harris, R. N.: *The police academy: An inside view.* New York, Wiley, 1973.

Hiatt, D. P.: The benefits of psychological testing to the applicants. In J. T. Reese & H. A. Goldstein (Eds.), *Psychological services for law enforcement.* Washington, DC., US Government Printing Office, 1986.

Hunt, R. G.; McCadden, K. S., & Mordaunt, T. J.: Police roles: Content and conflict. *Journal of Police Science and Administration, 11*: 175-184, 1983.

Hyatt, D. & Hargrave, G.: MMPI profiles of problem police officers. *Journal of Personality Assessment, 52*: 722-731, 1988.

Kazak, A. E.: The social context of coping with childhood chronic illness: Family systems and social support. In A. LaGreca, L. J. Siegel, J. L. Wallander & C. E. Walker (Eds.), *Stress and coping in child health.* New York, Guilford Press, 1991.

Kelling, G. E., & Pate, M.: The person-role fit in policing: The current knowledge and future research. In Kroes, W. & Hurrell, J. J. Jr. (Eds.), *Job stress and the police officer: Identifying stress reduction techniques.* Health, Education and Welfare Publication no. 76-187,NIOSH. Washington, DC, US Government Printing Office, 1975.

Kelling, G. E.; Wycoff, M. A., & Pate, T.: *Policing: A research agenda for national policy making.* Paper presented at the Cambridge Criminology Conference, University of Cambridge, England, July 12, 1979.

Kirschman, E.: *Wounded heroes: A case study and systems analysis of job-related stress and emotional dysfunction in three police officers.* Doctoral Dissertation, University of California at Berkeley, 1983.

Lefkowitz, J.: Psychological attributes of policemen: A review of research and opinion. *Journal of Social Issues, 31*: 3-26, 1975.

Lester, D., Babock, S. D., Cassisi, J. P., Genz, P., & Butler, A. J. P.: The personalities of English and American police. *Journal of Social Psychology, 11*: 153-154, 1980.

Lin, N.; Woelfel, M. W., & Light, S. C.: The buffering effect of social support subsequent to an important life event. *Journal of Health & Social Behavior, 26*: 247-263, 1985.

Lindy, J. D., Grace, M. C., & Green, B. L.: Survivors: Outreach to a reluctant population. *American Journal of Orthopsychiatry, 51*: 468-479, 1981.

Linville, P. W.: Self-complexity as a cognitive buffer against stress-related illness and depression. *Journal of Personality and Social Psychology, 52*: 663-676, 1987.

Madamba, H. J.: The relationship between stress and marital relationships in police officers. In J. T. Reese, J. T., & H. A. Goldstein (Eds.), *Psychological services for law enforcement*. Washington, DC, US Government Printing Office, 1986.

Manning, P. K.: Community policing. In R. G. Dunahm & G. P. Alpert (Eds.), *Critical issues in policing*. Prospect Heights, IL, Waveland, 1989.

Marks, S. R.: Multiple roles and role strain: Some notes on human energy, time, and commitment. *American Sociological Review, 42*: 921-936, 1977.

Meredith, N.: Attacking the roots of police violence. *Psychology Today, May, 1*: 12-19, 1984.

Neal, B.: The K-scale (MMPI) and job performance. In J. T. Reese & H. A. Goldstein (Eds.), *Psychological services for law enforcement*. Washington, DC: US Government Printing Office, 1986.

Niederhoffer, A.: *Behind the shield*. Garden City, NJ, Doubleday, 1967.

Paton, D., & Violanti, J.M.: *Traumatic stress in critical occupations: Recognition, treatment and consequences*. Springfield, IL, Charles C. Thomas, 1996.

Patterson, G. T.: *The effects of social factors, socialization, and coping on psychological distress among police officers*. Unpublished doctoral dissertation. State University of New York at Buffalo, NY, 1988.

Reiser, M.: Some organizational stressors on police officers. *Journal of Police Science and Administration, 2*: 156-159, 1974.

Regoli, R., & Poole, E.: Measurement of police cynicism: A factor scaling approach. *Journal of Criminal Justice, 7*: 35-51, 1979.

Repetti, R. L.; Mathews, K. A., & Waldron, I.: Effects of paid employment on women's mental and physical health. *American Psychologist, 44*: 1394-1401, 1989.

Schneidman, E. S.: *Definition of suicide*. New York, Wiley, 1986.

Skolnick, J.: A sketch of the policeman's working personality. In G. F. Cole (Ed.), *Criminal justice: Law and politics*. Belmont, CA, Wadsworth, 1972.

Solursh, L. P.: Combat addiction-PTSD re-explored. *Psychological Journal of the University of Ottawa, 13*: 451-462, 1988.

Stratton, J.: Pressures in law enforcement marriages: Some considerations. *Police Chief, November*: 44-47, 1975.

Stratton, J.: *Police passages*. Manhattan Beach, CA, Glennon, 1984.

Strawbridge, P., & Strawbridge, D. (1990). *A networking guide to recruitment, selection, and probationary training in major police departments in the United States*. New York, John Jay College, 1990.

Stryker, S., & Serpe, R. T.: Commitment, identity salience, and role behavior. In W. Ickes, & E. S. Knowles (Eds.), *Personality, roles, and social behavior* (8). New York, Springer-Verlag, 1982.

Thoits, P. A.: Multiple identities and psychological well-being: A reformulation and test of the social isolation hypothesis. *American Sociological Review, 48*: 174-187, 1983.

Thoits, P. A.: Multiple identities: Examining gender and marital differences in distress. *American Sociological Review, 51*: 259-272, 1986.

Turner, R. J., & Roszell, P.: Psychosocial resources and the stress process. In W. R. Avison, & I. H. Gotlib (Eds.), *Stress and mental health.* New York, Plenum, 1994.

Turvey, B,: Police officers: Control, hopelessness, and suicide. *World Wide Web, http://www.connix.com.*, 1996.

Van Der Kolk, B. A.: *Psychological trauma.* Washington, DC, American Psychiatric Press, 1987.

Verbugge, L. M.: Multiple roles and physical health of women and men. *Journal of Health and Social Behavior, 24*: 16-30, 1983.

Violanti, J. M.: *Police stress and coping: An organizational analysis.* Doctoral dissertation, State University of New York at Buffalo: Buffalo, NY, 1981.

Violanti, J. M.: Post-trauma vulnerability: A proposed model. In J. T. Reese & C. Dunning (Eds.), *Critical incidents in policing.* Washington, DC., U.S. Government Printing Office, 1990.

Violanti, J. M.: Suicide and the police role: A psychosocial model. *Policing: An International Journal of Police Strategy and Management, 20*: 698-715, 1997.

Violanti, J. M.; Marshall, J. R., & Howe, B.: Stress, coping and alcohol use. *Journal of Police Science and Administration, 13*: 106110, 1985.

Whisenand, P.: Personnel selection. In W. G. Bailey (Ed.), *The encyclopedia of police science.* New York, Garland, 1989.

SECTION II

SPECIAL POLICE POPULATIONS

Chapter 9

EFFECTS OF EXPOSURE TO VIOLENCE IN SOUTH AFRICAN POLICE

HEIDI KOPEL & MERLE FRIEDMAN

INTRODUCTION

South Africa's longstanding and continuing civil conflict is characterized by unprecedented levels of violence on a daily basis. "To be a policeman in South Africa's black townships is to spend much of the time acting as a mortuary assistant, picking up mangled and charred bodies, bodies with their faces shot off by AK-47 rounds, bodies that have been lying around for days and have become carrion for roving packs of dogs" (Barber, 1994, p. A2). As a result of intensified violence and unrest, the Internal Stability Unit (ISU) of the South African Police Force (SAP) was created in 1992. It functioned as a specialist riot squad, specifically located within the strife-torn black townships, where normal police patrols were withdrawn because of increasing danger. The ISU held a rather invidious position in the South African sociopolitical context. Inasmuch as there were continued allegations of police involvement in the perpetration of violence (Wits Trauma Clinic, 1993), members of the police force, in particular, the ISU, were also victims of violence. "From January to June 1993, 109 policemen were killed; 516 police homes were attacked; 916 personal police vehicles were destroyed; and 1720 policemen injured" ("109 policeman," 1993, p. A3). Thus beyond the normal duties of crime prevention, the ISU was exposed to a wide range of traumatic stressors.

Little is known about the psychological processes involved as a result of continuous exposure to violence. A study conducted by the SAPs Institute for Behavioral Sciences has found that stress-related trauma which results in police members being retired on medical grounds has increased (The Star, 1996). "Boarding" is the term used when members are declared unfit for service, due to physical or emotional factors, by a medical board. In 1993, "700 SAPS members were declared medically unfit and forced to retire because of stress-related psychological disorders" (Strachan, 1993: p. 1). According to police statistics, 184 policemen were boarded for stress and depression-related ailments in the first five months of 1996 (Thom, 1996). In 1994, a total of 540 (39%) of 1375 members who left the police did so on psychological grounds thus highlighting that stress-related cases constitute a high percentage of the total medical retirements in the police service. Massive increases in layoffs for psychological reasons since 1991 have been noted (The Star, 1996). These statistics serve as an indication of the growing contention that many police officers experience their circumstances as traumatic and feel unable to cope effectively.

A high suicide rate in the SAPS is also indicative of the distress experienced by its members. The suicide rate among police ranks in South Africa is 200 for every 100,000 members, compared with 22 in the United States (The Star, April 1996). The general rate of suicide in the SAPS has rapidly increased. At least "60 policemen had committed suicide in the first five months of 1996" (Thom, 1996: p. 6), and "some 172 police suicides were recorded in ten months between January and October of 1995" (Rodney, 1996: p. 7). In addition, "134 members of the SAPS took their lives in 1993, compared to 65 suicides in 1991" (Lazarus, 1994: p. 1). The majority of these suicides were reported in the Gauteng area (Thom, 1995). In more than 95 percent of these cases the officers used their service or private firearms to take their lives (The Star, 1996). In spite of these alarmingly elevated suicide rates, Cox (1996) reported that many traumatized and stressed policemen have been unwilling to make use of the SAPS Crisis Line which offers 24-hour counselling. This has been attributed to the stigma attached to social workers, psychologists, and counselling and the shame of seeking help. This discussion makes it clear that police officers in South Africa face a unique situation in exposure to daily and multiple stressors. Against this backdrop, it was expected that ISU members' exposure to traumatic stressors in the townships would lead to traumatic stress responses.

Posttraumatic stress disorder (PTSD) appears to be one of the most common outcomes to a traumatically stressful event (Breslau & Davis, 1987; Figley, 1986). Formulations about the psychological sequelae to extreme stress such as Horowitz's (1976) general stress response syndrome focuses on two major states: (1) intrusion—reliving, repeating, and remembering of the trauma as characterized by intrusive-repetitive thoughts, sleep disturbances including nightmares, and hypervigilance, and (2) avoidance—attempts to prevent the reemergence of traumatic reminiscences characterized by inattention, amnesia, emotional numbing, and constriction of the thought process which all function to reduce anxiety associated with intrusive imagery. These states do not always occur in a prescribed pattern but may oscillate with each other.

The criteria for PTSD in the *Diagnostic and Statistical Manual of Mental*

Disorders (American Psychiatric Association [APA], 1987;1994) include the above two mentioned dimensions. However, according to Laufer, Brett, and Gallops (1985b), little attention is given to the relationship between classes of war stress experiences and psychological stress reactions associated with them. Their study indicated that witnessing abusive violence contributes to higher rates of intrusive imagery or a re-experiencing-based stress disorder, as well as contributing to a diagnosis of PTSD independent of the effect of combat in Vietnam veterans. Yet, neither combat exposure nor witnessing violence were related to the denial-based stress disorder. Wilson and Krauss' (1981) research also found that the variable that accounted for the greatest proportion of variance of subsequent intrusive imagery was "exposure to scenes of violence," i.e., witnessing. Both these findings indicate that intrusive imagery is related to experiences of exposure to, or witnessing, violence. In light of the above findings, there are strong indications that there is a relationship between specific traumatic experiences and particular patterns of traumatic stress symptomatology which bear further investigation.

McFarlane (1992) highlighted that an important albeit acknowledged limitation of the study conducted by Laufer, Brett and Gallops (1985b) was its retrospective nature, as the data were being collected more than a decade after the Vietnam war. Thus, the relationship between specific war experiences and types of traumatic stress symptoms may well have been confounded by intervening variables.

While PTSD has been studied in the general population (Breslau, Davis, & Andreski, 1991) and among survivors of natural disasters (McFarlane, 1986), research has focused largely on abuse (Kemp, Rawlings, & Green, 1991) and on survivors of the Vietnam War (Kulka, Schlenger, Fairbank, Jordan et al., 1990b). PTSD has not, however, been studied extensively among police officers. Violanti and Aron (1994) surveyed a sample of police officers to obtain a ranking of police work stressors. These work stressors were described as those factors in the police environment external to the officer and perceived as bothersome or frustrating. Results of the study revealed that the two top-ranked stressors were killing someone in the line of duty and experiencing a fellow officer being killed. Of the top 20 ranked stressors, seven were organizational/administrative (e.g., shift work). Violanti and Aron (1994) theorized that police-shooting incidents may have been rated high due to the psychological trauma associated with such incidents. Perceptual distortion during the incident, a heightened sense of danger after the event, anger, flashbacks, isolation, emotional numbing, sleep difficulties, and depression are effects of shooting that have been highlighted (Solomon & Horn, 1986) which would be consistent with PTSD symptomatology following traumatic events. Hence, "the trauma experienced on the job can severely damage an officer's psychological and physical well-being" (Sewell,

Ellison, & Hurrell, 1988: p. 94). The identification of stressors such as threat of injury and physical danger in police work, as well as the exposure to levels of violence should therefore be recognized as crucial in preparing officers to better deal with stress. Police officers like those in the military are exposed to sadism, brutality, hostility, and carnage either as a participant, victim, or witness.

Williams (1987) has postulated that while there are remarkable similarities between types of stressors and responses of police officers and Vietnam veterans, there is also one crucial difference: "for cops, the 'war' never ends—they are out there 24 hours a day, 7 days a week to 'protect and serve'" (p.267). The police officer will not, however, always experience the high level of sustained stress that the combat soldier does, but rather repeated episodes of major or minor traumas over a prolonged period of time (McCafferty et al., 1990). Williams (1987) proposes that it is sometimes difficult to distinguish between the effects of traumatic, cumulative, protracted, and periodic or episodic stress. Clearly, there are interactive effects especially within a profession where the danger level and stress potential remain fairly high. Thus, the police officer is expected to be combat-ready at all times while remaining "normal" and socially adaptive away from the job. Consequently, the psychological toll for many is greater than acknowledged, and not well understood. The levels of stress that police officers endure can contribute to deleterious personality changes, specifically demoralization and brutalization and the traumatic stressors that are experienced may well predispose him/her to PTSD. Despite acknowledgement of the extremely high rate of constant alertness and exposure to traumatic stressors in general police service, thus far no research has investigated police officers in the environment of political and civil conflict that has characterized South Africa. Here the nature of exposure to trauma is current and ongoing. Thus, the notion of continuous traumatic stress (Straker, Moosa, & the Sanctuaries Counselling Team, 1988) may be a more appropriate conceptualization for these experiences than discrete prior stressors described in Criterion A of PTSD, and they may be similar to what Laufer (1988) termed the "routinized traumatization of war."

Despite the magnitude of traumatic stressors in this occupation, it would seem from an evaluation of the literature that little research is available which specifically explores the effects of exposure to such traumatic events. Nonetheless, as more research is conducted on PTSD with police officers, the psychological hazards connected to the job will be recognized. According to Williams (1987), it is being realized that psychological disturbances in officers are attributable to job-related hazards rather than preexisting personality traits at the time of recruitment.

To date, most research in the area of psychological distress in police officers have focused on the impact of fatal shooting incidents (Stratton, Parker, & Snibbe, 1984; Gersons, 1989; Manolias & Hyatt-Williams, 1993). A review of the literature also revealed one study which evaluated reactions of officers following a nonfatal shooting and a civilian death in an accident involving an officer (Curran, 1990). Nonetheless, there is broad agreement between these researchers and others that most American police officers view shooting as the most stressful event they could experience during their careers as police officers. Likewise, Violanti and Aron (1994) suggest that police officers consistently rate the duty related death of an officer as one of the most distressful events in their work. However, not all officers involved in a shooting incident will suffer serious adverse effects, the degree of reaction can range from mild shock to severe PTSD. It is important to also note that consistent with findings in America, shooting incidents have been identified as constituting a major source of trauma in the SAP (Rodney, 1996). Official police statistics have reflected that, in comparison to most Western European and North American law enforcement agencies, a greater number of police officials are more regularly involved in shooting incidents (Rodney, 1996).

This study examined the extent to which current and continuous exposure to traumatic experiences contributed to traumatic stress responses in a sample of South African police officers who are members of a specialist policing unit, the ISU. The specific traumatic experiences have been classified as involving (1) the exposure to the threat of injury or life-threatening situations and/or (2) witnessing violence, which includes death and destruction. Thus, the study aimed to empirically test whether continuous exposure to different types of traumatic township experiences, as measured by these two stressor variables differentially affected the two symptom categories, i.e., intrusion and avoidance.

METHODS

Subjects

The sample consisted of 55 male members of ISU units drawn from one of the most conflict ridden areas in South Africa which is today known as Gauteng (previously called the PWV: Pretoria-Witwatersrand-Vereeniging region). ISU units usually consist of approximately 600 members in total. There were approximately 80 ISU units in the PWV region. The sample was drawn from a unit from Pretoria, a unit from Johannesburg, and a unit from Vereeniging. About three-quarters were white (78%) and 22 percent were blacks. The home language of the subjects comprised Afrikaans (73%), English (6%), and various black languages (21%). Respondents ranged in age from 19 to 52, with a mean age of 23.16 years (SD = 5.01). All subjects had twelve years of education and had obtained a matriculation certificate. There were four different ranks from lowest to the highest rank: constable 73 percent, sergeant 22 percent, lance - sergeant 3 percent, and warrant officer 2 percent. Mean length of service in the South African Police Force was 3.69 years (SD = 4.25). Information on current marital status indicated 22 percent were married, 76 percent were single, while 2 percent were divorced. The major black townships of the PWV region were the areas in which the sample were deployed.

Procedure

Permission was obtained from a senior commander of the SAP to conduct this research. Respective ISU headquarters in the PWV region were then approached separately and the senior officer in command selected members who were not on duty at that time to participate in the study. Participation was voluntary and a consent form was signed by all the subjects indicating their agreement to participate. None of the subjects refused to participate in the study. Questionnaires were administered in groups. Subjects were informed that the purpose of the study was to identify stressors in the townships. The sampling procedure was not strictly random as respective units were selected on the basis of availability and accessibility, thus providing a convenience sample. To confirm that participants were in fact representative of the target population, ISU records were checked. Differences with respect to township duties, and demographic variables of age, race, education, and marital status were examined. No differences were found. Thus, these records indicated that the ISU participants did not differ significantly from nonparticipants in their sociodemographic and policing background. Questionnaires were completed between September and October of 1992. No identifying data was placed on the questionnaires, which guaranteed anonymity. The questionnaire was a structured self-report scale consisting of three discrete sections. These are described blow.

Demographic Information

Age, current marital status, rank and length of service in the police force, adapted from Part I of the Vietnam Era Stress Inventory (VESI), were measured.

Stressor Scale

This instrument was adapted from Laufer, Brett, and Gallops' (1985a,b) Combat Scale, and Part III of the VESI (Wilson & Krauss, 1981), with the addition of items that addressed stressors specific to the ISU, e.g., how often have you seen a person being necklaced? (A particularly gruesome form of killing where the victim is immobilized, a car tire filled with petrol is placed around the victim, who is then set alight from the feet upwards). Twenty items pertained to life/injury threat (e.g., How often do you feel in danger when dispersing a rioting crowd?) and 21 items addressed exposure to violence (e.g., How often are you concerned by the sight and sound of dying people?). Respondents rated the frequency of occurrence of each item of life/injury threat and exposure to violence (during the past year and including that day) on a Likert-type response scale, ranging from: experience did not occur (0), rarely (1), occasionally (2), often (3), very often (4). Total stressor scores were obtained by summing item scores.

Impact of Event Scale (IES; Horowitz, Wilson & Alvarez, 1979)

The IES measures traumatic stress symptomatologies and comprises two subscales, one measuring intrusive thinking while the other estimates avoidance tendencies. Zilberg, Weiss, and Horowitz (1982) reported the interscale correlation to be 0.42, indicating that these dimensions assess separate but related phenomena. Subjects reported the frequency of experiencing avoidance and intrusive thoughts in relation to a traumatic experience or event in the townships. Although Horowitz et al. (1979) specified the time frame for the IES as one week, it was decided to extend the time frame to one year on the assumption that this longer period permitted reports of less frequently experienced, albeit significant symptoms that might be missed with the shorter sampling period. Three separate scores were derived by summing items: an Intrusion, an Avoidance and a total IES score. Reliability and validity data for the extended time frame of the IES did not exist at the time of this research effort. Cronbach alphas for the IES scales were .79 for Intrusion, .69 for Avoidance, and .79 for the composite score.

RESULTS

Almost half of the respondents (47%) reported positive feelings about going into the townships, although 35 percent of the sample reported feeling neutral. Eighty-four percent had not suffered from any injuries or disabilities in the townships compared to 15 percent who had. One person failed to answer this question.

Mean scores for the stressors were as follows: life/injury threat (M = 32.0, SD = 9.9) and exposure to violence (M = 36.7, SD = 12.6). The most frequently reported traumatic stressors were seeing dead people in the townships (69%), hearing colleagues talking about other SAP members who had died or been wounded while doing township duty (64%), seeing SAP members wounded by a rock/stone throwing crowd (60%), and being bothered by the sight of burning property of township residents (56%). The least reported stressors (all less than 30%) were being wounded in the townships, collecting/handling the corpses of SAP members, encountering landmines and booby traps in the townships, and being part of a unit patrol which was ambushed.

Twenty-seven of the 55 subjects (49%) met the IES criteria for a diagnosis of PTSD using a diagnostic cut-off score of 25 recommended by Horowitz et al. (1979). The total IES mean score was 24.4 (SD = 12.56). Mean scores for Intrusion and Avoidance subscales were 8.7 (SD = 7.0) and 15.7 (SD = 7.9) respectively. Thus items on the Avoidance scale were endorsed more frequently. Mean scores of the IES subscales were compared with other normative data that used the same scoring method. Scores obtained by Wilson, Smith, and Johnson (1985) from a nonclinical volunteer sample of Vietnam war combat veterans were 20.32 for Avoidance and 20.42 for Intrusion, with a total IES score of 40.74. In a sample of firefighters (McFarlane, 1992), Intrusion was 11.5 (SD = 9.6), Avoidance 6.1 (SD = 7.4) and a total IES mean 17.4 (SD = 15.3). The IES data for the ISU when viewed in the context of previous findings suggest that their mean scores are comparable with firefighters and less than Vietnam war combat veterans.

Pearson Product - Moment correlations between the two stressor categories (life/injury threat and exposure to violence) and the IES subscales were calculated. Exposure to violence correlated significantly (r = 0.32, p < .01) with Intrusion but not with Avoidance (r = 0.09, p < .01). Life/injury threat did not correlate significantly with either IES subscales. The two stressor categories were significantly correlated (r = 0.42, p < .01), as were the two traumatic outcomes (Intrusion and Avoidance) (r = 0.41, p < .01).

Hierarchical regression analyses were conducted with the independent variables addressing type of stressor, i.e., life/injury threat and exposure to violence. Demographic variables such as age, rank, length of service were controlled. The dependent measures were Intrusion and Avoidance. Consistent with correlational results, exposure to violence remained a substantially important predictor of intrusion, even when the other predictors were statistically controlled (Beta = .17, p < .01). A significant effect was also found for length of service (Beta = .67, p < .05); the longer the length of service the higher the scores. Avoidance was not statistically accounted for by any of the predictors.

DISCUSSION

Unlike with other IES findings, in this study, there was a large discrepancy between Intrusion and Avoidance scores with Avoidance scores being almost twice as high as those of Intrusion. This was unlike previous noted studies of Vietnam veterans, where the two scores were more similar, or studies of firefighters, where Intrusion was more prominent. There are a number of potential explanations for this phenomenon. First, it may be attributed to the extension of the time frame of the IES which may have confounded results. Further, Lindy (1988) described an avoidance-numbing continuum whereby numbing/denial is an unconscious process to disconnect events, while avoidance is a conscious and deliberate aspect of this process. Measuring only intrusion and avoidance responses to traumatic stressors does not take into account other main features of PTSD, specifically disturbed arousal/affect (McFarlane, 1992), and it is suggested here that the ISU members may utilize these denial-avoidance processes as a defensive strategy against both the intrusive and disturbed arousal effects of traumatic exposure. Unfortunately the disturbed arousal effects were not measured in this study. It may be argued that for those police officers who are currently involved in a level of traumatic exposure that may be described as continuous, the use of processes of denial and avoidance during these periods may be perceived as adaptive.

A number of studies of PTSD in police officers following shooting incidents have found that their macho images and police culture results in the common use of denial or psychic distancing as a mechanism for coping with traumatic stress (Gersons, 1989; Maniolas & Hyatt-Williams, 1993; Williams, 1987). Police officers tend to exaggerate their abilities, emphasizing physical strength and ruggedness, believing they are invulnerable and able to handle any danger (Williams, 1987). As suggested above, these behaviors and attitudes can serve a survival function and protect the subject in a physically dangerous and psychologically threatening environment. There are costs to the use of these "defense mechanisms." Negative outcomes associated with these behaviors and attitudes may be repressed/dissociated effect, cynicism, or emotional distancing. Further, shame is involved in seeking help, and according to Williams (1987, p. 273), "they fear they are losing their minds" and therefore their problems remain untreated as they try even harder to suppress any pain.

When exposed to ongoing traumatic stressors like violence, these officers must continue to keep up a brave front so that it appears they are unaffected by such incidents. Given this, high ISU avoidance scores and lower intrusion scores point to the use of denial and self-preservation mechanisms to block out intrusive images of violence. This feature may also explain the surprising findings that 47 percent of the sample actually felt positive towards going into the townships. Together with another 35 percent who felt neutral about going into the townships, 82 percent of the sample did not feel negative about almost certain exposure to the threat of death and violence on a daily level. Another finding of interest from the regression analysis is that as length of service increased, so did scores of intrusion. On the one hand, that is to be expected, as with traumatic exposure almost daily, the arithmetic sum of incidents would imply an increased possibility of intrusive memories and cues. However, the importance of this finding is, that despite the shortcomings of self report, and the need for officers to deny symptoms, as the sum of exposures increase over time, it becomes more difficult for those defense mechanisms to shut out the effects of the experiences, and there is an increase in reportage of symptoms of intrusion. This finding indicates that the use of such coping mechanisms, may be useful in the short term, but become less effective as traumatic exposure increases.

The multiplicity of trauma to which the ISU are exposed may explain why the overall rate of probable PTSD for this sample was high (50%). But the totality of the responses may be more complex. Green (1993) suggested that "prolonged or multiple trauma would result in more complicated and/or more severe responses than acute events" (p. 141). Continuous traumatic exposure would explain findings of increased avoidance as reflecting the psychological need to deny the impact of trauma in the service of resilience. Therefore, the subject who does not report intrusive imagery but who exhibits numbing may be showing high levels of defensive behavior. Despite the high IES Avoidance score, the regression results were consistent with the findings of Laufer et al. (1985b,c). Neither of the predictors, life/injury threat nor exposure to violence, predicted voidance. McFarlane (1992) has suggested that avoidance phenomena represent a "response to the distress and pain caused by the trauma, rather than a primary link to symptoms" (p. 443). These findings tend to confirm that suggestion.

Laufer et al. (1985b) found that severe forms of numbing were related to personal complicity in atrocities. Fontana, Rosenheck, and Brett (1992) found that psychiatric symptoms and suicide were related to traumas high in personal responsibility, i.e., being an active agent or failure to prevent death or injury. As already noted, the suicide rate in the South African Police Force has doubled with increasing levels of violence. Coupled with this, there have been and continue to be very strong allegations of police complicity in perpetrating and/or failing to prevent acts of violence by the ISU. In this regard, despite the unsubstantiated causal relationship, it may be of heuristic value to postulate a relationship between high Avoidance scores and both alleged levels of complicity and a high suicide rate. Although Wilson and Krauss' (1981) study included questions regarding the participation in violence, in this study, given the political implications of disclosure in the perpetration of acts of violence, such questions were excluded.

Both intrusion and avoidance appear to be the primary features of both the normal and pathological responses to trauma. As the nature of work of members of the ISU represents ongoing and multiple traumatic stressors, as described above, it may be in their interest to avoid or deny such reactions. However, a caveat should be noted. One might speculate that ISU reactions to traumatic experiences may well in some cases be delayed. Like many Vietnam Veterans, they may appear to handle a trauma well initially, and assistance seems unnecessary. It is only as time passes and as the ISU members are continuously exposed to more stressful events that their ability to utilize the denial-avoidance process breaks down, as is intimated by the increasing Intrusion symptoms with the passage of time. Thus, individuals who do not present with the full range of traumatic stress symptomatology or qualify for the diagnosis under DSM IV should not be dismissed as people who ought not to be treated as trauma victims. At the time of treatment one set of symptoms may be dominant and/or there might be a consistent but limited symptom pattern related to the specific type of traumatic experience.

There are several limitations within this study. Persistent symptoms of arousal warrant measurement. Also, the use of clinical interviews or a more in-depth instrument that encompasses all dimensions of traumatic stress responses might have yielded different results. The question of social desirability in self-report measures should have been directly addressed in the light of the evidence for a macho culture in the police, the use of denial and distancing for self protection (Gersons, 1989), and the significant relationship found with social desirability and reported symptoms (Pickett, 1994). To substantiate the notion that the ISU's high Avoidance scores reflect the use of denial processes, it would have been advisable to have a scale measuring denial or coping. The present study also points to the need for more research on clinical samples of ISU members to determine generalizability of the findings of this investigation. Finally, the notion of continuous traumatic exposure that is presented in this chapter is clearly an area that bears further investigation.

In summary, the present study revealed, using correlation and regression analyses, that different traumatic stressors were related to different patterns of traumatic stress responses, which were consistent with Laufer, et al's. (1985b) finding that exposure to violence was directly related to the symptoms of intrusion.

REFERENCES

American Psychiatric Association: *Diagnostic and statistical manual of mental disorders* (3rd ed.- revised) (DSM III-R). Washington, D.C., Author, 1987.

Barber, S.: Up with men in firing line. *The Daily News, 19 April:* A2-A3, 1994.

Breslau, N., & Davis, G. C.: Post traumatic stress disorder: The specificity of wartime stressors. *American Journal of Psychiatry, 144:* 578-583, 1987.

Breslau, N.; Davis, G. C., & Andreski, P.: Traumatic events and post-traumatic stress disorder in an urban population of young adults. *Archives of General Psychiatry, 48:* 216-222, 1991.

Cox, A.: Stressed police seem unwilling to grasp lifeline. *The Star,* April: p.1, 1996.

Curran, S. F.: *Assessment of stress reactions following police officer exposure to traumatic incidents.* Paper presented at the meeting of the Association for Advancement of Behavior Therapy. San Francisco, CA, November, 1990.

Figley, C. R. (Ed.): *Trauma and its wake (Vol. I): The study of post-traumatic stress disorder.* New York, Brunner/Mazel, 1985.

Figley, C. R. (Ed.): *Trauma and its wake (Vol. II): Traumatic stress theory, research and intervention.* New York, Brunner/Mazel, 1986.

Fontana, A.; Rosenheck, R., & Brett, E.: War zone traumas and posttraumatic stress disorder symptomatology. *Journal of Nervous and Mental Disease, 180:* 748-755, 1992.

Gersons, B. P.: Patterns of post traumatic stress disorder among police officers following shooting incidents : A two dimensional model and treatment implications. *Journal of Traumatic Stress, 2:* 247-257, 1989.

Green, B. L.; Wilson, J. P., & Lindy, J. P.: Conceptualizing post-traumatic stress disorder: A psychosocial framework. In C. R. Figley (Ed.), *Trauma and its wake (Vol. I): The study of post-traumatic stress disorder.* New York, Brunner/Mazel, 1985.

Green, B. L.: Identifying survivors at risk: Trauma and stressors across events. In J. P. Wilson, & B. Raphael (Eds.), *International handbook of traumatic stress syndromes.* New York, Plenum, 1993.

Horowitz, M. J.: *Stress response syndromes.* New York, Jason Aronson, 1976.

Horowitz, M. J.; Wilner, N., & Alvarez, W.: Impact of event scale: A measure of subjective stress. *Psychosomatic Medicine, 41:* 209-215, 1979.

Kemp, A.; Rawlings, E. I., & Green, B. L.: Post-traumatic stress disorder (PTSD) in battered women: A shelter sample. *Journal of Traumatic Stress, 4:* 137-148, 1991.

Kulka, R. A.; Schlenger, W. E.; Fairbank, J. A.; Jordan; B. K., Hough, R. L.; Marmar, C. R., & Weiss, D. S.: *Trauma and the Vietnam war generation: Report of findings from the National Vietnam Veterans Readjustment Study.* New York, Brunner/Mazel, 1990.

Laufer, R. S.; Brett, E., & Gallops, M. S.: Dimensions of posttraumatic stress disorder among Vietnam veterans. *The Journal of Nervous and Mental Disease, 173:* 538-545, 1985a.

Laufer, R. S.; Brett, E., & Gallops, M. S.: Symptom patterns associated with post-traumatic stress disorder among veterans exposed to war trauma. *American Journal of Psychiatry, 142:* 1304-1311, 1985b.

Laufer, R. S.; Frey-Wouters, E., & Gallops, M. S.: Traumatic stressors in the Vietnam war and dimensions of posttraumatic stress disorder. In C. R. Figley (Ed.), *Trauma and its wake (Vol. I): The study of post-traumatic stress disorder.* New York, Brunner/Mazel, 1985.

Laufer, R. S.: The serial self: War trauma, identity, and adult development. In J. P. Wilson, Z. Harel, & B. Kahana (Eds.), *Human adaptation to stress from the holocaust to Vietnam.* New York: Plenum, 1988.

Lazarus, J.: Police suicides take their toll. *The Saturday Star, 12 February*: p. A1, 1994.

Lindy, J. D.: *Vietnam: A casebook.* New York, Brunner/Mazel, 1988.

Manolias, M. B., & Hyatt-Williams, A.: Effects of postshooting experiences on police-authorized firearms officers in the United Kingdom. In J. P. Wilson, & B. Raphael (Eds.), *International handbook of traumatic stress syndromes.* New York, Plenum, 1993.

McCafferty, F. L.; Domingo, G. D., & McCafferty, E. A.: Posttraumatic stress disorder in the police officer: Paradigm of occupational stress. *Southern Medical Journal, 83*: 543 - 547, 1990.

McFarlane, A. C.: Post-traumatic morbidity of a disaster. *Journal of Nervous and Mental disease, 174*: 4-14, 1986.

McFarlane, A. C.: Avoidance and intrusion in posttraumatic stress disorder. *The Journal of Nervous and Mental Disease, 180*: 439-445, 1992.

109 policemen killed this year. *The Star,* July 12: p. A3, 1993.

Pickett, G., Resick, P. A., & Griffin, M. G.: *Methods of coping used by police officers following traumatic events.* Paper presented at the International Society for Traumatic Stress Studies Annual Meeting, Chicago, 1994.

Rodney, D.: Violent society hits policemen hardest. *The Star,* January: p.7, 1996.

Schwarzwald, J.; Solomon, Z.; Weisenberg, M., & Mikulincer, M.: Validation of the Impact of Event Scale for psychological sequelae of combat. *Journal of Consulting and Clinical Psychology, 55*: 251-256, 1987.

Sewell, J. D.; Ellison, K. W., & Hurrell, J. J.: Stress management in law enforcement: Where do we go from here? In J. D. Sewell (1993). Traumatic stress of multiple murder investigations. *Journal of Traumatic Stress, 6*: 101-117, 1988.

Solomon, R. M., & Horn, J. M.: Post-shooting traumatic reaction: A pilot study. In J. M. Violanti, & F. Aron (1994). Ranking police stressors. *Psychological Reports, 75*: 824-826, 1986.

SA police suicide rate 9 times higher than US figure. *The Star,* 22 April: p.3, 1996.

Strachan, K. (1993, October 15). 700 policemen retire early because of stress. *Business Day, October 15*: 1-2, 1993.

Straker, G.; Moosa, F., & Sanctuaries Counselling Team: Post traumatic stress disorder: A reaction to state - supported child abuse and neglect. *Child Abuse and Neglect, 12*: 383-395, 1988.

Stratton, J. G.; Parker, D. A., & Snibbe, J. R.: Post-traumatic stress: Study of police officers involved in shootings. *Psychological Reports, 55*: 127-131, 1984.

Thom, A.: Fivaz upset by police suicides. *The Star,* 8 August: p.3, 1995.

Thom, A.: Severely stressed sergeant may have quit after transfer refused. *The Star,* 3 July: 6, 1996.

Violanti, J., & Aron, F.: Ranking police stressors. *Psychological Reports, 75*: 824-826, 1994.

Williams, C.: Peacetime combat: Treating and preventing delayed stress reactions in police officers. In T. Williams (Ed.), *Post - traumatic stress disorders: A handbook for clinicians.* Cincinnati, OH, Disabled American Veterans, 1987.

Wilson, J. P., & Krauss, G. E.: Predicting post-traumatic stress disorder among Vietnam veterans. In W. E. Kelley (Ed.), *Post-traumatic stress disorder and the war veteran patient.* New York, Brunner/Mazel, 1981.

Wilson, J. P.; Ken Smith, W., & Johnson, S.K.: A comparative analysis of PTSD among various survivor groups. In C. R. Figley (Ed.), *Trauma and its wake (Vol. I): The study of post-traumatic stress disorder.* New York, Brunner/Mazel, 1985.

Wits Trauma Clinic: *Unpublished statistics for 1993.* Johannesburg, Centre for the Study of Violence and Reconciliation, 1993.

Zilberg, N. J.; Weiss, D. S., & Horowitz, M. J.: Impact of Event Scale: Cross validation study and some empirical evidence supporting a conceptual model of stress response syndromes. *Journal of Consulting and Clinical Psychology, 50*: 407-414, 1982.

Chapter 10

THE EMOTIONAL AFTERMATH OF THE WACO RAID: FIVE YEARS REVISITED

ROGER M. SOLOMON & PETER MASTIN

INTRODUCTION

On February 28, 1993, 76 Bureau of Alcohol, Tobacco, and Firearms (ATF) agents raided the Branch Davidian Compound near Waco, Texas. The ATF agents were attempting to execute lawful search and arrest warrants at the compound where David Koresh and over 100 of his followers lived. The agents, teams from three geographically separate field divisions, were supported by other ATF personnel at the command post, in helicopters, at forward observer posts, and by agents providing security.

The raid had lost the element of surprise due to Koresh being tipped off. Despite an undercover agent warning the commanders that the Davidians knew ATF was coming, ATF commanders thought they could still surprise the Davidians and not encounter significant resistance. After a firefight which killed four agents and wounded sixteen, a cease-fire was called. The next day, the Federal Bureau of Investigation (FBI) took over responsibility for the inner perimeter while ATF maintained responsibility for the outer perimeter, providing security with additional support from McClennon County Sheriff's Department, the Texas Department of Public Safety, and the Texas National Guard. The Davidians refused to leave the compound, although some women and children were released. The standoff lasted 51 days, ending when the Davidians burned the compound down after the FBI used tear gas in an attempt to get them out. Over 80 residents killed each other or were killed by fire. This was the worst tragedy in ATF's history. Further, the trauma was compounded by the administration denying that the element of surprise had been lost, ATF personnel being relegated to a secondary role (e.g., outer perimeter), perceived insensitivity on the part of some administrators, the negative press, and second guessing from multiple sources.

One might expect that five and one-half years later there would be a number of agents who have retired on medical disabilities. At the present time, there has been only one medical retirement where Waco was a factor. Eight other agents retired, having reached retirement age. One agent who survived the Waco Raid was tragically killed in an automobile accident over a year after. No other personnel have prematurely left or quit the agency. This is not to say that premature retirements or emotional disabilities will not occur in the future. The Waco Raid impacted all who were involved and will never be forgotten. The effects of past and future traumatic incidents can accumulate resulting in severe symptoms in forthcoming years. But as we approach the sixth anniversary of the raid, it is remarkable that there have not been more medical disabilities or instances of leaving the agency because of Waco. One agent who did not take part in the raid, but was involved in the early investigation of the Davidians died of a selfinflicted gun shot wound. It can be conjectured that this death was related to the Waco raid, and will be discussed later.

The decisions and judgements that led to the tragic consequences will be studied for a long time. Ongoing investigations and civil legal matters make discussion of these factors beyond the scope of this chapter. However, it is important to discuss the organizational factors that may have contributed to the agents staying on the job. The lessons learned from this experience may help law enforcement organizations better handle the emotional aftermath of a future major tragedy.

The following observations result from the perspective of the first author who provided psychological services on site and on an on-going basis, and the second author being the Deputy Incident Commander of the raid. The second author was also the Special Agent in Charge of the division that took the most casualties—three killed and six wounded. He also was one of the coordinators of the ATF critical incident peer support team. Discussion will also draw upon survey data gathered a year following the raid. The survey asked respondents to rate the level of support received from peers, the special agent in charge (SAC), assistant agent in charge (ASAC), investigators, and headquarters administrators, and to add comments. Level of traumatic stress was measured by the Penn Inventory. The general implications of the findings from this survey will be discussed. The specific data will be discussed at a later date, after all civil and legal matters have been settled.

PRIMARY REASON

The agents were highly-trained professionals who had a strong degree of competence, camaraderie, cohesion, and dedication to their mission. Though many organizational, training, and personal factors combine to create the strong solidarity and positive identity so important in emotional recovery, the single greatest factor is the agents themselves. Their determination and desire to work through their pain, to support and care for each other, and to stay on the job, provide tangible evidence of the strength of the agents involved specifically, and the ATF organization generally. Some of the main factors instrumental in facilitating recovery are described below.

The Existence of a Critical Incident Program

ATF implemented a critical incident program in 1988. A peer support team, composed of agents previously involved in traumatic incidents who have received three days of training, is available to provide confidential support to fellow agents following critical incidents. The team is backed up by a clinical psychologist with expertise in law enforcement. The team was immediately deployed following the raid.

The program is coordinated by a SAC. Having high level administrators involved gives the program the organizational credibility for rapid deployment, access to resources, and efficient negotiation of organizational hurdles. At Waco, the SAC coordinator was extremely valuable in organizing the delivery of services and consulting with commanders and administrators on personnel matters. Further, the SAC team member was able to provide peer support to high ranking personnel involved in the tragedy.

The program also provides education on critical incident trauma and positive coping strategies. A video tape called the "Psyche of Survival" was made to introduce the peer support team, educate agents surviving critical encounters ("just because you're shot does not mean you have to die"), and teach strategies on dealing with fear and vulnerability (the "dynamics of fear," Solomon, 1991). This tape was seen by most agents prior to the raid. The tape is routinely presented at new agent training by peer support team members who also talk about critical incident trauma, positive coping, and the critical incident program. This education program proved its value at Waco. The agents shot at Waco had anywhere from forty-five minutes to two and one-half hours to wait before a cease fire was arranged. Several agents remarked that the strategies taught by the videotape and the peer support instructors aided their coping while waiting to be rescued.

A second video tape entitled "When the Shooting Is Over" was in production at the time of the Waco incident and was available to all ATF personnel after the incident. This video presentation, designed by the peer support group, dealt with trauma phenomenon such as time, visual, and auditory distortion, memory difficulties, and other reactions during moment of peak stress. This video is now used as a portion of the preincident awareness program utilized by the ATF.

Program Utilization

Program utilization was an important variable in recovery. The agents were from three different locations, allowing comparisons to be made between teams. Survey results show differences in emotional recovery among the three teams that may be due, in part, to the degree of followup services. Results suggest that immediately after the raid, the team that took the most losses (three agents killed, six wounded) was the most severely impacted. However, a year later, the Waco investigation team who interviewed all agents involved in the raid, ATF administrators who met with all involved agents, and Penn Inventory scores indicated that this team appeared to be doing better emotionally than the other two teams. Further, results show that this team felt significantly more positive about the ATF organization and felt more supported by their SAC and ASACs.

One reason for the differences in results may be that this team received the most CISDs, psychological services, and peer support over the year following the raid. The enhanced recovery of the team hardest hit illustrates the value of a critical incident program and the availability of followup support. Several aspects of the program's services and intervention will be described below.

However, having a program does not mean everyone will utilize the available services. The investigation of the raid revealed: "Although many agents did use those services, other agents who could have benefited from such services chose not to. Some of those who did not seek counseling apparently feared that if they did, they would be stigmatized as weak or troubled" (Department of the Treasury, 1993, p.117). The program needs to increase education to reduce the stigma associated with seeking counseling.

Concerned Leadership

Differences in level of traumatic stress among the three teams may also be attributable to the degree of administrative support and leadership concern. The team with the lowest level of trauma also had the highest ratings for the ATF organization, SAC, and supervisors. This implies that administrative support played an important role in the emotional recovery of the team. Indeed, there were differences among the teams in the presence of leadership. The two teams with the higher level of traumatic stress symptoms did not have their SACs fully available because of their involvement in the Waco investigation and subsequent suspension. The SAC of the team having the lowest trauma symptoms was the deputy incident commander at Waco. He was also on the line during the firefight. He was respected for his leadership and actions at Waco. He demonstrated caring leadership in the months following the raid by frequently checking the welfare of the agents, being available and encouraging talking about what happened, taking the initiative in getting information and facts about the raid out to all involved agents, and attempting to provide what ever services were needed. This level of involvement and support by the SAC appears to have had a positive impact on emotional recovery.

Many agents were deeply hurt and angry at the administration for perceived insensitivity and lack of demonstrable support. The team with the highest ratings for their chain of command having the lowest trauma scores underscores the importance of concerned, caring leadership to take the initiative in detecting needs, arranging for the delivery of services, and providing ongoing support.

Peer Support

Survey results indicate that peer support was the most effective strategy for coping with the emotional aftermath. Peers who have been through a similar critical incident can legitimize and validate each other's reactions with more credibility, perhaps, than anyone else (Solomon, in press; Mitchell & Everly, 1993; Horn & Solomon, 1988; Solomon & Horn, 1986). Although the established peer support team was helpful, survey results indicate it was more beneficial to talk with other agents who were at Waco. Involved agents felt closer to, and better understood by, fellow agents who had experienced the raid. Indeed, when officers survive threatening operations, they develop close personal ties, deep trust, and enduring friendships. Consequently, any activity or decision that reinforces positive group support will have a beneficial impact on recovery.

Reinforcement of Group Cohesion and Support

War research has taught us that unit cohesiveness, morale, and mutual support are critical factors in determining psychological casualties (Antonovsky & Bernstein, 1986; Milgram & Hobfoll, 1986). Consequently, in the aftermath of Waco, it was important to reinforce group cohesion and support.

In the days following the raid, organizational decisions were made that reinforced group cohesiveness. The morning after the raid the agents were mandated to meet as a group. The purpose of this meeting was to provide the agents some informal time to get together. Though a few agents resented having a mandatory meeting, most benefited from the opportunity to talk to one another and piece together what happened. It was the first chance for the whole group to get together.

An initial crucial decision was whether to immediately send the agents involved in the raid home and utilize fresh agents to continue duty. The decision was made to utilize the agents already present. It was thought that to send the agents home in shock would be destructive to the agents and their families. Further, sending them home may have precipitated feelings of isolation, abandonment, failure, and caused significant symptomatology. An abrupt transition can cause adverse stress reactions (Mitchell & Everly, 1993; Milgram & Hobfoll, 1986). The agents were given meaningful duty that reinforced their law enforcement identity. They remained on duty until they went home to attend funerals.

Hindsight, and feedback from agents, have taught us that keeping the agents on scene was the correct decision. Sending them home immediately would have undermined cohesiveness and given the message that the agents failed and were to blame for what happened. Consequent decisions to send the agents to funerals and organize group debriefings also reinforced group cohesiveness and support.

An Opportunity to Mourn

Funerals for the deceased agents took place three and four days after the raid. Another crucial decision was whether the agents could be spared to attend funerals. Agents on duty at Waco strongly wanted to attend. Because of manpower needs, it was difficult gaining permission for agents to go to funerals. Thanks to the cooperation of local law enforcement, and ATF going the extra mile to get more manpower, most agents who wanted to attend the funeral were able to do so. Being able to attend the funeral in units and mourn together was important in working through the traumatic event. The many memorial services held in different parts of the country in subsequent months, including a major ceremony at the Police Memorial in Washington D.C., further enabled appropriate grieving and working through the trauma.

MULTIFACETED INTERVENTION

Immediate Availability of Peer Support and Psychological Services

Psychological services and peer support were available the day after the raid. Numerous low key, informal individual and group sessions took place in the week following the raid. The peer support team was very useful in providing defusings (Mitchell & Everly, 1993) and referring agents with significant symptoms for further services.

Some agents were emotionally overwhelmed in the days following the raid. Psychological services were immediately available in a private setting in close proximity to duty stations. The goal of treatment was restoration of functioning and return to duty. Brief treatment procedures, such as Eye Movement Desensitization and Reprocessing (Shapiro, 1995), in conjunction with traditional crisis intervention strategies, proved effective in relieving severe intrusive symptoms. Appropriate relief and assignment recommendations were made according to the needs of the individual. No agent was sent home prematurely and all agents were able to carry out their postraid assignments.

Peer support personnel were also assigned to the local hospitals where wounded ATF personnel were recovering. The team was active with the wounded agents and their families. Many peer support contacts were made at the hospital as agents came to visit. Special sessions were held for family members of wounded agents. However, family services would have been enhanced with the availability of support from spouses of agents who had previously survived critical encounters.

Psychological Services upon Returning Home

Critical incident stress debriefings (CISD) were provided shortly after the agents returned home. Several police psychologists gave generously of their time and hearts in conducting multiple CISDs in the weeks following the raid. These psychologists along with other mental health professionals in the community also provided individual sessions as needed. Agents who were not at Waco and other ATF staff were included in debriefings. Indeed, many ATF personnel not present physically at Waco were present emotionally, and had deep emotional reactions. Debriefings were also held for spouses, although this was not done consistently for all involved. Survey results revealed that talking to family members about what happened was very healing. Such results underscore the need for broader family services and support teams that include spouses.

The debriefings appear to have decreased the development of severe symptoms and enhanced recovery. The majority of agents who later needed specialized services had not been able to attend debriefings. Scheduling problems, wounds prohibiting travel, or some people "falling through the cracks" despite efforts to contact everybody, prevented all personnel involved at Waco from attending a CISD.

The Availability of Specialized Psychological Services

Specialized mental health resources with expertise in law enforcement trauma were available for agents who experienced severe symptoms. This was particularly helpful for agents who had missed group debriefings, were suffering severe reactions, who did not feel comfortable utilizing resources within their community, or who lived in communities lacking appropriate resources. At the present time, programs are still in place to provide specialized treatment to agents suffering from trauma.

Access to the Facts

Knowledge of the facts about what happened and how it happened is crucial to emotional recovery. The denial by ATF administrators about losing the element of surprise heavily impacted the agents and was thought by some to be the most traumatic part of the incident. Restoration of a sense of control and the rebuilding of trust could not take place until the agents could understand how the incident happened and the reasons behind the decisions.

Within two months of the raid, special presentations by an administrator, investigators, and one of the raid planners were made to the involved agents to explain the facts, the reasons behind the actions taken and decisions made, to dispel rumors, and answer questions. The results of the investigation, completed about seven months after the raid, were released in its entirety to the agents. Investigators met with agents after the report was released to go over their findings and answer questions. Though these presentations could not undo the negative impact of the denial, they did enable the agents to further process and work through what happened.

Alleviating Agents of Blame

Issues such as how the tragedy happened, what went wrong, and the experience of responsibility guilt were evident in comments such as "did we fail?", "is it my fault?", "did I do my job?", and the like. These feelings exercised a powerful effect on personnel. Responsibility guilt is a normal reaction following critical incidents (Solomon & Horn, 1986). The immediate, continual, and consistent feedback from all levels of ATF, the outside investigators, and high ranking United States government officials was that the line agents performed their job well and bravely, and were not responsible for the tragedy. Though there was, and still is, much anger about tactical decisions, alleviation of guilt and responsibility for the tragedy was healing for the line agents. However, there were instances where individuals were criticized for their role. One agent initially was wrongly blamed for his role in undercover work, which caused much distress. He was later exonerated by the Treasury Department investigation. The agent who committed suicide was criticized by the Department of Treasury investigation. It is conjectured that the criticism may have been one factor, among many, that contributed to the suicide.

An Opportunity to Remember

Integration and resolution of a traumatic event comes from remembering what happened and dealing actively with it. Recall of the details, understanding what happened, facing the emotional impact, honoring the dead, and supporting the living, is often assisted by going to the site of a tragedy. On May 8, 1993, several weeks following the burning of the compound and after the scene investigation was completed, all involved agents gathered at Waco and spent several hours at the scene. This was a very healing experience for many. As one agent put it, "a purging took place when I was able to walk through the scene and not feel afraid." The agents had a private memorial ceremony at the scene and a more public memorial service later that day. The Waco community sponsored a dinner for the agents that night to demonstrate their support.

Support from the Law Enforcement Community and Concerned Citizens

The citizens of Waco were particularly supportive in the aftermath of the raid. They brought food, were demonstrably friendly toward the large law enforcement presence, and openly expressed their sorrow over the tragedy and their appreciation for what ATF was attempting to do. Such support and hospitality from the community created many bright spots in otherwise gloomy times. The positive support and caring from the law enforcement community was heart felt, needed, and healing. Fellow officers from all over the country were concerned, sympathetic, and were there for the agents. In the survey many agents commented how helpful it was to talk to officers from other agencies.

Learning from It

An important aspect of integrating a traumatic experience is learning from it. A formal time for dealing with lessons learned came during National Police Week in May, 1994. All involved agents gathered for a two-day meeting where they could express their perspective, critiques, and recommendations about the operational and technical aspects the raid, and the future. The meeting ended with an award ceremony. This meeting and ceremony brought a conclusion to Waco for many. It was time to get on with life. The Waco raid will never be forgotten and the impact will always be felt. Some agents are forever scarred. However, the agents and the organization are coping with the tragedy and are continuing to fulfill their mission.

CONCLUSION

In conclusion, the fact that there has been only one medical retirement among agents involved in the raid is a testimony to their fortitude, bravery, professionalism, and strength. The families of the agents need to be acknowledged, not only for what they had to go through, but also in regard to the crucial role they played in the healing process.

There are several organizational considerations that can facilitate emotional recovery following a major tragedy. The Waco experience substantiated the value of a critical incident program. The team with the highest level of recovery had received the most services. An important lesson learned was the need for family services and support teams that include spouses.

Group cohesion and support were major factors in the emotional recovery of agents. Organizational decisions that reinforced group cohesion and opportunity for interaction, such as keeping the agents together at Waco for a few days before rotating them home and having group debriefings, proved to be important in facilitating emotional recovery. It is important to provide all relevant facts about what happened to involved personnel as soon as is feasible. Closure and resolution of a critical incident cannot be completely attained until all questions have been answered.

Following a traumatic event it is crucial that there be immediate and enduring administrative support. Lack of support and person-to-person communication from administrators following a critical incident leaves personnel feeling very hurt, angry, abandoned, unimportant, and wondering if they did something wrong that the people they work for are not communicating with them. As one officer put it years ago, "If they don't care, why should I care?". This same dynamic was operating in the aftermath of Waco, only the negative impact of perceived lack of support was greater because of the magnitude of the tragedy. Lack of administrative support, or impersonal handling of the incident, can create secondary traumatization and compound the negative impact of the event. A potent healing force is set in motion when the people a law enforcement officer works for demonstrate they appreciate what the officer has been through, are concerned about his/her welfare, and genuinely care. The differential recovery among the teams involved in the raid confirms this principle.

It is conjectured that criticism of the performance of an undercover agent contributed to his suicide. If this is true, the tragedy of the aftermath did not stem from the horror of the raid, but from the investigative aftermath. Performance needs to be critiqued and lessons learned from mistakes. However, there can be increased support to help the involved person avoid overpersonalizing the criticism. While specific steps to provide this support are beyond the scope of this chapter, the organization must realize that how criticism is handled is a crucial variable in recovery. The negative impact of being second guessed can be greater than the trauma of the incident.

REFERENCES

Antonovsky, A., & Bernstein, J.: Pathogenesis and salutogenesis in war and other crises: Who studies the successful coper? In N. Milgram (1986) *Stress and coping in times of war.* New York, Brunner/Mazel, 1986.

Department of the Treasury: *Report on the Bureau of Alcohol, Tobacco, and Firearms Investigation of Vernon Wayne Howell also known as David Koresh*; page 117, Washington, DC, Author, 1993.

Horn, J. M., & Solomon, R. M.: Peer support: A key element for coping with trauma, *Police Stress, Spring.* 1988.

Milgram, N., & Hobfoll, S.: Generalizations from theory and practice in war-related stress. In N. Milgram (Ed.), *Stress and coping in times of war.* New York, Brunner/Mazel, 1986.

Mitchell, J. T., & Everly, G. S.: *Critical incident stress debriefing.* Ellicott City, MD, Chevron, 1993.

Shapiro, F.: *Eye movement desensitization and reprocessing: Principles, protocols and procedures.* New York, Guilford, 1995.

Solomon, R. M.: Critical incident stress debriefing in law enforcement. In G. Everly & J. Mitchell (Eds.), *Critical incident stress management.* Ellicott City, MD, Chevron, in press.

Solomon, R. M.: The dynamics of fear in critical incidents: Implications for training and treatment. In J. T. Reese, J. M. Horn, & C. Dunning (Eds.), *Critical incidents in policing, Revised,* Washington DC, U.S. Government Printing Office, 1991.

Solomon, R. M.: Mental conditioning: The utilization of fear. In J. T. Reese, & J. M. Horn (Eds.), *Police psychology: Operational assistance.* Washington, DC., United States Department of Justice, Federal Bureau of Investigation, 1988.

Solomon, R. M., with Horn, J. M.: Post-shooting traumatic reactions: A pilot study. In J. Reese, & H. Goldstein (Eds.), *Psychological Services In Law Enforcement.* Washington, DC., United States Government Printing Office, 1986.

Chapter 11

INCIDENT RESPONSE AND RECOVERY MANAGEMENT

DOUGLAS PATON, RHONA FLIN, & JOHN VIOLANTI

INTRODUCTION

While the direct impact of critical incidents and disasters on police officers has, in general, been well documented, response and recovery management issues, particularly at the level of the incident commander, have been surprisingly neglected (Flin, 1996). This chapter seeks to redress this imbalance. Despite the lack of dedicated research and literature pertaining to police organizations, we can draw upon the military and aviation literatures to explore the implications for police officers. The first section of this chapter will discuss the causes of stress for those in command positions.

INCIDENT-RELATED STRESS FOR COMMANDERS

The following discussion deals with the subject of acute stress rather than occupational stress, which has been well documented (e.g., Alexander & Walker, 1994; Kurke & Scrivner, 1995). Acute stress is the more intense experience of psychological and physiological effects stimulated by exposure to high demand situations, such as a major emergency or disaster. There is a paucity of literature on the causes and long-term effects of acute stress on police incident commanders. Consequently, little consideration has been given to understanding the specific stressors likely to affect them or their implications for their thinking and management skills during an operation. Flin (1996), after reviewing the available evidence, concluded that the factors shown in Figure 11.1 represent the principal causes, moderators, and effects of stress for incident commanders. If the elements of this generic command stress model are examined with particular reference to police commanders, then it seems that all the stressors (causes) are likely to be applicable to operational policing situations.

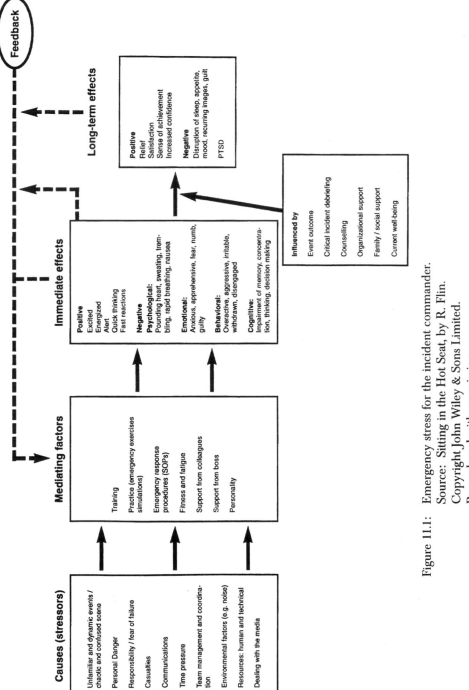

Figure 11.1: Emergency stress for the incident commander.
Source: Sitting in the Hot Seat, by R. Flin.
Copyright John Wiley & Sons Limited.
Reproduced with permission

Unfamiliar, escalating events are particularly difficult to manage and many police officers can describe the feeling of arriving on a chaotic and messy scene that characterizes a major emergency or disaster. A British police emergency procedures manual states: "Officers are most at risk from stress when confronting unfamiliar situations. Stress will undermine their confidence and their performance. Whilst there will be natural anxieties in the face of the unforeseen, experience indicates that the inadequate communication of information, lack of preparedness and training and a lack of experience will significantly affect stress levels. In the event of a major disaster all these conditions are even more pronounced" (Association of Chief Police Officers, 1989, quoted in Home Office, 1992, p 30).

The degree of personal danger varies depending on the incident, but commanders must also assess the risks to members of their team as well as members of the public. In the UK, new health and safety legislation for police forces, places a clear duty of care and the concomitant need for risk assessment on commanding officers. Time pressure is a common stressor in certain types of event (e.g., bomb threat), in others, the time may be controlled to some degree such as in a hostage negotiation or siege. The ability to assess available time and level of risk is an important element of command decision making, and one which appears to distinguish expert over novice commanders. Environmental factors such as noise or visibility can add extra pressure. In some situations, heat acts as an unwelcome stressor. Vrij, van der Steen, and Koppelar (1994) found that increased temperature in police-offender interactions causes increased tension, and more aggressive behavior. There are other stressors for the commander, including responsibility, sight of casualties, communications (or the lack of them), dealing with the media, and managing the team and the available resources.

What is most relevant for the management of the police response is to identify which of these potential stress factors can be controlled or reduced and how officers can be trained to deal with the others. There are marked individual differences in how people react to emergency stressors, principally due to "mediating factors" which influence the extent of stress reactions. These include personal factors, not only in terms of personality but also in relation to transient states of fitness and fatigue. Commanders who are less than fully fit, perhaps due to minor illness (e.g., colds and flu), or who are already tired when called to the incident are likely to be more prone to the effects of stress in this condition. The effects of fatigue on commanders' decision making are only beginning to be understood (Flin, Wyn, Ellis, & Skriver, 1998) and this is particularly relevant for long run police operations such as hostage or siege situations which can last for several days. Psychological fitness is also a relevant mediating factor. An officer who is suffering from occupational stress or a personal worry may be more vulnerable when faced with an acute stress situation. While such factors affect fitness for duty, in reality most commanders are unlikely to declare themselves unfit. They must, however, be aware that these limiting factors will affect their performance and increase their need to rely on other members of the command team (see below).

The question of personality differences in command ability (or stress resistance) is often raised. The limited research available (see Flin, 1996) suggests that beyond obviously unsuitable characteristics (nervousness, shyness, instability) for leadership there is no one standard command personality profile. What is important is that commanders have the required skills to manage this role. They must also be aware of their personal strengths and limitations, and have some knowledge of how they react in stressful environments and what they have to do to control negative effects. This insight cannot be taken for granted.

Psychological research has shown that some airline pilots were not properly aware of the effects that exposure to stressors (and mediating factors such as fatigue) could have on their performance. To counter these "invincibility" attitudes, special human factors training called crew resource management (CRM) specifically teaches pilots to recognize the personal limiting factors inherent in stressful situations, and to utilize the resources of the whole crew (Gregorich, Helmreich, & Wilhem, 1990). It is possible that some police commanders would lack awareness of such limiting factors in stressful command situations.

Difficulty recognizing limitations can arise for other reasons. In prolonged, complex incidents, a mix of role expectations and intense physical, psychological, and emotional demands can interact to create a situation where the incident commander perceives their active involvement as essential for the successful resolution of the incident (Raphael, 1986). The net effect of the ensuing overinvolvement is excessive fatigue, a decline in cognitive capabilities, and a significant decline in operational effectiveness and well-being. Time spent actively managing incidents should, therefore, be limited, adequate rest breaks taken, and performance/outcome expectations should be realistic, given the limitations under which commanders are operating (Duckworth, 1986; Paton, 1994).

INCIDENT COMMAND AND CONTROL

Command and control in routine police operations should ideally be a smooth running process where the plan or standard procedures meet the needs of the situation. Policing unexpected or escalating incidents is a far more difficult challenge, placing much higher demands on the personal resources and competence of the incident commander (Shaw, 1997; Stewart & Flin, 1996). Even with the best incident command system, functioning communications and a team who know their roles, the commander will have to make decisions "in the heat of the moment", often on the basis of incomplete information and ambiguous intelligence about the unfolding events. More senior commanders called to attend a serious incident may have had relatively little recent exposure to operational policing and this can enhance the task difficulty for them and their team. In these types of situations, the risk of experiencing acute stress begins to increase for both senior and junior ranks. This risk, however, can be minimized by planning and establishing operational systems to support the management of the potentially high stress components of emergency response (e.g., coordination, communication, decision making), and training for emergency and disaster work.

PLANNING FOR MAJOR EMERGENCIES AND DISASTERS

Police organizations generally appreciate the value of planning to manage major incidents. Plans should be linked to action (e.g., training programs, resource allocation, simulation exercises) and tested regularly. Plans based upon implicit and untested assumptions will be less effective than anticipated and, consequently, increase the ad hoc demands made on commanders (Flin, 1996; Paton, 1996, 1997; Powell, 1991). Detailed and comprehensive anticipation of operational demands, the testing of plan assumptions, and exercises and simulations that examine procedural and conceptual issues at operational and organizational level, should thus be integral to the planning process. Planning will also facilitate the development of operational and organizational response systems.

Operational Systems and Structures

Operational systems will be required to cover several atypical demands, including the management of emergency resources, delegation, novel and dynamic demands on communication and decision systems, interagency coordination, and media and community liaison (Paton, Johnston, & Houghton, 1998). Nor is it just the demands made upon systems that may differ from the routine. Short-term changes in operational structure may also be required (Flin, 1996; Powell, 1991). A capacity for adopting a more responsive structure when managing crisis demands should not be assumed, but it can be developed through planning and exercises (Hightower & Couta, 1996; Paton, 1997).

When responding to major emergencies and disasters, police organizations will interact with several agencies (e.g., other emergency services, the media), requiring that effective liaison mechanisms are established (Hodgekinson & Stewart, 1991; Walsh, 1989). Where possible plans should integrate the respective roles and operating practices of these agencies within planned response strategies. Consequently, the organizational, job and role analyses that will accompany response planning should extend beyond the police organization and accommodate the patterns of interorganizational relationships that will emerge in multiagency, emergency response situations.

COORDINATION AND TEAM WORK

The demands encountered when responding to a major incident transcend the capabilities of any one individual and their effective management requires the collective and coordinated activities of several individuals and groups. Two issues emerge in this context. One relates to the management of the police team and the other involves consideration of the implications of operating within a multiagency context.

With the exception of first responders, police officers will work in teams to deal with an incident of any size. The presence of a well-trained, experienced team will obviously reduce the impact of stressors on the commander as tasks can be delegated, second opinions sought, and tactics discussed and agreed. Good team work is very dependent on a proper analysis of the required team roles, training in team skills, and an open work climate. A major military psychology project in the USA has been studying Tactical Decision Making Under Stress (TADMUS) in order to identify critical skills for teams performing under stress and to design decision support systems for their commanders (Brannick, Salas, & Prince, 1997). Many of the findings from these military projects would translate directly to police operations. Similarly, adopting the principles of Crew Resource Management (CRM), used by most major airlines to identify problems in crew coordination, may prove beneficial as a means of facilitating the considerable resources of the other team members (particularly their brain power) in difficult stressful situations. The need for delegation, workload sharing, and joint problem solving is greatly heightened in situations of stress, and this likely to be as true of police incident grounds as it is of flight decks. In addition to their having a responsibility for coordinating the roles and tasks of police officers, incident commanders may also find themselves responsible for coordinating representatives of several agencies.

The diversity of the demands created by a disaster means that the coordinated response of several agencies, some of whom may have little contact with one another under normal circumstances, is required. Managing a multiagency response is a demanding task. Having to deal with, for example, interagency conflict, will constitute an additional source of stress. Response effectiveness relies heavily upon the activities of these agencies being integrated and their respective roles accommodated in a planned and systematic·manner (Auf der Heide, 1989). Establishing who exactly is in charge of a multiagency response at tactical and operational levels of command needs to be agreed in advance and rehearsed.

The management of a multiagency response can be facilitated by conceptualizing it as a team-based activity. A cohesive and integrated team provides the mechanism by which complex and diverse demands can be effectively managed. Psychological research into multidisciplinary team development and operation has identified several problems in getting diverse professional groups to work together. Team development issues are particularly salient here because incident commanders operate collectively with representatives of other professions only during the period of an emergency.

While conflict and diverse views represent a strength of teams, their constructive use requires education, negotiation, and the management of team development and performance (Northcroft et al., 1995). One crucial factor in team development and cohesion operation is social (professional) identity (Northcroft et al., 1995). Social identity processes, particularly the stereotyping of in- and out-groups, can limit the ability of official multiagency relationships to operate cohesively. Developing a coherent sense of identity thus represents an important preparatory activity (Hogg, 1992).

Realizing the benefits accruing from a multidisciplinary team effort and promoting effective and cohesive team work requires consideration of: (a) how participants define group membership and how it influences cohesion; (b) patterns of interaction between group members in relation to institutional policies, structures and culture, and the language and terminology used; and (c) contextual factors such as understanding of integrated emergency management policies and practices, the status and power accorded to different members, and resource constraints. Unless team development activities have been activated, behaviors associated with the operation of these factors operate during the response and constitute a source of stress for incident commanders. On the other hand, these points can serve as guidelines for multidisciplinary team development activities and underline the need for this process to be managed.

In addition to addressing team development issues, team management must be considered. Psychological research into multidisciplinary teams has developed models to assist this process (Paton et al., 1998). These models provide a framework for the kind of transitory organization required to manage the diverse and multijurisdictional demands that typify the disaster environment.

COMMUNICATION AND INFORMATION

The effectiveness of response coordination is a function of the quality of the information and communication systems which support it. Communication systems also affect the quality of decision making and decision implementation in an environment characterized by multiagency involvement; large numbers of personnel; and conflicting, diverse, and dynamic demands. Communication problems can represent a significant stressor for commanders. While some problems reflect hazard activity (e.g., damage to communication infrastructure), others reflect inadequacies in crisis communication systems and/or the expertise available to use them (Paton et al., 1998). A lack of processing capability, or the need for additional information processing, will introduce (unnecessary) response delays and constitute an additional source of stress for operational commanders.

Training programs may be required to develop the capability of commanders, and their counterparts in other key response agencies, to specify information needs, interpret them appropriately on receipt, and, if required, adapt them for different functions and end users over time (e.g., incident response, liaison with other agencies, media requests). A role for computerized decision support systems is also indicated here. However, care should be taken to ensure that personnel do not become overreliant on them, to ensure that commanders can function in their absence (e.g., if a disaster knocks out this capability).

Making effective use of information underlines the importance of appropriate decision-making processes. The scale of hazard impact and its multijurisdictional implications signals a need for using distributed decision-making procedures (Flin, 1996). In addition, it is pertinent to examine decision style and its implications for decision making within a high stress environment.

STRESS AND DECISION MAKING

The immediate and long-term effects of acute stress can be positive or negative, and individuals may experience a mixture of both. Performance enhancing effects include alertness, faster reactions, increased energy, and accelerated thinking skills. These are likely to improve a commander's ability to react to the occasion and to take decisions while under a degree of pressure. If the level of demand increases, or the commander has already started to experience a negative reaction, the effects resemble physiological and psychological symptoms of anxiety and fear, and a detrimental impact on performance and decision making will ensue. Typical problems, under these circumstances, include: "tunnel vision," failure to prioritize, "freezing," and loss of concentration (Flin, 1996, Flin et al., 1997; Klein, 1996; Orasanu, 1997; Orasanu & Backer, 1996).

The impact of stress on decision making may depend on the type of decision process used. A range of thinking skills can be used to reach a decision. First, there is the technique which experienced police officers call intuition or gut feel, and which psychologists label recognition-primed decision making (Klein, 1997). This is where the officer recognizes the type of situation encountered and from previous experience knows what course of action is appropriate. Secondly, there are situations where the officer may have to spend more time thinking about the situation to remember the appropriate rule or procedure to use. A third style is the most mentally labor intensive, analytical decision making, where the officer must think about a number of possible courses of action and then select the best option. This is the style that should be used during operational planning phases.

In policing operations, these three basic styles may be used to varying degrees depending on the situation and the role of the commander. Strategic commanders should use the analytic style to accommodate the broader perspective required of strategic command. In certain types of police operations, tactical commanders may need to switch their style of decision making. For example, a hostage or siege incident may have slow periods where optional response plans can be carefully evaluated and compared. In this case, analytical decision making should enable selection of the best option. If the hostage taker suddenly begins to attack the hostages, then very rapid decisions will have to be taken within minutes, making any new analytical decision making almost impossible.

Klein (1996) argued that the fast, intuitive decision style is less affected by stress than the more intellectually demanding analytical approach. He also has emphasized that properly trained and experienced commanders actually show adaptive reactions to stressors. "They include the selection of simpler and more robust decision strategies, narrowed and focused attention, use of heuristics, increased conservatism, and rapid closure on a course of action. To help decision makers avoid potential disruption due to stressors, it may be useful to train them to better manage time pressure, distracting levels of noise and high workload" (p 83).

INCIDENT COMMAND TRAINING

Without doubt, the key factor in training incident commanders to cope with stress is experience of demanding operational situations. Where this is achieved during routine operations, maximum learning is achieved if officers are prepared for the event, have realistic expectations of what will be required of them, and then are properly debriefed afterwards in a blame-free climate. A range of techniques has been tested for "stress-proofing" individuals, usually based on controlled exposure and careful debriefing and reported benefits appear to justify costs (see Driskell & Salas, 1996).

Training programs should be based on an all-hazards approach and designed to facilitate both technical and psychological preparedness and the development of a flexible and adaptable response capability (Auf der Heide, 1989; Paton, 1997). In addition to developing an appropriate knowledge and skill base (e.g., information analysis, decision making), training should address how the disaster context influences the applicability of expertise and the initiation and control of response activities. This has implications for the design of training simulations. For example, Paton (1994) demonstrated how management capability, developed in routine contexts, was ill-suited to the disaster response role, but training, designed specifically to prepare for disaster work, reduced stress and enhanced performance effectiveness. According to this model, training program and simulation design require two inputs. One involves the detailed analysis of emergency response roles, tasks, and responsibilities to define the skills and knowledge required for effective response. The second involves considering how the disaster operating context can render operational procedures and expectations inadequate or inappropriate to the needs of the disaster response.

The characteristics of the routine operating environment (e.g., clear role/task expectations, hierarchical reporting, and command structures) are incorporated into the psychological frameworks (schemata) that guide response and become implicit, or "taken for granted," facets of routine operations. However, their importance as determinants of well-being and performance effectiveness may go unrealized until faced with atypical operational demands (e.g., scale of infrastructure disruption, multiagency operating environments, rapid role change) which challenge these assumptions (Flin, 1996; Paton, 1994). This signals a need to develop procedures, and expectations, that accurately reflect the disaster operating context in which they will be applied (Paton, 1994).

Managing these issues has implications for training needs analysis (TNA). Not only must it consider atypical demands, disaster training needs analysis must also accommodate multiagency involvement and interaction to facilitate the development of knowledge, skills, systems and procedures capable of supporting an integrated response. While a capability for training needs analysis may exist, it will have to be developed specifically to identify atypical demands and contextual factors that fall outside usual operating demands. Consequently, a broader range of analytical techniques than those used in routine contexts will be required and the process will extend beyond organizational boundaries to include analysis of nonorganizational personnel who have experienced particular kinds of hazard activity. This ensures that the TNA process identifies the demand characteristics (Paton, 1997) and competencies (Flin, 1996; Paton et al., 1998) likely to be encountered and used when responding. These outputs also represent the demands and competencies that should be modeled in simulations.

In recent years, increasing use has been made of specially designed simulations where commanders can practice dealing with high pressure situations in a safe and supportive environment. This not only allows technical and managerial skill development but also lets the individual know how he or she is likely to react to stressors and how to minimize negative reactions (Flin, 1996). Obviously, experience of command roles in major emergencies and disasters is limited by their infrequent nature. Developing effective training programs requires that we understand the nature of the demands faced by incident commanders and how this expertise is used to initiate and control response activities. Armed with this knowledge, we are in a position to develop and evaluate training simulations and exercises.

In the UK, different types of simulation are used to train commanders, from table top to more realistic exercises (Home Office, 1997). The metropolitan police force in London developed a special computer based training system, called MINERVA, for training senior police officers in critical incident management (Crego, 1995). The MINERVA system is a fast-time command and control training simulator which uses a network of computers to present full motion digital video and computer graphics to a number of different groups of officers representing sectors in a large-scale operation. It has been programmed for football crowds and public order scenarios as well as armed siege.

One issue in simulation training is whether they expose commanders to realistic levels of stress. Crego and Spinks (1997) compared the heart rates of commanders in the MINERVA simulator programmed for the Notting Hill Carnival in London (the biggest street carnival outside Rio) and when they were in command of the real event, and found them to be broadly similar. They also analyzed video recordings of the simulations and log sheets of the real event to determine the type of decision making commanders were using. The found that the command environment does not produce a constant level of demand; rather, it has a phased quality, with periods of varying time pressure.

Training, supported by exercises and simulations to practice skills and use knowledge in a wide range of realistic scenarios and conditions, provides opportunities to generalize understanding, and promote predictability, control, adaptability, and effective performance under a range of circumstances. Detailed process and context evaluation should follow training exercises.

These should be conducted by an outsider or an officer with the independence or rank to be sufficiently critical.

RECOVERY MANAGEMENT

Responding to critical incidents can be stressful for all officers concerned. Officers who do experience a stress reaction may find that it persist well beyond the termination of their direct involvement. Managing these reactions requires that recovery resources are put in place. Senior officers also have a role in recovery management.

Management Style

The hierarchical, autocratic management style prevailing within police organizations (Violanti, 1996) can hinder recovery and adaptation (Alexander & Wells, 1991). Although ideally placed to facilitate adaptation, police supervisors may lack the capability or willingness to provide support to officers involved in traumatic events (Violanti, 1996). Consequently, this capability must be developed.

Recovery is facilitated by senior officers acting as role models (e.g., acknowledging their own feelings) and providing feedback to staff (Alexander & Wells, 1991; Duckworth, 1986). This behavior also demonstrates how officers can reconcile the personal impact of the event with the process of returning to work, and provides a framework for the positive resolution of their experience. The latter can be facilitated by helping officers identify strengths that helped them deal with the event or using the experience to discuss how future incidents could be dealt with more effectively. Senior officers can also promote recovery by providing accurate information about what happened, what may happen (e.g. criminal proceedings), and opportunities to discuss experiences and attend funerals and memorial services.

Returning to Work

Returning to work and getting back into normal routines can be therapeutic. This helps officers put their experience into perspective, allows access to support networks, and facilitates their regaining a sense of perceived control. However, managing the gradual return and reintegration into work requires careful planning and judgement. Senior personnel should ensure that staff do not take on too much too soon and, because cognitive capacities may be temporarily diminished, remind them to take care when, for example, driving or making complex decisions.

At a more general level, organizational analyses can help define the climate of relationships between senior officers and staff and determine its implications for support and recovery (Paton, 1997). In the longer term, such analyses can contribute to organizational development programs through, for example, identifying response constraints within organizational systems (e.g., lack of policy and procedures for managing line-of-duty deaths, insufficient managerial knowledge to manage reintegration and recovery (Paton, 1997)). This information can be fed back into management and organizational development programs to promote not only future response effectiveness but also the creation and maintenance of a supportive organizational climate.

CONCLUSION

Psychological research into the causes and impact of acute stress on police commanders is almost nonexistent. Nevertheless, this is an important issue particularly for the more unusual and demanding operational situations that emerge when responding to major emergencies and disasters. In the absence of appropriate empirical data, we can turn to research findings from other domains such as disaster management, military and aviation fields where commanders also have to take decisions under pressure to inform this debate. This literature suggests many potential stressors for police commanders but also offers methods of training, stress proofing, and team working likely to reduce the risks of commanders making errors when functioning under pressure. We discussed how planning, communication and co-ordination, team development and management, training, and decision making systems and capabilities can be implemented to reduce stress and promote effective response management. Senior officers also have a role to play in facilitating recovery in offices experiencing stress reactions. There is a clear need for more systematic research into response and recovery management issues for senior police offices, particularly those fulfilling command roles at major incidents.

REFERENCES

Alexander, D., & Walker, L.: A study of methods used by Scottish police officers to cope with work-induced stress. *Stress Medicine, 10*: 131-138, 1994.

Alexander, D. A., & Wells, A.: Reactions of police officers to body handling after a major disaster: A before and after comparison. *British Journal of Psychiatry, 159*: 517 - 555, 1991.

Auf der Heide, E.: *Disaster Response.* St. Louis, C.V. Mosby, 1989.

Brannick, M.; Salas, E., & Prince, C. (Eds.): *Team performance, assessment and measurement.* Mahwah, NJ, Lawrence Erlbaum, 1997.

Crego, J.: Wisdom's way. *Police Review, 28*: July, 24-25, 1995.

Crego, J., & Spinks, T.: Critical incident management simulation. In R. Flin, E. Salas, M. Strub & L. Martin (Eds.), *Decision making under stress.* Aldershot, Ashgate, 1997.

Driskell, J., & Salas, E.: *Stress and human performance.* Hillsdale, NJ, Lawrence Erlbaum, 1996.

Duckworth, D.: Psychological problems arising from disaster work. *Stress Medicine, 2*: 315-323, 1986.

Flin, R.: *Sitting in the Hot Seat. Leaders and teams for critical incident management.* Chichester, UK, Wiley, 1996.

Flin, R.; Wynn, V.; Ellis, A., & Skriver, J.: *The effects of sleep loss on commanders' decision making: A literature review.* Report to Defense Evaluation Research Agency, Centre for Human Sciences, Farnborough (Project CHS7381), 1998.

Flin, R.; Salas, E.; Strub, M., & Martin, L. (Eds.):*Decision making under stress.* Aldershot, UK, Ashgate, 1997.

Gregorich, S.; Helmreich, R., & Wilhelm, J.: The structure of cockpit management attitudes. *Journal of Applied Psychology, 75*: 682-690, 1990.

Hightower, H. C., & Couta, M.: Coordinating emergency management: A Canadian example. In R. T. Sylves and W. L. Waugh (eds) *Disaster Management in the US and Canada: The politics, policymaking, administration and analysis of emergency management* (2nd ed). Springfield, IL, Charles C. Thomas, 1996.

Hodgekinson, E., & Stewart, M.: *Coping with catastrophe.* London, Routledge, 1991.

Hogg, M. A.: *The social psychology of group cohesiveness: From attraction to social identity.* New York, New York University Press, 1992.

Home Office: *The Human Elements of Disaster Management.* London: Home Office Advisory Facility on Organizational Health and Welfare, 1992.

Home Office: *Dealing with disaster* (3rd ed). London, Home Office, Emergency Planning Division, 1997.

Klein, G.: The effect of acute stressors on decision making. In J. Driskell & E. Salas (Eds.), *Stress and human performance.* Hillsdale, NJ, Lawrence Erlbaum, 1996.

Klein, G.: Recognition-primed decision making. In C. Zsambok & G. Klein (Eds.), *Naturalistic decision making.* Mahwah, NJ, Lawrence Erlbaum, 1997.

Kurke, M., & Scrivner, E. (Eds.): *Police psychology into the 21st century.* Hillsdale, NJ, Lawrence Erlbaum, 1995.

Northcraft, G. B.; Polzer, J. T.; Neale, M. A., & Kramer, R. M.: Diversity, social identity, and performance: Emergent social dynamics in cross-functional teams. In S. E. Jackson, & M. N. Ruderman (Eds.), *Diversity in work teams: Research paradigms for a changing workplace.* Washington, DC, American Psychological Association, 1995.

Orasanu, J.: Stress and naturalistic decision making: Strengthening the weak links. In R. Flin, E. Salas, M. Strub & L. Martin (Eds.), *Decision making under stress.* Aldershot, Ashgate, 1997.

Orasanu, J., & Backer, P.: Stress and military performance. In J. Driskell & E. Salas (Eds.), *Stress and performance.* Hillsdale, NJ, Lawrence Erlbaum, 1996.

Paton, D.: *Dealing with traumatic incidents in the workplace* (3rd ed). Queensland, Australia, Gull, 1997.

Paton, D.: Disaster Relief Work: An assessment of training effectiveness. *Journal of Traumatic Stress, 7*: 275 - 288, 1994.

Paton, D.; Johnston, D., & Houghton, B.: Organizational responses to a volcanic eruption. *Disaster Prevention and Management, 7*: 5-13, 1998.

Powell, T. C.: Shaken, but alive: Organizational behavior in the wake of catastrophic events. *Industrial Crisis Quarterly, 5*: 271 - 291, 1991.

Raphael, B.: *When Disaster Strikes.* London, Hutchinson, 1986.

Shaw, R.: Decision making under stress: Forming effective police commanders. *Police Research and Management, Autumn*: 51-59, 1997.

Stewart, E., & Flin, R.: Taking action. *Policing Today, December.* 14-17, 1996.

Vrij, A.; van der Steen, J., & Koppelaar, L.: Aggression of police officers as a function of temperature: An experiment with the fire arms training system. *Journal of Community and Applied Psychology, 4*: 365 - 370, 1994.

Violanti, J. (1996) Trauma stress and police work. In D. Paton, & J. M. Violanti, J. (Eds.), *Traumatic stress in critical occupations: Recognition, consequences and treatment.* Springfield, IL, Charles C. Thomas., 1996.

Walsh, M.: Disasters: *Current planning and recent experiences.* London, Edward Arnold, 1989.

Chapter 12

DEATH ON DUTY:
POLICE SURVIVOR TRAUMA*

JOHN M. VIOLANTI

INTRODUCTION

Approximately one million police officers have been assaulted since 1960, resulting in the murder of 2,129 police officers and injury to 328,000 others. Some 631,000 other incidents also occurred where officers suffered attacks without physical injury. Within the last decade, 801 police officers were feloniously murdered and 713 killed in duty-related accidents (FBI Uniform Crime Reports, 1996). Since 1990, there have been 915 officers killed in the line of duty (Concerns of Police Survivors, 1997). This chapter outlines the psychological impact on survivors of police duty-related death. The sudden and often violent death of a loved one in the line of duty can be a traumatic experience for survivors. Such deaths are a reminder of the dangers that officers face each day they go to work. While the loss of a police officer to a community is serious, it is emotionally devastating to family, friends, and other officers.

Stillman (1987) pointed out that police departments are often unaware of the impact of an officer's death on survivors. Many mistakenly believe that police survivors are somehow more emotionally prepared for such losses than survivors in civilian occupations. In fact, police survivors may be more at risk for psychological distress and trauma than their civilian counterparts. Family members often believe that they must "tough it out" because it is expected of them as part of the police culture. They may not seek professional help if needed and tend to rely on police agencies for support. Unfortunately, such support is not always available as many departments lack policy for helping survivors. However, sensitive police agency policies for death notification, emotional support during and after the ordeal, profes-

* This research was supported by the Bureau of Justice Assistance, Office of Justice Programs, U.S. Department of Justice, Grant Number 96-DD-BX-0027, and Concerns of Police Survivors (COPS).

sional psychological referrals, and explanation of benefits may all help to reduce trauma and pathological grief in survivors.

IMPACT ON POLICE SURVIVORS

Despite the incidence of violence against police officers, few studies have examined the effects of duty-related police deaths on surviving spouses and family members. An early study by Danto (1975) involved a small descriptive study of widows of police officers from Detroit and found reported weight loss, sleep difficulties, loss of interest in activities, and suicidal thoughts among these survivors. Niederhoffer and Niederhoffer (1978) commented that a lack of understanding by those outside the police profession contributes to problems experienced by surviving spouses of slain police officers.

Shaw (1986) noted that the successful recovery of the police spouse and family is directly related to events which follow the death; emotional and tangible support was essential for survivors. Shaw (1986a) described the difficulties that police widows must face such as public scrutiny, military style funerals, hesitancy of other officers in talking, and misperceptions of their vulnerability. Stillman (1986) commented that the psychological impact of death on the officer's family has been neglected by police administrators, mental health professionals, and society in general. Police officers, as well as their families, are expected to be invulnerable to psychological harm. Mitchell (1994) described obligations of critical incident support teams to police survivors, including funeral preparations, immediate psychological support, safe places for survivors to go, follow-up services, and possible psychological referral.

Stillman (1986a) was among the first to empirically measure psychological distress and trauma in police spouse survivors. She found that 58 percent of survivors met the criteria for Posttraumatic Stress Disorder (PTSD) after the death of their husband. On a psychological symptomatology measure, surviving spouses demonstrated greater levels of depression, anxiety, hostility, and guilt. No significant differences in measures of PTSD or psychological symptoms were found between spouses of officers killed accidentally and those killed feloniously. The suddenness of the death appeared to make no difference. Spouses exhibited similar high levels of negative psychological symptoms whether the death was sudden or extended.

In a secondary analysis of Stillman's data, Violanti (1996) found that that social interactions with police groups after the death of an officer affected trauma and distress in surviving spouses. Trauma Reaction Index (Frederick, 1985) global scores showed a statistically significant decrease as positive interaction with police departments increased (beta = -.336), followed by police friends (beta = -.157) and police fraternal groups (beta = -.115) Spouse interaction with the community was significantly associated with increased trauma global scores (beta = .212). Police fraternal groups were significantly associated with decreased "trauma fixation" in survivors (beta = -.271), followed by police friends (beta = -.188) and police departments (beta = -.156). Increased positive interaction with the police department was associated with decreased "behavior manifestations of trauma" scores (beta = -.335), police fraternal groups (beta = -.288), and police friends (beta = -.246). Positive interactions with the police department was associated with a significant decrease in "psychological disruption" (beta = -.336).

THE NATIONAL POLICE SURVIVOR STUDY

A recent study of police survivors by this author was conducted to help clarify the impact of duty death on survivors. The goals of this study were to: (1) compare results with Stillman's (1987) study to ascertain an updated status of survivors, (2) compare police survivors to a control group, (3) measure additional factors of grief, coping strategies, self-esteem, and physical health, and (4) determine policies of police agencies towards line-of-duty deaths. The sample of police survivors and departments for the study were drawn from the U.S. Department of Justice Public Safety Officer Benefits database. This office maintains records on officers who died in the line of duty and whose departments have filed for death benefits. Survivors and departments included in this study applied for benefits between 1990-1995. Survey information was obtained from 256 surviving police spouses. An additional 63 police spouses who had not experienced the on-duty death of a loved one were surveyed and utilized as a control group. Information on departmental line-of-duty death policies was collected from 298 police agencies throughout the United States.

Survivors from the 1997 survey were, on average, older than those in 1987 (Table 12.1). Approximately 25 percent of survivors were over 46 years of age, compared with 13 percent in 1987. The average age of 1997 surviving spouses was 39.8 years. Age differences between the two studies are likely accounted for by the higher average age officers who died (1997- 38 years; 1987- 35 years). A greater percentage of survivors were male in 1997 than in 1987. This may be attributed to the increase in women police officers in the United States over the past ten years. Similarly, the number of minority survivors increased in 1997, a statistic that reflects increasing minority group representation in police agencies. Survivors in the 1997 study were on average more educated, had been married approximately the same average num-

Table 12.1.
Demographic characteristics: A comparison between 1987 and 1997 survivors.

Characteristic (N = 256)	Percentage of Survivors	
	1987	1997*
Age		
Less than 25	8.0	0.8
26-30	17.6	12.9
31-35	27.8	22.7
36-40	23.9	19.1
41-45	9.6	18.8
46 or over	13.1	24.6
Sex		
Female	99.2	96.9
Male	0.8	2.7
Ethnic Origin		
Caucasian	84.8	83.2
African-American	5.6	5.1
Hispanic	4.0	5.9
Native-American	—	3.5
Asian-American	—	0.8
Other	—	1.2
Marital Status		
Widowed	97.6	82.8
Remarried	2.4	12.9
Education		
Less than High School	6.5	—
High School	58.9	28.1
Two-year college	13.7	12.5
College	11.3	18.8
Graduate Study	4.0	10.7
Number Years Married		
Less than 5	20.1	30.1
6-10	22.3	19.9
11-15	26.2	15.6
16-20	9.8	14.5
21-25	6.4	9.4
25 or more	15.2	9.0
Number of Marriages		
1	77.8	64.5
2	18.2	27.7
3	4.0	5.5
4 or more	—	0.8

* Percentages may not total to 100% due to missing cases

ber of years at the time of death (11.9 years), and were more likely to have had more than one marriage.

PSYCHOLOGICAL IMPACT ON POLICE SPOUSE SURVIVORS

Symptoms of Psychological Distress

Using the Derogatis Brief Symptom Inventory (BSI) (1992) to measure psychological symptomatology, the 1997 study found that police spouse survivors experienced heightened symptoms of psychological distress after the death of the officer. Figure 12.1 compares reported symptoms of survivors in 1987 and 1997 with a group of police spouses who had not experienced the on-duty death of a loved one (control group). Ten psychological symptoms and an overall symptom score are reported in Figure 12.1.

Figure 12.1. Comparison of Psychological Symptoms: Surviving Police Spouses and a Control Group.

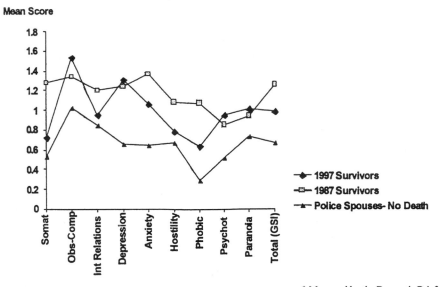

Mean Score

Legend:
- → 1997 Survivors
- ▫ 1987 Survivors
- ▲ Police Spouses- No Death

* Measured by the Derogatis Brief Symptom Inventory (BSI) 1992.

Survivors whose spouses died from duty-related incidents in both 1987 and 1997 were higher on all psychological symptoms compared with a police control group (Figure 12.1). The 1997 survivors scored highest on the following: Obsessive-Compulsiveness (trouble remembering things, feeling blocked, difficulty making decisions, mind going blank, trouble concentrating); Depression (feeling lonely, feeling blue, lost interest, feeling hopeless, feeling worthless); and Paranoia (feelings other were to blame, people cannot be trusted, others are talking about you, people taking advantage of you).

Symptoms of anxiety, hostility, phobia, and interpersonal relationship problems were lower among 1997 compared to 1987 survivors. Total psychological symptom scores (GSI) were also lower in 1997 survivors, although still higher than the police spouse control group. One might speculate that an increased awareness of police spouse survivor problems over the past ten years by nationally based organizations such as Concerns of Police Survivors (COPS) helped to decrease some distress symptoms in survivors.

Posttraumatic Stress Disorder

Such a traumatic event as the death of a loved one may result in Posttraumatic Stress Disorder (PTSD). In Stillman's 1987 study, 59 percent of the survivors met the criteria for Post Traumatic Stress Disorder. In the present study, we compared survivors with control spouses on the PTSD Check List (Weathers et al., 1993). Results showed that surviving spouses were on average 10 percent higher on PTSD scores than the control group. Approximately 32 percent of survivors met the criteria for PTSD, while only 8 percent of the control group met such criteria. Table 12.2 compares PTSD

Table 12. 2.
Comparing Trauma Stress Symptoms Between Survivors and a Police Spouse Control Group*

Traumatic stress symptom	Police Survivors affected "quite a bit" %	Police Spouse Control Group affected "quite a bit" %
Repeated disturbing memories	22	9
Disturbing dreams	8	6
Relive experience	9	3
Upset when reminded of experience	17	10
Physical reaction when reminded of experience	11	3
Avoided thinking about experience	9	5
Avoid activities reminding of event	10	7
Trouble remembering event	11	3
Loss of interest in activities	18	7
Feeling distant from others	21	10
Feeling emotionally numb	14	3
Feeling future will be cut short	17	3
Difficulty concentrating	22	14
Trouble with sleep	23	11
Being super-alert or watching	11	10
Feeling jumpy or easily startled	13	7
Feeling irritable or angry	18	10

*Measured by the "PTSD Check List" (Weathers, et al., 1993)

symptoms between 1997 survivors and the spouse control group. This table reflects items which spouses in both groups stated bothered them "quite a bit."

It is evident from Table 12.2 that there were differences between survivor and control spouses in trauma symptoms. A substantially greater percentage of surviving spouses experienced repeated disturbing memories of the death, were upset when reminded of the experience, felt distant from others, and had difficulty concentrating. Overall, surviving spouses reported a higher percentage in all trauma symptoms, and symptoms remained elevated for as long as five years after the death of the officer. These results indicate evidence of PTSD symptoms among line-of-duty survivors.

Grief Responses

Grief reactions to a police line-of-duty death may be more severe than other types of loss. The 1997 police survivor study compared reactions of survivors with those of the police spouse control group using the Grief Experience Questionnaire (GEQ) (Barret & Scott, 1989). The GEQ measures various components of grief, including somatic reactions, general grief reactions, loss of social support, stigmatization, responsibility, shame, and rejection. The control group comprised spouses who reported the recent loss of a loved one unrelated to police work. Survivors of line-of-duty deaths experienced significantly higher scores for the factors associated with grief described in Figure 12.2.

Figure 12.2.
Factors associated with grief reported at a significantly higher rate by survivors of line-of-duty deaths.

General grief reactions -	numbness, denial, panic attacks, crying, hostility, feelings of emptiness.
Somatic reactions -	physical reactions, including chest pains, palpitations, sick feeling, nervousness, dizziness/fainting, trembling.
Search for explanation -	more intense, more solitary, and less easily resolved.
Loss of social support -	feeling abandoned, avoided, and unsupported
Guilt -	guilt concerning things not said or done in the time before the death
Shame -	denial and an inability to talk openly about the death
Overall grief reaction -	Line-of-duty death survivors experienced a more intense overall grief response than did control police spouses.

Ways of Coping

The ways that persons cope with tragedy may differ according to the nature of the event and previous learning. We were interested in how 1997 survivors coped with the line-of-duty death of their spouse and how such coping compared to the police spouse control group. Coping was measured with the Folkman and Lazurus (1985) "Ways of Coping" revised scale. Line-of-duty death survivors used the coping strategies described in Figure 12.3 at a significantly higher rate than control group spouses.

Self-Esteem

Self-esteem is a fundamental psychological resource that people draw upon in times of distress and trauma. Self-esteem refers to positive attitude toward one's self and represents a characteristic can be overwhelmed in tragic situations. A damaged self-esteem may impair the ability to cope with the officer's death. We analyzed self-esteem scores of survivors based on a scale developed by Pearlin and Schooler (1978) and compared them to the police

---

Figure 12.3:
Coping strategies used more frequently by line-of-duty death survivors, compared with a control spouse group.

- Mentally distanced themselves
- Tried to go on as if the death didn't happen
- Tried to forget the whole thing
- Tried to find something positive for the future
- Became self-controlled
- Kept my feelings to myself
- Kept others from knowing how bad I felt
- Tried to keep my feelings from interfering with other things
- Sought social support
- Talked to someone to find out more about the death
- Asked a friend or relative for advice
- Talked with someone about how I was feeling
- Accepted sympathy and understanding from someone
- Sought escape
- Wished the situation would just go away
- Tried to make myself feel better my eating, drinking, etc
- Avoided people in general
- Took it out on other people

---

spouse control group. Overall, line-of-duty death survivors demonstrated that survivors had a significantly more negative attitude toward themselves. Survivors strongly agreed with the following statements:

- I have little control over things that happen to me
- There is no way to solve the problem I have
- There is little I can do to change my life
- I often feel helpless
- Sometimes I feel like I am pushed around in life
- All in all, I feel like a failure
- I feel useless at times

Physical Health

We assessed the physical health status of survivors and compared it to the police spouse control group. The results (Table 12.3) indicate that survivors reported poorer physical health than spouses in the control group. Only 26.6 percent of survivors reported that their health was presently "excellent" compared with 38.7 percent of control spouses. A larger percentage of survivors reported that their health was excellent prior to the death of the police officer (40.2%). Some 15.6 percent of survivors reported that they presently

Table 12.3.
Comparing physical health between survivors and the police spouse control group

	Survivors	Control Group
How is your health today?		
Poor	6.6%	3.2%
Fair	16.8%	9.7%
Good	48.8%	46.8%
Excellent	26.6%	38.7%
How was you health two years ago?		
Poor	2%	6.5%
Fair	9.4%	11.3%
Good	47.3%	46.8%
Excellent	40.2%	33.9%
Any current health problem?		
Yes	15.6%	12.9%
No	80.5%	82.3%

had a health problem. This finding suggests that line-of-duty survivors should obtain medical as well as emotional support following the death.

SURVIVORS AND RESPONSES TO THE DEATH

Death Notification

For the most part, survivors were satisfied with death notification procedures, policies, and practices. Some 69 percent of survivors stated that the notification was done with sensitivity and understanding, 11 percent said that notification was cold and informal, and 10 percent said they wished someone else would have told them. The majority of death notifications were done by someone from the police agency. When survivors were asked who they would most have liked there at notification, 33 percent chose a relative, 15 percent wanted a friend present, and 20 percent wanted their children at the scene.

Support after the Death

Survivors ranked those most supportive after the death of the officer in the following order: (1) parents, (2) nonpolice friends, (3) children, (4) police friends, (5) coworkers, and (6) in-laws. Survivors were asked how satisfied they were with responses of certain groups after the death. Table 12.4 provides results from 1997 survivors and compares them to 1987 survivors. We can infer from Table 12.4 that 1997 survivors were much less satisfied than 1987 survivors with the responses of police departments and other police officers. Satisfaction was similar in 1987 and 1997 concerning responses from other groups.

POLICE AGENCY SURVEY RESPONSES

A national sample of 298 police agencies responded to the COPS survey. Questions were asked about policies and practices concerning duty-related death survivors. Responding agencies had all experienced line-of-duty deaths within the past 10 years. Approximately 85 percent reported accidental deaths, 69 percent felonious deaths, 76 percent deaths due to illness, and 32 percent suicide.

Table 12.4.
Percent *"very satisfied"* with responses after the death of the officer:
A comparison of 1987 and 1997 police survivors.

	Survivors	
Responses:	*1987*	*1997*
Police Department	53.7%	35.9%
Other officers	56.6%	33.2%
Death notification	35.4%	32.8%
Funeral arrangements	66.9%	66.4%
Community response	70.3%	73.0%
Police benevolent groups	55.4%	54.7%
Trial proceedings	10.3%	10.9%
Final verdict	13.1%	16.8%
Media coverage	30.3%	24.6%

Death Notification and Follow-up

Most police agencies (51%) sent more than one officer to the survivors residence. Only 10 percent sent one officer. Some 77 percent stated that they sent the chief or a high ranking official, 57 percent sent clergy, 13 percent the officer's partner, and 4 percent a physician. Overall, 29 percent of departments contacted relatives and brought them to the residence. Regarding training, only 13 percent of responding agencies said that their personnel were trained in death notification. Some 73 percent said they assigned a family liaison officer after an officer's death, and 70 percent supported survivors during the death investigation and trial. Only 39 percent of the agencies had a policy to maintain contact with survivors after the funeral. In general, the length of contact ranged from one to two years. Some departments stated that they maintained contact for as long as survivors felt it was necessary. Some 49 percent of departments said they maintained formal contact (high ranking official) and 65 percent stated they initiated informal contact by patrol officers. If the deceased officer was single, surviving parents were afforded the same services by 90 percent of the departments surveyed.

In the 1997 survey, 39 percent of police agencies had some general orders in place for line-of-duty deaths. Approximately 20 percent of the departments stated that formal policy was initiated as a direct result of a line-of-duty death. This was a very slight improvement from 1987, where 33 percent had formal officer death policies. Departmental size was a factor in whether or not the department had a formal policy. Approximately 72 percent of large departments (1001-6274 officers), 46 percent of medium departments (51-1000 officers), and 28 percent of small departments (2-50 officers) had a formal policy for line-of-duty deaths.

In general, it appears that police agencies are lagging in having structured, formal policy for managing duty deaths and meeting the needs of survivors. The 1987 study noted that lack of formal policy leaves departments and survivors unprepared to deal with the funeral, benefit explanation, and the emotional distress of the officer's death.

IMPACT OF DEATH ON THE DEPARTMENT

Several questions were asked concerning the effect of line-of-duty deaths on the department (see table 12.5). Some 93 percent stated that an officers death had an emotional impact of other officers. In addition, personnel at the scene of the death were reported to have experienced psychological distress and trauma. Incidents of death lead to 25 percent of departments initiating psychological services for officers. These results emphasize the need for services for coworkers as well as family survivors. Police agencies often consider themselves as a "family," and the death of a fellow or sister officer can have a profound psychological impact on officers, dispatchers, and civilian personnel.

INTERVENTION

A surviving police family never forgets the tragedy of a traumatic death. They continue on with the tragedy now a part of their lives (Lindemann, 1944; Raphael; 1977; Burnett, et al., 1994). The trauma of a death experience is somehow integrated into their lives. Each time the death anniversary occurs, the family's sense of loss may surface. In instances of felonious death,

Table 12.5.
Line-of-duty deaths: Effects on the police department.

Effect	% *Departments Responding* *"yes"*
Emotional impact on officers	93
Trauma in those close to the scene	73
Changes in operational procedures	32
Changes in family notification	14
Identified need for additional officers	12
Implementation of psychological services	25

every retrial, appeal, or parole forces the family to relive the injustice dealt to the fallen officer and their loved ones (van der Kolk, 1990; Stillman, 1987). Within the police family, intervention may best occur on (1) the group level, which Violanti (1996) suggests may be associated with reduced distress and trauma, and (2) the individual level, where specific characteristics of the death and individual grief responses must be dealt with.

Group Level Intervention

The essence of trauma is loss of safety (van der Kolk, 1990). The first step in intervention should therefore be to ensure that police survivors can retreat to a safe place of physical and psychological support. Our findings suggested that police groups may be such a safe place. Others (Figley, 1988; Ochberg, 1995, Violanti, 1996) have found that a supportive group or family is ideal for trauma recovery.

Figley (1988b) described how such groups promote recovery by detecting trauma stress, confronting the trauma, urging recapitulation of the incident, and facilitating resolution. Figley (1989; 1995) presented a generic model for treating traumatized families. The goal of his therapy is to empower the family (or group in the case of the police) to overcome and learn from their ordeal with duty-related death and in doing so be better prepared for future occurrences. Empowerment is a result of the development of social supportiveness among members of the group.

Unfortunately, not all police agencies are aware that they may be of benefit to survivors. Police agencies should strive to develop timely policies and practices that promote the development and maintenance of a supportive climate (Paton, 1996). Stillman (1987) found that some 67 percent of law enforcement agencies lacked guidelines for continued emotional support for the survivors beyond the wake and funeral. Stillman commented that failure to provide continued support gave survivors the impression that they had been abandoned by the department. This may account for our finding that trauma in survivors does not significantly decrease over time. It is important that supportive groups provide help with a wide scope of problems associated with the death.

Cook and Bickman (1989) found high correlation between satisfaction with cohesive groups and support with tangible factors (i.e., the provision of concrete favors such as funeral arrangements, guarding the house, transporting children to school, etc.). A national group named Concerns of Police Survivors (COPS), organized in 1984, provides support to police survivors and assists law enforcement organizations with developing plans to help survivors. COPS developed tangible (policy suggestions) and intangible (emotional support and counseling) organizational guidelines designed to mediate the impact of duty-related death. Below are suggestions made by COPS to help reduce the trauma of police survivors (Concerns of Police Survivors, 1997).

Death Notification

In many cases, the death of a law enforcement officer is sudden and unexpected. It is important for officers who notify survivors to be sensitive and caring. The name of the deceased officer should never be released to the media before immediate survivors are notified. Notification must always be made in person and never alone. The chaplain, psychologist, head of the agency (or representative), or another public safety survivor could appropriately accompany the informing officer. Gather everyone in the home and ask them to sit down. Inform them slowly and clearly of the information you have on the incident. Make sure to use the officer's name during the notification. If the officer has already died, relay that information and do not give the family a false sense of hope. Use words like "died" and "dead" rather than "gone away" or "passed away." The department should be prepared to handle immediate family needs. This is where coworkers' spouses or a spouse support group can be used. It is most reassuring to the family when the chief or another highranking designate responds to the home or hospital. In some cases, the absence of this figurehead was viewed by both the family and fellow coworkers as both insensitive and indicative of poor leadership.

Supporting the Family During the Ordeal

The appointment of a police officer to liaise between the family and the department may help survivors feel that they are still part of the police family. Liaison officers provide a "connection" to the police agency and allow survivors to feel more comfortable in asking questions and making arrangements. This may be beneficial in reducing trauma. The liaison officer should meet with the family regarding funeral arrangements and be constantly available to the family throughout this traumatic time. Since most officers have not prearranged their wishes for the handling of their funeral, the family will most likely need to make decisions regarding all aspects of the funeral. The department should only make the family aware of what they can offer in the way of assistance.

If there is a family support group within the police department, this group should have the responsibility of ensuring that the needs of survivor families and their visitors are attended to. Departmental vehicles should be made available to the family if they desire transportation to and from the funeral home. The family should have access to other public safety survivors or other support groups (Concerns of Police Survivors, Survivors of Homicide Victims, Compassionate Friends, Parents of Murdered Children, etc.). Although some police agencies may provide survivors access to the staff psychologist immediately following the death of the officer, the psychologist should provide only supportive services for the present. Arrangement can be made for future sessions. Survivors have a definite need to talk to someone about the incident.

Follow-up with the Police Family

Based on our finding that trauma remains high in police survivors over time, it is important to help all survivors feel part of the police family for which the officer gave his/her life. Departments can easily keep in touch with the family through monthly phone calls the first year after the death and less frequently thereafter. Coworkers of the deceased officer should be encouraged to visit survivors on a regular basis. The department should always observe the officer's death anniversary date with a short note to the family. Keep in mind that all holidays are traumatic events for the family during the first year. The department should maintain support as long as the family feels the need for the support. The family will let you know when they are ready to move on with their lives without assistance from the department.

The police agency should be sensitive to the long-term needs of other family members as well as the spouse. When plaques/memorabilia are given to the surviving spouse, the same should be made available to the surviving parents. They have lost a child who can never be replaced. Remember to invite the surviving family to agency activities. Parents, adult-aged or younger children, siblings, and others are all experiencing grief (Gold, 1994). Realize that grief is a process and that everyone handles grief differently. It might be beneficial to have the psychologist see the entire family for a supportive service session shortly after the funeral. Do not set time limitations on when the family should recover from the death. The grief process has no timetable and many survivors may experience a complicated grief process.

Individual Treatment Issues

While it is important to establish and maintain a supportive police group environment, it is also important to consider individual therapy for police survivors. The suddenness of duty-related death is an exacerbating factor in the impact of trauma. Sudden deaths are usually more difficult to grieve than deaths which occur with some prior warning (Parkes, 1975). A sudden death will generally leave the police survivor with a sense of unreality about the loss. A first appropriate intervention might be to heighten the reality of the event (Worden, 1991). This may be accomplished by allowing the body to be openly viewed and explaining the circumstances of the death to survivors. I recall an incident where a chief of police was murdered and his body so badly mutilated that the coffin was closed. Police investigators were extremely wary about talking to the widow about the gruesome details of the incident. Upon learning of this, the police psychologist called a family meeting some three months after the death and requested that police detectives explain how the chief was killed. Both the widow and family members were afforded closure and considerable relief was expressed by them.

Guilt feelings are also common among survivors of sudden deaths. I recall a police officer's surviving spouse repeatedly blaming herself for his death because she was unable to persuade him to put on his bullet-proof vest before he went on duty. Worden (1991) points out that the need to blame someone for the sudden death is very strong and often survivors will either blame themselves or react harshly towards other family members or close friends. A sense of helplessness and rage is often associated with blame. An important intervention issue in these cases is to help the survivor focus on issues of the reality of responsibility for the death. The counselor should also be aware that the desire for retribution may be a psychological defense against both the reality and pain of the officer's death (Rynearson & McCreery, 1984).

One of the most difficult obstacles for police survivors are the legal issues associated with duty-related deaths. Getting on with the task of mourning is sometimes impossible until legal aspects are resolved. Many police survivors feel they have been traumatized over and over again by the courts and the criminal justice system. Delays in the trial of the accused murderer can delay the grief process. Concerns of Police Survivors (1997) made several suggestions to help survivors through the ordeal of the legal process.

First, it is the police department's responsibility to keep the family informed of the legal proceedings. Public safety's surviving families are no different than any other victim. They must know how the incident occurred, down to the smallest detail. Many departments keep the family in the dark about the incident stating that it could influence the outcome of the trial if the family is informed of the investigation. If this is the case, the department should sit down with the family and explain their reasons for not sharing information. At the earliest opportunity following the trial, the investigators should sit down with the family and answer their questions about the ordeal. The facts will be far less shocking than what they have already imagined happened during the incident. Should the department show a reluctance to share information about the incident, the survivors may view it as an attempt to hide something from the family.

Police Coworkers

Although the immediate family suffers greatly the loss of a loved one, co-workers should also be considered. They are all part of the extended work family of policing. Departments must provide emotional support and debriefing sessions for friends of slain officers; from the partner and shift co-workers, to the station clerks and the dispatchers. Departments should develop in-depth, general orders that deal with the logistics of the department's handling of an officer's funeral. They should also develop a system whereby timely reviews of beneficiary papers are afforded the officer. Important considerations like continued health insurance coverage for the family after the officer's death, educational benefits for surviving children, and arranging surviving spouse pension benefits, should be included as part of policy.

CONCLUSION

The job of policing presents a clear danger for traumatic death. When such deaths occur, police survivors are left behind in the wake of trauma. This chapter described a recent study on the effects of duty-related death on surviving spouses. The results suggest that police survivors experience increased levels of many negative psychological symptoms as well as Posttraumatic Stress Disorder. In addition, we suggest that police agencies are important support groups and, as such, should improve and formally solidify their policies towards survivors of duty-related death. Results of previous research have indicated that an increase in the quality of interaction with police groups after the death of the officer decreases psychological distress and trauma in survivors. Positive interaction with police friends, the department, and police fraternal groups was statistically associated with a decrease in distress in police spouse survivors. This may indicate that cohesiveness and a sense of belonging to the police culture somehow influences experiences of distress and trauma (Stillman, 1987; Violanti, 1996; Violanti, in press) .

Effective intervention and treatment for survivor families of police deaths may be important for the amelioration of distress and trauma. Intervention was viewed as occurring on the group as well as individual level. It is important, however, for police groups to understand specifically what they must do to assist survivors. Emotional as well as tangible support through the entire process of grieving is essential. The police group must therefore be available for the survivor during the ordeal and afterwards. A police widow commented to me: "When my husband was alive, we were told that we would always be part of the police family. Now that he is gone, where is our police family when we need them the most ?". Perhaps future longitudinal research will help to confirm that support over time is important in reducing trauma. Increased representation of minority groups also has implications in this context. Research and intervention procedures must investigate cultural differences in the grieving process, grieving rituals, and in the expression of grief. Once obtained, this knowledge can be used to develop culturally sensitive and appropriate interventions.

Treatment for police survivors on an individual level must address many of the same problems associated with anyone who has suffered a loss. Along with these are special problems involving the suddenness and violence of the officer's death, public notice of the death, and dealing with an often slow, unresponsive criminal justice system. Quite often, psychological closure is delayed for many years as legal issues concerning the death are argued in the courts and discussed in the media. Recent research on the exposure of police officers to stress and trauma often overshadows the effects of residual exposure on their families. The impact of police duty-related death touches all in its wake and leaves a discernible path of grief. It is important that we understand and attempt to lessen the pain of those left behind.

REFERENCES

Barret, T. W., & Scott, T. B.: Development of the grief experience questionnaire. *Suicide and Life-Threatening Behavior, 19*: 201-215, 1989.

Burnett, P.; Middelton, W.; Rapheal, B.; Dunne, M.; Moylan, A., & Martinek, N.: Concepts of normal bereavement. *Journal of Traumatic Stress, 7*: 113-128, 1994.

Concerns of Police Survivors: *The trauma of law enforcement deaths.* Handbook published by C.O.P.S. Bureau of Justice Assistance public safety officer's benefits program, 1997.

Cook, J. D., & Bickman, L.: Social support and psychological symptomatology following a natural disaster. *Journal of Traumatic Stress, 3*: 541-556, 1989.

Danto, B. L.: Bereavement and the widows of slain police officers. In J. Shoenberg (Ed.), *Bereavement: Its psychological aspects.* New York, Columbia, 1975.

Derogatis, L. R.: *Administration, scoring, and procedures manual-II for the SCL-90R,* Baltimore, Clinical Psychometric Research, 1992.

Federal Bureau of Investigation: *Uniform crime reports: Law enforcement officers killed and assaulted.* Washington, DC: U.S. Dept. of Justice, 1996.

Figley, C. R.: Post-traumatic family therapy. In F. M. Ochberg (Ed.), *Post-traumatic therapy and victims if violence.* New York, Brunner/Mazel, 1988.

Figley, C. R.: *Helping traumatized families.* San Francisco: Jossey-Bass, 1989.

Figley, C. R.: Systemic PTSD: Family treatment experiences and implications. In G. S. Everly & J. M. Lating (Eds), *Psychotraumatolgy: Key papers and core concepts in post-traumatic stress.* New York, Plenum, 1995.

Folkman, S.; Lazarus, R. S.; Dunkel-Schetter, C.; DeLOngis, A., & Gruen, R.: The dynamics of a stressful encounter: Cognitive appraisal, coping, and encounter outcomes. *Journal of Personality and Social Psychology, 50*: 992-1003, 1985.

Frederick, C. J.: Selected foci in the spectrum of post traumatic stress disorder. In J. Laube & S. Murphy (Eds.), *Perspectives on disaster recovery.* Norwalk, CT, Appleton-Century, 1985.

Gold, D. N.: I had no room to breath: Line-of-duty death of the adult child. In J. T. Reese, & E. Srivner (Eds.), *Law enforcement families: Issues and answers.* Washington, D.C., U.S. Government Printing Office, 1994.

Lindemann, E.: Symptomatology and management of acute grief. *American Journal of Psychiatry, 101*: 141-148, 1944.

Mitchell, J. T.: Critical incident stress interventions with families and significant others. In J. T. Reese, & E. Srivner (Eds.), *Law enforcement families.* Washington, D.C., U.S. Government Printing Office, 1994.

Niederhoffer, A., & Niederhoffer, E.: *The police family: From station house to ranch house.* Lexington,KY, D.C. Heath, 1978.

Ochberg, F. M.: Post-traumatic therapy. In G. S. Everly & J. M. Lating (Eds.), *Psychotraumatolgy: Key papers and core concepts in post-traumatic stress.* New York, Plenum, 1995.

Parkes, C. M.: Determinants of outcome following bereavement. *Omega, 6*: 303-323, 1975.

Paton D.: Traumatic stress in critical occupations: Current status and future issues. In D. Paton & J. M. Violanti (Eds.), *Traumatic stress in critical occupations: Recognition, consequences and treatment.* Springfield, IL, Charles C. Thomas, 1996.

Pearlin, L. I., & Schooler, C.: The structure of coping. *Journal of Health and Social Behavior, 19*: 2-21, 1978.

Rapheal, B.: Preventative intervention with the recently bereaved. *Archives of General Psychiatry, 34*: 1450-1454, 1977.

Rynearson, E. K. & McCreery, J. M.: Bereavement after homicide: A synergism of trauma and loss. *American Journal of Psychiatry, 150*: 258-261, 1984.

Shaw, J. H.: Duty-related deaths: Family policy considerations. In J. T Reese, J. M. Horn, & C. Dunning (Eds.), *Critical incidents in policing.* Washington, D.C., U.S. Government Printing Office, 1986.

Shaw, J. H.: The death of an officer: Surviving the first year. In J. T Reese, J. M. Horn, & C. Dunning (Eds.), *Critical incidents in policing.* Washington, D.C., U.S. Government Printing Office, 1986a.

Stillman, F. A.: The invisible victims: Myths and realities. In J. T Reese & H.T. Goldstein (Eds.), *Psychological services for law enforcement.* Washington, D.C., U.S. Government Printing Office, 1986.

Stillman, F. A.: *Psychological responses of surviving spouses of public safety officers killed accidentally or feloniously in the line of duty.* Unpublished doctoral dissertation, Baltimore, MD, John Hopkins University, 1986a.

Stillman, F. A.: *Line-of-duty-deaths: Survivor and departmental responses.* Brief Report, Washington, DC: National Institute of Justice, pp. 1-4, 1987.

Van der Kolk, B. A.: The psychological processing of traumatic events: The personal experience of post traumatic stress disorder. In J. T. Reese; J. M. Horn, & C. Dunning (Eds.), *Critical incidents in policing.* Washington, D.C., U.S. Government Printing Office, 1990.

Violanti, J. M.: The impact of cohesive groups in the trauma recovery context: Police survivors and duty-related death. *Journal of Traumatic Stress, 9*: 379-386, 1996.

Violanti, J. M.: Duty-related deaths and police spouse survivors group support affect. In C. Figley (Ed.), *Traumatology of grieving.* Philadelphia, Taylor & Francis, in press.

Weathers, F. W.; Litz, B. T.; Herman, D. S.; Huska, J. A., & Keane, T. M.: *The PTSD checklist: Reliability, validity, and diagnostic utility.* Presentation at ISTSS annual conference, San Antonio, Texas, 1993.

Worden, J. W.: *Grief counseling and grief therapy: A handbook for the mental health practitioner.* New York, Springer, 1991.

Chapter 13

IMPACT OF DUTY-RELATED DEATH ON OFFICERS CHILDREN: CONCEPTS OF DEATH, TRAUMA REACTIONS, AND TREATMENT

MARY BETH WILLIAMS

INTRODUCTION

The impact of a duty-related death of a police officer is widespread. The officer's partner, coworkers, and officers from other jurisdictions respond in a variety of ways, ranging from expressing shock and/or rage to giving financial support. Media personnel generally descend upon the scene and funeral services receive widespread attention. But what of the officer's family in general and children in particular; what is the impact of the death upon them? How do the children process the event and how can they be helped to survive the loss?

Children of law enforcement officers who have died in duty-related deaths are direct victims of the trauma as well as secondary victims as they are exposed to the posttraumatic symptoms of others around them, including the remaining parent. These children suddenly learn that life is not permanent. In the case of a duty-related death, daddy or mommy went to work, often at night, and suddenly was violently killed. The children of that officer had no time to prepare for this event or to say goodbye (Walsh & McGoldrich, 1991), and their symptoms of loss and trauma may be even more intense than those in children whose parents have died from natural causes. In addition, media response to and focus upon the death, as well as any coverage of subsequent legal proceedings, re-exposes the children and often retriggers their symptoms, leading to a posttraumatic stress reaction. The horrible images may remain indelibly inscribed on the children's brains (Pynoos, 1993). The death also challenges the child's ability to maintain an internal locus of control, disturbing his/her sense of historical continuity and ability to make plans for the future.

What individual characteristics of children influence whether or not they develop post-traumatic stress reactions? Shirk (1988) noted that age, cognitive ability, level of ego development, conceptualization of death, developmental stage, and other similar factors influence coping responses and understanding. More recently, Bowman (1997) noted that factors of the event alone may not be sufficient in and of themselves to lead to PTSD. Individual differences in children must also be taken into account including age and stage related beliefs about the world, sources of other danger in the child's world, the child's beliefs about the self, previous life experiences, personality traits (e.g., resilience), and cognitive competencies. A combination of event characteristics, personal attributes, and belief systems therefore must be considered.

Children develop, epigenetically, in a series of stages. If a major trauma interferes with that development, then regression, fixation, or acceleration of development may occur (Erikson, 1967; 1973). How do children at various stages of development conceptualize death and what are their typical traumatic reactions to death? What symptoms do they exhibit and how can they be helped to heal. The initial part of this chapter examines conceptualizations of death of children at preschool (0-5), elementary school (6-10), and preteen and teenage (11-18) stages of development. The second part examines posttraumatic reactions in children, and the third presents short- and long-term interventions to help a child after the duty-related death of a parent.

A CHILD'S VIEW OF DEATH

A child's understanding of the death of a slain police officer parent depends upon a variety of factors, including level of cognitive development, perception of the death-related events, previous resolution of developmental tasks, and previous experiences with death (Wass & Corr, 1984). As Staudacher (1987) noted, however, these descriptions are approximate and depend upon the factors previously mentioned; "there are no age limits, which can be homogeneously applied to every child's understanding of death" (p. 310).

Corr (1995), recognizing that death as a concept has a number of components, identified five central concepts for children. The first concept involved in a child's view of death is universality, the recognition that all living things die. This includes recognition of the "all inclusiveness" of death, the "inevitability" of death, and the "unpredictability" of death. When the death of a parent occurs in the line of duty, this latter notion is particularly vivid. The second concept is that of irreversibility; once a body is dead, it can never again return to life (i.e., after all resuscitation attempts have failed). This concept includes both the process/transition from life to death and the state of death that is an outcome (Speece & Brent, in press). The third concept is nonfunctionality. Once something living is dead, it can never again perform the functions or have the capabilities it had when alive. These functions are of two types: external functions such as breathing, playing, talking, moving, and internal indirectly observed functions of feeling, thinking, imagining, intuiting, or dreaming. The fourth concept is causality. Trying to understand what causes death can be a challenge for children. To truly understand causation requires fairly developed thought processes in a child. The final aspect of death is the understanding/belief that something exists after death, whether as a soul in heaven/hell or a soul in a reincarnated body. The questions children ask about each of these five concept areas will vary according to age and stage.

The Preschool Child

Infants from birth to about age three have no concept of death but have fears of separation, the dark, and being dropped. Preschool children are generally interested in immediate rewards of behavior (Selman, 1980). The preschooler who is well-adjusted has resolved developmental crises of trust vs. mistrust and autonomy vs. shame and doubt (Erikson, 1967; 1973). The child therefore has reasonable trustfulness toward others and trustworthiness toward the self and feels secure in the permanence of a nurturing object (generally the mother). This child is beginning to explore the world and has learned to exhibit some self-control without loss of self-esteem. Being autonomous is a source of pride. The line-of-duty death of a parent challenges trust and autonomy and impairs the child's ability to work through and resolve these developmental crises, limiting the child's ability to find direction and purpose, impairing the formation of relationships outside the family.

Preschoolers express feelings primarily through play that is often spontaneous and communicate needs through words. Their active imaginations lead them to create visual images of what they believe others experienced (NOVA, 1990). They may recreate pictures of the death of the parent in their mind repetitively.

Preschool children see death as temporary, impermanent, and reversible (Staudacher, 1987), as well as unpleasant and bad. Their view of the world rests upon outward appearances (Lagorio, 1991). They "play dead" and have fantasies of death that may involve magical thinking. They often believe they can make things happen by wishing them to happen, including death or regeneration. They also exhibit animistic thinking and give everything characteristics of being alive. They tend to idealize the dead parent (Worden, 1991) and view him/her as merely absent. The parent's aliveness is diminished and he/she is "away" (Kastenbaum, 1992). They expect him/her to come back. Many preschoolers believe that the dead are still able to eat, play, or sleep (Beckman, 1990). Death has some permanent ramifications but the preschool child has little coping capacity to death with the death as a finality or with the reactions of traumatized others. Still the child's reactions are influenced by the responses of adults in the child's environment, adults who often are in denial. According to Schowalter (1975), even a four-year-old has the capacity to mourn and tries to defend against the pain of mourning. Exposure to death threatens the preschooler's security (Vondra, 1990), even though it is a departure and not a finality.

Preschoolers are dependent on others and are vulnerable, yet they hold fantasies of invulnerability and model themselves after their superheros. Death reminds them of their vulnerability and they may replay a death repeatedly to regain a sense of control or may rely on dissociation to get them through traumatic events. If a remaining parent is also extremely traumatized, the child has (at least temporarily) lost two parents and may have extreme fears of being abandoned permanently (Catherall, 1992).

Elementary Age Children

Elementary age children (ages 6-11) are working through the stage of development known as industry vs. inferiority (Erickson, 1967). They are able to criticize themselves and their personal behaviors as well as express self-disgust. They have a better understanding of time and space as well as some sense of both past and future. They are beginning to develop strong peer relationships and their major concerns are social rather than physical (NOVA, 1990; Catherall, 1992). Older elementary-age children have begun to think abstractly, introspectively, and to process information through deductive reasoning.

Young, elementary age children may not grasp the finality of death. Between ages of 5 and 9, they recognize that all living things die but do not associate the concept with themselves (Ayalon, 1992). By approximately age 10, children recognize that death is irreversible. They have become aware of their own mortality and have fears of death (Lagorio, 1991). They seek facts about a death and, if not given that information, create scenarios to provide explanations and may exhibit intrusive thoughts or nightmares (Beckman, 1990). They understand the changes that death brings and, as they mourn, become less interested in play and increase the distance between them and friends (Pynoos & Nader, 1988). These isolating behaviors are in contrast with the normal developmental tasks of developing peer relationships and functioning academically in a school community. They are aware that the roles of a family change after a death and that death impacts the family as a system (Catherall, 1992).

Elementary age children tend to jump to conclusions and are blind to inconsistencies. They also try to avoid issues directly, yet may be preoccupied with the morbid, gory details of a death (van Ornum & Mordock, 1990). In the early elementary years (ages 5-9), they tend to see death as due to an external source, e.g. the bogeyman or a monster, a creature that can be avoided through cunning and skill (Staudacher, 1987). In later years, death is viewed as a biological process that may be painful; in addition, death has consequences both to the self (the deceased) and others. Children see the relationship between life and death. They may fear being buried alive or have fantasies of horrible body mutilation occurring to them. School-age children may be very angry with the dead parent because that parent has abandoned them. They understand concepts of forever, irreversibility, and transformation (Worden, 1991). To these children, death has become a natural, universal event that must be grieved. They are also able to understand the stages of grief (confusion/denial; sadness, anger, fear; bargaining and solution searching; and acceptance (Kubler-Ross, 1992; Lagorio, 1991).

Preteen and Adolescent

The preadolescent child and the adolescent have advanced language capabilities and may tend to be judgmental about the world and the self. They often communicate by "acting out." Their primary needs are support and positive regard that builds self-esteem; the primary source of relationships for them moves between family and peers (Erikson, 1967). Preadolescents are entering the stage of Identity vs. Identity Diffusion and are attempting to internalize moral judgement, are experimenting with roles of work and play, and are learning to make decisions involving interactions with others. This stage of development is generally resolved by the close of the teen years. The most typical reaction to trauma at this stage is outrage, which may be communicated creatively through art, poetry, and drama (Hindman, 1989). This preoccupation with the expression of anger may lessen the impact of death (van Ornum & Mordock, 1990). Preadolescents, in particular, are more likely to act out deep feelings and exhibit behavioral extremes. They tend to be introspective and think of alternative coping options to situations (Lagorio, 1991). Adolescents also tend to resolve grief through self-destructive behaviors. However, helping them to talk about the meaning of life and death, often within the peer group, is an important intervention. The teen years are a time of emotional turmoil. The group serves to provide a sense of identity for the teen and limits their sense of isolation.

If a teen has lost a parent through death, in most instances, that teen does not fit in with others who have not lost a parent. Finding a group of others who understand can help facilitate healing.

Preadolescents and adolescents understand the reality of death but may challenge its existence. They want to know all the distasteful details about a death, including the changes the body experiences to control their anxious fears. They may inoculate themselves by watching violent, death-filled movies and television shows. They seek to find meaning to life and death and search for or avoid explanations of why a death occurred. They also may imagine what it is like to be dying.

The tasks of grief for teens are similar to those of adults (Worden, 1991). Teens must learn to accept the reality of the loss of the parent, experience the pain of grief, adjust to the changed environment without the parent, develop a new sense of self, relocate the parent emotionally through ritual to lessen emotional attachment, and move on with life. At this time, adolescents are also developing the capacity to question existentially. They are aware of the social context and cultural system of death and dying that is surrounding them and is part of their world. Death of a parent often challenges their acquisition of abstract thought and conflict resolution abilities (Pynoos, 1993). Death is supposed to remain distant; the death of a parent changes that schema/belief (Staudacher, 1987). Teens try to defend against the personal impact of death and their own vulnerability. However, by the end of the teenage years, death is generally seen as permanent, inevitable, universal, and a biological process they cannot escape.

REACTIONS AND SYMPTOMATOLOGY

The child's most common reactions to the death of a parent are emotionally-based and center on feelings of fear, guilt, anger, and confusion. The ways these emotions are expressed and resolved vary with the age and stage of development of the child, the amount and quality of support given to that child, the coping abilities and belief systems of the child (including the meaning of the death to the child) and the child's previous experiences with trauma. The most common fears are fear of losing the remaining parent; fear of one's own death; fear of sleep (if sleep becomes equated with death [if the death occurred at night, often the case in duty-related incidents] or if the child has frequent nightmares); fear of being separated from others; fear of being unprotected; or the fear of consequences of sharing these fears with others (Staudacher, 1987). Emotions related to guilt often surround beliefs that the child is somehow being punished for misdeeds by the death; that the child may have caused the death by wishing ill-will on the parent; that the child did not love the dead parent enough to protect him or her; or that the child should be dead instead of the parent. Feelings of anger frequently are manifestations of these fears and fears of abandonment as well as manifestations of beliefs about powerlessness and vulnerability.

Traumatized preschool children exhibit both trauma-specific behavioral disturbances and more generalized fears, aggressive behaviors, regressions (e.g., toileting), distractibility, frozen watchfulness, sleep disorders, and repetitive talk and play as they attempt to find meaning in the sudden death of the parents (Green et al., 1991). Posttraumatic play may be a form of obsessive repetition to relieve anxiety through re-enactment of what the child imagines to be the death scene. The death may challenge moral development, may disturb narrative coherence (the ability to tell the beginning, middle, and end of a story), and may lead to cognitive confusion (Pynoos, 1993). Preschool children are extremely vulnerable to reports of the death in the media and exposure to the traumatic reactions of other family members, particularly when the reactions threaten their security and safety. They tend to withdraw as their anxiety grows and are prone to unlearn previously learned skills and behaviors.

If the young child continues to grieve and does not get help, if the child does not cope and process to assimilate the loss and death of the parent, personality disorders may occur. A child may get stuck in magical thinking and fantasy thinking. Magical thinking in young children is often associated with a child's attempts to gain control over a situation or make the parent come back. Mood changes which accompany loss can impact personality development as well. Many children with unresolved grief may become driven workaholics as adults (Fogarty, 1993). Unresolved grief may lead to psychosomatic disorders and unresolved anger may lead to oppositional defiant disorders.

Elementary-Age Children

Elementary school children feel powerless in the face of a traumatic death and may lose control over their own lives. Davidson and Smith (1990) reported that children who experienced traumatic events prior to age 11 were three times more likely to develop PTSD than those who experienced similar events after age 19. Elementary-age children continue to exhibit regressive symptoms associated with earlier developmental stages, such as excessive clinging, crying, or previously extinguished behaviors (Erikson, 1967). They may become irritable and aggressive or may react to specific fears or triggers that "set off" certain emotions including rage reactions. They may have elaborate fantasies, dreams, and/or nightmares about the death. They may lose interest in school and demonstrate concentration problems. They may not report that they felt numb directly but may say that they felt more distant from others or wanted to avoid awareness of their feelings (Pynoos & Nader, 1988).

In severe cases, if the young child or early elementary school child becomes very dissociative, reactions may be seen in five areas. In the cognitive domain, there may be cognitive distortions that interfere with the child's ability to develop a language to understand death and thereby retell the story of what happened. Flashbacks may also occur. In the emotional domain, the child may have a damaged capacity for expression of emotion; feelings may be too intense and too labile. The child may not have a socially appropriate way to channel and discharge intense emotions or express ambivalence. In the physical domain, the child may have difficulty grasping and understanding the body's reactions to trauma and may try to retraumatize the self in physical ways. In the interpersonal domain, the child may find that the capacity for trust, safety, and intimacy has been damaged; alienation rather than healthy attachment becomes the norm. And, finally, in the spiritual domain, the child may find himself or herself demoralized and without the benefit of a belief in God or a supreme being. Despair exists in the place of faith and optimism (Silberg, 1996).

Startle and nervous reactions, as well as jumpiness, are typical in elementary-age children. At times, they appear to be hyperactive and may be diagnosed as having Attention Deficit Disorder or Attention Deficit Hyperactivity Disorder. They may have sleep disorders and/or psychosomatic complaints. These children may fantasize retributions and revenge toward perpetrators. Their defenses may become more primitive, and impulse control may become impaired, particularly if stability or routine is threatened (Ackerman, 1983). Intrusive symptoms of posttraumatic stress reactions may be indirectly demonstrated through limit testing, obsessive play, secrecy about what "really happens" in their lives; avoidant symptoms center around withdrawal from peer and play groups. In addition, they worry about how their needs will be met (Heegaard, 1992).

Preadolescents and Adolescents

Preadolescents and adolescents, when traumatized, may exhibit sleep and appetite disturbances as well as psychosomatic symptoms (e.g., headaches). They question the fairness of the death of the parent and are self-judgmental. They may express emotions through aggressive, rebellious behaviors including sexual acting out or substance abuse (the latter, often to numb themselves) and their patterns of reactions tend to resemble those of adults. They may be suspicious and guarded, extremely self-conscious about their own vulnerability while not wanting to appear "different" to others.

They may resort to self-mutilation, suicidal thoughts, suicidal gestures, or even suicide attempts to stop their pain. In addition, they may exhibit feelings of "futurelessness," anxiety, apathy, and/or depression (NOVA, 1990).

The perceived meaning of that death also influences the impact of the death of a parent on any age child. Beliefs that are challenged by the death are those of the five fundamental need areas of safety, trust, power/control, esteem, and intimacy (McCann & Pearlman, 1990). The task of healing is always greater when family members are also traumatically impacted by the death (e.g., the remaining parent). The ability of the surviving parent to provide support to the child is often limited, particularly if the parent has a history of trauma. Frequently, the parent turns his/her focus inward to personal reactions (Williams, 1992). If that parent cannot function in a positive, supportive manner for the child/children, then other adults must be called upon to provide support. Perhaps another member of the police force as well as friends' parents, other relatives, teachers, counselors, and others can help provide nurturing, security, and support at this time, as well as later.

HEALING STRATEGIES AND TECHNIQUES

Ayalon (1992), explaining the rationale for helping children deal with death, wrote: "A child's encounter with death is usually random, unplanned and unprepared for. The child's reactions to such an event are frequently unheeded. The adults who usually care for the child's welfare are either too stricken by their own sorrow to answer his questions or consider death too morbid a subject for a child's scrutiny. Yet gaining access to information about death and learning to deal with it in a socially acceptable manner is very important for children (p. 135)." O'Rourke and Worzbyt (1996) add that all children need to receive accurate information about what happened to the parent; share and understand their feelings; share their beliefs about death, whether cultural, religious, imaginative, or reality-based; grieve; and take constructive action in response to their loss. One way to take action is to participate in some type of ritual.

The use of rituals is an important healing tool. Rituals establish order to what the child is reexperiencing. They may reaffirm meaning and answer the child's questions; they bond together those who participate in a shared world view. They serve as a way to handle ambivalence about the death and function as a safe way to express emotions and often introduce spirituality (Putter, 1997). They are also a way to include children in the grieving process. Van Si and Powers (1994) developed a workbook which encourages children to use a variety of expressive techniques and rituals to describe feelings about the death, to say goodbye, to list memories and dreams, and to celebrate the life of the dead parent. It includes a place to hold keepsakes and becomes an everlasting keepsake itself when finished. The act of completing the workbook is a ritual in itself, and serves as a way to commemorate the deceased, record the loss, and remember the dead parent (Fox, 1985).

The death of a parent in the line of duty is a public event that is kept alive by media portrayals and a legal system that may take years to resolve the murder. Similarly, resolution of the loss of the parent may require years of grieving and recovery (Monahon, 1993). Anniversary reactions also are frequent and occur on the dead parent's birthday, during special family activity times, on holidays, and on the date of the event.

Immediate crisis intervention and debriefing for the remaining parent and the children is essential in the wake of a duty-related death. This debriefing can be done within the first 72 hours after the death and is part of a more comprehensive Critical Incident Stress Management program that triages the type of intervention to be used with each family member and the family as a whole. Many persons may offer support to the children and remaining spouse immediately after a shooting. Among these persons are fellow officers and their families, families of other officers killed in the line of duty, crisis response teams, school counselors, teachers, school social workers, relatives, and friends, among others. It is important that these interventions are not restricted to the period immediately after the death. Instead, children (and the remaining spouse) need assistance at regular intervals afterwards. If the school does not know of the child's trauma, it is important that someone notify the principal and the children's teachers.

It is extremely important not to hide the death from a child. The child needs to be told in language that is appropriate, truthful, and free of religious platitudes. Death can be described in understandable terms that reflect the level of comprehension and understanding of death as a concept. Death is not just "going to sleep" or "going away." Children also need age appropriate explanations about what happened, without the provision of excessive or gruesome details. The child also needs an opportunity to ask questions after he/she is told. Each question needs to be answered in an honest, open manner (Staudacher, 1987).

Children must feel safe and have some semblance of normalcy immediately following the death and death notification. Bedtime needs to remain as bedtime, for example. Catherall (1992) noted that children not only need to know what happened (to make sense of the death) and why the death happened (an explanation), they also want to know how their lives and beliefs will change due to the death (e.g. life is no longer predictable might be a new belief), why they are reacting as they are (provided through education about reactivity), and what will happen next (funerals, family changes, changes in routines, changes in residence, and others).

Children need opportunities to say goodbye to their dead parent. It is important to allow children to attend the funeral in order to gain a better understanding of the meaning of death. In fact, France (1996) has stated that children above the age of 2 should attend. Funerals help to dispel fantasies about death and give children an opportunity to grieve and mourn. Funerals of officers killed in the line of duty are generally intense, extremely large events that honor the memory and sacrifice made by the individual. As Staudacher (1987) noted, attending this type of funeral gives the child confirmation of the parent's value through the honors afforded to him/her. If the child is going to attend the funeral, it is very important to prepare him/her about the setting, ceremony, cortege, response, and customs. The child can also be encouraged, ahead of time, to create personal healing rituals for the funeral. Perhaps the child wants to draw a picture to place in the coffin. Perhaps an older child or adolescent wants to read a poem written in honor of the parent during the service.

Children may also be encouraged to complete workbooks about death and grief. Some of the exercises might be begun prior to a funeral, if time allows, or the book may be completed later with appropriate support. One book for younger children is *My Memory Book, A Journal for Grieving Children* (Gaines-Lane, 1997). This book is designed to help the child understand grief, legitimatize connections to the dead parent, and talk about that relationship and how the death has changed it. This book, and others, recognize that traumatized children have symptoms similar to adults, though feelings of numbness are unusual.

Many of the workbooks for children and teens include art activities. Drawing a traumatic event empowers a child and presents an opportunity to begin to overcome fear and helplessness (Heegaard, 1992). Creative art as a tool expresses fears of death and feelings of grief, suffering, and mourning and helps children understand the impact of the traumatic event upon themselves. It also helps the child come to resolution and develop knowledge that death is a part of life while he/she is attempting to build an understanding of (and even an acceptance of the reality of the death (Williams, 1994b).

One resource for teens is *Fire in My Heart, Ice in My Veins* (Traisman, 1992). This book provides a journal in which the teen can record details of the relationship with the deceased parent, the loss involved, and the effect on the teen's life. The workbook helps the respondent look at how to make sense of what happened through a search for meaning. It helps memorialize and helps the teen decide what to do or begin to do to take care of self in the deceased parent's memory. It also has a place for poetry, short stories, and writing about unfinished business with the parent. The teen then has the opportunity to write a goodbye letter to the parent and record how the death has changed his/her life.

Teens are primarily group-oriented. As was noted earlier, when a teen's parent dies, there are frequently few others in the peer group with similar experiences. Developing a supportive/ educational group for teens, whether in the community or within the school, can serve a variety of functions for teens. The group can provide information about the process of grief, about trauma, and about the impacts of traumatic events. The group can address issues related to trauma and grief through structured activities and can expand the teen's support system if the teen so desires. The group can also encourage peer consultation and identification with others who have had similar experiences as a way to alleviate isolation (Purchy, 1997). Some teens need additional help after the group and may be triaged into individual counseling, or may work with peer facilitators who are more experienced (Fox, 1985).

Any individual who works with a child who has suffered the death of a parent in the line of duty needs to help the child mourn and grieve losses. This includes allowing the child to ask questions, discussing feelings with the child, and providing correct and factual information about the parent's death, when that information is available. Helping persons (counselors, pastors, adult friends, teachers) can also ask the child about previous experiences with death as well as the child's conceptualization of death and what happens thereafter. Through these conversations, a child's misperceptions can be clarified and the finality of death can be reinforced. Teaching children and teenagers how to mourn, providing debriefing when indicated, and presenting a model that is within a framework of acute stress and posttraumatic stress is also very important. A trauma model helps the child or teen to realize that grief, mourning, and traumatic reactions are normal in these circumstances. Every child needs to be able to mourn in a personal way with the goal in mind of accepting the reality of the loss (Bertman, 1984). Children need to respond to the death cognitively (talking about what happened), emotionally (venting feelings), behaviorally (doing things to memorialize the parent, exercising, acting out), and morally (looking at fundamental values and beliefs that the death has challenged).

SCHOOL INTERVENTIONS

When schools begin group programs for children who have lost parents through death or as school personnel work with those children, it is important that the school be a care-giving environment that is predictable, organized, and supportive. Classroom discussion with classmates of the child whose parent has died about what happened can be helpful, particularly when conducted before the child returns to school. Having appropriate books available for reading also can be appropriate. The use of the following principles of posttraumatic counseling (Williams, 1994a) will be helpful to build trust and work through the traumatic deaths:

- Establish a safety milieu for the children;
- Be empathic to the children;
- Educate children about the nature of grief and posttraumatic stress responses;
- Help children remember the trauma and find personal meaning;
- Help children release emotions in an atmosphere that acknowledges that emotional expression is a necessary part of the healing process;
- Help children identify and deal with losses that have occurred because of the death;
- Help the child build appropriate peer and adult relationships;
- Help the child build self-enhancing beliefs and expectations, adding to feelings of empowerment and control.

The school functions as a care-giving environment for the child who has lost a parent in a line-of-duty death. Predictability, organization, and support are three important aspects of the classroom that promote stability in a traumatized child.

FINAL CONSIDERATIONS

One goal for those who work with children who have lost a parent in a line-of-duty death is to help the child manage his/her psychological distress without incurring a major deviation in development. Teaching the child coping skills and providing education about normal reactions after traumatic loss are also important tasks (Pynoos, 1993). Over time, if it becomes obvious that the child is exhibiting more than the normal grief or acute stress reactions, or if that child has developed a posttraumatic stress disorder, then it is important to arrange group or individual counseling for that child. In therapy, when the child learns more about PTSD, that child may feel validated and less damaged. Talking about death and ventilating emotions may help the child reestablish personal control. Social skills training, while focusing on taking concrete action, is also a helpful strategy (Harris, 1991). Therapy teaches children alternative ways to resolve problems and deal with tensions (Catherall, 1992). Therapists may use the workbooks mentioned previously as well as others (Alexander, 1992, 1993; Hammond, 1981; Heegaard, 1991). Therapists also may design counseling groups (Hannaford & Popkin, 1992; Lagorio, 1992; Landy, 1988) or use play therapy techniques (puppets, art, dolls, stories, sand trays) to help children and teens work through defenses,

verbalize feelings, and resolve the trauma (Webb, 1992). An additional healing strategy is helping children to use writing skills to express anxieties,
death-related fictions or fantasy, as well as anger (Staudacher, 1987); another is to use books with death-related themes to stimulate discussion and provide information.

Resolution of the death of a parent in the line-of-duty is often a life-long
process. Recovery may never have been totally complete. However, the
trauma-based life of a child will become more "routine" and "normal" with
the passage of time and through the use of the healing strategies previously
mentioned. Helping children live with the reality of the death of their parent is essential if they are to return to a measure of "ordinary" existence. A
concerted effort made by those who support the child (parent, relatives,
friends, teachers, therapists, counselors, fellow officers of the deceased adult)
is crucial to that process. The ultimate goal, however, is to build resilience
in the child so that the child, eventually, will face life with a sense of humor,
view him/her self as competent, and solve problems creatively.

REFERENCES

Ackerman, R. J.: *Children of alcoholics: A guidebook for educators, therapists, and parents*
(2nd Ed). Holmes Beach, FL., Learning Publications, 1983.
Alexander, D. W.: *It happened to me.* Huntington, NY: Bureau for At-Risk Youth,
1992.
Alexander, D. W.: *It happened in autumn.* Huntington, NY: Bureau for At-Risk
Youth, 1993.
Ayalon, O.: *Rescue! C.O.P.E. handbook: Helping children cope with stress. Guided Group
Activities.* Ellicott City, MD, Chevron, 1992.
Beckman, R.: *Children who grieve: A manual for conducting support groups.* Holmes
Beach, FL., Learning Publications, 1990.
Bertman, S.: Helping children cope with death. In J. C. Hansen & T. T. Frantz,
(Eds), *Death and grief in the family.* Rockville, MD, Aspen, 1984.
Bowman, M.: *Individual differences in posttraumatic response: Problems with the adversi-
ty-distress connection.* Mahwah, NJ., Lawrence Erlbaum, 1997.
Catherall, D. R.: *Back from the brink: A family guide to overcoming traumatic stress.* New
York, Bantam Books, 1992.
Corr, C. A.: Children's understandings of death: Striving to understand death. In
K. J. Doka (Ed.), *Children Mourning, Mourning Children.* Bristol, PA, Taylor &
Francis, 1995.
Davidson, J., & Smith, R.: Traumatic experiences in psychiatric outpatients. *Journal
of Traumatic Stress, 3:* 459 - 475, 1990.
Erikson, E. H.: Identity and the life cycle. *Psychological Issues, 1:* (Whole Issue), 1967.
Erikson, E. H.: *Childhood and society.* New York, Norton, 1973.

Fogarty, J. A.: *The grieving child: Comprehensive Treatment and Intervention Strategies.* Tucson, AZ, Carondelet Management Institute, 1993.

Fox, S.: *Good Grief: Helping groups of children when a friend dies.* Boston, MA, New England Association for Education of Young Children, 1985.

France, K.: *Crisis intervention: A handbook of immediate person-to-person help* (3rd Ed.). Springfield, IL, Charles C. Thomas, 1996.

Gaines-Lane, P.: *My Memory Book: A journal for grieving children.* Gaithersburg, MD., Chi Rho Press, 1997.

Green, B. L; Korol, M.; Grace, M. C.; Vary, M. G.; Leonard, A. C.; Glaser, G. C., & Smitson-Cohen, S.: Children and disaster: Age, gender and parental Effects on PTSD symptoms. *Journal of the American Academy for Child & Adolescent Psychiatry, 30*: 945-951, 1991.

Hammond, J. M.: *When my dad died: A child's view of death.* Ann Arbor, MI, Cranbrook, 1981.

Hannaford, M. J., & Popkin, M. (1992). *Windows: Healing and helping through loss.* Atlanta, GA, Active Parenting, Inc., 1992.

Harris, C. J.: A family crisis-intervention model for the treatment of post-traumatic stress reaction. *Journal of Traumatic Stress, 4*: 195-207, 1991.

Heegaard, M. E.: *The drawing out feelings series: Facilitators guide for leading grief support groups.* Minneapolis, MN, Woodland Press, 1992.

Heegaard, M.: *When someone very special dies.* Minneapolis, MN, Woodland Press, 1991.

Hindman, J.: *Just before dawn.* Ontario, OR, Alexandria Associates, 1989.

Kastenbaum, R.: *The psychology of death,* (2nd ed.). New York, Springer, 1992.

Kubler-Ross, E.: *On death and dying.* New York, Macmillan, 1992.

Lagorio, J.: *The life-cycle education manual.* Solana Beach, CA, Empowerment In Action, 1991.

Landy, L.: *Child support through small group counseling.* Mount Dora, FL, Kids Rights, 1988.

McCann, I. L, & Pearlman, L. A.: *Psychological trauma and the adult survivor.* New York, Brunner/Mazel, 1990.

Monahan, C.: *Children and trauma: A parents' guide to helping children heal.* New York, Lexington Books, 1993.

National Organization of Victims Assistance (NOVA): Syllabus: National Crisis Response Team Training Institute: Participant's manual. *Children's reactions to trauma.* Washington, DC, Author. Class 16, July 1990.

O'Rourke, K., & Worzbyt, J. C.: *Support groups for children.* Washington, D.C., Taylor & Francis, 1996.

Purchy, M. K.: *Helping teens work through grief.* Washington, D.C., Taylor and Francis, 1997.

Putter, A. M.: (Ed.). *The memorial rituals book for healing and hope.* Amityville, N., Baywood, 1997.

Pynoos, R.: *Children and trauma.* Bergen, Norway: Presentation at the European Conference on Traumatic Stress, 1993.

Pynoos, R., & Nader, K.: Psychological first aid and treatment approach to children exposed to community violence. Research Implications. *Journal of Traumatic Stress, 1*: 445-474, 1988.

Schowalter, J. E.: Parent death and child bereavement. In B. Schoenberg, I. Gerber, A. Wiener, H. Kutscher, D. Peretz, & A. C. Carr (Eds.), *Bereavement: Its psychological aspects.* New York, Columbia University Press, 1975.

Selman, R.: *The growth of interpersonal understanding: Developmental and clinical analysis.* New York, Academic Press, 1980.

Shirk, S. R. (Ed): *Cognitive development and child psychotherapy.* New York, Plenum, 1988.

Silberg, J. R.: The five-domain crisis model: Therapeutic tasks and techniques for dissociative children. In J. L. Silberg (Ed.), *The dissociative child: Diagnosis, treatment, and management,.* Lutherville, MD, Sidran Press, 1996.

Speece, M. W., & Brent, S. B.: The development of children's understanding of death. In C. A. Corr & D. M. Corr (Eds). *Helping Children Cope with Death and Bereavement.* New York, Springer, in press.

Staudacher, C.: *Beyond grief: A guide for recovering from the death of a loved one.* Oakland, CA., New Harbinger, 1987.

Traisman, E. S.: *Fire in my heart, ice in my veins.* Omaha, NE, Centering Corporation, 1992.

Van Ornum, W., & Mordock, J. B.: *Crisis counseling with children and adolescents: A guide for non-professional counselors.* New York, Continuum, 1990.

Van Si, L, & Powers, L.: *Helping children heal from loss: A keepsake book of special memories.* Portland, OR, Portland State University Continuing Education Press, 1994.

Vondra, J. I.: Sociological and ecological factors. In R. T. Ammerman & M. Hersen (Eds.), *Children at risk: An evaluation of factors contributing to child abuse and neglect.* New York, Plenum Press, 1990.

Walsh, F. & McGoldrick, M.: *Living Beyond Loss: Death in the family.* New York, Hemisphere, 1991.

Wass, H., & Corr, C. A. (Eds.): *Helping children cope with death: Guidelines and resources* (2nd Ed). New York, Hemisphere, 1984.

Webb, N. B (Ed.): *Play therapy for children in crisis: A casebook for practitioners.* New York, Brunner/Mazel, 1992.

Williams, G.: Children of the Wall. *The American Legion, 132*: 30-31, 1992.

Williams, M. B.: Intervention with child victims of trauma in the school setting. In M. B. Williams, & J. F. Sommer, Jr. (Eds.), *Handbook of Post-Traumatic Therapy.* Westport, C., Greenwood Press, 1994a.

Williams, M. B.: Impact of duty-related death on officers' children: Concepts of death, trauma reactions, and treatment. In J. T. Reese & E. Scrivner (Eds.), *Law enforcement families: Issues and answers.* Washington, DC., United States Government, 1994b.

Worden, J. W.: *Grief counseling and grief therapy: A handbook for the mental health practitioner.* New York, Springer, 1991.

Chapter 14

INTERGENERATIONAL LEGACIES OF TRAUMA IN POLICE FAMILIES

Yael Danieli

What cannot be talked about can also not be put to rest; and if it is not, the wounds continue to fester from generation to generation (Bettelheim, 1984, p. 166).

INTRODUCTION

This chapter examines intergenerational aspects of trauma as they apply to law enforcement families. Following a brief presentation of the author's framework for viewing trauma and the intergenerational context, it will draw relevant comparisons among different populations, i.e., Nazi Holocaust survivors, veterans, and police officers. This intergenerational perspective has been largely neglected in the law enforcement literature. This chapter emphasizes that trauma is an integral part of the job of law enforcement, and that it reverberates in the officer's family. This fact carries policy, selection (screening), training, preventive and therapeutic implications.

TRAUMA AND THE CONTINUITY OF SELF

The multidimensional, multidisciplinary framework (TCMI) was formulated to delineate and encompass the nature and extent of the destruction of catastrophic massive trauma, account for its different contextual dimensions and levels, the diversity in and in response to it, and to guard against the reductionistic impulse to find unidimensional explanations for such complex phenomena. An individual's identity involves a complex interplay of multiple spheres or systems. Among these are the biological and intrapsychic; the interpersonal; the ethnic, cultural, ethical, religious, spiritual, natural; the educational/professional/ occupational; the material/economic, legal, environmental, political, national, and international. These dimensions overlap and dynamically coexist along the time dimension to create a continuous conception of life from past through present to the future. Ideally, the individual should simultaneously have free psychological access to and movement within all these identity dimensions.

Exposure to trauma causes a rupture, a possible regression, and a state of being "stuck" in this free flow, which I have called fixity. The time, duration, extent, and meaning of the trauma for the individual, the survival mechanisms/strategies utilized to adapt to it (Danieli, 1985), as well as postvictimization traumata (Danieli, 1982; Keilson, 1992; Johnson et al., 1997) will determine the elements and degree of rupture and the severity of the fixity. Fixity may render the individual vulnerable to further trauma/ruptures throughout the life cycle. This (TCMI) framework allows evaluation of whether and how much of each system was ruptured or proved resilient, and may thus inform the choice of optimal systemic interventions.

An essential aspect of the establishment of such perspective is that integration of the trauma must take place in all of life's systems and cannot be accomplished by the individual alone. Systems can change and recover independently of other systems. For example, there may be progress in the social system but not in the political system. While there can be independent recovery in various systems, they may also be related and interdependent (Matussek, 1975). To fulfill the reparative and preventive goals of psychological recovery from trauma, perspective and integration through awareness and containment must be established so that one's sense of continuity, belongingness, and rootedness are restored (see also Krystal, 1988; Lifton, 1979). For healing to occur, the integration of traumatic experiences must be examined from the perspective of the totality of the trauma survivors' and family members' lives (Danieli, 1998).

THE INTERGENERATIONAL CONTEXT

The intergenerational perspective reveals the impact of trauma, its contagion, and repeated patterns within the family. It may help explain certain behavior patterns, symptoms, roles, and values adopted by family members, family sources of vulnerability as well as resilience and strength, and job choices (following in the footsteps of a relative) through the generations. The family is a carrier of conscious and unconscious values, myths, fantasies, and beliefs that may not be shared by the larger community or culture. Yet, the role of the family as vehicle for intergenerational transmission of core issues of living and of adaptive and maladaptive ways of defining and coping with them may vary among cultures. In addition, family interactions and relationships tend to be highly reciprocal, patterned, and repetitive and changes therein can reverberate in other parts of the system. Moreover, what happened in one generation will, as the trauma and its impact are passed down as the family legacy, affect subsequent generations, though the actual behavior may take a variety of forms. The awareness of (the possibility of) pathogenic intergenerational processes and the understanding of the mechanisms of transmission (Danieli, 1998) should contribute to our finding effective means for preventing the transmission of pathology to succeeding generations (Danieli, 1985, 1987, 1993).

Findings by Klein-Parker (1988), Kahana, Harel, and Kahana (1989), Kaminer and Lavie (1991) and Helmreich (1992) confirm a heterogeneity (Danieli, 1985, 1988) of adaptation and quality of adjustment to the Holocaust and post-Holocaust life experiences. It follows that to understand posttrauma adjustment, it is critical to examine fully pretrauma background, including the family's trauma history. For example, Holocaust parents, in the attempt to give children their best, taught them how to survive and, in the process, transmitted to them the life conditions under which they had survived the war. Thus, one finds children of survivors, who psychologically, and sometimes literally, live in hiding, or run from relationships with people, commitment to a career, or from one place of residence or country to another. These modes of being are manifested in their language, behavior, fantasy life, and dreams. Like their parents, many children of survivors manifest these Holocaust-derived behaviors, particularly on the anniversaries of their parents' traumata. Moreover, some survivors' offspring have internalized as parts of their identity the images of those who perished. Beyond their psychosocial implications, multigenerational effects of trauma may carry legal (e.g., issues of compensation and restitution, the current debate with regard to the need to form an international criminal court) and political (e.g., wars and cycles of violence, ethnic and racial strife) implications.

VULNERABILITY AND/OR RESILIENCE?

Two contrasting perspectives exist regarding the role of prior trauma in subsequent response. The vulnerability perspective holds that trauma leaves permanent psychic damage that renders survivors more vulnerable when subsequently faced with extreme stress. The resilience perspective (Harel, Kahana, & Kahana, 1993; Helmreich, 1992; Kaminer & Lavie, 1991; Whiteman, 1993) postulates that coping well with initial trauma strengthens resistance to the effects of future trauma, making survivors more resilient when faced with adversity. Both perspectives recognize individual differences in response to trauma, that exposure to massive trauma may overwhelm predisposition and previous experience, and that posttrauma environmental factors play important roles in adaptation (see also Eberly, Harkness & Engdahl, 1991; Engdahl et al., 1993).

With survivors it is hard to draw conclusions based on outward appearances. Survivors often display external markers of success (i.e., occupational achievement or establishing families) that in truth represent survival strategies. Clearly, these accomplishments may facilitate adaptation and produce feelings of fulfillment in many survivors. Thus, the external attainments represent significant adaptive achievement in their lives. However, there are also other facets of adaptation that are largely internal and intrapsychic (see also Engdhal et al., 1997).

Similarly, while some of the child survivor literature reports good adjustment (e.g., Leon et al., 1981), Solomon, Kotler, and Mikulincer (1988) demonstrated in them a special vulnerability to traumatic stress. Even survivors in the "those who made it" category still experience difficulties related to their traumatic past, and it is amongst this group that we observe the highest rates of suicide among survivors as well as their children. It is important to note that disagreement in the literature regarding vulnerability and/or resilience could reflect professionals' countertransference reactions (Danieli, 1984). The findings that survivors and their offspring have areas of vulnerability and resilience is no longer paradoxical when viewed within a multidimensional framework for multiple levels of posttraumatic adaptation. Tracing a history of multiple trauma along the time dimension at different stages of development reveals that while for many people time heals ills, for those traumatized, time may not heal, but may magnify their response to further trauma (Danieli, 1997; Yehuda, et al., 1995) and carry intergenerational implications.

For example, the daughters (23 and 17 years old) of JL, a New York City policeman residing on Long Island, who constantly frightened them of the City, insisted that they would "absolutely never come to New York City" other than to therapy, despite their great attraction to things in it. Moreover, they would come to therapy only when driven by their father and no one else. When their father, after much testing, approved of the therapist, he extended his overprotectiveness to her, and in addition to giving her a can of Mace, lectured and interrogated her frequently about how to detect danger ("Look for bad people doing bad things. They are out there, everywhere.") and how to protect herself. FH, whose officer father was murdered when FH was six years old, resolved to join the force after a rather rebellious adolescence "to get to know Dad as a real person rather than as the saint you [his mother] always described him." The other profession he had considered "in order to get the story straight" was crime reporting.

LEGACIES OF TRAUMA TO THE FAMILY

In recent years, following studies on three generations of families of survivors of the Nazi Holocaust (Bergman & Jucovy, 1982; Braham, 1988; Danieli, 1985, 1993; Rosenthal & Rosenthal, 1980; Rubenstein, 1989; Sigal & Weinfeld, 1989), the effect of PTSD on family relationships and children of combat veterans has been examined. A variety of negative family problems (e.g., loss of family cohesion and expressiveness) has been associated with combat-related PTSD (Solomon, Mikulincer, Fried & Wosner, 1987).

Among wives of veterans with PTSD, Verbosky and Ryan (1988) found increased levels of stress as a result of attempts to cope adequately with the veteran's PTSD symptoms; they also found that the majority of the wives verbalized feelings of worthlessness. Both Williams (1987) and Matsakis (1988) reported that about 50 percent of all Vietnam veterans' wives that they treat have been battered. According to Matsakis (1988), the problems most commonly reported by wives of Vietnam veterans were coping with the veteran's problems; loneliness and social isolation; feeling confused, overwhelmed, and responsible; feeling a loss of identity and a loss of control over one's life; and self-blame. Children of Vietnam veterans may present low self-esteem; aggressiveness; developmental difficulties; impaired social relationships; and, symptoms mirroring those of the veteran; "secondary traumatization" (Rosenheck & Nathan, 1985) and elevated risk of behavioral or psychiatric problems (Davidson, Smith, & Kudler, 1989).

Nonetheless, the researchers (Jordan et al., 1992) conclude that "the pervasiveness and severity of problems vary substantially among the families of Vietnam veterans with PTSD" and do not suggest that all of the families of veterans with PTSD are "extremely chaotic, desperately unhappy, and severely disturbed"(p. 924). But, although background variables do have some effect on the development of family problems, PTSD is more strongly related to exposure to combat trauma, which greatly overshadowed the effect of any predispositional variable.

Many wives of veterans with PTSD function reasonably well and often assume the major financial, parental, and domestic responsibilities within the relationship (Verbosky & Ryan, 1988; Williams, 1987) which may mitigate some its effects on the children. Also, many spouses might have entered the relationship in a rescuer role. Hartsough (1991) discusses how the spouses of law enforcement personnel relate to the stresses of police work, and identified three major sources of stress they experience: occupational, organizational, and traumatic incident sources.

In her empirical study of 40 families of Vietnam veterans with combat-related PTSD, Harkness (1993) interprets the similarity between a child's and his/her fathers' behavior as the child's possible attempt to identify with or understand his/her fathers' behavior, or as indicative of the offspring's secondary traumatization to having a father with PTSD. A major finding was that the destructive effect of the violent behavior on the children appears to be more influential than either the father's PTSD or the level of family functioning. She also delineates the father's PTSD related difficulties during life cycle transitions (e.g., adolescence), which are experienced by the fathers as recapitulations of prior ruptures. Maslach and Jackson (1979) similarly report that the wives of burned-out cops [of which younger officers seem to be in the greatest jeopardy, (p. 60)] described their children as feeling anxious, irritable, and isolated, and their husband's relationship with the children as most difficult during the teenage years, because of "getting a double dose of upsetting experience" and having to "struggle with youthful criminals on the job" (p. 61). In these families, wives reported that children are four times as likely to look exclusively to their mother for support: "His work created a distance. We were a family—he was a stranger" (p. 61).

A preliminary impression of the children's perceptions portion of Harkness' study is that almost every child responded positively to her question, "Have you ever thought about your father killing somebody?" and was quite open to discuss further and to offer his or her understanding of it. This is particularly poignant since so many of the fathers, like Holocaust survivors and police officers, avoid sharing their traumatic experiences for fear that the memories would corrode their and their children's lives. This created an intrafamilial conspiracy of silence (Danieli, 1985) in which the children avoided asking questions to protect their parents and themselves against the hurt of knowing, remembering, and reliving, even though some of them want to know all the details, who, what, why, where, and read everything they can, "trying to make it real" and constructively integrate their parent's trauma (for example, see Fisher, 1991). Six (15%) of the veterans in Harkness' study were police officers, all of whom subsequently lost their job due to alcohol and drug abuse (Harkness, personal communication).

Rosenheck and Fontana (1998) considered whether Vietnam veterans whose fathers served in combat had an increased risk of Posttraumatic Stress Disorder (PTSD) and other postwar adjustment problems when compared with other Vietnam veterans. In the total National Vietnam Veterans Readjustment Study sample there were no differences between these two groups. However, within the subgroup of veterans who met criteria for PTSD, those whose fathers had been exposed to combat had more severe problems on several measures. In the Department of Veterans Affairs sample, too, veterans whose fathers served in combat scored higher in PTSD symptoms, suicidality, guilt, and loss of religious faith. They concluded that intergenerational effects of trauma emerge when the second generation itself has PTSD, and show that these transgenerational effects are related to intergenerational processes during the homecoming period rather than to differences in premilitary experience.

Hunter-King (1998) examined the possibility of the transmission of these effects to future generations of children of American military personnel declared missing in action (MIA) during the Vietnam era. Her research indicated that the response of the wives of MIAs was the key variable in predicting the effects on their children, effects that can be either positive or negative. Her findings suggest that adequate support of families who are coping with the MIA experiences can play a preventive role in the transmission of longterm negative intergenerational effects.

Williams (1987) states "While there are remarkable similarities between the types of stresses on and the responses of [veterans and cops], there is also one crucial difference: for cops, the 'war' never ends–they are out there 24 hours a day, 7 days a week to 'protect and serve,' to fight the criminal–our peacetime enemy. The police officer is expected to be combat-ready at all times while remaining 'normal' and socially adaptive away from the job. The psychological toll for many is great, unexpected, and not well understood [(see also Smith, et al., 1996; Violanti & Aron, 1994)]. Their families and friends have been adversely affected and emotionally wounded, as well" (p. 267).

Concluding that both the immediate and long-term reaction patterns they found closely coincided with those reported in American studies, Manolias and Hyatt-Williams (1993) examined the impact of the following on postshooting experiences on police-authorized firearms officers in the United Kingdom: (1) attitudes toward firearms, (2) training, (3) reactions in the officers, (4) perceptual distortions during the shooting, (5) official actions and senior officers' attitudes, (6) attitudes of colleagues, (7) press and public, (8) reactions of families of officers, and (9) legal litigation and appearance in court. They found that the effects of the shooting incident spread to all immediate family members, and that the quantity and quality of sharing and communication determined the outcome, particularly with the spouse and children. The in-laws frequently reacted with shock or distress, but were supportive in all instances and sometimes proud of their son-in-law's bravery. For one officer, the shooting incident followed very closely the death of his father. "The cumulative effect of the two shocks was overwhelming for his mother and completely demolished her efforts to retain any semblance of composure" (p.392).

A LEGACY CHANGE?

Until 1983, the preference points allocated in civil service merit systems to war veterans made it very hard for nonveterans to compete for positions as police officers. Since most police officers retire at 50-55, Vietnam veterans will be leaving within the next 8 years. Even if Desert Storm veterans join, the change in the civil merit system makes it less likely that new combat-addicted veterans—to drug, street, domestic wars—will join law enforcement, unless they are crisis and trauma addicted child survivors of alcoholic or abusive homes. (For a review of findings on intergenerational transmission of child abuse, see Oliver, 1993 and Buchanan, 1998, and of domestic violence, see Simon & Johnson, 1998.) Liebert (1991) describes police officers whose job performance was severely impaired by overidentifying with, and wanting to rescue, victims whose lives resembled theirs, or by identifying with their parents'/father's brutality.

Introducing a predicted shift in the composition of "the 21st century cop," Maghan (1989) reports that college education affects the psychological profiles of police recruits. It produces recruits who are not authoritarian at the outset of their police training (Lundman, 1984). Comparing authoritarianism in police college graduates and noncollege police, Smith, Locke and Fenster (1970) found college educated police officer less likely to have an authoritarian attitude, and that newly appointed officers who choose to attend college scored lower than their noncollege peers on the "F" scale [a measurement of authoritarianism]. The 1986 class of the New York City Police Academy recruit population (some 1,900) reflected the changing demographics of future police officers, with a historic high number of minority and female entry level recruits (Maghan, 1989). These recruits will have had thirteen years of policing in the year 2000. Consequently, they may represent an important reference profile of the 21st century cop.

Approximately one-half, 50.4 percent, of the class has some family member (father, mother, brother, sister, uncle, aunt or cousin) currently (or previously) in police service. The demographic profile of police family background shows recruits who are (1) younger than those from nonpolice backgrounds, (2) less likely to have worked full-time previously, (3) more likely to live at home and less likely to have served in the military. The majority of police family background recruits are white and predominantly Catholic. Police family background recruits generally have some college education as compared to nonpolice background recruits. Mothers and fathers of police family recruits tend to be better educated than the parents of recruits from nonpolice backgrounds. Like other recruits, fathers/stepfathers are cited as the most influential persons affecting the decision to become a police officers. However, police family mothers are the only subgroup favorable towards the recruit's decision to become a police officer.

Like others, their most important reason for becoming a police officer was the ability to help people. Compared to nonpolice background recruits, they ranked "wearing a uniform" as less important and "carrying a gun" as the least important factor in their decision to become a police officer. They are also more like other entry recruits in changing their enforcement and service orientations as a result of training.

While these results suggest the possibility of a drastic cultural and normative shift, it is still far too soon to predict how these young officers will fare after a significant period of police service. Cumulative evidence, however, suggests that a legacy of trauma—on the job as well as within one's family tree (e.g., community and domestic violence, alcoholism, crime)—is highly likely to render its victims vulnerable, particularly to further trauma/rupture.

SUICIDE AND TRAUMA

One of the most poignant consequences as well as causes of trauma to the (police as well as one's own) family is suicide. One police officer committed suicide right after his retirement. He was "a 100 percent pure policeman, and there was nothing left." During his service he had "too much to do" and had neither the time nor the emotional resources available for his family, which he lost a while back. Another law enforcement officer recalled a "suicide agent [who] sat in his supervisor's chair, wrote a note and then ate his gun. While 'getting even with his supervisor' he didn't remotely comprehend the life-long pain he inflicted on his family and what a lesson he taught his children about how to deal with problems" (see also Horvitz, 1994; Janik & Kravitz, 1994). Another colleague reported four suicides of policemen's sons, all of whom shot themselves with their fathers' guns (John M. Violanti, personal communication).

Suicide ruptures the family, and exacerbates previous family ruptures. In his paper on the illegacy of suicide, Kamerman (1993) reports preliminary results of his beginning follow-up study of the families of over 90 New York City police officers who committed suicide between 1934 and 1940. Since this was more than double the rate of the previous 6 years, data were collected on these families in the past. His research led him to conclude that "these suicides have affected the lives of wives, sons and daughters, grandchildren, and great-grandchildren."

SOME CONCLUDING REMARKS

The central reparative and preventive goal of understanding and integrating trauma is the multigenerational family tree (Guerin & Pendagast, 1976; McGoldrick & Gerson, 1985) which can map individuals' and families' unique dynamics, history, and culture (Danieli, 1993; Wachtel & Wachtel, 1986). Although constructing a family tree may trigger an acute sense of pain and loss, it reaffirms the importance of continuity. Exploring the family tree opens communication within families and between generations, making it possible to work through toxic family secrets. Breaking the silence about the trauma, and pre- and posttrauma experiences within and outside the family is generally helpful, but it is particularly crucial for aging individuals and their offspring (Danieli, 1989, 1997), particularly those entering a profession where the risk of exposure to other trauma is high

An overwhelming clinical finding with police family members is that losses not worked through render the police officers and/or their families vulnerable, and sometimes even incapacitated, in confronting and engaging constructively new loss and trauma situations. While space constraints make it impossible to elaborate further, one cannot overestimate the psychological importance of "survivor guilt," its commemorative function (Krystal & Niederland, 1968; Carmelly, 1975), and its functions related to helplessness, loneliness, loyalty, mourning, and a sense of justice (Danieli, 1981, 1985, 1989; Goodman, 1978) in understanding the obstacles to grief and bereavement in individual officers and their families. For example, it is common for a son or a daughter to carry on the military service tradition for a dead or injured veteran parent, just as in law enforcement for heroic police service to become the family legacy.

Part of the difficulty in understanding stems from the ceremonial public appearance that they are not lonely in their grief, that the memory and the legacy of their trauma and loss is shared by the law enforcement family, the community, and sometimes even the whole nation; that they share the pain and mourning, and their need to bear witness, and transform them into a part of its global consciousness. But the real transformation that is called for in the law enforcement family and culture is in the full recognition and acknowledgement of trauma and its (possibly preventable) lifelong and intergenerational effects. Trauma is an integral part of the work(life) of the police officer and his or her family. It must therefore carry policy, selection (screening), training, preventive and therapeutic implications at all levels.

REFERENCES

Bergman M. S., & Jucovy, M. E. (Eds.): *Generations of the Holocaust.* New York, Basic Books, 1982.

Bettelheim, B.: Afterward. In C. Vegh, *I didn't say goodbye* (R. Schwartz, Trans.). New York, E. P. Dutton, 1984.

Braham, R. L. (Ed.): *The psychological perspectives of the Holocaust and of its aftermath.* New York, Columbia University Press, 1988.

Buchanan, A.: Intergenerational child maltreatment. In Y. Danieli (Ed.), *International handbook of multigenerational legacies of trauma.* New York, Plenum, 1998.

Carmelly, F.: Guilt feelings in concentration camp survivors. Comments of a "survivor." *Journal of Jewish Communal Service, 2*: 139-144, 1975.

Danieli, Y.: *Therapists' difficulties in treating survivors of the Nazi Holocaust and their children.* (Doctoral dissertation, New York University, 1981). University Microfilms International, #949-904, 1982.

Danieli, Y.: Psychotherapists' participation in the conspiracy of silence about the Holocaust. *Psychoanalytic psychology, 1*: 23-42, 1984.

Danieli, Y.: The treatment and prevention of long-term effects and intergenerational transmission of victimization: A lesson from Holocaust survivors and their children. In C. R. Figley (Ed.), *Trauma and its wake.* New York, Brunner/Mazel, 1985.

Danieli, Y.: Treating survivors and children of survivors of the Nazi Holocaust. In F. M. Ochberg (Ed.), *Post-traumatic Therapy and Victims of Violence.* New York, Brunner/Mazel, 1987.

Danieli, Y.: The heterogeneity of postwar adaptation in families of Holocaust survivors. In R. L. Braham (Ed.), *The psychological perspectives of the Holocaust and of its aftermath.* New York, Columbia University Press, 1988.

Danieli, Y.: Mourning in survivors and children of survivors of the Nazi Holocaust: The role of group and community modalities. In D. R. Dietrich & P. C. Shabad (Eds.), *The problem of loss and mourning: Psychoanalytic perspectives.* Madison, International Universities Press, 1989.

Danieli, Y.: Diagnostic and therapeutic use of the multigenerational family tree in working with survivors and children of survivors of the Nazi Holocaust. In Wilson, J.P. & Raphael, B. (Eds.), *International handbook of traumatic stress syndromes.* New York, Plenum, 1993.

Danieli, Y.: As survivors age: An overview. *Journal of Geriatric Psychiatry, 30*: 9-26, 1997.

Danieli, Y. (Ed.): *International handbook of multigenerational legacies of trauma.* New York, Plenum, 1998.

Davidson, J.; Smith, R., & Kudler, H.: Familial psychiatric illness in chronic post-traumatic stress disorder. *Comprehensive Psychiatry, 30*: 339-345, 1989.

Eberly, R. E.; Harkness,A. R., & Engdahl, B. E. (1991). An adaptational view of trauma response as illustrated by the prisoner of war experience. *Journal of Traumatic Stress, 4*: 363-380, 1991.

Engdahl, B. E.; Dikel, T. N.; Eberly, R., & Blank, Jr., A.: Posttraumatic stress disorder in a community sample of former prisoners of war: A normative response to severe trauma. *The American Journal of Psychiatry, 154*: 1576-1581, 1997.

Engdahl, B. E.; Harkness, A. R.; Eberly, R. E.; Page, W. E., & Bielinski, J.: Structural models of captivity trauma, resilience, and trauma response among former prisoners of war 20 to 40 years after release. *Social Psychiatry and Psychiatric Epidemiology, 28*: 109-115, 1993.

Fisher, C. R.: Critical incident trauma treatment of an officer/son of a slain officer. In Reese, J. T., Horn, J. M. & Dunning, C. (Eds.), *Critical incidents in policing*. Washington, D.C., U.S. Department of Justice, Federal Bureau of Investigation, 1991.

Goodman, J. S.: *The transmission of parental trauma: Second generation effects of Nazi concentration camp survival.* (Doctoral dissertation, California School of Professional Psychology, 1978). University Microfilms International No. 7901805., 1978.

Guerin, P. J., Jr., & Pendagast, E. G.: Evaluation of family system and genogram. In P. J. Guerin, Jr. (Ed.), *Family therapy: Theory and practice*. New York, Gardner Press, 1976.

Harel, Z.; Kahana, B., & Kahana, E.: Social resources and the mental health of aging Nazi Holocaust survivors and immigrants. In J. P. Wilson & B. Raphael (Eds.), *International handbook of traumatic stress syndromes*. New York, Plenum, 1993.

Harkness, L. L.: Transgenerational transmission of war-related trauma. In Wilson, J. P. & Raphael, B. (Eds.), *International handbook of traumatic stress syndromes*. New York, Plenum, 1993.

Hartsough, D. M.: Stresses, spouses, and law enforcement: A step beyond. In Reese, J. T., Horn, J. M. & Dunning, C. (Eds.), *Critical Incidents in Policing*. Washington, D.C., U.S. Department of Justice, Federal Bureau of Investigation, 1991.

Helmreich, W. B.: *Against all odds: Holocaust survivors and the successful lives they made in America*. New York, Simon & Schuster, 1992.

Horvitz, L. A.: Can police solve their epidemic of suicide? *Insight, November 7*: 9-12, 1994.

Hunter-King, E. J.: Children of military personnel missing in action in Southeast Asia. In Y. Danieli (Ed.), *International handbook of multigenerational legacies of trauma*. New York, Plenum, 1998.

Janik, J., & Kravitz, D. O.: Police suicides: Trouble at home. In J. T. Reese & E. Scrivner (Eds.), *Law enforcement families: Issues and answers*. Washington, D.C., U.S. Department of Justice, Federal Bureau of Investigation, 1994.

Johnson, D. R.; Lubin, H.; Rosenheck, R.; Fontana, A.; Southwick, S., & Charney, D.: The impact of the homecoming reception on the development of posttraumatic stress disorder: The West Haven Homecoming Stress Scale (WHHSS). *Journal of Traumatic Stress, 10*: 259-277, 1997.

Jordan, B. K.; Marmar, C. R.; Fairbank, J. A.; Schlenger, W. F.; Kulka, R. A.; Hough, R. L., & Weiss, D. S. (1992). Problems in families of male Vietnam veterans with posttraumatic stress disorder. *Journal of Consulting and Clinical Psychology, 60*: 916-926, 1992.

Kahana, B.; Harel, Z., & Kahana, E.: Clinical and gerontological issues facing survivors of the Nazi Holocaust. In P. Marcus, & A. Rosenberg (Eds.), *Healing their wounds: Psychotherapy with Holocaust survivors and their families*. New York, Praeger, 1989.

Kamerman, J.: The Illegacy of Suicide. In Leenaars, A. A. (Ed.), *Suicidology: Essays in honor of Edwin S. Shneidman*. New Jersey, Jason Aronson, 1993.

Kaminer, H. & Lavie, P.: Sleep and dreaming in Holocaust survivors: Dramatic decrease in dream recall in well-adjusted survivors. *Journal of Nervous and Mental Disease, 179*: 664-669, 1991.

Keilson, H.: *Sequential traumatization in children.* Jerusalem, The Hebrew University, Magnes Press, 1992.

Klein-Parker, F. (1988). Dominant attitudes of adult children of Holocaust Survivors toward their parents. In J. P. Wilson, Z. Harel, & B. Kahana (Eds.), *Human adaptation to extreme stress.* New York, Plenum, 1988.

Kleinplatz, M. M.: *Contribution of support to the adaptation of survivors' children in two cultures.* Paper presented at the annual meeting of the American Psychological Association, Montreal, 1980.

Krystal, H.: *Integration and self-healing.* Newark, NJ, Analytic Press, 1988.

Krystal H., & Niederland, W. G.: Clinical observations on the survivor syndrome. In H. Krystal (Ed.), *Massive psychic trauma.* New York, International Universities Press, 1968.

Leon, G.; Butcher, J. M.; Kleinman, M.; Goldberg, A., & Almagor, M.: Survivors of the Holocaust and their children. *Journal of Personality and Social Psychology, 41*: 303-316, 1981.

Liebert, J.: Prevention of stress disorders in military and police organization. In J. T. Reese, J. M. Horn, & C. Dunning (Eds.), *Critical incidents in policing* (pp. 169-177). Washington, D.C., U.S. Department of Justice, Federal Bureau of Investigation, 1991.

Lifton, R. J.: *The broken connection.* New York: Simon & Schuster, 1979.

Lundman, R. J.: *Police and policing.* New York, Holt, Rinehart & Winston, 1984.

Maghan, J. L.: *The 21st century cop: Police recruit perceptions as a function of occupational socialization.* Doctoral dissertation, City University of New York, 1988. University Microfilms International, 49(8), 1989.

Manolias, M. B., & Hyatt-Williams, A.: Effects of postshooting experiences on police-authorized Firearms officers in the United Kingdom. In Wilson, J. P. & Raphael, B. (Eds.), *International handbook of traumatic stress syndromes.* New York, Plenum, 1993.

Maslach, C., & Jackson, S. E.: Burned-out cops and their families. *Psychology Today.* 59-62, 1979.

Matussek, P.: *Internment in concentration camps and its consequences* (D. Jordan, & I. Jordan, Trans.). New York, Springer Verlag (Original work published 1971), 1975.

McGoldrick, M., & Gerson, R. (1985) *Genograms in Family Assessment.* New York, W.W. Norton, 1985.

Oliver, J. E.: Intergenerational transmission of child abuse: Rates, research, and clinical implications. *American Journal of Psychiatry. 150*: 1315-1324, 1993.

Rosenheck, R., & Nathan, P.: Secondary traumatization in children of Vietnam veterans. *Hospital and Community Psychiatry, 36*: 538-539, 1985.

Rosenheck, R., & Fontana, A.: Warrior fathers and warrior sons: Intergenerational aspects of trauma. In Y. Danieli (Ed.), *International handbook of multigenerational legacies of trauma.* New York: Plenum, 1998.

Rosenthal, P. A., & Rosenthal, S.: Holocaust effect in the third generation: Child of another time. *American Journal of Psychotherapy. 34:* 572-580, 1980.

Rubenstein, I.: *Psychic trauma as a result of the Holocaust in three generations.* Paper presented at the Fifth Annual Meeting, Society for Traumatic Stress Studies, San Francisco, CA, 1989.

Sigal, J. J., & Weinfeld, M.: *Trauma and rebirth: Intergenerational effects of the Holocaust.* New York, Praeger, 1989.

Simon, R. L., & Johnson, C.: An examination of competing explanations for the intergenerational transmission of domestic violence. In Y. Danieli (Ed.), *International handbook of multigenerational legacies of trauma.* New York, Plenum, 1998.

Smith, A. B.; Locke, B., & Fenster, A.: Authoritarianism in policemen who are college graduates and non college police. *Journal of Criminal Law, Criminology and Police Science. 61:* 313-315, 1970.

Solomon, Z.; Mikulincer, M.; Fried, B., & Wosner, Y.: Family characteristics and posttraumatic stress disorder: A follow-up of Israeli combat stress reaction casualties. *Family Process, 26:* 383-394, 1987.

Solomon, Z.; Kotler, M., & Mikulincer, M.: Combat-related post-traumatic stress disorders among second generation Holocaust survivors: Preliminary findings. *American Journal of Psychiatry, 145:* 865-868, 1988.

Verbosky, S. J., & Ryan, D. A.: Female partners of Vietnam veterans: Stress by proximity. *Issues in Mental Health Nursing, 9:* 95-104, 1988.

Violanti, J. M., & Aron, F.: Ranking police stressors. *Psychological Reports, 75:* 824-826, 1994.

Wachtel E. F., & Wachtel P. L.: *Family dynamics in individual psychotherapy: A guide to clinical strategies.* New York, The Guilford, 1986.

Whiteman, D. B.: Holocaust survivors and escapees–their strengths. *Psychotherapy, 30:* 443-451, 1993.

Williams, C. M.: Peacetime combat. In Williams, T. (Ed.), *Post-traumatic Stress Disorder.* Cincinnati, OH, Disabled American Veterans, 1987.

Yehuda, R.; Kahana, B.; Schmeidler, J.; Southwick, S. M.; Wilson, S., & Giller, E. L.: Impact of cumulative lifetime trauma and recent stress on current Posttraumatic Stress Disorder symptoms in Holocaust survivors. *American Journal of Psychiatry, 152:* 1815-1818, 1995.

Chapter 15

TRAUMA OF WORLD POLICING: PEACE-KEEPING DUTIES

CLAY FOREMAN & LIISA ERÄNEN

INTRODUCTION

This chapter describes the working conditions of the Civilian Police Unit (CIVPOL) of the United Nations (UN) in the active war zone of the former Yugoslavia. Hermeneutic methodology (Lofland & Lofland, 1995; Ricoeur & Kearney, 1996) was used to provide a theoretical framework for understanding personal accounts and illustrating core themes from data collected through interaction with the subjects of the research. A hermeneutical approach begins with understanding the context within which phenomena of interest present themselves. The inquiry must consider the many factors which come to bear on the experience, including personal, professional, social, cultural, and historical aspects. Hence, any single account must be interrogated and then interpreted with respect to other accounts until a coherent facsimile is produced.

A clinician must be cognizant of psychological distress among individuals exposed to traumatic incidents, yet an exclusive focus on pathology is a disservice to the person. Even when faced with extreme levels of threat (e.g., combat), adverse reactions need not necessarily develop (Orner, 1993; Williams, 1987). The point is not to discount the possibility of significant life disruption, but rather to question the lack of attention given to learning from people who do well following combat experience and to determine what contributes to this resilience. For example, Solomon (1993) concluded that aspects of the group experience (group cohesion, leaders' skill and moral purpose) were influential in mitigating concurrent and subsequent reactions. This knowledge has implications for developing selection, training, support, and readjustment programs. In this context, the "trauma membrane" may prove useful as a guide for understanding reactions to extreme situations, and provide a useful alternative to a pathological model.

TRAUMA MEMBRANE

Lindy, Grace and Green (1981) and Lindy (1985) used the "trauma membrane" metaphor to illustrate intrapsychic and interpersonal dynamics following trauma that serve to protect victims from additional distress. The membrane represents an expression of the victims' feeling that only those who were there themselves can understand what they went through. A common, intense emotional experience becomes the basis of their social identity, the criterion for in-group membership, and a means by which empathy and sharing of emotional experience help safeguard the person (Eranen & Liebkind, 1995).

When considering police officers, we must accommodate the role of the police culture and organization as a form of membrane that confers upon officers a unique and strong self- and social identity (Violanti, 1996). The police subculture represents a response to extreme working conditions that helps officers to manage threatening situations.

SURVIVOR GROUPS AS SYSTEMS

A sense of group identity is ubiquitous within police culture. Officers from different countries recognize their affinity and form bonds that denote mutual trust. This can be construed as an extension of the highly cohesive nature of police organizations that becomes an implicit aspect of offices operational expectations (Paton, 1994). As such, its disruption would constitute a significant additional stressor for officers faced with considerable adversity. Thus it is important, when researching intense experiences in atypical contexts, to examine whether the operating context sustains or inhibits the availability or use of this important coping resource. On the other hand, this sense of cohesion can have other implications during the postevent period.

A strong group unity, based on internal system structures of mutual meaning, trust, acceptance, similarity of experience and a clear sense of "us" and "them," can exist (Paton & Stephens, 1996) and otherwise healthy processes of mutual validation and mutual nurturing can maintain the traumatic theme. Accordingly, it may be difficult to leave these highly cohesive and self-maintaining systems, yet doing so may be vital for adjustment and reintegration. In other words, intense experiences, and the sense of identity it forges with those similarly involved, can make it difficult for those involved to fit back into "routine" systems, necessitating the establishment of support systems that assist officers reintegrate into normal family and organizational environments.

UNITED NATIONS MILITARY OPERATIONS

The lack of information on police officers in this context necessitates our looking elsewhere to gain insights into differences between routine and UN policing duties. Lundin and Otto (1989) found that UN military assignments presented stressors which differed significantly from those anticipated from military training (e.g., adopting a passive role that left them feeling vulnerable to attack and unable to intervene when civilians were attacked). Weisaeth et al. (1993) noted irritability and symptoms of high autonomic activity in response to "suppressed aggressiveness" in troops on UN duty, as well as a high frequency of stressful life events and divorce following completion of duty. Clearly, the working conditions of UN soldiers differs from ordinary military situations (Lundin & Otto, 1989). Consequently soldiers' reactions may differ from those expected. UN personnel must play a role of mediation, not confrontation, and maintain neutrality, even under intense provocation.

Two conditions associated with UN duty that were predictive of later psychiatric difficulties were repatriation before the end of a tour and a high level of alcohol use (Lundin & Otto, 1992; Weisaeth et al., 1993). Alcohol-related problems were noted by several contingents. Most afterhours recreation included alcohol consumption, so nonparticipants did not fully socialize. Surprisingly, a number of Moslem officers had begun abusing alcohol, largely from pressure to "socialize" with their CIVPOL peers.

Weisaeth et al., (1993) concluded that some early repatriation was caused by a preexisting condition of "severe introversion," and argued that troops should be screened accordingly during predeployment. While personality characteristics may interact with extreme conditions, or interfere with social reintegration following exposure to trauma, a lack of systematic knowledge in this area makes it premature to consider exclusion from duty solely on personality grounds.

The UN studies suggest that psychological problems follow from suppression of responses learned during traditional military training. Exposure to extreme situations which do not conform to previous experience, expectations, or which are too ambiguous to be understood, act to heighten vulnerability to stress reactions (Paton, 1994). Faced with events that are inconsistent with their preexisting self-image, individuals must struggle to impose psychological coherence upon their trauma experience. Thus, UN personnel are faced with both traumatic experiences and the task of imposing coherence (meaning) upon activities which conflict with role and personal expectations. This may introduce problems relating to other officers while on CIVPOL duties and/or make it more difficult to discuss problems with either loved-ones or valued colleagues back home (Gersons, 1989; Paton,

1994). Such uniqueness could signal an enduring trauma system closed to the usual support for reprocessing unusual experiences.

First encounters with UN police officers in the war zone often began with an overview of the culture, history, and people of the region. The officers found such historical reviews to be an important grounding for their struggle to understand the wanton destruction and genocide perpetuated on neighbors, comrades, and relatives. The convoluted history of deception and violence was an important shared knowledge within the UNPROFOR system which also supported a pessimistic expectation for mission success.

Dynamics of Interpersonal Violence

According to Staub (1993), violent social movements often develop in countries following significant environmental impact (e.g., war, political upheaval, economic collapse, community disaster, or rapid social change). The ensuing chaos encourages membership in strongly led groups (Staub, 1993) that sharply define social constructs. News accounts indicated clear antagonists identified as Slovenia, Croatia, and Serbia, with Bosnia as a battleground. Often termed "balkanization," a breakdown into local factions increased isolation, decreased communication, and heightened fear of attack. Since ethnic differences were not previously evident, a vocal minority of hate-mongers may have exerted powerful intragroup influence (Moscovici, 1985).

An important caveat suggested by Staub (1993), for sustaining this process, is international indifference. European loyalties were divided, preventing their taking unilateral action. This, in turn, encouraged an ambivalent stance by the United States towards a military intervention, creating a context in which international politics allowed the wanton destruction and ethnic cleansing that came to epitomize the conflict.

CIVPOL CONTEXT

CIVPOL duty required close personal interaction with combatants and civilians within war zones. Responsibilities included reporting criminal activities, monitoring human rights abuse, locating vulnerable civilians, and identifying humanitarian needs. CIVPOL recruited officers from 30 countries with cultures that differed vastly in traditions, values, and beliefs. Consequently, officers arrived with different policing styles, procedures, and expectations. A national contingent of officers would arrive together and would meet every six weeks. Otherwise, individual officers were assigned to multinational units across the region, and were subject to frequent reassignment, making the formation of coherent bonds important for coping. CIVPOL volunteers were to have a working knowledge of English, five years of policing experience, and good driving skills.

Cross-Cultural Issues

Officers' working knowledge of English was left to the interpretation of the sending country. Language skills thus varied widely, and meeting this criterion resulted in some countries sending offices with limited or no patrol experience. Although UN Headquarters tried to discourage the practice, some CIVPOL administrators informally screened for English proficiency, and continued to do so despite Headquarters concerns.

Teamwork is an important part of an officer's operating context, particularly in dangerous situations. Language difficulties restricted information exchange and casual conversations and reduced opportunities for officers to bond. This made the process of establishing a common culture difficult, and staff often devolved into regional cliques. Lack of bonding also reduced the level of trust between members of these ad hoc groups, added to feelings of isolation, and meant that the expected sense of safety (cohesion and trust) within an operating context was absent.

Conflicts between egalitarian and hierarchical cultures appeared in numerous ways, and political and racial discrimination was also evident. African officers experienced disregard and disrespect from local people. Some officers encountered comments to the effect that it was hypocritical for a Nigerian officer to investigate Yugoslavian human rights abuse when Nigeria was accused of human rights abuse. Asian officers were also ignored by local people who preferred to deal with white officers. As it was, the white officers took the lead in many interactions with local people.

No Weapons

In Bosnia and UNPROFOR officers did not carry guns on their person or in their vehicles. Most officers had to adjust to this policy, as only Norwegian police do not routinely carry guns. An often repeated phrase was, "They know I am not armed, so I am not a danger." These phrases were an important part of a common belief system. In the Balkans everyone except CIVPOL and humanitarian workers openly carried automatic rifles, which is quite different from normal patrol duty. Not carrying a gun in such dangerous circumstances could well create some cognitive dissonance for officers, forcing them to reframe this "no gun" policy in a positive manner to reduce the dissonance.

Driving on Patrol

Some officers arrived with little actual patrol experience. Routine police skills were not easily adapted to the Balkan situation. Individual officers developed ad hoc operating procedures to fulfill the general CIVPOL mandate. The Yugoslavian terrain challenged the driving skills of many officers. Many officers lacked the necessary driving skills, and others were so uncomfortable, or so poorly skilled, that they traveled only with others willing to do the driving. Traffic accidents were frequently cited as stressors. Accidents occurred for various reasons, such as poorly lighted farm vehicles at dusk, drunken drivers (including CIVPOL officers), poor pavement, and pedestrians who inexplicably wandered across busy streets. Poor driving conditions compounded the dangers of a war zone.

Living Environment

Officers were not garrisoned. Being accommodated within the community meant they experienced the same difficulties as local people. The absence of running water and electricity made any semblance of normal life impossible. On and off-duty, officers were subject to threats, kidnapping, robbery, and serious physical injury. On patrol, officers were impeded by checkpoints, delays, detours, and aborted missions. Few officers understood the local language, and local interpreters went on all patrols. However, divisions between CIVPOL officers and local people were imposed for several reasons.

UN staff also had to exclude local people from CIVPOL membership. In the war context their loyalties could be divided by their vulnerability to hostile forces. Hence, UN personnel could not trust the interpreters or local staff. Officers maintained liaison with counterparts in the local militia. Yet, local officials from a morning meeting, later might be heavily-armed, masked bandits who robbed the officer and stole his vehicle.

Danger also came from snipers and buried landmines. The former were assumed to observe all CIVPOL activities. The latter were laid throughout the landscape, confining travel to roads and stone paths. Areas with trees indicated possible sniper fire or mortar attack. Most streets were lined with battle-damaged buildings. The gunfire that accompanied local weekend celebrations indiscriminately rained bullets. Officers lay awake listening for nearby impacts.

Police officers working in these conditions were imperiled day-in-day-out for 6-week stretches. Officers were completely focused on their immediate surroundings. This acute awareness of any danger further distanced themselves from formal routines and expectations. In short, this was not typical police work. However, operating under these conditions did not always result in apprehension and concern for one's safety.

An English officer described how uncomfortable he was at home, how ill-informed his friends back home were about "important world issues," and how they were unable to understand his experiences. The impression was of a young man utterly disconnected from his previous life, and seemingly enthralled with the tensely dangerous work. His expressed pleasure with negotiating passage of relief supplies through roadblocks and past other dangers was indicative of stress addiction (see Chapter 7).

Corruption

Confounding other difficulties was corruption and private marketeering by UNPROFOR contingents. This was extremely disturbing for officers and affected development of a sense of coherence within CIVPOL. Police are not used to dealing with such widespread and blatant corruption within their midst, and, where weapons were involved, having their comrades assisting to heighten the prevailing danger.

Thus danger was outside and inside the unit, and a protective membrane could not solidify at the CIVPOL perimeter. Even a sense of being a survivor could only cautiously include other officers. Group identification remained with the country contingents and regional kinship. Shared beliefs are structural vehicles for group cohesion and communication. In this way, the operating context provides important interpersonal coping mechanisms. CIVPOL did not generate much communality. If an operating context does not exist, or is dysfunctional under extreme conditions, a spontaneous trauma membrane may define group membership in ways that reflect offices' perceptions of the context in which they find themselves rather than in the manner that might have been anticipated from observing offices in routine contexts.

Planning for Catastrophe

UN officers often described their evacuation plans. Although the UN had clearly defined evacuation routes along principle roads, some officers formed separate contingency plans to evade detection during hostilities. These plans spoke the officers' need to anticipate personal control in the event of future danger.

HUMAN RIGHTS ABUSE AND OTHER CRIMES

Encountering inhumane acts towards other people was part of the fabric of the experience. While initially shocking and provocative, as one gained war zone experience such accounts became commonplace and part of the expected background of the lived experience. Intentionally slaughtered children and purposefully defiled women were high crimes that, consistent with one's expectations, one hoped would be punished later.

Delayed retribution was the psychological compensation for salient encounters with inhumane acts and represented attempts to reconcile a police officer arc of experience with a CIVPOL arc. The hope for later retribution, with war criminals being held accountable for their wartime actions, was encouraged by an understanding that all sides participated in atrocious treatment of other people. Under war zone conditions perpetuators are not easily identified, especially when the aggressors come from within the same group as the victims. Several well-publicized incidents of mass death and injury were later determined to have been perpetuated by local power-holders against their ethical group to engender world sympathy. Such incidents are indicative of the long convoluted history of duplicity within the Balkan region. In this regard, understanding the regional history can lead to pessimistic expectations for a just outcome.

Criminal Activity

Various war zone areas were controlled by "local warlords," who welded significant power over local inhabitants. A warlord could equally have been an officer in the Yugoslavian army or a common criminals. Lack of any overarching political or military structures for the three principle ethnic groups engendered fear amongst local people and made it relatively easy for warlords to establish their positions. Under these conditions people fall in behind whatever leadership exists and allow group norms to dictate appropriate behavior. When political leaders encourage the dehumanization of another group and direct mistreatment, average people become perpetrators. A war zone comprising various power groups and uncertain alliances made for very chaotic conditions and unrestrained criminal activity. This made it difficult for CIVPOL officers to feel any personal control however much they understood the situation.

PSYCHOLOGICAL REACTIONS

Intrapsychic defense mechanisms were noticed, but were often appropriate to the context of their occurrence. There was a pronounced use of denial and avoidance of awareness of the immediacy of personal danger. Trauma survivors use these mechanisms (Horowitz, 1976; Williams, 1993) to fend off awareness of fear, to avoid psychological reactions that might interfere with effective action (Solomon, Mikulincer & Benbenishty, 1989), and to fend off fears of personal rejection if others learn of certain inner feelings, thoughts or desires. However, other explanations are also possible.

Despite the danger they faced, officers needed to maintain a sense of invulnerability in order to function effectively. Instead of directing this towards themselves, fears for personal safety appeared to be deflected by concern for local people. Local people were distinct and separate from an officer's own identity. This separation may have allowed concern for the welfare of other people to substitute for fear about one's own safety, without the deception being obvious to the officer. Certainly, there was little evidence of officers being able to call upon any group identity or cohesion to assist coping.

CIVPOL was divided by interpersonal boundaries defined by national or regional origin. Personal exposure to danger and trauma appeared to intensify intergroup distinctions. Cultural differences, operational conditions, and limited UN structures interacted with the experience to divide groups. While a sense of similarity was conveyed by, for example, UN compliments to the national police uniforms, UN vehicles, and CIVPOL assignments, this communality did not extend to operating procedures, culture or a clear sense of common purpose or teamwork.

This fragmentation was also evident in local people not viewing CIVPOL as a unified force. They dealt with officers according to expectations derived from their nationality. Accordingly, they showed gratitude to Norwegian officers in remembrance of Norwegian resistance fighters helping Serbs escape WWII concentration camps in Norway. Black officers were disrespected due to racial stereotypes.

Lack of coherent power structure, in the region and within UN units, was problematic for officers accustomed to interfacing with hierarchically-structured organizations and compounded officers' difficulty in fulfilling their overall mission. The absence of usual formal structures also diminished the potential for a common operating context. Lines of communication differed from those expected and could not provide the secure intelligence police agencies rely on to predict and control situations in their local jurisdictions. The opportunity for officers to develop informal conduits for information was severely hindered by sudden and frequent reassignment. If any local people wanted to assist or warn UN personnel, they were thwarted by the inability to sustain relationships long enough to develop the necessary trust.

Teamwork should be automatic and reliable, especially in danger or confusing confrontations. The lack of expected operational structures provided little support for personnel to cope with the grave difficulties of their mission. Such contextual deficits contributed to an officer's sense of vulnerability. Multinational teams had an unrealized potential for creative problem solving. Ironically, even as they intervene in international ethnic conflicts, multinational UN organizations must take steps to acknowledge and reduce their own internal cross-cultural conflict.

UN member countries did not provide predeployment orientation or training specific to UNPROFOR. Many officers arrived wholly unprepared for this duty. It is likely that police will continue to work internationally under such extreme conditions. It is incumbent on the organizing authority to address the potential for officers to develop a detrimental survivor identity. Traditionally, police find protection in an existing operating context, which includes an insulating organizational identity, as well as on-duty crisis intervention, counseling, debriefing, and conflict resolution.

CONCLUSION

From this brief review, it is clear that the CIVPOL experience was unlike any civilian police operation. On a personal level, officers encountered isolation, danger, and discomfort. At a professional level, the CIVPOL situation was devoid of routine policies and procedures typical of police operations. Organizationally, CIVPOL was derelict with regards to providing preparation, training, secure communication, and a coordinated command structures. These deficiencies must be addressed. It would also be beneficial to install a high-ranking leadership to protect CIVPOL from direct political interference by member nations, and allow some measure of selfdetermination. Common codes of conduct need to be defined as well as sanctions for infractions. UN standards of civil and criminal law should be established to guide CIVPOL officers in regions without effective local law enforcement agencies. Officers need some enforcement capacity with regard to recognized international laws, although perhaps, limited to investigations and reports of wrongdoing. International laws should address criminal acts and human rights violations.

The CIVPOL system should encourage officers' resilience during extreme duties by providing a supportive operating context and reducing organizational stress factors. While crisis intervention and debriefing services address psychic rupture, organizational development must attend to structural integrity and the mitigation of long-term psychosocial consequences. Specifically, CIVPOL needs to develop a group identity and common expectations and explore how this experience can be better integrated into the officers' home policing contexts, including maintaining regular information exchange with family, friends, and colleagues.

Training programs should be based on an accurate mission description, be provided prior to leaving for duty, and be designed to facilitate integration within the region of operation. Induction training should familiarize officers with CIVPOL policy and procedures. Officers' capability for duty (e.g., patrol experience, driving, language competence) should be assessed. Team-building exercises should play a vital part in CIVPOL training as should the development of conflict resolution and negotiation skills. Training should also familiarize officers with local conditions and its cultural and social milieu. Multinational groups could be trained as mission components and dispatched to the field to work together and be demobilized as intact transnational units.

Training should also increase officers' awareness of the implications of CIVPOL duty for significant others. Integration between home and mission must be encouraged and supported throughout the tour of duty, with renewed emphasis during demobilization. Ideally, family and colleagues can be involved in training and reintegration programs to facilitate communication and recognition of the issues that have to be addressed on return and how they can facilitate this process.

Psychological preparation should be integrated to the training program. It would also be pertinent to develop mechanism to monitor condition of units in the field, including organizational dynamics and system responses to stressors, the results of which trigger dispatch of support appropriate to need. Psychological services should be a permanent on-duty component of CIVPOL operations.

A research component should be built into the CIVPOL operations to address, for example, pre- and postdeployment psychological measurement, correlation of these indices with later difficulties, and follow-up studies of readjustment difficulties to determine causes and identify predisposing conditions. Instruments should be refined to assess onduty levels of individual stress, operating unit stability, and overall effectiveness.

REFERENCES

Eränen, L., & Liebkind, K.: Coping with disaster: The helping behavior of communities and individuals. In J.P. Wilson & B. Raphael (Eds.), *International handbook of traumatic stress syndromes.* New York, Plenum, 1993.

Gersons, B. P. R.: Patterns of PTSD among police officers following shooting incidents: A two-dimensional model and treatment implications. *Journal of Traumatic Stress, 2*: 247-257, 1989.

Horowitz, M.: *Stress response syndrome.* New York, Jason Aronson, 1976.

Lindy, J. D.: The trauma membrane and other clinical concepts derived from working with survivors of natural disaster. *Psychiatric Annul, 15*: 153-160, 1985.

Lindy, J. D., Grace, M., & Green, B. L.: Survivors: Outreach to a reluctant population. *American Journal of Orthopsychiatry, 51*: 468-478, 1981.

Lofland, J., & Lofland, L. H. (1995). *Analyzing social settings: A guide to qualitative observation and analysis (3rd ed.)* Belmont, CA, Wadsworth, 1995.

Lundin, T., & Otto, U.: Stress reactions among Swedish health care personnel in UNIFIL, South Lebanon 1982-1984. *Stress Medicine, 5*: 237-246, 1989.

Lundin, T., & Otto, U.: Swedish UN soldiers in Cyprus, UNFICYP: Their psychological and social situation. *Psychotherapy and Psychosomatics, 57*: 187-193, 1992.

Moscovici, S.: Social influence and conformity. In G.Lindsay, & E. Aronson (Eds.), *Handbook of social psychology, Vol.2 (3rd ed.)* New York, Random House, 1985.

Orner, R.J.; Lynch, T., & Seed, P: Long-term traumatic stress reactions in British Falklands War veterans. *British Journal of Clinical Psychology, 32*: 457-459, 1993.

Paton, D.: Disaster relief work: An assessment of training effectiveness. *Journal of Traumatic Stress, 7*: 275-288, 1994.

Paton, D., & Stephens, C.: Training and support for emergency responders. In D. Paton, & J. M. Violanti (Eds.), *Traumatic stress in critical occupations: Recognition, consequences and treatment.* Springfield, IL, Charles C. Thomas, 1996.

Ricoeur, P., & Kearney, R. (Eds.): *The hermeneutics of action.* London, Sage, 1996.

Solomon, Z.: *Combat stress reaction: The enduring toll of war.* New York, Plenum, 1993.

Solomon, Z.; Mikulincer, M., & Benbenishty, R.: Locus of control and combat-related Post-traumatic Stress Disorder: The intervening role of battle intensity, threat appraisal and coping. *British Journal of Clinical Psychology, 28*: 131-144, 1989.

Staub, E.: The psychology of bystanders, perpetrators, and heroic helpers. *International Journal of Intercultural Relations, 17*: 315-341, 1993.

Violanti, J.: Trauma stress and police work. In Paton, D., & Violanti, J. (Eds.), *Traumatic stress in critical occupations: Recognition, consequences and treatment.* Springfield, IL, Charles C. Thomas, 1996.

Weisæth, L.; Aarhaug, P.; Mehlum, L., & Larsen, S.: *The UNIFIL study, positive and negative consequences of service in UNIFIL contingents I-XXVI, report part I, results and recommendations.* Oslo, Norwegian Defense Command Headquarters, The Joint Medical Service, 1993.

Williams, T.: Trauma in the workplace. In J. P. Wilson, & B. Raphael (Eds.), *International handbook of traumatic stress syndromes.* New York, Plenum, 1993.

Williams, T.: Diagnosis and treatment of survivor guilt. In T. Williams (Ed.), *Post-traumatic stress disorders: A handbook for clinicians.* Cincinnati, OH, Disabled Veterans of America, 1987.

SECTION III

PREVENTION, RECOVERY
AND TREATMENT

Chapter 16

TRAUMA PREVENTION IN THE LINE OF DUTY

Joseph M. Rothberg & Kathleen Wright

INTRODUCTION

In this chapter, we will discuss duty-related traumas in military and police departments using the public health prevention concepts of primary, secondary, and tertiary prevention. As applied to disasters and other traumatic events, primary prevention addresses preparation and training prior to an event; secondary prevention focuses on the needs of participants in the event(s) during or shortly afterwards; and tertiary prevention considers how to limit the long-term effects and better prepare for, and manage, future events.

The police and the military are similar but not directly comparable institutions. Police officers are in "combat" every day and differ from soldiers with respect to the training received and exposure to trauma during their career. A police officer with two months of patrol time probably has conducted more mount operations than Special Operations Forces do in a career. Both institutions are characterized by hierarchical organization with a focus on leadership and by the exposure of their personnel to uniquely stressful environments, which, for both, may regularly include dealing with violence, injury, and death. The organizational philosophy in both professions emphasizes the importance of training in preparation for dealing with threatening situations. In reality, there are only selected subsets of personnel in both of the organizations who are at-risk for exposure. In the military, the "tooth to tail" ratio as the description the combat and supporting components is echoed in the division of police responsibilities.

Traumatic events originate from many sources, from a coordinated firefight or the response to an armed robbery in progress. It could involve a sniper attack on a mess hall in Vietnam or a shooter on the upper floors of the DC police headquarters. It could originate from a natural disaster or a mass casualty accident. Thus, for both groups, in general, traumatic events are unexpected and their consequences are unplanned. Further, the psychological recovery process is similar in police and military situations. While the unique characteristics of each of these groups, the police and the military, should be borne in mind throughout this discussion, there are sufficient general similarities between them to afford some interesting comparisons which can both assist understanding the nature of traumatic experiences and aid the formulation of management strategies.

ARMY TRAINING FOR TRAUMA

The basis of military training for response to trauma can be summarized in the phrase that "you can't prepare today to do today." One part of the program whose task is to provide the best possible health care to the military is the Uniformed Services University of the Health Sciences (USUHS) with its associated medical school. To carry out the unique mission of training military physicians and allied health personnel, USUHS has its own textbook series, *The Textbook of Military Medicine* (TMM). Of particular relevance within the series are the two TMM volumes relating to the education of military health personnel to deal with trauma.

War Psychiatry (Jones et al., 1995a) deals with the delivery of mental health services during wartime. It is organized around the assumption that, despite the significant stresses of combat, prevention and treatment can keep the majority of soldiers functioning as fully integrated members of their units. *Military Psychiatry: Preparing in Peace for War* (Jones et al., 1995b) addresses the multiple mental health services provided by the military during peacetime. The continual "war" footing of contemporary police organizations makes the philosophy described in these volumes of considerable relevance for managing duty-related traumatic stress in police officers. The prevention and treatment issues that apply to the military's peacetime missions, such as peacekeeping, realistic training, and natural disaster assistance resemble wartime in their potential for trauma. The following paragraphs briefly touch on some of the trauma-related topics presented in those volumes.

As a general model of the normal functioning of soldiers, we assume that various permanent (trait) and transient (state) personality and situational factors (e.g., cohesion, leadership) interact with external events (stressors) to determine behavior. The focus of the TMM volumes is the military group as it supports the individual and provides resources for dealing with the stresses and trauma associated with the military itself.

One way in which the mental health and performance of military group members is maintained is by the active outreach activities of military medicine referred to as command consultation or unit consultation. There are two distinctive aspects of this form of mental health care. One is the aggressive presentation of the mental health resources, almost to the point of case solicitation. The other is the focus on the group as the client with the emphasis on the restoration of the group rather than the individual. This form of consultation usually entails the health professional going to the unit or group rather than being office-based and awaiting the arrival of the client.

The Army actively encourages command consultation to reach out to the leaders as well as the soldiers to maintain mental health and stress resistance. In a hierarchical organization such as the Army, the behaviors of the leaders are an important component in the way subordinate personnel deal with stress. The leaders in the Army have the resource of mental health workers to deal with matters of stress management. Considerable attention is focussed on educating the mental health personnel in the nature of stress management for the leader, the soldier, and the soldier's family.

As with other components of Army education and training, the focus is on the practice of what could be expected to occur in reality. Field training exercises include a medical component with realistically presented "casualties" and "snafus." Because of limited medical resources, the immediate tasks in the field are the timely characterization of the physical state of the soldiers. Combat stress casualties are included in the planning and the simulated psychiatric impact of combat (or the real disasters of training accidents) serves to familiarize everyone involved with the way people and systems function in response to stress. Developing holistic approaches to trauma and stress management, which involve the leader, personnel, and their families, describes a model that has some utility in police organizations.

DISASTERS, TRAUMATIC EVENTS AND MASS CASUALTIES

The mass casualties and other combat consequences are not unlike individual disasters. Military medicine teaches that the psychiatric dynamics of the military and civilian responses are similar. In both situations, the abnormal circumstances (rather than individual psychopathology) are the origin of the dysfunction. A general approach considers the time span before, during, and after the disaster. The interval of the event is referred to as the impact period and is forewarned by the preimpact or threat period. A warning period immediately precedes the impact period. A recoil period follows the impact which, in turn, leads to the postimpact period. There is no reason to believe that the future will have fewer natural and human-made disasters. A case can be made that the advances in communications will result in more people being emotionally involved, including those beyond the physical site of the disaster. In this era of competitive coverage, disasters may be exaggerated by "newsworthy" statements drawn out of context that do not reflect the intent at the time they were made. Reasonable guidance for the participants of such situations is to recognize the realities of media presence while attending to one's own professional role within the group.

While the trauma of the impact period is most visible, the effects of a disaster may extend throughout the community during the postimpact period in unanticipated ways. In the case of the Gander disaster of December, 1985, where 248 soldiers died in a fiery airplane crash, the morgue operation at Dover Air Force Base experienced extreme stress reactions requiring replacement of personnel and a mini-epidemic of suicides and suicide attempts among the adolescents. It is of interest that the survivors at the home base of the soldiers who perished did not report such postimpact problems. The highly traumatized home base community had the active support of the Chaplain's office, the Mortuary Affairs, the Veterans Administration, the Red Cross, the Army Mutual Aid, Army Community Services, the Judge Advocate General's office, the finance office, and the mental health services. The Dover Air Force Base community did not have the same levels of aggressive outreach activities that took place at the home base. Attention to outreach is an issue that may have some relevance for police organizations. While they may not live on a base, the close knit relationships that exist between police officers, and between officers and their families, can result in a substantial "ripple effect." This describes how an event which involves one group or individual can extend its influence to affect those in close personal or professional relationships with those affected. Getting assistance to this wider group would be important. Although this represents an appropriate role for outreach, careful attention would have to be directed to establishing and managing administrative procedures in police organizations.

DISASTER ON GREEN RAMP

Process in Action

To illustrate the utility of mental health intervention and to provide a focus for the discussion of lessons learned, we will draw upon the highly detailed material published from a recent military disaster. The nature and magnitude of the awesome human consequences of the fire fuelled by the collision of two aircraft is briefly described by the Army's Center of Military History. This work describes the Army's exceptionally effective response to the tragic events on 23 March 1994 at Pope Air Force base, North Carolina. On that day a large number of Army paratroopers from nearby Fort Bragg had assembled in an area adjacent to the airstrip known as Green Ramp, preparing to board a transport that would carry them aloft for a training parachute jump. They never made that jump. Shortly after 1400 hours two aircraft attempted to land simultaneously at Pope. The resulting crash produced a massive fire that brought death or injury to more than 100 paratroopers, the worst peacetime loss of life suffered by the 82nd Airborne Division since World War II (Condon-Rall, 1996, p. vii).

Primary Prevention

Training Prior to the Event

The realistic nature and effectiveness of Army training is evident from the following description of the responses of trained units. One month before the accident, the 2nd Battalion, 504th Infantry, had to simulate evacuating dead and wounded during maneuvers at the joint Readiness Training Center at Fort Polk, Louisiana. Lessons learned during those exercises helped the battalion to evacuate soldiers and account for fallen comrades on Green Ramp. "Most of the things (at the crash site) were exactly as we had trained" said Lt. Col. Stanley A. McChrystal, the battalion commander who had served with a special operations unit during the Gulf War. "We had to figure out who we had, and that's much harder than you think because of the confusion on the site" (Condon-Rall, 1996, p.22).

At the level of the individual participant, the effectiveness of training as preparation for heroic acts was clear. S. Sgt. Timothy J Gavaghan of the 82d Airborne Division's Headquarters and Headquarters Company, 3d Brigade, had a similar story. He was sitting outside the jumpmaster school when he heard the explosion. As the fireball came toward him, he lay on the asphalt with his hands over his face. After feeling the intense heat pass over him, he got up and for the next twenty minutes "operated on auto pilot." He "dragged people to safety, patted out fires, carried litters, whatever was needed." His "training took over," [emphasis added] Gavaghan said. The "mere process of repetition" kept him "going." Gavaghan was one of many heroes (Condon-Rall, 1996, p.11).

And at the organizational level, the ability of the multitude of responders to coordinate is seen in the following summary. While terrible misfortune sometimes just happens, a professional response to crisis is no accident. Training, hard work, esprit, and dedication in the everyday routine of soldiers can pay off in emergencies. Such was the case at Fort Bragg, where Womack [hospital] medical personnel, with the help of volunteers, triaged the Green Ramp casualties, gave them life-supporting treatment, and advanced them to the next level of care within two hours. The timing of the accident, coming at a change in hospital shifts, allowed for maximum staffing, and the presence of other medical units on post provided additional people and equipment. Womack's Colonel Timboe believed that the experience gained by his medics in Panama, the Persian Gulf, Honduras, and Somalia, as well as the training received at Womack's December 1993 mass casualty seminar when department chiefs discussed responsibilities and preparations for the upcoming Haiti contingency operation enabled the hospital to respond with confidence to the disaster. Colonel Weightman, who agreed with Timboe, also credited the usefulness of the advanced trauma life support and combat casualty care courses, taught at Fort Sam Houston, and recent mass casualty exercises in Honduras and at Fort Bragg. Teamwork was possible because the 44th Medical Brigade "had built up the links" that ensured an organized and efficient response. As stated by General Peake, "It's one Army Medical Department, not multiple chunks that never talk" (Condon-Rall, 1996, pp.44-45). The value of widespread training as a form of primary prevention could not be described in more vivid language, nor could it make a more compelling case than was seen above in the language of those involved in the disaster. The training and teamwork described here are similar to those prevailing in police organizations. Attention to developing these strategies can confer considerable benefits, both in terms of safeguarding the well-being of officers and in promoting effective incident response.

Command Consultation

The organizational emphasis of both police and military on leadership places a large burden on individuals in that role and attention to the potential for the loss of the leader from burnout must be kept in mind. An efficient use of limited behavioral sciences resources has been found to be the paradoxical "Command Consultation" mode of mental health outreach. By going around to contact the units and personnel, problems can be resolved at an early phase before they become troublesome and require more time and manpower. Although it would seem that sitting in one's office and not soliciting contacts would be the best way to deal with an excessive workload, the military has found that a modest investment in prevention yields the healthiest overall force. Preventive activities can thus confer considerable benefits. However, the unpredictable and atypical nature of critical incidents, and their implications for those involved, also requires that due consideration is given to providing resources designed to prevent reactions reaching serious proportions.

Secondary Prevention

Critical Incident Stress Debriefing

A disaster is traumatic for the participants and distressing for others. The function of critical incident stress debriefings is to resolve the trauma and prevent the development of extended disruption from the unfortunate event. The caregivers are a group who are as vulnerable to such posttraumatic problems as the nonprofessionals. The continued functioning and avoidance of burnout requires attention to the stresses of the event.

The military use the formal critical incident stress debriefing (CISD) process wherein the participants share their involvement in the event with their (organizationally) closest mental health consultant. In most cases, this is a behavioral sciences specialist who is a member of the unit and perceived by the participants as an integral part of the system and not an unknown outsider. As well as being an insider, the consultant has training and clinical skills in the debriefing process. The function of the reconstruction process is to clarify the who-did-what-when events and to share the what-it-meant experiences of the participants. Fear, anxiety, and terror seem to have less impact over time if they are confronted and resolved soon after the event. Staff debriefings and other police policies, such as an automatic review after every shot fired in the line-of-duty, may function as a form of CISD in the nonmilitary environment. The written report by an individual may also provide an outlet for the lower impact events.

Outreach to Soldiers

The surviving on-scene participants in the tragedy were the priority focus for mental health efforts. To heal emotional wounds, Fort Bragg's mental health professionals conducted formal debriefings. Strong emotional reactions to abnormal situations, psychiatrists believed, were best handled by people talking about their experiences with others who had gone through the same thing. The 1985 air crash at Gander, Newfoundland, in which 236 members of the 101st Airborne Division (Air Assault) perished, had taught the Army that "it doesn't work to have people with different uniforms, with different patches, not knowing what's going on, conduct the debriefings," said Colonel Plewes, Womack's psychiatry and neurology chief. Hence, Fort Bragg used its own mental health resources, which were considerable. Although the 82d was primarily responsible for debriefing the troops, other Fort Bragg mental health specialists and chaplains assisted. Womack's social workers and chaplains dealt primarily with family issues, and the nearby

Rumbaugh Child and Adolescent Mental Health Clinic took care of the emotional needs of adolescents and children.

Formal critical incident stress debriefings began on the afternoon of 24 March. Four teams, consisting of two individuals each, met with the soldiers and divided into small groups. The debriefings lasted between thirty and sixty minutes. Within seventy-two hours every soldier involved in the accident had attended at least one session. Debriefings continued on a daily basis for about a week. By then the mental health specialists had debriefed forty-nine separate units and about 500 troops.

The debriefings were cathartic experiences, where the soldiers shared information about their location at the time of the crash, what they saw, and what they felt. Psychiatrists were able to differentiate between normal and abnormal reactions to trauma and identify those who were not coping well. The latter often were individuals who had experienced an earlier trauma but had never been debriefed, and thus the Green Ramp episode rekindled their pain. Psychiatrists also offered special counseling to soldiers who witnessed the accident and were not hurt, but who felt guilty for having been spared.

Therapy for the soldiers came in other forms as well. Colonel Plewes believed that the memorial service "shored up their mores, as it were." Ceremony and ritual also provided closure. Colonel McChrystal's personal therapy was to focus on the nearly 620 paratroopers in his battalion who were not killed and who needed a commander.

The psychiatrists decided to take the soldiers back to the crash site as therapy, especially since many expressed interest in returning to Green Ramp. Unit commanders and hospital nurses worked together to organize the effort. One week after the accident, the soldiers returned to Green Ramp. As far as Colonel Plewes could tell, no one was retraumatized. The paratroopers were supportive of one another and seemed to handle well the visit to the crash location (Condon-Rall, 1996, pp. 108-110).

Outreach to Staff

The reality of a disaster is that it has profound effects on all involved, including the helping professions. Their efforts to provide aid and comfort to the victims exacts a toll of its own. Womack's mental health specialists took care of the hospital staff. Colonel Plewes gave top priority to debriefing emergency room and operating room personnel, followed by nurses on the wards that received the injured. Formal critical incident stress debriefings for hospital staff began two days after the accident. Psychologists emphasized the normalcy of the painful feelings and responses to a tragedy like Green Ramp. After attending a session, Major Light, who helped to triage the casualties, shed her initial skepticism and reported, "Talking about what happened is crucial." Psychiatrists and hospital chaplains contacted pathologists conducting autopsies in the morgue to offer encouragement. Hospital custodial staff, who had cleaned up an excess of blood and debris after emergency treatment, also received debriefings one week after the incident (Condon-Rall, 1996, p.110).

Chaplains directly immersed in the response were debriefed with those immediately involved on Green Ramp. Mental health specialists and chaplains in a support role talked to each other about their experiences during the debriefing sessions, which was itself a form of debriefing. Colonel Plewes found it difficult to erase the memories of the casualties screaming when he tried to administer intravenous fluids into their burned skin. Talking about it helped him to process the experience (Condon-Rall, 1996, p.111).

Outreach to Families

As with the civilian police community, many soldiers are married and their families frequently socialize. Their off-duty lives are interrelated as is their on-duty performance. The families of the victims received formal debriefings and individual counseling from chaplains and social workers at Womack's Weaver Conference Room or the family assistance activity in the Fort Bragg Community Center. Major Clark, the surgeon of the 82d, coordinated with the Rumbaugh Clinic on debriefings for adolescents and children because, according to Colonel Plewes, the division "likes to take care of its own." Counselors also visited the Fayetteville schools and allowed the youth to tell their classmates how they felt. Lt. Col. Sherry Conner, a social worker, understood the healing process, stating that "adaptation to catastrophic events comes in stages over time." Colonel Plewes reported that with each patient and family he tried to show that the accident, "while tragic, [was] just one event in the person's life." Womack kept its outpatient clinic opened on the weekend to conduct individual debriefings or perform crisis intervention. Handouts on stress and trauma were available. Formal debriefings ended about a week after the accident, although counselors continued to be available for anyone who still needed to talk (Condon-Rall, 1996, pp. 110-111).

Outreach to Community

The boundaries of a tragedy are hard to define. The efforts to alleviate the effects of the disaster extended beyond the individual participants to those in the community who were in need. Fort Bragg's mental health professionals, chaplains, and social workers had come together to help the Army community deal with the Green Ramp Disaster. At "business-like meetings" they divided up the workload and shared resources. Formal critical incident stress debriefings became "cooperative and multidisciplinary" undertakings, providing opportunities for psychiatric, social, and spiritual healing. Margaret Tippy remembered Colonel Plewes saying: "Everybody worked together handling the emotional needs of people involved in the accident". Tippy added: "It wasn't personality driven. It wasn't ego driven. It was mission oriented and mission focused and that was wonderful" (Condon-Rall, 1996, p. 111).

Tertiary Prevention

Army After-Action Report Process

To prepare for and manage future events, the military provides institutional self-evaluation on an on-going basis. This form of tertiary prevention is the driving force for the training that was seen to be so effective in the discussion above. In addition to various special investigative studies, the most consistently generated document is that of the after-action report (AAR), a reporting format that all officers are trained to utilize. Regular staff meetings provide the opportunity for the definition and discussion of the events to be characterized in the AAR. The events of the AAR are the basis of training (since the only reasonable predictor of future behavior is past behavior) and considerable effort is expended to keep the training cogent to the organizational needs. Assessment of the effectiveness of the training is a regular component of the military training process. A continuing conflict within the training environment is to determine the level of stress which will prepare the individuals for the on-the-job requirements without washing out too many individuals due to excessively stressful training. The lesson for police agencies is to use a formal review and evaluation of operations as a learning device.

The military actively supports historical documentation of its activities (referred to as lessons learned) as a form of continuous self-evaluation. With regard to trauma management of military disasters, many of the recent events have been investigated and documented by the Department of Psychiatry of the Uniformed Services University of the Health Sciences which has an on-going program. These sources of data provide an institutional setting that allows the interested professional to benefit from the historical experiences of prior efforts to deal with the traumatic effects of disasters.

Research Opportunities

There are a number of research and evaluation issues that emerge from this discussion. In broadest scope, the education and training for disaster and trauma management of different levels of personnel in both the Army and in Police Departments could be assessed and evaluated. In addition to the usual end-of-class testing for the student's acquisition of the learning objectives, there is a need for continuing assessment to determine how long the knowledge lasts, and how well it transfers tom operational situations. The harder question is whether the training is realistic in terms of the evolving risks in today's society.

CONCLUSION

This chapter described an effective response to an incident involving mass casualties and how we can draw upon the experience of diverse groups, in this case the military, to inform the process of developing philosophies, strategies, and procedures to assist the management of stress and traumatic stress in police officers. Solomon's discussion (this volume) of the experience of officers who responded to the Waco incident presents a scenario where the lessons described in this chapter could be applied. While differences between groups limits our ability to transfer his expertise automatically, this discussion demonstrates how looking beyond the group under immediate consideration can facilitate research and intervention development.

REFERENCES

Jones, F. D.; Sparacino, L. R.; Wilcox, V. L.; Rothberg, J. M., & Stokes, J. W. (Eds.): *War psychiatry. The textbook of military medicine.* Washington, D.C., Office of The Surgeon General, U.S. Dept Army and Borden Institute, 1995.

Jones, F. D.; Sparacino, L. R.; Wilcox, V. L., & Rothberg, J. M.: Military psychiatry: Preparing in peace for war. In Jones, F. D.; Sparacino, L. R.; Wilcox, V. L.; Rothberg, J. M., & Stokes, J. W. (Eds.), *The textbook of military medicine.* Washington, D.C., Office of The Surgeon General, U.S. Dept Army and Borden Institute, 1995.

Condon-Rall, M. E.: *Condon-Rall, 1996.* Washington, D.C., Center of Military History, US Army, 1996

Chapter 17

COPING EFFECTIVENESS AND OCCUPATIONAL STRESS IN POLICE OFFICERS

GEORGE T. PATTERSON

INTRODUCTION

How individuals cope with stressful events is a topical issue and one which reflects the assumption that it is not the event alone which affects well-being. Rather, well-being is also affected by how the individual copes following exposure to a stressful event. In fact, this view has resulted in a paradigm shift in stress and coping theory. Consequently, research has shifted away from causal reductionism, which posits that stress is the primary cause of stress outcomes, to the use of models based on transactionism which views stress outcomes such as psychological distress as resulting from the interaction between events and appraisal and coping processes. Moreover, while social factors such as gender, race, and social identity influence exposure to stressful events, social factors and coping strategies can also protect individuals from the negative effects of stressful events on psychological well-being (Aldwin, 1994).

A common approach to investigating the effectiveness of coping strategies has been to examine whether psychological distress has been reduced. If it has, the coping strategies used are considered to be effective (Menaghan, 1983). While a framework for investigating stress and coping has thus been established, it has scarcely been investigated among the police. Given the negative implications of distressed officers for their department and the citizens whom they serve, this framework is worth investigating. It would be important to know whether the coping strategies that police officers use increase or decrease psychological distress, and to determine whether social factors differentially affect exposure to stressful events.

214

A REVIEW OF THE LITERATURE

The use of effective coping strategies and a strong social support system protect individuals from psychological distress by reducing or eliminating distress. Folkman and Lazarus (1988a) describe two ways in which this process occurs. First, by changing the stressful event which is the source of the distress (problem focused coping strategies), and/or second, by regulating the distress which arises as a result of experiencing the stressful event (emotion focused coping strategies). Individuals are more likely to use emotion-focused, coping strategies in response to unchangeable events. These strategies function to regulate the emotions which arise in response to the event or changed the individual's thoughts about the event. On the other hand, if the situation is appraised as changeable, problem-focused coping strategies that functioned to resolve the circumstances of the stressful event are more likely to be used (Folkman & Lazarus, 1980). Coping strategies can function in problem-focused and emotion-focused coping strategies simultaneously (Folkman & Lazarus, 1991) and individuals use both forms of coping to manage stressful events (Folkman & Lazarus, 1988a) .

Choice of coping strategy may also be influenced by personality and dispositional factors. For example, Kirmeyer and Diamond (1985) found Type A officers tended to use problem-focused strategies, regardless of whether the situation was appraised as changeable or unchangeable, although most appraised the stressful event as changeable. While most Type B officers appraised stressful events as changeable, Type As and Type Bs did not differ in their use of emotion-focused coping.

STRESSFUL OCCUPATIONAL EVENTS AMONG THE POLICE

Traumatic occupational events such as being shot in the line of duty or the shooting of a partner, are often ranked by officers, despite their infrequent occurrence, as the most stressful field events (Coman, 1987; Coman & Evans, 1991; Gudjonsson & Adlam, 1985; Sewell, 1983). Referring to traumatic events as "outside the range of the average human experience," McCafferty, Godofredo, and McCafferty (1990) drew comparison between police officers in large urban areas and military personnel. Both may be exposed to booby traps, snipers, and other physical and emotional dangers which may be common to military personnel are experienced by urban police officers as well. Other examples of traumatic events include a partner being critically injured or killed in the line of duty, exposure to abused or dead children, severe motor vehicle accidents and plane crashes, exposure to human body parts, and shooting another person. They argued that some officers do not develop posttraumatic stress disorder (PTSD) symptoms due to the geographic location of the police department, the extent and use of a social support system, and personality characteristics. Thus, exposure to traumatic events would also depend upon rank, assignment, and other social factors.

Routine tasks, such as shift work and excessive paperwork, are rated as highly stressful (Coman, 1987; Coman & Evans, 1991; Cooper, Davidson, & Robinson, 1982; Sewell, 1983). Patterson (1997) found that stressful organizational events were more highly correlated with psychological distress than were stressful field events. Furthermore, field events involving the potential for danger occurred less frequently than field events which threatened the officer's image or authority. While traumatic events have been shown to affect psychological well-being, it would be important to investigate the effects of exposure to routine and frequently occurring stressful events, and explore the relationship between the type of traumatic event and the coping strategy used.

COPING AMONG POLICE OFFICERS

The police stress literature has identified numerous coping strategies used by police officers to manage occupational stress. Aloofness, alcoholism, authoritarianism, cynicism, depersonalization, emotional detachment, and suspiciousness are all factors which have been identified as either coping strategies or personality characteristics that develop in police officers over the length of their careers (Bonifacio, 1991; Davidson & Veno, 1980; Kroes, 1985; Niederhoffer, 1967; Violanti & Marshall, 1983). Despite being used on the assumption that they will assist coping, these factors are rarely effective in helping officers manage stressful occupational events (Violanti, 1983; Violanti, Marshall, and Howe, 1985; Alexander and Walker, 1994). Furthermore, research has not clearly established whether these factors are coping strategies, personality traits, or in the case of alcoholism, a disease (Dishlacoff, 1976).

Taken together, this evidence supports calls for the systematic investigation of officers' coping strategies. While police coping studies have conceptualized and measured coping strategies in various ways, several significant patterns have emerge. First, maladaptive behaviors such as alcoholism and cynicism have been found to be ineffective and maladaptive as coping strategies among the police. Second, police officers tend to use more problem-focused coping strategies aimed at changing stressful occupational stressful events. Officers also use less emotion-focused coping strategies aimed at regulating their distress (Evans et al., 1993). Lastly, the use of emotion-focused coping strategies results in higher levels of psychological distress and the use of problem-focused coping strategies results in lower levels of psychological distress (Violanti, 1992).

THE PRESENT STUDY

Hypotheses

While most studies investigating police occupational stress have investigated how officers rate or rank occupational stressful events, this study first investigates the frequency of exposure to stressful events. Next, the appraisals which officers assign to these events, and finally coping strategies and levels of psychological distress are examined. It was hypothesized that officers would appraise stressful occupational events which originate within the organizational structure of the police department as unchangeable. It was also hypothesized that officers would use different coping strategies depending on social factors and socialization. Overall, it was expected that officers would report greater use of problem-focused coping strategies and less use of emotion-focused coping. Furthermore, greater use of problem-focused coping would be associated with lower levels of psychological distress while greater use of emotion-focused will be associated with higher levels of distress.

Methods

Sample

The present study makes use of a cross-sectional survey of a sample of 233 police officers from a mid-sized city located in the northeastern United States. The response rate was 67 percent. While a nonrandom convenience sample was used, participants were recruited from every unit of the police department and included officers who held both administrative and operational positions. Some 89 percent of the respondents were male, 11 percent female. Seventy-two percent are white, 15 percent African American, 8 percent Hispanic, 2 percent Asian American, and 1 percent Native American. Two percent of the respondents did not provide response for their race. Seventy-nine percent held operational positions and 18 percent held administrative positions. Three percent of the respondents did not provide a response for their rank. The average age of the sample was 37 years and the average length of police experience was 12 years.

Procedures

Officers in each of the police department units were approached during roll call periods. The supervisors of each unit were contacted by the researcher in advance and a day was arranged for the researcher to attend every roll call within the unit to request participants for the study. Officers were told that the study was concerned with stress and coping among police officers and that their participation was voluntary and that the data were for research purposes unrelated to departmental business.

Measures

A Police Stress and Coping Questionnaire (PSCQ) was developed for use in this study. The PSCQ consists of an occupational stress checklist including both routine organizational and routine field events, an appraisal item assessing whether the event was either a changeable or unchangeable situation, the Ways of Coping Questionnaire (Folkman and Lazarus, 1988b), items measuring psychological well-being, and the last section of the questionnaire asked demographic information.

Stress

Stress and stressful events are conceptualized according to Lazarus and Folkman (1984) as "a relationship between the person and the environment that is appraised by the person as taxing or exceeding his or her resources and endangering his or her well-being" (p. 21). Participants were asked to indicate whether or not a particular occupational or personal stressful event occurred within the past 6 months, and, if an event did occur, to rate the event on a 3-point scale ranging from (1) "not stressful" to (3) "very stressful." Examples of field events include: involvement in a high-speed car chase, situations requiring the use of force, handling domestic disputes, and child abuse/neglect situations. Examples of organizational events include: lack of say about departmental policies and procedures, inadequate supervision, conflict with a supervisor, insufficient personnel, and inadequate equipment. The alpha reliability for the field events scale is .83, and for the organizational events scale, it is .65.

Secondary Appraisal

Secondary appraisal is conceptualized as the process an individual uses to assess whether something either can or cannot be done to change the stressful event. This process occurs after exposure to a stressful event. During this process, an individual attempts to determine what impact the stressful event has for their psychological or physical well-being. More importantly, outcomes of psychological well-being, such as psychological distress, depend on the individual's appraisal of the event (Lazarus & Folkman, 1984). Participants selected a single item from the stressful occupational events checklist, designated this event as their most stressful event, and then rated the stressful event as either changeable or unchangeable by answering the following question: was the event one that "you could change or do something about" (Lazarus & Folkman, 1984). This item was measured using a binary scale of (1) "yes" or (2) "no."

Coping

Coping is conceptualized as "constantly changing cognitive and behavioral efforts to manage specific external and/or internal demands that are appraised as taxing or exceeding the resources of the person" (Lazarus & Folkman, 1984, p. 141). Coping was measured using the Ways of Coping Questionnaire developed by Folkman and Lazarus (1988b). The questionnaire contains 66 items and the response format is a 4-point Likert Scale ranging from (0) "does not apply or not used" to (3) "used a great deal." Examples include "I came up with a couple of different solutions to the problem" and "I wished the situation would go away or somehow be over with." The alpha reliability for the emotion-focused coping scale is .87. The alpha reliability for the problem-focused coping scale is .79, and for the social support scale, it is .67.

Psychological Distress

Mirowsky and Ross (1989) conceptualized psychological distress as "unpleasant subjective states of depression and anxiety" (p. 7). Psychological distress was measured using some items from the Center for Epidemiological Studies' Depression Scale (CES-D; Radloff, 1977) and some from the Langner index (1962). Respondents were asked to indicate how often they had been "bothered or troubled" by 15-items indicating psychological distress during the past 6 months. They were asked to rate items on a scale ranging from (1) "never" to (4) "frequently." Examples include: "I had periods of time when I could not get going" and "I had nightmares." A total of 15 items comprised the psychological distress scale. It has an alpha reliability of .90.

Strategy of Analysis

Hypotheses were tested using multiple regression analysis. First, in separate analyses, the effects of education, gender, marital status, race, rank, and the number of years of police experience on psychological distress were examined. Next, these variables were regressed on emotion-focused, problem-focused, and social support coping strategies in order to determine their effects on the use of the 3 coping strategies.

RESULTS

From table 17.1, officers were more likely to choose an organizational event as the single most meaningful event from a list of both field and organizational events. Traumatic events and field events involving dangerous situations or the potential for danger were appraised as less meaningful for officers. The data presented in table 17.2 demonstrate that the majority of officers in each social category appraised their most meaningful stressful occupational events as unchangeable. Rank is associated with the greatest percentage of officers appraising that a stressful occupational event is unchangeable with lieutenants and captains more likely to appraise events as unchangeable. Gender was associated with the lowest appraisals that events were unchangeable with females less likely to appraise events as unchangeable.

The results of four separate multiple regression equations are presented in Table 17.3. Each equation contained the independent variables education, marital status, police experience, race, rank, and sex. The independent vari-

Table 17.1.
Occupational events appraised as meaningful during a 6-month period.

Occupational event	Percent
Insufficient personnel to handle all the calls for service	17.6
Working with an incompetent co-worker	6.8
Inadequate process of decision-making	6.3
Conflict with supervisor(s)	5.9
Lack or respect for police authority	5.9
Exposed to a negative image of police by the media	5.0
Child abuse/neglect	5.0
Lack of say about departmental policies	4.5
Inadequate supervision	4.1
Inadequate equipment	4.1

Table 17.2.
Percentage appraising that a stressful occupational event is changeable/unchangeable.

	Changeable	*Unchangeable*
Age		
20-30 years	25.0	75.0
31-40 years	17.4	82.6
41-50 years	22.7	77.3
51-60 years	20.0	80.0
Education		
H.S. Graduate	21.7	78.3
Associates	22.5	77.5
B.S/B.A	20.0	80.0
M.S/M.A.	28.6	71.4
Years Experience as Police Officer		
0-5 years	23.5	76.5
6-13 years	20.2	77.8
14-20 years	21.2	78.8
20 years or more	28.6	71.4
Sex		
Male	21.5	78.5
Female	28.6	71.4
Race		
white	22.4	77.6
Non-white	18.5	81.5
Rank		
Patrol	21.2	78.8
Investigator	11.1	88.9
Sergeant	38.0	62.0
Lieutenant/Captain	9.0	91.0

ables were separately regressed on the dependent variables: psychological distress, emotion-focused coping, problem-focused coping, and social support. The unstandardized regression coefficients, standard errors, constant, and adjusted $R2$ value for each equation are presented in the table. As indicated in the table, higher rank is associated with greater levels of psychological distress. Higher rank also resulted in less use of emotion-focused coping strategies. Higher education resulted in greater use of emotion-focused, problem-focused, and social support coping strategies. Finally, years of police experience resulted in greater use of emotion-focused coping strategies.

Table 17.3.
The effects of demographic factors on levels of psychological distress, and the use of
emotion-focused, problem-focused, and social support coping strategies
(unstandardized coefficients and s.d.).

Independent Variable	Psychological Distress	Emotion-Focused Coping	Problem-Focused Coping	Social Support
Education	.01	1.9**	.99*	.66**
	(.77)	(.65)	(.56)	(.28)
Marital Status	1.4	.92	1.1	.56
(0=Married,	(1.4)	(1.2)	(1.0)	(.52)
1=Non-Married)				
Police Experience	-.07	1.4**	.41	.26
(years)	(.77)	(.65)	(.55)	(.28)
Police Rank	1.3*	-1.4**	.76	.07
	(.76)	(.65)	(.55)	(.28)
Race	-1.2	1.6	-.01	-.13
(0=white,	(.1.5)	(1.2)	(1.1)	(.53)
1=non-white)				
Sex	-.90	-1.5	-.82	.62
(0=Male,	(2.1)	(1.7)	(1.5)	(.75)
1=Female)				
Constant	30.82	-5.97	-4.50	-2.40
Adjusted R²	- 0.00	.04	0.01	0.01

* $p < .10$, **$p < .05$, ***$p < .001$

As indicated in Table 17.4, exposure to stressful organizational events resulted in higher levels of psychological distress, such that the greater the number of events, the greater the distress. While exposure to a greater number of field events also resulted in higher levels of distress, this relationship was not significant. From Table 17.5, it is evident that greater use of emotion-focused coping results in higher levels of psychological distress. Greater use of social support also results in higher levels of distress. While greater use of problem-focused coping results in lower levels of psychological distress, this relationship is not significant.

Table 17.4.
The effects of stressful occupational events on levels of psychological distress
(unstandardized coefficients and s.d.).

Independent variable	Distress
Number of organizational events	1.3***
	(.24)
Number of field events	.04
	(.15)
Constant	32.62
Adjusted R^2	0.12

* p <.10, **p<.05, *** p<.001

Table 17.5.
The effects of coping strategies on levels of psychological distress
(unstandardized coefficients and s.d.).

Independent variable	Distress
Emotion-focused coping	.21**
	(.09)
Problem-focused coping	-.01
	(.12)
Social support	.36*
	(.22)
Constant	32.64
Adjusted R^2	0.06

* p <.10, ** p<.05, *** p<.001

CONCLUSION

The data show that in general, officers were more likely to appraise stressful occupational events as unchangeable. The majority of officers chose an organizational event as the most meaningful occupational event that occurred within the last 6 months. This was true for officers regardless of age, education, years of police experience, sex, race, and rank.

Theoretically, if stressful events are appraised as unchangeable, we should observe greater use of emotion-focused coping strategies associated with lower levels of distress. The present data show that both emotion-focused and social support coping strategies resulted in higher levels of distress. While the use of problem-focused strategies did result in lower levels of distress as theoretically predicted, this relationship was not significant.

When officers appropriately used emotion-focused coping in responses to unchangeable events to regulate the effects of distress, the coping strategies appear to be ineffective. Because numerous subscales of coping are contained within the emotion-focused and problem-focused categories, these results may in part be due to the fact that the broad categories were used.

The data also show that levels of distress and use of coping strategies among the police varies according to social characteristics. This suggests that it is important to investigate both occupational stress and coping among the police in relationship to social categories since police officers as an occupational groups do not all experience these events in similar ways.

Finally, appropriate coping strategies can be learned and perhaps unlearned as methods for managing stressful occupational events. Since high levels of distress can be psychologically and physically harmful to officers, learning effective and appropriate strategies will benefit both the officer and the community. Perhaps the coping strategies which officers use to manage their routine stressful events are also used to manage infrequently occurring events. More research is needed to determine whether police officers use the same type of coping strategies to manage traumatic stress that they use to manage routine occupational stressors.

REFERENCES

Aldwin, C. M.: *Stress, coping, and development: An integrative perspective.* New York, Guilford, 1994.

Alexander, D. A., & Walker, L. G.: A study of methods used by Scottish police officers to cope with work-induced stress. *Stress Medicine, 10:* 131-138, 1994.

Bonifacio, P.: *The psychological effects of police work.* New York, Plenum, 1991.

Carter, D., & Stephens, D.: *Drug abuse by police officers: An analysis of critical policy issues.* Springfield, IL, Charles C. Thomas, 1988.

Coman, G. J.: *An analysis of factors in the resignation of Australian Federal Police Personnel.* Unpublished postgraduate thesis, Chisholm Institute of Technology, Melbourne, 1987.

Coman, G. J., & Evans, B. J.: Stressors facing Australian police in the 1990s. *Police Studies, 14:*153-165, 1991.

Cooper, C. L.; Davidson, M. J., & Robinson, P.: Stress in the police service. *Journal of Occupational Medicine, 24:* 30-36, 1982.

Davidson, M. J., & Veno, A.: Stress and the policeman. In C. L. Cooper & J. Marshall (Eds.), *White collar and professional stress.* New York, John Wiley, 1980.

Dishlacoff, L.: The drinking cop. *The Police Chief, 43:* 32-39, 1976.

Evans, B. J.; Coman, G.; Stanley, R. O.,& Burrows, G. D.: Police officers' coping strategies: An Australian police survey. *Stress Medicine, 9:* 237-246, 1993.

Folkman, S., & Lazarus, R. S.: An analysis of coping in a middle-aged community sample. *Journal of Health and Social Behavior, 21:* 219-239, 1980.

Folkman, S., & Lazarus, R. S.: The relationship between coping and emotion: Implications for theory and research. *Social Science Medicine, 26:* 309-317, 1988.

Folkman, S., & Lazarus, R. S.: *Ways of coping questionnaire: Permissions set.* Palo Alto, CA, Consulting Psychologists Press, 1988.

Folkman, S., & Lazarus, R. S.: Coping and Emotion. In A. Monat, & R. S. Lazarus (Eds.), *Stress and coping: An anthology.* New York, Columbia University Press, 1991.

Gudjonsson, G. H., & Adlam, K. R.: Occupational stressors among British police officers. *The Police Journal, 58:* 73-80, 1985.

Kirmeyer, S. L., & Diamond, A.: Coping by police officers: A study of role stress and Type A and Type B behavior patterns. *Journal of Occupational Behavior, 6:* 183-195, 1985.

Kroes, W. H.: *Society's victims: The police* (2nd ed.). Springfield, IL, Charles C. Thomas, 1985.

Langner, T. S.: A twenty-two item screening score of psychiatric symptoms indicating impairment. *Journal of Health and Social Behavior, 3:* 269-276, 1962.

Lazarus, R. S., & Folkman, S.: *Stress, appraisal, and coping.* New York, Springer, 1984.

Lazarus, R. A., & Folkman, S.: *Stress, appraisal, and coping.* New York, Springer, 1984.

McCafferty, F. L.; Godofredo, D. D., & McCafferty, E. A.: Posttraumatic stress disorder in the police officer: Paradigm of occupational stress. *Southern Medical Journal, 83:* 543-547, 1990.

Menaghan, E. G.: Individual coping efforts: Moderators of the relationship between life stress and mental health outcomes. In H. B. Kaplan (Ed.), *Psychosocial stress: Trends in theory and research.* New York, Academic, 1983.

Mirowsky, J., & Ross, C. E.: Social causes of psychological distress. Hawthorne, NY, Aldine de Gruyter, 1989.

Niederhoffer, A.: *Behind the shield.* Garden City, NY, Doubleday, 1967.

Patterson, G. T.: *The effects of social factors, socialization, and coping on psychological distress among police officers.* Unpublished doctoral dissertation, State University of New York, University at Buffalo, 1997.

Radloff, L. S.: The CES-D scale: A self report depression scale for research in the general population. *Applied Psychological Measurement, 1:* 385-401, 1977.

Sewell, J. D.: The development of a critical life events scale for law enforcement. *Journal of Police Science and Administration, 11:* 109-116, 1983.

Violanti, J. M.: Stress patterns in police work: A longitudinal study. *Journal of Police Science and Administration, 11:* 211-216, 1983.

Violanti, J. M.: Coping strategies among police recruits in a high-stress training environment. *The Journal of Social Psychology, 132:* 717-729, 1992.

Violanti, J. M., & Marshall, J. R.: The police stress process. *Journal of Police Science and Administration, 11*: 389-394, 1983.
Violanti, J. M.; Marshall, J. R., & Howe, B.: Stress, coping, and alcohol use: The police connection. *Journal of Police Science and Administration, 13*: 106-110, 1985.

Chapter 18

FINDING MEANING IN POLICE TRAUMAS

INGRID V. E. CARLIER

INTRODUCTION

This chapter begins by reviewing the occupational hazards that police officers face as regards psychological traumas. A distinction can be drawn between the relatively high risk of traumatic experience in police work, and the relatively low risk of related psychopathology, such as post-traumatic stress disorder (PTSD). Next I will examine in greater detail how police officers cope with traumatic stress, with particular emphasis on how, as a step towards accepting their experience, they find meaning for their traumatic experiences. I will conclude by explaining how the process of giving meaning to trauma is used in the professional treatment of PTSD in police officers.

TRAUMA EXPERIENCED BY POLICE OFFICERS

People in trauma-sensitive occupations can regard traumatic experiences encountered in the course of their work, as well as their associated psychological after-effects, as occupational hazards. Of all the high-risk occupations, police work is probably the most trauma-sensitive. That is because police officers are frequently confronted with very sad as well as very violent incidents (Carlier & Gersons, 1992; Carlier, Lambert, & Gersons, 1994). The sad (or depressing) events include natural disasters and other calamities, confrontations with sexually abused children or adults, failures to save lives, and suicides by colleagues. Violent events include shooting incidents, escalating riots, hostage situations, and other situations of threatened or actual brutal violence. People in other trauma-sensitive occupations tend to have traumatic work experiences less often, and these are usually confined to one of the two categories. Firefighters, for instance, almost only experience depressing events such as seeing victims badly burned or killed in a fire.

227

Bank tellers and taxi drivers almost only face violent events such as rob-
beries, sometimes combined with hostage-takings. Public transport or prison
workers may be subject to both types of events, but less frequently than
police officers.

In the present context, the term "trauma-sensitive" carries no implications of extreme psychopathology or emotional instability in the members of
these professions. It simply means there is a greater risk of their experiencing traumatic events at work. In view of this risk status, it is a wonder that
the percentage of police officers with a severe disorder, in this case PTSD,
should be as low as 7 percent (Carlier, Lamberts, & Gersons, in press;
Marmar et al., 1996). After all, an estimated 9 percent of the general public
is affected by PTSD (Breslau, Davis, Andreski, & Peterson, 1991; Norris,
1992; Resnick et al., 1993; Kessler et al., 1995). This difference can be attributed to the operation of factors such as education, training, selection, and
self-selection which probably play an important preventative role with
respect to the development of psychopathology in police officers.

Despite the horrific or threatening nature of traumatic incidents, by no
means all of them are perceived by experienced police officers as emotionally intense. For PTSD or other trauma-related psychopathology to develop,
potent emotions such as fear, rage, disgust, or grief must have been evoked
by the traumatic event. Such emotions arise out of the meaning that a subject attributes to the traumatic experience. How a police officer interprets
the event is crucial to the issue of attributing meaning. I shall return to this
theme at length when I deal with coping with trauma and the treatment of
PTSD.

A traumatic event is usually not the sole cause of PTSD. The risk of
PTSD is generally governed by a combination of personal and environmental factors (Davidson & Foa, 1993; Carlier et al., in press). Such a risk model
goes a long way towards explaining why two police officers can experience
the same traumatic incident, with one of them developing PTSD and the
other not. More specific examples of personal PTSD risk factors among
police officers include social introversion, excessive difficulty in expressing
emotions, lack of an outlet to vent feelings outside work, and lack of hobbies.
Environmental risk factors include inadequate social support networks, emotional exhaustion at the time of the traumatic event, and prior experience of
traumatic incidents. Certain PTSD risk factors, such as insufficient time
allowed for coping with traumatic incidents, dissatisfaction with the support
provided, uncertain career prospects, and discontent and brooding about
work, can also be present within the work situation of police officers. The
latter two factors, in particular, are key targets in the prevention of PTSD in
police officers.

CONSEQUENCES OF POLICE TRAUMA

The ways that traumas can affect the police force are wide-ranging. To begin with, there are the effects on the traumatized officers themselves. Immediately after a traumatic experience, officers tend to exhibit a cluster of characteristic reactions as part of a natural coping process. Among these are shock, nightmares, irritability, concentration problems, emotional instability, and physical symptoms. Such stress reactions are manifestations of a usually temporary disturbance in their balance, which they have to try to restore. In most cases it takes them several weeks and sometimes several months to regain their emotional equilibrium. With support from those around them, most people manage to come to terms with the traumatic event and get on with their lives and careers. As part of this process, they give the traumatic experience a meaning and accept it as part of their lives. For example, the knowledge of having successfully dealt with a life-threatening situation at work could boost their self-confidence. Or it might prompt them to finally go off on that dream vacation. Religious aspects can also play an important part in giving meaning to a traumatic experience (Scurfield, 1994).

As I have noted above, it is only in a minority of cases that this coping process stagnates. A blocked coping process manifests itself in persistent, intensive, and unmanageable stress complaints that can come to completely dominate a person's life. Such is the case, for example, with PTSD (Carlier, Fouwells, Lamberts, & Gersons, 1996; Carlier & Gersons ,1995, 1997). Despite all their efforts to bypass any reminder of it through avoidance mechanisms, police officers with PTSD have the traumatic event on their mind day and night. They are constantly on edge and perceive danger at every turn, of unexpected violence, of escalations, of confrontations with mutilated victims. Traumatic stress reactions, including PTSD, can radically change them, making them more fearful, aggressive, indifferent, depressed, distracted, or self-absorbed than they were before the traumatic event. Clearly these changes affect the quality of their lives. In extreme cases, officers might even conclude that life is futile and not worth living. This is the main reason why it is crucial to provide adequate information about effective treatment for police officers, and others, who are traumatized, and to detect PTSD early. Effective treatment can help people with simple PTSD to enjoy their lives and their work again within a reasonably short time. After successful treatment, they can finally relegate the traumatic event to its proper place in their life history, in the sense of having "gained" an experience. This might seem paradoxical in view of the horror of the experience, but it is nonetheless essential if one is to find meaning in the traumatic event and accept it. One must, as it were, put a positive twist on something negative, for instance by learning something from it. How this attribution of meaning is achieved will be explained below when I discuss the treatment of PTSD.

Quite often, PTSD has a detrimental effect on police officers' private lives as well. Relationships with spouses and children often suffer severe blows, even leading to divorce or serious child-raising problems. For this and other reasons, it is wise to invite officers' partners or other significant persons in their lives to attend some of the treatment sessions, thus getting them involved in the treatment. Close relationships can be of vital importance in finding meaning for the traumatic experience.

Apart from the effects on officers and their loved ones, there may also be ramifications at work (Carlier & Gersons, 1994). PTSD can cause officers to react less alertly and less appropriately, have trouble interacting with other people, take too many or too few risks at work, or have persistent concentration problems. In other words, PTSD can result in unsafe situations for the officers themselves and for the colleagues they work with, as well as in complaints from members of the public, low individual productivity, absenteeism, and ultimately even disablement. In certain cases, in consultation with their superiors, it might be wise for police officers with PTSD to be given a temporary desk job on therapeutic grounds. Dutch labor legislation, which stipulates that employers bear responsibility for the safety, welfare, and health of their personnel, allows for alternate employment options and for professional treatment.

CONSTRUCTING MEANING IN THE TREATMENT OF POLICE OFFICERS WITH PTSD

This section examines how meaning can be constructed during the treatment of PTSD in police officers. A short description of the treatment is followed by a more detailed discussion of the therapeutic process of finding meaning.

A randomized, controlled study among police officers has recently demonstrated the efficacy of an individual psychotherapeutic treatment protocol for PTSD (Carlier & Gersons, 1994). The therapeutic effect was assessed on the basis of the resolution of PTSD, the return to or reintegration in the work environment, and the stabilization of the police officer's home situation. The effectiveness of the treatment was not influenced by the number of traumas or by the point in time when they occurred. The treatment consists of sixteen sessions, normally held weekly. A necessary condition for the treatment is a good working relationship between the client and the therapist, which is more easily achieved when the therapist is thoroughly familiar with police work.

The objective of the treatment is to enable the client to adequately come to terms with his/her hitherto repressed thoughts, feelings, and memories about the event (Gersons & Carlier, 1997). As noted above, giving a meaning to the trauma plays a crucial role in enabling a person to deal with it. The construction of meaning proceeds in five steps: (1) creating a frame of reference for the symptoms, (2) working through the feelings that were avoided, (3) existential questions and insight, (4) personal growth, and (5) acceptance and farewell ritual. These five steps are elaborated upon below.

1. Frame of Reference for the Symptoms (Treatment Session 1 with Partner)

The first step in giving meaning to the traumatic experience entails learning to understand the why of the psychological complaints and the how of the treatment, in other words how the treatment is to address the symptoms. This is also known as psychoeducation. Basically this means the client is offered a frame of reference to help him/her understand his/her complaints. His/her partner, or another significant person, is invited to attend the first session.

At the start of the treatment, the client is told how his/her symptoms are connected to the traumatic event. Clients often have never thought nor heard of any relationship between their symptoms and traumatic experiences. It is important to explain both how PTSD symptoms can be brought on by a traumatic experience and how they can influence the client's functioning. He/she is told that the main focus will be on the following issues:
- The client acts as if the traumatic event or events can occur again at any time (a constant feeling of danger lurking).
- The PTSD symptoms keep recurring because extreme, and therefore frightening, emotions linked to the life-threatening experience are being repressed, and thus are obstructing the resolution of the symptoms.
- Relaxation exercises, combined with a gradual journey back into the client's mind to the traumatic memories (by means of imaginary guidance or exposure), allow him/her to feel and express his/her intense emotions.
- Writing down the traumatic experience and using mementos (things that remind the client of the event) can be helpful.
- After the client has reexperienced the emotions linked to the trauma, he must describe how he now sees the world and him/herself and how he is going to adjust to that world.
- It is often extremely difficult for people with PTSD to leave the traumatic experience behind them, assigning it a place in their personal life history. However, this is crucial for giving meaning to the trau-

ma. A farewell ritual at the end of the treatment is a useful way to achieve this.

To someone plagued by PTSD symptoms, these essentially symbolize a terrifying loss of control over their own thoughts (involuntary reexperiencing, catastrophic fantasies, or flashbacks of the traumatic event), over their own feelings (emotional volatility and inability to hold back tears), and over their own behavior (sudden anxiety about performing certain activities, unanticipated fits of rage). Such a loss of control can be extremely disconcerting and disheartening for a police officer, since it is usually so contrary to his/her original self-image and expectations. He or she might mistakenly jump to the conclusion that he/she is unfit to be a policeman or, even worse, has failed as a human being.

Once a frame of reference is provided for the PTSD symptoms at the first treatment session, this makes the officer aware that PTSD is an occupational hazard that even healthy, stable people can come up against. The sense of relief engendered by this fresh view of things opens the way for the hope and courage to regain control. The process starts by working through all the emotions associated with the trauma.

2. Working Through Emotions Hitherto Avoided (Treatment Sessions 2 to 6)

A second step in the process of finding meaning is based on the fact that insight (see Stage 3 and further) must always be preceded by a catharsis of emotions that have not yet been felt. It is abundantly clear by now that simply talking about feelings sometimes just serves to repress them. It is essential to bring to the surface the intense emotions of rage, guilt, concern, and grief that the client has not yet fully felt (if he has even felt them at all). The important thing is to finally give in to the feelings he/she has so stubbornly been avoiding.

The chronological and moment-to-moment reliving of the entire traumatic experience by means of imaginary guidance usually requires four to six sessions. If the client has had more than one traumatic experience, he/she will usually choose the most prominent of them, which is referred to as the "core" traumatic experience. The others can generally be left aside, since the main purpose of the treatment is to uncover and reexperience the most extreme emotions, such as fear.

First a short relaxation exercise is performed. As soon as the client indicates he/she is sufficiently relaxed, the therapist asks him/her to go back gradually in their mind to the traumatic experience, helping him/her with a few suggestions. For example: "What is the first thing you remember about that day? What kind of weather is it? What are you wearing? What exactly is happening? What do you feel? What do you see? What do you hear?" This helps to evoke memories of the day the trauma took place. The technique allows the client to feel how frightening and shocking the experience was by making him/her reexperience every last detail of it. That is why it is not the therapist who describes the traumatic event, but the client. The client gives as exact a description as possible of what he/she sees, hears, feels, and experiences. This makes recalling the trauma a painstaking process, which occupies only fifteen to twenty minutes of each session. The therapist encourages the client to recount the experience as animatedly and graphically as possible, concentrating on sensations such as fear, confusion, pain, rage, and grief. The client will usually recall new details that are charged with extreme fear or pain, and discover feelings that have not surfaced before. It is important for the therapist to listen carefully to the client, supporting him/her as he/she relives his/her oppressive, terrifying emotions and not interfering with or curbing these emotions. Interpretations should not yet be formulated at this stage.

As additional aids in activating the memories of the traumatic event and the feelings associated with it, two techniques can be used: mementos and writing assignments. Mementos are objects that bear a concrete or symbolic link to the traumatic event, such as the clothing the client was wearing at the time, newspaper articles and photographs, objects such as a gun. Some mementos can be used for the farewell ritual at the close of the treatment (see Stage 5).

Writing assignments can also be helpful in uncovering extreme emotions, but they are prepared outside the sessions. It is good for the client also to be actively involved with the treatment outside the sessions, and to feel emotions without having the therapist nearby. Writing assignments are not only designed to record the traumatic experience. This technique is explicitly intended to evoke feelings of rage, for example towards certain individuals or organizations linked in some way to the trauma. That is why the writing assignment is often referred to as an "ongoing letter" in which difficult or aggressive feelings can be expressed. But it is a letter that will never be sent, so there is no need to censor its contents. It is meant to be destroyed along with other mementos in the farewell ritual. It makes it possible to express aggressive emotions in a controlled fashion. Clients are advised to purchase something special for the writing assignment, such as a small notebook, and to write practically every day for half an hour, always in the same place and at the same quiet moment. Sensations of rage, grief, and guilt often surface in the process.

3. Existential Questions and Insights
(Treatment Sessions 7 to 9, with Partner at 9th Session)

After the difficult emotions have been released, most of the PTSD symptoms will remit, and the client will realize for the first time that his/her life has been drastically altered. This is the third step in the process of finding meaning. No matter how well informed many people are about traumas, people who have not experienced one first hand are still apt to view their own lives as reasonably stable, predictable, and manageable. Experiencing a traumatic event confronts a person with his/her own vulnerability and helplessness, and with the often extreme and terrifying sides of human behavior. They can develop a deep distrust in humanity. After these intense, frightful emotions have been released and experienced in therapy, the clients may go on to ask themselves certain fundamental existential questions. They will talk about how they see the world, themselves, their family, their work (their "view of the world"). They must now specify the extent to which, and in what sense, the traumatic experience has changed their life and influenced how they look at the world, themselves, and others.

Sometimes a link can be drawn between the traumatic experience and the client's personal life history. The client now begins to perceive the trauma as part of his/her life and to liberate him/herself from the feelings, thoughts, and acts that were geared to avoiding it (e.g., steering clear of places that remind him/her of it, or detached emotions). If relevant, the therapist can draw a connection between this traumatic experience and earlier traumas in the client's life. For example, a police officer might have felt abandoned by the police force after being wounded in a shooting incident (e.g., no support from his/her superiors). Or it could be clear from his/her biography that the client had an extremely authoritarian father, who also failed to support him/her. This client-parent link can be drawn if the client seems to be searching for this type of explanation. As part of the treatment, attention is also devoted to matters related to everyday life, such as returning to work or problems with insurance. It is important to avoid dependence and to spend time testing the client's sense of reality and ability to take responsibility. Practical ramifications of the trauma also need to be discussed, such as resuming work, how other people will react, how the client will talk about the treatment, and any fear they have of being stigmatized because of the treatment.

4. Personal Growth (Treatment Sessions 10 to 12)

The purpose of these sessions is to devote more attention to the aftermath of the traumatic event. How has it affected the client's life? What has he/she learned from it? Has he/she benefited from it in any way? This is the fourth step in the process of finding meaning. Relevant themes and emotions in the individual case of the client should be pinpointed, such as his/her feelings of anger, grief, and powerlessness, or his/her loss of trust in the goodness of their fellow human beings. The client is also given an opportunity to vent his/her "negative" emotions and understand them better. The therapist provides ample leeway for this. Then the therapist shifts the focus to the "positive" side of having experienced a trauma, if the client is able to perceive that as existing. This positive aspect can vary from a feeling that the traumatic experience has somehow fostered a new attitude towards life, to a resolution to seize the day, or do more to help others. Not forgetting the traumatic experience can perhaps be defined as a healthy sign, an expression of inner strength and courage. The client can see the treatment as a way to develop a stronger personality. One police officer learned from his/her traumatic experience what the most important thing was in his/her life: his/her family. What matters in this stage is that, after the catharsis of emotions, the client feels better than before and begins to appreciate life and love more. This often serves as the basis for a new start at work or in some other activity.

5. Acceptance and Farewell Ritual
(Treatment Sessions 13 to 16, with Partner at Final Session)

The treatment is closed with a farewell ritual. As the therapist explains to the client, and his/her partner, the purpose of the ritual is to accept the traumatic experience and say farewell to it. This is the last step in the process of finding meaning. The idea is not to forget the experience altogether, but to give it a place in the client's personal life history. At the first stage of the treatment, the therapist explained that the client's behavior was still being shaped by past events, that he/she was standing with his/her back to the future as it were. At the farewell ritual, the time has come to face the future with new energy.

The technique used for the farewell ritual is as follows. First the client has to decide whether or not he/she wants to perform a farewell ritual. It is good to explain to the client at this point how the ritual is usually performed. There are people who, under safe conditions, burn letters, clothing or drawings in their garden, out in the country or at home, or throw them into the sea. It is important for the client to decide for themselves, together with their partner or another significant person, about what approach to choose. The decision about when to perform the ritual is also made by the client. Only when he/she feels the traumatic experience is a thing of the past has the time come to unambiguously express this feeling in a farewell ritual. It is the last time the feelings of grief and aggression are expressed, this time in the presence of someone who plays an important part in his/her life. This act represents the return to normal life. The farewell ritual is closed with a symbolic gesture of moving on, for example taking a shower or celebrating with a dinner or a walk on the beach or in the woods with a loved one.

Psychoeducation also plays a role in this final stage of treatment, but in a different way than at the start. The client is now asked how he looks back at the relationship between the trauma and the symptoms. He/she is told that the PTSD symptoms can come back if he/she is faced again with events or situations where he/she is vulnerable. The therapist also discusses with the client what he/she has learned from the treatment and how he/she can apply this knowledge in other situations in the future.

CONCLUSION

Most police officers cope with traumatic experiences on their own, often with the support of the people around them. Sometimes they learn from the experience and undergo positive changes. For example, they may decide to worry less about the future. In this way, they "inscribe" and integrate the traumatic experience into their life history. This is part of the process by which they give meaning to their traumatic experience.

For a minority of traumatized police officers, however, the natural coping process stagnates and they develop symptoms of PTSD. Professional treatment is called for in such cases. Basically the treatment can be viewed as a structured process of constructing meaning (see also Clarke, 1993), which consists of five main components. This is illustrated in the followed diagram.

Figure 18.1.
Finding meaning in trauma in the treatment of PTSD.

Stage 1: Frame of reference for the symptoms

Stage 2: Working through emotions hitherto avoided

Stage 3: Existential questions and insights

Stage 4: Personal growth

Stage 5: Acceptance and farewell ritual

The foundation for the search for meaning is laid by creating a theoretical framework in which the client learns to understand his/her symptoms in relation to their traumatic experience. This specification and explanation of the PTSD symptoms, also called "framing," is done by way of psychoeducation (see Stage 1, Figure 18.1). The client can then begin to emotionally work through the traumatic experience. This involves bringing to the surface, in a gradual and carefully controlled manner, the intense emotions attached to the traumatic experience which have been avoided up to now. The catharsis of emotions is central at this stage, and interpretations should not yet be given (Stage 2). After the pent-up emotions have been released, most of the PTSD symptoms will disappear. This is the moment when the client will be open to insightful interpretations, for example, interpretations of his/her reactions to the traumatic event in relation to his/her life history, or his/her altered view of the world. Some fundamental questions may be raised. "Why did this have to happen to me? Who can I still trust? How can I ever feel safe again? Am I fit to do police work? How can I live with the idea that I needed therapy?" (Stage 3) At the fourth stage of the process, the client consciously considers what he/she has learned from his/her traumatic experience, and whether this exploration of meaning has resulted in personal growth. This implies an explicit pursuit of positive aspects of the traumatic experience (Stage 4). The final stage in the process entails the acceptance of the traumatic experience, symbolized in a farewell ritual. With this, the client puts the traumatic experience behind him/her for good, and takes an active step into the future (Stage 5).

The recognition of positive aspects of the traumatic experience as part of the search for meaning is crucial to the resolution of PTSD (Scurfield, 1994; Egendorf, 1982, 1985; Card, 1983; Hendin & Haas, 1984; Lifton, 1979; Lyons, 1991; Sorenson, 1988). It is therefore surprising that so little research has been devoted to this process. One important study is that by Draucker (1992), who viewed the pursuit of positive aspects of the traumatic experience as an internal coping strategy. She conducted a study among a relatively large group of traumatized people who were currently in treatment. Her results showed that the positive aspects of a traumatic experience could be expressed in four possible themes or "benefits" (see also Stage 4, figure 18.1): (a) altruism, (b) guilt and forgiveness, (c) strength and survival, and (d) self-knowledge. The most frequently reported "benefit" was a more altruistic attitude to life, varying from showing more understanding for other people to being more helpful (see also Gelinas, 1983).

This helpfulness was also evident in police officers who wanted to give their fellow officers a chance to benefit from their learning experience after their trauma treatment, for example, by giving an interview in the police force magazine or becoming a counselor for their colleagues. Draucker's respondents cited the issue of guilt and forgiveness as a second benefit of the traumatic experience (see also Taylor, 1983). In the trauma treatment described here, this is addressed at the first session, when clients are offered a frame of reference for their symptoms. They are informed that PTSD can be seen as an occupational hazard. That helps reduce their guilt feelings, and it can also enable them to more or less forgive the aggressor who was to blame for the traumatic incident. This opens the way for coping and acceptance on the part of the police officer. The third benefit cited in Draucker's study involved discovering or rediscovering one's own strength and survival instinct (see also Andreasen & Norris, 1972; Janoff-Bulman & Wortman ,1977; Silver et al., 1983). This was illustrated by statements like "I had the inner strength to survive that nightmare." A traumatic experience often means a person is left completely to their own resources. If they get through it all right, that can enhance their sense of independence, autonomy, and self-reliance. The fourth and least frequently mentioned benefit of a traumatic experience involved gaining more self-knowledge (see also Schulz & Decker, 1985; Taylor, 1983). In particular, clients who formerly had trouble expressing their feelings had learned in the course of the treatment to better appreciate and understand their own emotions and to be less apprehensive about them.

The most shocking, and very crucial, part of a traumatic experience involves realizing how vulnerable you and your loved ones are. It might occur to a police officer now and then that his/her colleagues could get hurt or develop PTSD, but he/she thinks the chance is negligible that they will be the victim. Thus, if it does happen, they start doubting themselves and indeed the whole world. If police officers were constantly occupied with their own physical and emotional vulnerability, they would not be able to do their jobs. Fear and tension would dominate their lives. The much talked of "macho" aspect of the police is unjustly seen as a purely negative phenomenon. A macho mentality is a handicap if it causes officers to bottle up their emotions and not confront their problems. The advantage of the macho culture, however, is that it can shield them from the less agreeable, sometimes harrowing aspects of their work.

In the course of trauma treatment, police officers with PTSD learn more or less to reconcile this awareness of their own vulnerability with their self-image, especially the image they formerly had of themselves: "I thought I was a good cop! I used to know no fear!" Trauma treatment cannot make police officers invulnerable, nor can it change their character. These are widespread misunderstandings. And despite successful treatment, PTSD symptoms or other complaints may inevitably reappear, especially if new stressors emerge. But the treatment will have taught clients how to cope with any new complaints, provided, of course, that they can count on support from the people at work. If such support, for example from superiors, is lacking, that can undermine the whole success of the treatment. One last benefit of the treatment is that it teaches clients to better understand and handle certain of their own character traits. Viewed in this way, the traumatic experience has heightened their awareness, and in some sense it has made them more mature persons and police officers.

REFERENCES

Andreasen, N. J. C., & Norris, A. S.: Long-term adjustment and adaptation mechanisms in severely burned adults. *Journal of Nervous and Mental Disease, 154*: 352-362, 1972.

Breslau, N.; Davis, G. C.; Andreski, P., & Peterson, E.: Traumatic events and post-traumatic stress disorder in urban populations of young adults. *Archives of General Psychiatry, 48*: 216-222, 1991.

Card, J.: *Lives after Vietnam: The personal impact of military service.* Lexington, MA, Lexington Books, 1983.

Carlier, I..V..E., & Gersons, B. P. R.: Development of a scale for traumatic stress incidents in police work. *Psychiatrica Fennica (Supplementum), 23*: 59-70, 1992.

Carlier, I. V. E., & Gersons, B. P. R.: Trauma at work: Post-traumatic stress disorder: An occupational health hazard. *The Journal of Occupational Health and Safety—Australia and New Zealand, 19*: 254-266, 1994.

Carlier, I. V. E., & Gersons, B. P. R.: Partial PTSD: The issue of psychological scars and the occurrence of PTSD symptoms. *The Journal of Nervous and Mental Disease, 183*: 107-109, 1995.

Carlier, I. V. E., & Gersons, B. P. R.: Stress reactions in disaster victims following the Bijlmermeer plane crash. *The Journal of Traumatic Stress, 10*: 329-335, 1997.

Carlier, I. V. E.; Lamberts, R. D., & Gersons, B. P. R.: *Traumatic events in police work. A study of the risk factors for PTSD and the effect of a treatment programme in police officers with PTSD.* Gouda Quint, Arnhem; Kluwer Rechtsweten-schappen, Antwerp (in Dutch only), 1994.

Carlier, I. V. E.; Fouwels, A. J.; Lamberts, R. D., & Gersons, B. P. R.: Post-traumatic stress disorder and dissociation in traumatized police officers. *The American Journal of Psychiatry, 153*: 1325-1328, 1996.

Carlier, I. V. E.; Lamberts, R. D., & Gersons, B. P. R.: Risk factors for post-traumatic stress symptomatology in police officers: A prospective analysis. *The Journal of Nervous and Mental Disease, in press.*

Clarke, K. M.: Creation of meaning in incest survivors. *Journal of Cognitive Psychotherapy: An International Quarterly, 7*: 195-203, 1993.

Davidson, J. R. T., & Foa, E. B. (Eds.), *Posttraumatic stress disorder, DSM IV and beyond.* Washington D.C./London, England, American Psychiatric Press, 1993.

Draucker, C. B.: Construing benefit from a negative experience of incest. *Western Journal of Nursing Research, 14*: 343-357, 1992.

Egendorf, A.: The post-war healing of Vietnam veterans: Recent research. *Hospital and Community Psychiatry, 31*: 13-23, 1982.

Egendorf, A.: *Healing from the war: Trauma and transformation after Vietnam.* Boston, Houghton Mifflin, 1985.

Gelinas, D. J.: The persisting negative effects of incest. *Psychiatry, 46*: 312-332, 1983.

Gersons, B. P. R., & Carlier, I. V. E.: *Protocol for an integrated individual treatment of post-traumatic stress disorder.* Department of Psychiatry, Academic Medical Centre, University of Amsterdam, The Netherlands, 1997.

Hendin, H., & Haas, A. P.: Combat adaptations of Vietnam veterans without post-traumatic stress disorders. *American Journal of Psychiatry, 141*: 956-960, 1984.

Janoff-Bulman, R., & Wortman, C. B.: Attributions of blame and coping in the "real" world: Severe accident victims react to their lot. *Journal of Personality and Social Psychology, 35*: 351-363, 1977.

Kessler, R. C.; Sonnega, A.; Bromet, E.; Hughes, M., & Nelson, C. B.: Posttraumatic stress disorder in the national comorbidity survey. *Archives of General Psychiatry 52*: 1048-1060, 1995.

Lifton, R. J.: *The broken connection: On death and the continuity of life.* New York, Simon & Schuster, 1979.

Lyons, J. A.: Strategies for assessing the potential for positive adjustment following trauma. *Journal of Traumatic Stress Studies, 4*: 93-112, 1991.

Marmar, C. R.; Weis, D. S.; Metzler, T. J.; Ronfelt, H. M., & Foreman, C.: Stress responses of emergency services personnel to the Loma Prieta earthquake Interstate 880 freeway collapse and control traumatic incidents. *The Journal of Traumatic Stress, 9*: 63-85, 1996.

Norris, F. H.: Epidemiology of trauma: Frequency and impact of different potentially traumatic events on different demographic groups. *Journal of Consulting and Clinical Psychology, 60*: 409-418, 1992.

Resnick, H. S.; Kilpatrick D. G.; Dansky B. S.; Saunders B. E., & Best, C. L.: Prevalence of civilian trauma and posttraumatic stress disorder in a representative national sample of women. *Journal of Consulting and Clinical Psychology, 61*: 984-991, 1993.

Scurfield, R. M.: War-related trauma: An integrative experiential, cognitive, and spiritual approach. In M. B. Williams, J. F. Sommer, Jr. (Eds.), *Handbook of post-traumatic therapy.* Westport, CT/London, Greenwood Press 179-204, 1994.

Schulz, R., & Decker, S.: Long-term adjustment to physical disability: The role of social support, perceived control and self-blame. *Journal of Personality and Social Psychology, 48*: 1161-1172, 1985.

Silver, R. L.; Boon, C., & Stones, M. H.: Searching for meaning in misfortune: Making sense of incest. *Journal of Social Issues, 39*: 81-101, 1983.

Sorenson, G.: Survey measures symptoms among successful veterans. *Vet Center Voice, 11*: 2-24, 1988.

Taylor, S. E.: Adjustment to threatening events. A theory of cognitive adaptation. *American Psychologist, 38*: 1161-1173, 1983.

Chapter 19

POLICE SUICIDE: THE ULTIMATE STRESS REACTION

Robert Loo

INTRODUCTION

Policing is a high stress occupation with exposure to occupational demands and critical incidents manifesting itself posttraumatic stress reactions, burnout, and suicide (e.g., Bedian, 1982; Violanti, Vena, & Marshall, 1986). This chapter focuses on the ultimate stress reaction, suicide. Some reported police suicide rates are extremely high, creating the impression that suicide has reached epidemic proportions in some police forces (e.g., France reels, 1996; Police Suicide, 1995). We will systematically examine police suicide by first reviewing the recording and reporting of police suicide rates, examining societal changes and cross-national differences associated with differing suicide rates, and assessing the fit between police suicides and theoretical models that attempt to understand suicide. Finally, key suicide prevention measures that police departments can implement to minimize suicides and help manage the impacts of suicides on survivors will be discussed.

ISSUES IN ADDRESSING POLICE SUICIDE RATES

While much of the police literature portrays policing as a high suicide occupation, there are several issues concerning the reliability and validity of reported suicide rates in police departments that need to be addressed.

Public Image

First, relatively little is published on the prevalence and causes of police suicide compared to other populations. Not surprisingly, police forces are sensitive about their public image and tend to take care of such problems in-house. However, those police forces that have brought the problem into the open deserve recognition for their efforts to confront police suicide. For example, the Los Angeles Police Department (LAPD) addressed this concern years ago and continues to work towards minimizes suicide (e.g., Dash & Reiser, 1978; Josephson & Reiser, 1990). Another example is the Royal Canadian Mounted Police (RCMP), Canada's largest police force, which felt that suicide was a priority issue for its new psychological services program in 1982 (Loo, 1986a).

Suicide Data and Misclassification

Second, police departments have historically not obtained and kept comprehensive data on suicide or suspected suicides. Given the stigma against suicide in North America and other cultures and in some religions, it is not surprising to find underreporting of police suicide just as one finds a general underreporting of suicide (e.g., O'Carroll, 1989). Also, some suicides might be easily misclassified as accidental deaths (e.g., Lester, 1992; Violanti, 1996), for example, death in a single-vehicle accident where there is no obvious road hazard or vehicle defect. Violanti, Vena, Marshall, and Petralia (1997) recently provided an important insight into the issue of misclassification in police suicides. Using four simple statistical adjustments to death classification data, they demonstrate that the true suicide rate was higher than the officially-reported rate.

Calculating Suicide Rates

Some police suicide rates published in the open literature present a chilling picture of a serious problem. For example, Nelson and Smith (1970) reported an average annual suicide rate of 203 per 100,000 for the period 1960-68 for police in the state of Wyoming. Friedman (1968) indicated an average annual rate among New York City police officers of 80 per 100,000 for the period 1934-40. Finally, Richard and Fell (1975) reported a rate of 69 per 100,000 for 1972-74 for officers in the state of Tennessee. Such statistics suggest that policing is a high-suicide occupation; however, several methodological problems deserve comment. First, these studies, among others, use relatively short time periods, covering as little as two or three years (e.g., Richard & Fell, 1975). Second, if police forces with a small staff complement of a few hundred officers are used, even one suicide per year would present a chilling picture when a suicide rate per 100,000 is calculated. Generally, police suicide is a low probability event with most years marked by no suicides or just one suicide and the odd extraordinary year marked by several suicides.

Loo's (1986a) study tried to overcome these methodological problems by examining a relatively long time period, 23 years, in the Royal Canadian Mounted Police, Canada's largest police force. He found the suicide rate to be approximately half the comparable Canadian average with most years marked by no suicides. Several years could be described as "spike" years with three or four suicides. If a short period was used, reported rates would have been significantly distorted, particularly if a "spike" year were included, and two dramatic but contrasting pictures of police suicide could be obtained by differences in time sampling. The value of examining an extended time period is well-illustrated in a recent examination of police suicide in Queensland, Australia where the time frame covered the period 1843-1992 (Cantor, Tyman, & Slater, 1995).

National Differences and Cultural Change

The police suicide literature is largely based upon studies of United States police forces. However, the few studies from other countries present a different picture. For example, Heiman (1975) reexamined Friedman's (1968) data and added more recent data covering the period 1960-73 for the New York City police and 1960-66 for the London Metropolitan police force in England. Heiman noted the contrasting low suicide rates for the British police force and the British general population as compared to rates in the U.S.A. and considered differences in access to firearms as contributing factors to the marked differences in police suicide rates.

The same rationale could be applied to Canada and Loo's (1986a) finding that suicide in the Royal Canadian Mounted Police (RCMP) was half that of the comparable Canadian population. Although police are armed in Canada, access to firearms in terms of gun control and ownership is much more restricted than in most U.S. states (e.g., Lester, 1988; Lester & Leenaars, 1993) and attitudes toward firearms are conservative.

Besides cross-national and cross-cultural differences, cultural changes within nations are worthy of additional exploration. For example, Violanti (1995) suggested links between the fluctuations in police suicide over a 40-year period in a U.S. police department and cultural changes in the U.S.A., including changing attitudes toward the police.

Women and Visible Minorities

Historically in many countries, only men were admitted to policing and even then, it was men drawn from the dominant society (e.g., white men in many European and North American countries). Over the past few decades, women have been admitted to police work in increasing numbers, as have members of visible minorities (e.g., nonwhites, aboriginal peoples). The changing face of police forces has implications for our understanding of suicide because women and visible minorities confront not only the typical sources of police stress (e.g., Loo, 1987), but additional stressors because they are new minorities in a traditionally male-dominated profession and because of credibility concerns in dealing with the public. The question to be raised is "Will suicide patterns and rates differentiate the various groups in policing?". This concern was raised by Josephson and Reiser (1990) in their follow-up of suicide in the LAPD where, more and more, women and minority officers make up the force.

A TYPOLOGY OF POLICE SUICIDE

With the exception of Friedman's (1968) study which used a psychodynamic or Freudian approach and Violanti's (1996) recent development of the Police Role Constriction Model, studies of police suicide tend to be atheoretical even though there are some 15 theories of suicide (e.g., Lester, 1994a). Although descriptive studies are important, there is a need to develop a theoretical framework in order to truly understand police suicide and link it to the broader field of suicidology.

Loo (1986a) attempted to fit his findings on suicide in the RCMP to established frameworks including psychodynamic, sociological, and psychological models. He found that Baechler's (1979) treatment of suicide made the best fit to his data. Baechler views suicide as a positive act of a relatively normal person struggling with life's problems and trying to resolve them. For Baechler, the focus of suicidal behavior is the individual's personality, coping skills, and logic. Within Baechler's typology, Loo's (1986a) findings indicate that most RCMP suicides can be described as serving an "escape" function. Officers committed suicide as a maladaptive response to intolerable personal, family, or work situations they felt they could not resolve. Most RCMP suicides resulted from chronic stress (e.g., the combination of marital problems and career disappointments with the resulting deterioration of self-confidence and self-worth). This theme of "suicide as escape from self" has received greater attention recently (Baumeister, 1990).

While police suicides usually occur within the context of chronic stress, the importance of a traumatic event must be recognized as either the precipitating event to a suicide or as a major contributing factor (e.g., Violanti, 1996). For example, Loo (1986a) found that a traumatic event was a contributing factor in five of the 35 (14%) RCMP suicides.

PREVENTION AND POSTVENTION

Prevention

Regardless of whether or not one believes that suicide is a serious problem in police forces, from both humanitarian and management perspectives, it is necessary to consider prevention and postvention measures to minimize suicides and their negative impacts on all involved stakeholders. For the purposes of this chapter, prevention avoids explicit distinctions among the primary, secondary, and tertiary levels of prevention; distinctions among the public health, operational, antecedent conditions, and injury control models of prevention (see Silverman & Felner, 1995 a; b); and a strict definition of whether prevention targets suicidal ideation of behaviors. Practitioners may find the questions posed by Silverman and Maris (1995, see their Tables 2 & 3, pp. 18-19) useful in developing preventive interventions. In the planning process for developing preventive measures in police departments, consider the points described in Figure 19.1.

Prevention Measures

Several preventive measures can be used to minimize police suicides. Police organizations should take a systematic approach to this issue, focusing

---

Figure 19.1.
Points to consider in planning preventative measures in
police departments.

- How to define the risk conditions that officers face.

- How and when to identify those officers most at risk.

- What measures would likely be effective in reducing the risk status of officers in the short term and long term?

- When should these measures be applied to effectively reduce risk in the short term and long term?

- What types of measures are officers more likely to accept?

- What are the costs of the various measures and the expected cost-effectiveness of the measures?

not just on suicide itself but also on comprehensively building people's work and life competencies to enhance their resilience to stressors while recognizing that no single type of intervention can be universally effective (e.g., Loo, 1986a & b, 1987; Silverman & Felner, 1995a & b). Suicide prevention must be integrated into a comprehensive model which emphasizes physical, psychological, and spiritual well-being throughout an officer's career from recruitment to retirement. It must also be recognized that suicide can result not just from a single traumatic event or crisis but also from the accumulation of apparently minor life events, thus making the prediction of suicide and its prevention more difficult (e.g., Lester, 1994b; Loo, 1986a).

Another key issue in prevention is understanding the role of ready access to firearms. The majority of police suicides in countries where police are armed is by their personal sidearm (Loo, 1986a; Violanti, 1996). Consequently, preventive actions must address the issue of removing an "at risk" officer's firearm and access to other force weaponry. Such actions fit with Haddon's injury control strategies (see Silverman & Maris, 1995, Table 1, p. 16). Fortunately, some police forces are adopting at least some of these practices. Much more could be done by forces worldwide if a comprehensive rather than piecemeal approach is adopted (e.g., Loo, 1987; Violanti, 1996).

The Public Health Model (e.g., Potter, Powell, & Kachur, 1995; Silverman & Felner, 1995b) is a widely-accepted comprehensive approach to prevention. From our perspective on suicide prevention, primary prevention seeks to reduce the incidence of new suicides (e.g., by offering stress management programs to recruits and supervisors where suicide is one key topic), secondary prevention targets those showing early warning signs of being at-risk for suicide (e.g., by offering medical and counselling services to an officer who is depressed or talks about death). Finally, tertiary prevention focuses on those already severely distressed (e.g., by providing medical and psychological services perhaps on an in-patient basis to officers who may be evaluated as unfit for duty or denied access to weapons).

The effectiveness of such measures must be evaluated (e.g., Tierney, 1994). Effectiveness should focus not just on the reduction in suicide rate over time but also on reducing the undesirable antecedent conditions that lead to suicide (e.g., perceived lack of departmental, superior and community support for officers) and the increase in the number and variety of protective factors (e.g., peer and family support groups–e.g., Loo, 1987; Silverman & Felner, 1995a & b). The following measures are standard preventive actions that any police department should consider.

Recruit Selection Criteria

Set selection criteria that are clearly bona fide occupational requirements and in line with human rights legislation. Police applicants usually cannot be screened-out because of familial or personality factors associated with suicide. However, predisposing (e.g., personality factors) or precipitating (e.g., history of family violence, alcohol abuse) factors can be noted in the successful applicants' medical/service file for tracking as high-risk officers.

Stress Management Training

Provide a comprehensive stress-management training program that starts in recruit training (Violanti, 1993) and ends with preretirement counselling. Such training must be a component of training for special, high-risk duties such as tactical teams.

Stress Inoculation Training

A category of stress management training that focuses on specific sources of occupational stress is stress inoculation training. For example, despite their training in firearms use, involvement in shooting incidents can be traumatic for officers (e.g., Loo, 1986b; Violanti, 1996). Stress inoculation training for shooting incidents could involve presentations by officers who had been involved in shootings and health professionals with expertise in dealing with postshooting stress reactions. It could also involve guided group discussions (e.g., using the above sources) about reactions to death and dying among other relevant topics.

Supervisor Training

Police supervisors, at all levels, should be trained to identify the early warning signs of suicide ideation or intention, along with the common precipitating events (e.g., facing disciplinary charges) and to take appropriate management action. A supervisor's action should include contacting a health professional for advice and assistance and an injury control action such as having the officer turn in firearms to remove the most commonly-used method of suicide among police. This can be linked to stress management training.

Identify and Track High-Risk Officers

Police forces should develop criteria to identify high-risk officers (e.g., major marital, financial, work, legal, or drug abuse problems) and a tracking or surveillance system to unobtrusively monitor such officers so that timely support can be provided. Stillion and McDowell's (1991) model of suicide trajectory can be a useful model to help identify at risk officers because their model emphasizes four assessable categories of risk factors (biological, psychological, cognitive, and environmental—see their Figure 1, p. 329) that can promote suicidal behavior. Given that suicide by service sidearm is the most frequent method of suicide, departments must address the difficult issue of removing an officer's sidearm, and any access to firearms when officers are judged by a health professional or their supervisor to be at significant risk for suicide. In an impulsive moment, the almost effortless squeeze of a trigger can bring a life to an end.

Psychological Assessments for Special Duties

Psychological assessments should be conducted for officers designated for high-stress duties (e.g., undercover drug squads) so that their suitability can be evaluated. There should also be periodic psychological assessments (e.g., annual assessments) for officers in these duties and an assessment at the end of such duties and before they are reassigned to other policing duties.

Critical Incidents

Psychological debriefings or assessments should be conducted following critical or traumatic incidents (e.g., Loo, 1986b) or, more generally, encounters with death (Henry, 1995), with follow-up assessments and counselling being provided as required.

Psychological Services

In-house or externally-contracted psychological services must be available to all officers for primary, secondary, and tertiary prevention actions. It is critical that service providers be thoroughly familiar with the nature of policing, the confidentiality and ethical issues related to this occupation, and the role of medication and other therapies on the officers' ability to do their job (e.g., Loo, 1985). Police organizations may find a model such as the Suicide Trajectory model within a life-span perspective (Stillion & McDowell, 1991) useful in guiding services over the career life cycle of police officers.

Drug Abuse and Life-Styles

Historically, policing has been a male-dominated occupation characterized by a macho image. Thus, it is not surprising that alcohol, tobacco, and other self-destructive behaviors are part of this macho police culture. These kinds of self-destructive behaviors eventually take their toll on the officer's health, work performance, and family or social relationships. Several studies have shown that alcohol played a key role in police suicide (e.g., Loo, 1986a; Violanti, 1996), so programs that promote healthy life-styles (e.g., fitness programs; smoking cessation programs) and help officers with drug abuse problems would also help prevent suicides.

Suicide Hotlines

Hotlines (e.g., Seeley, 1994) and crisis centers, whether provided by the police force or externally-contracted in the case of small departments, available 24 hours a day, can provide a timely point of intervention to help the distressed officer. One issue that a department needs to address, whether the hotline is operated within the department or contracted externally, is the degree of confidentiality of the telephone conversations.

Peer Support Programs

Social supports can act to "buffer" the officer against the impacts of stress (e.g., Haines, Hurlbert, & Zimmer, 1991; Loo, 1987). Peer support networks and peer counselors enable suitable police officers to be trained to support their fellow officers and complement the work of health professionals. Such a program could also use carefully selected and trained civilian volunteers (e.g., Whiting, 1994). Personnel selection and training are the two key steps in peer support programs. Personnel who volunteer must be themselves psychologically healthy, emotionally stable, altruistic, and accepting of others with all their shortcomings. In terms of personal suitability to be a peer counselor or volunteer, that is a lot to ask for in a candidate, but one cannot help others through traumatic periods without having a high level of psychological hardiness and altruism. Another key step is managing the confidentiality issue because officers may be wary of using peer counselors. For example, an evaluation of the peer support program in the Ontario Provincial Police Force in Canada showed that only 44 percent of those surveyed believed the program was confidential (Loutzenhiser & Hoath, 1991).

Spousal Support Program

A spouses' network can provide social supports for the spouses and children of officers as well as a network for disseminating information and familiarization on policing (e.g., "ride-along" experiences). Such a program may also help reduce domestic problems, an area that has been linked to higher suicide attempts among police officers (Janik & Kravitz, 1994).

Preretirement Counseling

Counselling (e.g., identifying potential retirement activities, addressing health issues among retirees) and information (e.g., financial/tax planning for retirement) sessions.

Postvention

At least three key actions that should be taken following a suicide, suspected suicide, or attempted suicide. Here, postvention may be viewed as tertiary-level prevention. Such actions would help minimize the negative impacts on survivors and help provide a data base to develop and revise Departmental policies, programs, and services.

Psychological Autopsies

A psychological autopsy (e.g., Loo, 1986a) should follow every suicide and suspected suicide. A psychological autopsy is a systematic procedure for reconstructing the suicidal death through interviews with key survivors (e.g., family members, friends, and coworkers) to understand the suicide from physical, psychological, and social perspectives (e.g., Beskow, Runeson, & Asgard, 1990; Brent, 1989). Interviewers must be qualified health care professionals, have good interviewing and clinical skills and expertise in suicidology, and be sensitive to the implications of the suicide event for survivors and ethical issues (e.g., interviews possibly causing even greater distress for survivors). Skilled health professionals would also be attuned to issues of reliability and validity when collecting and analyzing interview data under these circumstances.

Ellis (1988; see Table 3, p. 366) provides a four-dimensional model of self-destructive behavior that can be applied in conducting the psychological autopsy. The *descriptive* dimension captures information about the suicide method, prior suicide attempts, and suicides threats or ideation. The *situational* dimension examines interpersonal, health, and financial factors, as well as identifying precipitating factor(s). The *psychological/behavioral* dimension focuses on moods (e.g., depression), attitudes and beliefs (e.g., hopelessness about one's personal situation), coping skills (e.g., poor problem solving or conflict resolution skills), and the like. Finally, the *teleological* dimension determines the reason or rationale for the suicide (e.g., elimination of pain and suffering, self-punishment). The analysis of any suicide note may also be informative in understanding the suicide (e.g., Leenars & Lester, 1991).

Findings from psychological autopsies help improve future prevention measures as well as let officers and others know that the police department cares. Participating in these interviews may also help survivors work through their loss and grief as well as help identify distressed survivors for referral to professional counselors.

Survivor Supports

Professional counselling and peer support should be provided to survivors (e.g., spouses and dependents) and other stakeholders (e.g., police supervisor and partners/coworkers) to ameliorate their distress, guilt, and grieving (e.g., Loo, 1987; Violanti, 1996). Pastoral counselling or spiritual assistance can be effective and welcomed by those with strong religious or spiritual beliefs. It is also commendable that a national organization, Concerns of Police Survivors (COPS), was established in the U.S.A. to help provide and coordinate such support.

Intervention Evaluation

The periodic and comprehensive evaluation of prevention and postvention measures must be undertaken to determine the efficacy of the measures and to take timely actions to improve the organization's efforts in minimizing police suicide and stress.

CLOSING COMMENTS

Given the methodological weaknesses in most studies of police suicide and the more optimistic findings of Loo (1986a) and Josephson and Reiser (1990), police suicide need not be as disturbing a phenomenon as the U.S. literature has painted over the years. Clearly, police organizations must implement both prevention and postvention actions to help minimize suicides and the negative impacts suicides have on all stakeholders.

REFERENCES

Baechler, J.: *Suicides.* New York, Basic Books, 1979.

Baumeister, R. F.: Suicide as escape from self. *Psychological Review, 97:*, 90-113, 1990.

Bedian, A. G.: Suicide and occupation: A review. *Journal of Vocational Behavior, 21:* 206-222, 1982.

Beskow, J.; Runeson, B., & Asgard, U.: Psychological autopsies: Methods and ethics. *Suicide and Life-Threatening Behavior, 20:* 307-323, 1990.

Brent, D. A.: The psychological autopsy: Methodological considerations for the study of adolescent suicide. *Suicide and Life-Threatening Behavior, 19:* 43-57, 1989.

Burge, J. H.: *Occupational stress in policing.* Ottawa, Ontario, Canada, American Educators Publishing, 1984.

Cantor, C. H.; Tyman, R., & Slater, P. J.: A historical survey of police suicide in Queensland, Australia, 1843-1992. *Suicide and Life-Threatening Behavior, 25:* 499-507, 1995.

Dash, J., & Reiser, M.: Suicide among police in urban law enforcement agencies. *Journal of Police Science and Administration, 3:* 267-273, 1978.

Ellis, T. E.: Classification of suicidal behavior: A review and step toward integration. *Suicide and Life-Threatening Behavior, 18:* 358-371, 1988.

France reels from police suicides: *The Globe and Mail, 18 March:* Toronto, Canada, p. A8, 1996.

Friedman, P.: Suicide among police: A study of ninety-three suicides among New York policemen, 1934-1940. In E. Shneidman (Ed.), *Essays in self-destruction.* New York, Science House, 1968.

Haines, V. A.; Hurlbert, J. S., & Zimmer, C.: Occupational stress, social support, and the buffer hypothesis. *Work and Occupations, 18:* 212-235, 1991.

Heiman, M. F.: The police suicide. *Journal of Police Science and Administration, 3:* 267-273, 1975.

Henry, V. E.: The police officer as survivor: Death confrontations and the police subculture. *Behavioral Sciences and the Law, 13:* 93-112, 1995.

Janik, J., & Kravitz, H. M.: Linking work and domestic problems with police suicide. *Suicide and Life-Threatening Behavior, 24:* 267-274, 1994.

Josephson, R. L., & Reiser, M.: Officer suicide in the Los Angeles police department: A twelve-year follow-up. *Journal of Police Science and Administration, 17:* 227-229, 1990.

Leenars, A. A., & Lester, D.: Myths about suicide notes. *Death Studies, 15:* 303-308, 1991.

Lester, D.: Gun control, gun ownership, and suicide prevention. *Suicide and Life-threatening Behavior, 18:* 176-180, 1988.

Lester, D.: Miscounting suicides. *Acta Psychiatrica Scandinavica, 85:* 15-16, 1992.

Lester, D.: A comparison of 15 theories of suicide. *Suicide and Life-Threatening Behavior, 24:* 80-88, 1994a.

Lester, D.: Reflections on the statistical rarity of suicide. *Crisis, 15:* 187-188, 1994b.

Lester, D., & Leenaars, A.: Suicide rates in Canada before and after tightening firearm control laws. *Psychological Reports, 72*: 787-790, 1993.

Loo, R.: Policy development for psychological services in the Royal Canadian Mounted Police. *Journal of Police Science and Administration, 13*: 132-137. 1985.

Loo, R.: Suicide among police in a federal force. *Suicide and Life-Threatening Behavior, 16*: 379-388, 1986a.

Loo, R.: Post-shooting stress reactions among police officers. *Journal of Human Stress, Spring*: 27-31, 1986b.

Loo, R.: *Police stress and social supports.* Paper presented at the Annual Conference of the Canadian Psychological Association, Vancouver, 1987.

Loutzenhiser, L. A., & Hoath, D. R.: *An evaluation of the Ontario Provincial Police employee peer support program.* Paper presented at the Canadian Psychological Association Annual Conference, Calgary, Canada, June 1991.

Nelson, Z., & Smith, W.: Law enforcement profession: An incident of suicide. *Omega, 1*: 293-299, 1970.

O'Carroll, P. W.: A consideration of the validity and reliability of suicide mortality data. *Suicide and Life-Threatening Behavior, 19*: 1-16, 1989.

Police suicide.: *The Globe and Mail, August 8*: Toronto, Canada, p. A6, 1995.

Potter, L. B.; Powell, K. E., & Kachur, S. P.: Suicide prevention from a public health perspective. *Suicide and Life-Threatening Behavior. 25*: 82- 91, 1995.

Richard, W. C., & Fell, R. D.: Health factors in police job stress. In W. H. Kroes & J. J. Hurrell, Jr. (Eds.), *Job stress and the police: Identifying stress reduction techniques.* Symposium paper presented for the Department of Health, Education and Welfare, Division of Biomedical and Behavioral Science, Cincinnati, 1975.

Seeley, M. F.: What are hotlines? *Crisis, 15*:, 108-109, 1994.

Silverman, M. M., & Felner, R. D.: Suicide prevention programs: Issues of design, implementation, feasibility, and developmental appropriateness. *Suicide and Life-Threatening Behavior, 25*: 92-104, 1995a.

Silverman, M. M., & Felner, R. D.: The place of suicide prevention in the spectrum of intervention: Definitions of critical terms and constructs. *Suicide and Life-threatening Behavior, 25*: 70-81, 1995b.

Silverman, M. M., & Maris, R. W.: The prevention of suicidal behaviors: An overview. *Suicide and Life-Threatening Behavior, 25*: 10-21, 1995.

Stillion, J. M., & McDowell, E. E.: Examining suicide from a life span perspective. *Death Studies, 15*: 327-354, 1991.

Tierney, R. J.: Suicide intervention training evaluation: A preliminary report. *Crisis, 15*: 69-76, 1994.

Violanti, J. M.: What does high stress police training teach recruits? An analysis of coping. *Journal of Criminal Justice, 21*: 411-417, 1993.

Violanti, J. M.: Trends in police suicide. *Psychological Reports, 77*: 688-690, 1995.

Violanti, J. M.: *Police suicide: Epidemic in blue.* Springfield, IL, Charles C. Thomas, 1996.

Violanti, J. M.; Vena, J. E., & Marshall, J. R.: Disease risk and mortality among police officers: New evidence and contributing factors. *Journal of Police Science and Administration, 14*: 17-23, 1986.

Violanti, J. M.; Vena, J. E.; Marshall, J. R., & Petralia, S.: A comparative evaluation of police suicide rate validity. *Suicide and Life-Threatening Behavior, 26*: 79-85, 1996.

Whiting, N.: Selecting and training volunteers for suicide prevention. *Crisis, 15*: 4-6, 1994.

Chapter 20

A CURRENT VIEW FROM THE UK IN POST INCIDENT CARE: "DEBRIEFING," "DEFUSING" AND JUST TALKING ABOUT IT

MARGARET MITCHELL

INTRODUCTION

This chapter reviews the origins, development, and current status of interventions, primarily Critical Incident Debriefing (CIDB), developed to assist police officers in the United Kingdom (UK) after a significant and potentially traumatic incident. The review describes how the practical necessity for UK forces to put in place some form of intervention may well have prevented a comprehensive evaluation of them.

Police work is a demanding and challenging profession (Anshel et al., 1997; American Institute of Stress, 1997; Dantzker, 1997; Mitchell et al., 1997; Ainsworth, 1995; Alexander et al., 1993; Brown & Campbell, 1993) exposing officers to chronic occupational stress and potentially traumatic incidents. Overall, such demands can significantly affect sickness absence rates (Her Majesty's Inspector of Constabulary, HMIC, 1997, p 22), alcohol abuse (Alexander et al., 1991) and mental health problems (Borrill et al., 1996), and retirement from service. Further, it is possible that some 25 percent of officers retire from police work for reasons of their "psychological health" (HMIC, 1997, p 62). If police management is to ensure that work standards are maintained, and to avoid the loss of trained and highly experienced officers, stress issues must be tackled.

Ainsworth (1995) states that little emphasis in the training of British police officers is placed on dealing with stress, in contrast to the US where "handling personal stress" is rated as the highest priority by police trainers (Manolias, 1988). More recently, however, greater understanding of, and vigilance about, the effects of workplace stress has resulted in the UK police vigorously remedying this omission. The spate of disasters in recent years, and recognition of their impact on the police involved, has heightened awareness of how this interacts with the managerial and social context of the

255

workplace. This has led to examining support provision in the workplace, as well as prompting the provision of interventions intended to ameliorate the effect of traumatic incidents in particular.

The hierarchical nature of police organizations can result in officers feeling uncomfortable about obtaining formal support, largely as a result of enduring concerns about confidentiality and the effect that seeking help may have on their career (Dantzker, 1997; Mitchell et al., 1997). Often support is only obtainable through the Occupational Health Unit, or through supervisors. Moreover, a deep seated belief exists that to obtain or seek formal support after an incident is an overreaction and officers express the view that the event they have experienced is not sufficiently "serious" to warrant formal assistance (Mitchell et al., 1997). This view persists despite evidence that minor incidents can be cumulatively distressing (Scott & Stradling, 1994). The efforts of employers to provide visible and more formal methods of support (both to support employees and be seen to be supporting employees) may have resulted in the more "simple" methods of making officers feel good about what they do being overlooked.

Growing awareness of the serious impact which traumatic incidents can have on officers' mental health has led to workplace initiatives aimed at preparing employees to deal with trauma, or providing support for them afterwards. The urge by police employers to "do something" reflects a recognition that duty of care extends beyond the physical well-being of employees, and includes mental health. It also reflects increasing expectations by officers themselves for a healthier, happier working life. Employers' concerns about potential legal action by employees because of exposure to trauma and lack of support following an incident is without doubt also a motivating factor.

Possibly central to this concern in the UK are the sequelae of the Hillsborough Football Stadium Disaster, in April 1989 at the Hillsborough Football Stadium, which claimed the lives of 93 football spectators as they succumbed to the physical pressure of the very large crowd. One view is that the police officers on duty at the grounds realized too late that things were going very badly wrong, thereby contributing to the disaster. Of relevance for the present purposes, however, was the effect that public criticism of the officers at the game, their exposure to death and injury, and their feelings of guilt and anger had on these officers. Several officers claimed compensation from their employer for posttraumatic stress disorder, and out-of-court settlements were reached. These decisions "brought home" to police employers the importance of taking reasonable steps to protect officers from psychological injury. However, developing an appropriate response has been hindered by difficulties in defining which stressors are likely to lead to psychological distress, the range of likely responses, the relative responsibilities of the employer vis a vis the officer, and how support can best be provided in a working context which requires toughness in order to get the job done.

CRITICAL INCIDENT DEBRIEFING IN THE UNITED KINGDOM

In an effort to clarify some of these issues, and to develop a set of guidelines for "best practice" in managing the consequences in the UK, the Health and Safety Executive commissioned an investigation by the Police Research Unit at Glasgow Caledonian University. This chapter reviews the "work in progress" regarding postincident care as practiced in the UK. The second part of the chapter reviews work on the "informal," or "natural," debriefing which often takes place spontaneously amongst groups of officers who have attended the same threatening incident (Mitchell et al., 1998). The support officers themselves say they want from their employer is also described from this same research, and the variety in the responses demonstrates the difficulty of serving all the perceived needs and preferences of the individuals who comprise any police force.

In the early eighties, several models, designed to manage the psychological effects of involvement in traumatic incidents, emerged (see Chapter 21 for an account of the development of debriefing models). While the initial view that interventions based on disclosure and education about reactions after the incident could prevent the onset of psychological symptoms, this view is no longer held to be axiomatic within the professional and academic mental health communities. However, police organizations may still hold on to that view. Police management requires a solution to the high exposure rates in order that operational standards are maintained with minimal disruption. The simplistic model perpetrated by medical and legal contexts of a single overwhelming event suggests that a "cure" to counteract the effects is available, in much the same way as a broken ankle requires early stabilization and physiotherapy. The early intervention of a CIDB is aimed at preventing the development of symptoms of posttraumatic stress disorder. In many ways, in a work place in which the rate of exposure to traumatic incidents is relatively high and in which there is a necessity to get employees back to full "working order" as soon as possible, CIDB appears to offer an ideal solution.

The form of postincident debriefing typically used in UK forces follows the model described by Dyregrov (1989). In one major UK force, which is the major source of information in this chapter, the model of trained peer debriefers is used. This procedure is offered following involvement in incidents involving: multiple casualties or fatalities; accidental/violent death of police officer off duty; extreme violence or threat of extreme violence towards a police officer (e.g., firearm presented, knife attack); an accumulation of several serious incidents; or any other incident which might be deemed to be critical (e.g., cot death, fatal road accident, incident involving children).

Geates (1996) found that this list agreed largely with what officers believed to be traumatic, and had found to be problematic. Other research (Mitchell & Hogg, 1997; Mitchell et al., 1998) found that officers can be deeply affected by other incidents, not all of which would fit the list above. Officers might find certain peculiar aspects of the incident difficult to stop thinking about, or would experience a considerable emotional response when thinking about it. Possible explanations for this might be the personal meaning they attribute to it (e.g., the person involved might remind them of a family member); or because it challenges their assumptions about police work or society (Janoff-Bulman, 1989). Equally, encountering an incident in which the officer felt their skills and previous knowledge seriously inadequate to the task can have a profound effect. Of course, not all incidents have an adverse effect, and this is the enigma for police management: the inability to predict outcome has presented real conceptual difficulties for police forces. The fact that some officers are affected and some are not leads to explanations concerning the character of the individual officer more often than the contextual and organizational issues discussed below.

THE CIDB MODEL

The model of debriefing most frequently used in UK forces, following typical triggering incidents, is a three-phase process.

The Facts

Participant's thoughts, impressions, expectations, and decisions are discussed, including their anticipation when getting to the incident, and their impressions immediately on arrival. This phase is fairly brief, and attempts are made by the debriefers to involve everyone by encouraging them to introduce themselves and describe their own involvement in the incident.

The Feelings

The second phase, which takes up the most time, considers participants' feelings and reactions. Experienced debriefers state that, contrary to expectations, officers find it easy to talk about the incident and express their feelings, apparently because they welcome the opportunity to get certain aspects "off their chest." Participants find that they talk about themselves and their work in a way which differs from what they do normally at work. Age and experience can influence the ease with which officers will talk about their emotions and reactions. Younger officers can talk in quite "personal" ways, while older officers have reported that they have never spoken to anyone in the way they do during the debriefing, not only to the debriefers but also to the relative strangers in the group. This demonstrates the importance of this phase, with perhaps the most important process being the sharing and "normalization." Possibly the sense of isolation about one's feelings is reduced by such a process (older participants have told the debriefers that they had previously found it difficult at work the day after an incident when, still feeling affected themselves, it would appear that everyone else was fine—they now know differently, and that is helpful). Feelings of helplessness when attending an incident can also be expressed, as can concerns of being unable to act, frustration at not being able to do more, or guilt. Anger, is also a frequent and very potent emotion expressed and must be managed very carefully in the group debriefing.

The Future

The final phase is "educational" and concerns how participants can move on from the incident and be able to deal with their feelings about it. Information leaflets give advice on likely time scales when any feelings might subside, and information on various facilities which officers can access later, if they feel it necessary, is provided.

THE PROCESS IN THE UK

Two "customer satisfaction" surveys of serving police officers in one UK force which uses trained peer debriefing have been conducted. The first (Gallagher, 1996) examined officers' awareness of CIDB and found it to be considerably higher among supervisory officers than constables. In terms of setting up a CIDB for groups of officers under their care, some line managers were found to assess the need for a debriefing based on their own possibly idiosyncratic criteria, or may even have attempted to form some "diagnosis" of the mental health of the officers under their care. Conversely, some supervisors misunderstand their role, or underestimate their responsibilities in caring for their officers. It appeared that given the number of serious incidents, the facility was greatly underused. During the period of the study, seventeen debriefings took place when very many more incidents, identified as potentially traumatic, occurred.

Geates (1996) surveyed perceptions of CIDB with the aim of confirming the definition of incidents after which a CIDB should take place. It was found that the criteria for judging an incident as "critical" are reasonable. Officers in the sample who had attended a CIDB had found it beneficial, although the precise way in which it was found to be beneficial was not assessed. Awareness was thought to be insufficient as CIDB was not used as often as it could be. Again, the study did not assess the impact of CIDB on the officer's psychological state, although it did produce instructive lists of what officers reported as the effect of traumatic incidents (e.g., sleeplessness, antisocial behavior), and the coping methods officers reported as useful. Interestingly, the two most frequently cited police incidents which officers found "affected them afterwards" were the Lockerbie Disaster (in December 1988) and road traffic accidents.

THE CURRENT SURVEY OF UK FORCES

As part of the current research, we have been asked to review current practice in managing trauma in the police service and examine how interventions are used. In particular, the aims of CIDB at organizational and individual levels are to be reviewed. As a first step, a phone-round of UK forces was conducted to establish the range of practices currently in use and to identify key issues with which to structure and inform the survey of practice. It quickly became apparent that there is variation in the reasons put forward for having interventions in place. The responses to a fairly simple question on whether the force had a written policy were instructive. Some had written policy while others had what could be termed an implicit policy, or understanding. A few had even discontinued their policy, while many were reviewing or rewriting policy. An important point raised in one force was that they had no formal policy as they had recognized a need to be flexible. These preliminary inquiries emphasized the complexity of the subject, and the difficulties of conducting a meaningful audit of current practice in the current state of flux, particularly in a climate of forthcoming change in HSE legislation (the Police Health and Safety Act (1997)), which took effect from mid 1998.

In general, forces are preparing their policy and practice to comply with this and several documents are being prepared in order to provide guidance on debriefing practice. The factors influencing the instigation and development of mechanisms to manage trauma in the police service are many and varied. The need to manage traumatic stress in police officers has long been recognized by some forces because of the particularly demanding nature of the work (e.g., London Metropolitan Police, Royal Ulster Constabulary (RUC) in Northern Ireland). For Strathclyde Police, the second largest force in the UK, the impact of the Lockerbie Disaster in 1988 in which over 2,000 officers from Strathclyde alone were involved, was a major impetus to setting up some form of care program for officers. Other forces have been required to act in response to major incidents, such as following the Hillsborough Disaster described above or the murders of the class of five-year-old children in Dunblane, Scotland in 1996. In a few forces, an influential individual, a "torch-bearer," provided the impetus. This can make it difficult to know who, exactly, should be contacted as the spokesperson for that force, an important consideration when policy and practice may be at some variance.

The type of support forces offer following incidents also differs widely. More or less formal networks of support are frequently reported including colleague support, peer group counselling, professional counselling, and access to a clinical psychologist. One-to-one counselling is common, and there is evidence that individuals may fare better using this modality. Most use some form of debriefing procedure which can include "defusing," a less intense form of CIDB. However, much confusion remains in the use of basic terminology. The terms defusing, debriefing, operational debrief, and counselling have been used by different individuals in different forces to refer to the same process. A further aim of the current work is to to generate a common lexicon on this subject so that interventions, aims, and outcomes may be compared UK wide.

Of the forces using CIDB, variation in practice is apparent, such as the timing of a debriefing following an incident; whether attendance is voluntary or mandatory; whether individuals can choose not to speak during the debriefing; who conducts debriefings (most often peer debriefers or welfare officers); who trains the debriefers; what debriefers are trained to do; what records are kept; and what monitoring and follow up is undertaken. Views also differ on the issue of confidentiality. In some forces, complete confidentiality is guaranteed; in others it is not. Different methods of initiating a CIDB are used. This has implications for who participates and who is missed out. Some rely only on a supervisor making a request to the Welfare Service, and this is dependent on the supervisor's understanding of what a potentially traumatic incident might be, their view of what available support is, and what it can "do."

There is some evidence that senior officers may not fully understand the purpose of CIDB (Gallagher,1996). Other forces rely on an alerting system from Force Control or the Communications Center to the Welfare Service which will then offer a debriefing, as necessary. In others, an individual, or group of officers may request a debriefing from the Welfare Service. In some instances, this is taken as an indication of the perceived value of the service by officers. On the other hand, debriefing is certainly not seen universally as a panacea. In one multiservice initiative in Lincoln, England, in which pioneering work in debriefing practices was developed, there is a move away from group debriefing towards such initiatives such as individuals conducting self-assessments using approved psychological instruments and managing their own rehabilitation in collaboration with Welfare and Occupational Health Services.

A legal issue which has influenced debriefing practice more than any other is the problem of "disclosure." During a debriefing, evidence may be disclosed which, because of its relevance in case, may not be held in confidence. Currently, the matter is being discussed and a guidance document is being prepared for police officers, the UK Crown Prosecution Service staff, and other interested parties. The differing interpretations of the legislation covering disclosure of evidence has led, in some forces, to their abandoning debriefing altogether or to their suspending the use of peer debriefers.

The implicit goals of trauma management suggested by forces involve the prevention of the onset symptoms, offering of support to colleagues, and a demonstration that the force is a caring employer. Without clearly defined goals, evaluation is impossible. This has led to some forces reporting perceptions of CIDB as very positive, although the actual effect on the emotional status of participants has never been examined. In individual terms, the aim could be preventative health in exactly the same way as cardiac exercise and nutrition programs. Employees also now have higher expectations for a safe and protected workplace, and this extends to their psychological well-being.

At an organizational level, aims include demonstrating a duty of care by taking reasonable steps to protect officers from potentially harmful effects. These aims could be operationalized into reducing sickness absence, reducing the potential for public complaints, enhancing performance, and creating overall improvements in health. Other incidental effects have been observed after group debriefing, for example, increasing group cohesion within a shift, and encouraging officers to use other sources of support. It is only once these aims are clearly stated that the effectiveness or otherwise of the intervention (or the demonstration of duty of care) can be evaluated.

CIDB, as a practice, may have been adopted for pragmatic reasons. This makes it essential that its aims are clearly defined and, once established, objectively evaluated (the "what can CIDB do" question). Similarly, the extent to which CIDB is effective in achieving these stated aims (the "what does CIDB do" question) must also be evaluated. Possible effects could simply be whether participants found it "helpful" according to a range of criteria, whether the onset of symptoms is actually prevented, or whether there is a reduction in sickness absence. While forces have established explicit aims, they may vary considerably between forces. Except in very few cases, no objective evaluation of effectiveness has been conducted. Appropriate evaluation would require the use of blind evaluations, reliable and valid measures, trained assessors, specifically defined methods of debriefing, and an unbiased assignment of individuals to different intervention conditions (Rick et al., 1998). Although our survey of practice is only in its infancy it appears that few forces actually assess effects in any systematic way.

In conclusion, the practical necessity of protecting officers from traumatic stress has led forces to implement initiatives quickly without the luxury of being able to evaluate them. Clear evidence that CIDB is helpful is lacking (see Hobbs & Adshead, 1997; Raphael, Meldrum & McFarlane, 1995; Bisson & Deahl, 1994). Although there appear to be some positive effects, a more detailed systematic analysis is required. An example would be the development of group cohesion and a demonstration on the part of the force that management recognizes that a significant incident has taken place. So, despite the attractions of an easy to organize, and relatively inexpensive intervention, it is likely not the panacea which was once hoped and several writers (e.g., Raphael et al., 1995) have suggested that debriefing cannot be made mandatory within occupational contexts while the effect on employees is still unclear. From this preliminary survey it appears that awareness and practice between, and even within, police forces varies significantly. The next section takes as its starting point the experience of individual officers, rather than the views of the policy makers.

NEW RESEARCH ON SOCIAL SUPPORT AMONG POLICE OFFICERS

Previous work (Mitchell et al., 1998) on what incidents officers construe as personally threatening provides some information about the degree to which posttrauma symptoms can result from more minor incidents. In this study, 300 officers from two UK forces were asked to describe an incident they had experienced in the "last year or so" which they had found personally threatening . An example of the sort of police-public interactions described is: "Answered a housebreaking call in plain clothes. A male who was in the house exited carrying a knife and stabbed me during the ensuing struggle/arrest."

The complexity and alarming nature of these incidents lead to the expectation that officers may require to review their actions, evaluate them, and explore their reactions and feelings. Of this sample, five (1.6%) scored above cut-off on the Impact of Events Scale, although CIDB had been offered in only seven instances (this seven did not include those with the elevated scores) and taken up in only three. This research presented a good opportunity to ask what had happened after the incident, specifically what conversations took place afterwards. The purpose of this was to find out if "informal" or "natural" forms of debriefing took place, whether operational debriefing was a norm, and what was the content of any conversations. Within police organizations there often exists an esprit de corps or "buddy system" (Fielding 1995) which provides appropriate informal social support. However, the occupational culture of the police force results in each generation passing on and maintaining beliefs about appropriate coping responses (Brown et al., 1989), and about the definition of roles within the service, such as what is appropriate for women or those younger in service (Anshel et al., 1997). Added to this, the reserve which officers may feel about seeking help formally makes informal sources of support most important and relevant as a focus of study.

This study examined assumptions about the informal support available to officers in the course of normal duty and after exceptional incidents; officers' perception of, and experience of, the informal and formal sources of social support; and the role of social support as a coping strategy. An open ended question was asked: "We are very interested in the informal support given by colleagues (and supervisors) to officers who have been involved in threatening and violent incidents. Usually this takes the form of talking about what happened after the incident, and the conversation can be positive and supportive, or quite negative. After the incident you have described, did this happen and, if so, what sorts of things were talked about?" The narratives were content analyzed and categorized into three groups according to their reported complexity. That no conversation of any significance took place following 114 (38%) incidents meant that such postincident discussion does not happen as a matter of course.

These aside, two-thirds of the sample (184; 62%) acknowledged a conversation or discussion after the incident. For the most part, accounts of discussions suggested that they involved recounting what had happened with the partner with whom they had attended the incident. In some instances, they took the form of a far more extensive operational debriefing which included supervisors (which may have actually been a CIDB, though, interestingly was not labeled as such—which makes one wonder if the officers were told that it was one!). Those categorized as "minimal" were described as "banter," or quite superficial (for example, "Just normal bravado / joking banter with colleagues"). A more detailed discussion of the event was categorized as a "review" (for example, "General conversation between the officers involved, some disagreeing with the course of action taken, others notably more experienced officers agreeing with action"). Those categorized as "analysis" were described as quite formal discussions of the operation, usually involving supervisors (for example, "The incident was discussed by members present including the shift supervisor. The incident was talked through and good and bad points discussed, with a view to learning from the incident," or, "The whole incident discussed afterwards with colleagues and supervisors. Discussed feelings and fears about entering the house")—the latter may have been a CIDB.

Three broad themes emerged from these discussions: (1) complaints about the organization; (2) mutual agreement on the course of action, as a form of mutual support and as reflective practice; and (3) a final interesting category of discussions about what *could* have happened. Some 12 percent specifically mentioned operational difficulties at the scene as an element of their postincident discussion, or the main focus of it. The ability to discuss the incident in this way and the development of a sense of cohesion by sharing difficulties may be helpful in coming to terms with the incident in the short term; however, it is equally likely that a steady stream of moaning, and reinforcing the sense of not being appreciated by the organization may lower moral. It is interesting that the enemy as the organization is mentioned far more than the enemy outside (the threatening incidents they have to deal with). Some 10 percent had a theme of a mutual patting on the back (e.g., considering the situation, officers had done as well as could be expected, and had made the right decisions). This is a form of reflection which, depending on the nature of the discussion, may have simply reinforced poor decisions or presented an opportunity to learn. As well as providing a sense of social support, postincident conversations allowed reflective practice to take place, and consolidated learning. Fourteen statements reflected a theme of catastrophizing the outcome and imagining what might have happened (if certain actions had not been taken, or had the suspect been different in some way). This may well serve the psychological function of coping with the more fortunate "real" outcome. Information seeking can serve as a coping mechanism (Evans, Coman, Stanley & Burrows, 1993; Carver, Scheier & Weintraub, 1989). It is clear from the number of discussions which the officers had spontaneously that many consisted of a dissection of the preceding events (Mitchell et al., 1998). This can result in reassessing the stressfulness of the incident (Taylor 1991) and may help officers to manage the situation, and even reduce any anxiety.

Discussing the incident provides an opportunity to check that one's actions were appropriate or even valued. The figures on postincident discussion suggest that it has at least two main functions, one "educational" in learning from, and reflecting on, the incident, and the other providing "social," or emotional support in the form of encouraging the officer that he or she had done the right thing, and in some instances even asking after their welfare. Enhancement of the *esprit de corps* is evident from some of the coping themes in talking about the appropriate management of the incidents in the face of perceived organizational and other difficulties of the job. Apparently, officers were conducting informal peer debriefings themselves. Further research would elucidate the degree to which the "facts," "feelings," and "future" elements of a CIDB occur naturally. It is also important to assess whether such discussions actually conferred social support upon participants and functioned to safeguard well-being.

Of the greatest significance to officers is the pivotal role of the supervisor in many aspects of the provision of social support. In accounts which specifically mentioned the supervisor, twenty-five evaluated the interaction with the supervisor positively, while nineteen evaluated it negatively. Although no outcome measures indicated the instrumental effect of social support, the conclusion that officers need and appreciate recognition for their work is unavoidable (Alexander et al., 1993; Childers, 1991).

Brown and Campbell (1993) found that lack of support from colleagues significantly influences how officers manage the physical and other dangers they face. A lack of social support, generally, results in officers feeling unappreciated. In one study of police officers, almost half the sample agreed with the statement that their Police Force had to some extent been "unaware of their efforts" in the previous four weeks, and about a quarter believed this to be the case to a "marked degree." Feelings of not being appreciated were found only in the lower ranks (Brown et al., 1996), and were associated with self-report of irritability, depression, anxiety, and feeling "stressed."

The postincident support needs of police officers are complex and vary with the individual, and the nature and outcome of the incident. In another part of our study, officers were asked what the force should do to support officers. Without presenting the details of this part of the work, suggestions from officers were very varied. Only 10 percent failed to provide an answer (indicating that it is an important topic for them). In terms of how to offer CIDB, the responses are instructive. Opinions were divided on whether the use of support interventions should be voluntary or mandatory. A minority explicitly felt that support should be provided only after certain more serious incidents (as is the basis of CIDB), and this view was implicit in many other responses. This of course, begs the question of who decides whether an incident is of sufficient significance to warrant a CIDB? Other issues concerned the timing of intervention, and views that it should be offered immediately or extended over a long period of time were expressed. Most officers would welcome some form of pos incident support, often through spontaneous, informal channels (e.g., discussion with peers individually or collectively).

Joseph, Williams, and Yule (1998) reviewed the putative "stress buffering" effects of social support, especially with reference to the amelioration of the effects of traumatic incidents. They point out that the social support needs (emotional, tangible, information) vary over time and that some of the inconsistencies found in examining the buffering effects of social support may be explained by this. In general, there is a reduction in the distress in the six or so weeks following an incident and a reduction in the need for social support, although immediately following there is high level of distress and a concomitant high need for social support, particularly emotional support. The different "types" of social support, variation in the need for support, who provides it and in what form, and the changes in symptoms over time all need to be considered when assessing the processes involved. Continued education about psychological health, and how that can be maintained by officers themselves, are both important. Equally, or even more important, is educating supervisors to create an occupational context which recognizes good work.

REFERENCES

Ainsworth, P. B.: *Psychology and policing in a changing world.* Chichester, UK, Wiley, 1995.

Alexander, D. A.; Innes, G.; Irving, B. L.; Sinclair, S. D., & Walker, L. D.: *Health, stress and policing: A study in Grampian police.* The Police Foundation, 1991.

Alexander, D. A.; Walker, L. G.; Innes, G., & Irving, B. L.: *Police stress at work.* Washington, D.C., The Police Foundation, 1993.

American Institute of Stress: *Top ten most stressful jobs.* (Quoted in *Police Beat* Volume 6, May/June), 1994.

Anshel, M. H.; Robertson, M., & Caputi, P.: Sources of acute stress and their appraisals and reappraisals among Australian police as a function of previous experience. *Journal of Occupational and Organizational Psychology, 70:* 337-356, 1997.

Bisson, J. I., & Deahl, M. P.: Psychological debriefing and prevention of post-traumatic stress; more research is needed. *British Journal of Psychiatry, 165:* 717-720, 1994.

Borrill, C. S.; Wall, T. D.; West, M. A.; Hardy, G. E.; Shapiro, D. A.; Carter, A.; Golya, D. A., & Haynes, C. E.: *Mental health of the workforce in NHS Trusts.* Phase 1 Final Report. National Health Service, London, 1996.

Brown, J., & Campbell, E.: *Stress and policing: Sources and strategies.* Chichester, UK, Wiley, 1993.

Brown, J.; Cooper, C., & Kirkcaldy, B.: Occupational stress among senior police officers. *British Journal of Psychology, 87:* 31-41, 1996.

Carver, C. S.; Scheier, M. F., & Weintraub, J. K.: Assessing coping strategies: A theoretically based approach. *Journal of Personality and Social Psychology, 56:* 267-283, 1989.

Childers, J.: Plateauing in law enforcement. *FBI Law enforcement Bulletin, 60:* 16-18, 1991.

Cutrona, C. E.: Stress and social support: In search of optimal matching. *Journal of Social and Clinical Psychology, 9*: 3-14, 1990.

Dantzker, M. L.: *Contemporary policing: Personnel, issues and trends.* Oxford, Butterworth-Heinemann., 1997.

Dyregrov, A.: Caring for helpers in disaster situations: Psychological debriefing. *Disaster Management, 2*: 25 - 30, 1989.

Evans, D. J.; Coman, G. J.; Stanley, R. O., & Burrows, G. D.: Police officers' coping strategies: An Australian police survey. *Stress medicine, 9*: 237-246, 1993.

Gallagher, B.: *Critical incident debriefing: Occupational health and welfare unit.* Glasgow, Strathclyde Police, 1996.

Geates, J.: *Critical incident stress.* Unpublished Internal Report. Glasgow, Strathclyde Police, 1996.

Her Majesty's Inspector of Constabulary: *Lost time: The management of sickness absence and medical retirement in the police service.* London, Home Office, 1997.

Hobbs, M., & Adshead, G.: Preventative psychological interventions for road crash survivors. In M. Mitchell (Ed.), *The aftermath of road accidents: Psychological, social and legal consequences.* London, Routledge, 1997.

Janoff-Bulman, R: Assumptive worlds and the stress of traumatic events: Applications of the schema construct. *Social Cognition, 7*: 113 - 36, 1989.

Joseph, S.; Williams, R., & Yule, W.: *Understanding post-traumatic stress: A psychosocial perspective on PTSD and treatment.* London, Wiley, 1997.

Manolias, M.: Training for stress. In P. Southgate (Ed.), *New directions in police training.* London: HMSO, 1988.

Mitchell, M., & Hogg, I.: The emotional impact of collecting crime evidence: The work of the scenes of crime officer. *Procedures in Criminal Justice: Contemporary Psychological Issues, 29*: 35 - 40, 1997.

Mitchell, M.; Cowan, M.; Hamilton, R.; Jackson, J., & Speed, E.: *Facing violence: Assessing the training and support requirements of police constables in Scotland.* Edinburgh, Scottish Office Central Research Unit, 1997.

Mitchell, M.; Cowan, M.; Jackson, J., & Speed, E.: *Facing violence: Assessing the training and support needs for police constables in Scotland.* Edinburgh, Scottish Office, 1998.

Mitchell, M.; Poole, D.; Stevenson, K., & Young, K.: *Managing post-incident trauma in the police service.* First Quarterly Report, Glasgow, Police Research Unit, Glasgow Caledonian University, 1998.

Raphael, B.; Meldrum, L., & McFarlane, A. C.: Does debriefing after psychological trauma work? Time for randomized controlled trials. *British Medical Journal, 310*: 1479 - 1480, 1995.

Rick, J.; Perryman, S.; Young, K.; Guppy, A., & Hillage, J.: *Workplace trauma and its management: Review of the literature.* Health and Safety Executive Contract Research Report: London, 1998.

Schaefer, C., Coyne, J. C., & Lazarus, R. S.: The health related functions of social support. *Journal of Behavioral Medicine, 4*: 381 - 406, 1981.

Scott, M., & Stradling, S.: Post-traumatic stress disorder without the trauma. *British Journal of Clinical Psychology, 33*: 71-74, 1994.

Taylor S. E.: *Health Psychology* (2nd ed.), New York, McGraw-Hill, 1991.

Chapter 21

POSTINTERVENTION STRATEGIES TO REDUCE POLICE TRAUMA: A PARADIGM SHIFT

CHRIS DUNNING

INTRODUCTION

History of Debriefing in Law Enforcement for Work-Related Mental Injuries

As the contents of this book have demonstrated, law enforcement officers are confronted daily with the reality of trauma: of responding to scenes of horrific and gruesome accidents and crimes as well as to the heartbreaking tragedy of physical and sexual child abuse, homicide, suicide, and rape. It is not surprising that police officers have been empirically found to suffer the mental injuries associated with traumatic stress as the result of their assigned duties (Violanti, 1996). Recognition by administrators of the fact that stress and traumatic stress have caused performance and financial costs has wrought acceptance for the need for some type of program to forestall such negative consequences. It is now common for police departments to incorporate a debriefing for workplace trauma as part of their employee assistance response.

Debriefing to mitigate stress was first introduced to the police field by Roberts (1975) and Davidson (1979). Roberts used the technique of debriefing learned from the military (Bourne, 1969). Where once conducted as an individual intervention modality, the debrief as a group process developed in response to the need to cover, with a minimum of intrusion and cost, a large group of responders to traumatic assignments. The benefits of group intervention following significant operations as a mechanism to reduce stress were being presented to police administrators and psychologists (Wagner, 1981a, 1981b).

The stress debrief sessions, as they were then called, had two purposes (Wagner, 1981). The first focused on the opportunity to talk about the experience as a means of lessening the intensity of any ensuing symptoms. The second was to facilitate a discussion of the incident and individual reactions among officers so that the participants could be educated about the nature of stress reactions and the various personal strategies and counseling resources available to them.

Historically, it is important to note that debriefing had its genesis in addressing stress, not trauma, and was widely reported in the law enforcement literature (Davidson, 1979; Dunning & Silva, 1980; Roberts, 1975; Wagner, 1979, 1981a, 1981b). The title "stress debriefing" speaks to its orientation toward reducing stress and anxiety in those involved in traumatic events. By 1984, debriefing was the accepted modality to reduce stress in police services and was discussed at numerous professional association conferences in the early 1980s. By 1985, the law enforcement professionals recognized stress as the norm and legitimized programs to mitigate its inevitable impact on police officers.

The use of the group debrief to mitigate trauma experienced by emergency workers was suggested by Dunning and Silva (1980) and Wagner (1979) in relation to the conventional use of the word trauma as defined as a "disordered psychic or behavioral state resulting from mental or emotional stress" (Woolf, 1977). At that time, the diagnosis of Posttraumatic Stress Disorder (PTSD) had yet to be codified by the American Psychiatric Association in its publication *Diagnostic and Statistical Manual of Psychiatric Disorders*, 3rd Edition (1980). Mitchell (1983) purported that the modality, retitled Critical Incident Stress Debriefing, was useful in mitigating Posttraumatic Stress Disorder. Being essentially the same Stress Debrief process put forth by Wagner (1981a), the modality had only changed in goal, not in process, from stress to trauma mitigation. What was not understood at that time, given the newness of the diagnosis of PTSD, was the difference between stress and trauma. It was common for lay persons, and most clinicians, to lack an understanding of the difference between stress, trauma, and posttraumatic stress.

DEBRIEFING FOR POLICE STRESS OR PTSD?

Stress and traumatic stress are distinct phenomena, representing different physiological, neurobiological, and psychological processes. It is unfortunate that the word stress even exists in the diagnosis of Posttraumatic Stress Disorder. It is common for many individuals, especially clinicians, to perceive stress and traumatic stress as existing on a continuum. This is a misconception. While stress relates to anxiety and the adrenaline response of "fight or flight," traumatic stress involves the way in which the brain in its physical structures and chemistry takes in information, encodes it, stores it, and is able to retrieve it as memory. People who experience trauma may present a blunt affect or be unable to regulate emotion and cognition as a result. When cued in a fashion similar to the original trauma, the traumatized person may experience the same emotional reaction, generally fear, and physiological arousal as if the event were reoccurring. It is important for any clinician involved in the intervention of trauma subsequent to crisis to have a basic understanding of the differences neurobiologically between stress and traumatic stress (Yehuda & McFarlane, 1997; Yehuda, 1998).

Since debriefing has been touted as a prevention aid concerning, or remedy to, Posttraumatic Stress, several evaluative studies have been undertaken. That police officers can be traumatized is well accepted, but the role of intervention in the acute phase of exposure is not. One side in the present debate suggests that immediate post-employment debriefing represents the state-of-the-art standard of reasonable care for mental injuries sustained by deployment in traumatic events. While anecdotal support for its efficacy has been proposed (Mitchell & Everly, 1995; Robinson & Mitchell, 1993), others have discounted such claims, pointing out that researching one's own modality introduces bias. What is clear is that other anecdotal and more methodologically rigorous research has seriously questioned the efficacy of debriefing for PTSD (Alexander & Wells, 1991; Bisson & Deahl, 1994; McFarlane, 1988; Hytten & Hasle, 1989; Creamer, et al., 1991; Griffiths & Watts, 1992; Deahl, et al., 1994; Kenardy, et al., 1996; Carlier, et al., 1997). In fact, many have concluded (Avery & Orner, 1998) that Critical Incident Stress Debriefing causes the very disorder that it was said to prevent, Posttraumatic Stress Disorder. Indeed, the previously mentioned researchers were surprised at the high levels of incidence and chronicity of the PTSD reported by those participating in debriefs.

POLICE TRAUMATIC DUTY ASSIGNMENT AND PATHOLOGY

Debate over the efficacy of debriefing has resulted in the understanding that exposure to a traumatic event produces reactions that occur along a continuum. To assume that traumatic exposure produces trauma, or even stress, ignores the reality that many individuals value their traumatic event as a learning and growth experience. The stress debriefing modality, following a medical model, suggested that its efficacy was in treatment for or to prevent pathology, in this case PTSD. CISD (Mitchell & Everly, 1995) was touted as a mental health mechanism to forestall the development of PTSD.

It is conceivable, however, that debriefing accentuated the stress response and exacerbated the traumatic stress response (Herman, 1992;

Dunning, 1995, 1988; Paton & Stephens, 1996). The traumatized person in group-debrief may be triggered into the same neurobiological response as the traumatic event when confronted by the disclosure of others. In affective overload, the cognitions involving imagery, sensory-motor memory, and interpretative sense of meaning held by persons who experienced the event, the traumatized police officer may confabulate and bring such material into their trauma set. This is especially likely to happen in the CISD model where participants are asked to relate to the group their worst moment, imagery, and fears. Participants may be contaminated by the trauma experience and meaning of other participants, with these being confabulated into their own traumatic memory. This is in contrast to the Raphael's (1986) model which asks members of the debrief to relate their successes, their strengths, and support of others. Where the CISD model predicts and reinforces negative outcomes, Raphael's model focuses on planning to prepare oneself for the future of reoccurrence.

What is problematic, then, is when group debriefing exacerbates or intensifies the physiological process that causes trauma. While stress may be mitigated by disclosure to another in a group, where the element of social sharing involve interpretation and feedback its helpfulness is diminished (Stuhlmiller & Dunning, in press). It must be remembered that the experience may well prove positive to many. In fact, it has long been administrative procedure in law enforcement to rotate as many officers as possible at a mass casualty scene to give them a "training experience." Here, trauma exposure is accepted as a source of growth and development. What is required is a paradigm shift away from considering the inevitable consequence of high-risk or disastrous situations as traumatic pathology, to one that presupposes posttraumatic growth as the predominant experience.

TRAUMATIC EXPOSURE AND POSTTRAUMATIC GROWTH

The protocols developed in the 1980s all had an orientation to disclosing the worst fear, sight, experience, or meaning. In addition, the educational component dwelt on pathology and the emergence of symptomatology associated with police duties at traumatic events. However, Higgins (1994) reminded us that those experiencing trauma are generally able to negotiate significant challenges as individuals and do consistently "snap back." This was consistent with research conducted on community or group-experienced disaster which consistently documents how survivors support and enhance a collective sense of strength. This strength supports the group and individual not only in what was just experienced but also in future ability to control and respond to the demands occasioned by the event (Dynes, 1970). Higgins suggested the term "resilience" to capture the active process of self-righting and growth. Higgins defined resilience broadly as the ability to function psychologically at a level far greater than expected given the individual's capabilities and previous experiences. By viewing resilience as a process in which the person experiences learned resourcefulness, the police officer can be seen to contribute internal strengths, which are validated by group process. Lyons (1991) supported this orientation in suggesting that it is imperative that we do not err in the opposite direction of attempting to identify pathology resulting from traumatization.

Higgins' (1994) conceptualization of resilience is of a process that builds on itself over time. While individuals may have differing core resilient dynamic capacities, all persons possess to some degree the ability to learn and grow from a traumatic experience. She suggested that there are natural "holding environments" (e.g., organizational culture) that promote the growth of these capacities, and maximizing resilience requires that attention be given to the environments that surrounds the event. Just as individual characteristics influence outcome, so too do group norms, values, interpretations, and meanings that are communicated to its members. Minimization and denial from external significant sources act to exacerbate trauma just as validation and normalization are suggested to act prophylactically to improve the course of trauma recovery. The group can act as a source of healing and recovery or of exacerbation and decline (Smith, 1985). Group process in its context has not been as widely examined, although benefits of the group for protective service personnel have been suggested (Paton & Stephens, 1996).

It is important that any formal organizational psychological response subsequent to a traumatic event builds upon the strengths and capabilities of those affected. The atypical nature of traumatic experiences makes it likely that officers will show some normal sign of emotional strain, but it does not necessarily imply mental illness or posttraumatic reaction. Few studies have explored how marginally-impaired and successful individuals cope with the aftermath of trauma. In fact, while the literature gives brief mention to hardiness (Bartone et al., 1989) and resiliency (Funk, 1992; Siebert, 1993), little attention has been paid to the assessment of positive outcome from traumatic experience. Tedeschi and Calhoun (1996) and Tedeschi, Park, and Calhoun (1998) suggested the possibility of positive impact of negative events and the potential, and possible prophylaxis, of resilient factors that can lead to posttraumatic growth. They assert that since growth is the antithesis of posttraumatic stress disorder, posttraumatic growth becomes a novel approach to pychotraumatology. Persons who discover or create the perception of positive changes and growth shed light on the problems of those who continue to suffer.

The positive effects of traumatic experiences include the enhancement or reinforcement of the ability to cope with adversity, development of self-discipline, an appreciation for the value of life, and a sense of accomplishment, competence, and resilience. Tedeschi and Calhoun (1996) found at least three broad categories of perceived benefit that individuals have identified in connection with their traumatic experience: changes in self-perception, changes in interpersonal relationships, and change in philosophy of life. Recognizing that trauma has salutary benefits, Tedeschi and Calhoun (1996) developed the Post Traumatic Growth Inventory (PTGI) which attempted to measure the extent to which survivors of traumatic events perceive changes in these characteristics following their traumatic experience.

The wording of the PTGI presented possible benefits as outcomes of coping with traumatic events with the coping process of positive, reinterpretation, positive reframing, interpretive control, or reconstrual of events as the coping process. Some empirical research currently exists to document that the process of posttraumatic growth acts to mitigate against the development of PTSD (Elder & Cliff, 1989; Joseph et al., 1993; Fontana & Rosenheck, 1998; Tedeschi, Park, & Calhoun, 1998). Yet, Tedeschi and Calhoun suggested that adopting these beliefs and seeing the traumatic event as an experience with some meaning and benefit provided comfort to the traumatized individual. Research by Kobasa (1979), Kobasa et al. (1982), and others (Taylor, 1983) have correlated the relationship between the existence of positive others and better physical and psychological outcome. Further, persons who have experienced exposure to horrific traumatic events have reportedly extolled the importance of consequent positive growth benefits, identification of meaning, and of connection with others as a salutary consequence of their sorrow (Frankl, 1963; Eitenger, 1964; Krystal, 1968). It would appear that the identification of benefits and measurement of growth add significantly to the perception of meaning that survivors derive from their trauma experience.

Clinicians who intervene in the acute stage of trauma must remember that it is the survivor's cognitive appraisal of the traumatic event that is the major determinant of subsequent adjustment (Breslau et al., 1991). Many models of acute intervention tend to focus on role and response to the trauma rather on the search for meaning, the question of "Why did this event happen, ...happen to the victim, ...happen to me?) (Taylor, 1983). According to Lyons (1991), cognitive restructuring that finds meaning in some outcome of the event such as increased self-knowledge or a revision of priorities is associated with positive adjustment and that the explanation upon which the survivor settles need not be reality-based. Taylor (1989) posited that it is a natural cognitive phenomenon to maintain one's competence by overestimating one's ability to respond to traumatic situations and to maintain an illusion of self-efficacy and self-esteem not consistent with reality in order to live with knowledge of the event. The process of developing resiliency depends in great part on retroactive reworking of the cognition and meaning that the survivor attaches to the event and their response.

It is important to note that resilience in adults has been conceptualized variously by a variety of clinicians and researchers (Siebert, 1994; Richards, 1989). Higgins' (1994) dynamic conceptualization of the resilient adult is described in Figure 21.1. Most importantly, resilient adults have gradually relaxed their initial, over-determined sense of self-interpretation and self-reliance and have moved collaboratively into experiencing the event as a member of the group. What is significant, according to Higgins, is that resilience can be cultivated, that the group can influence the individual, that "good company" can change the course of individual reaction from traumatic decline to traumatic growth. The salutogenic effects of resilience and social perception suggests that the group can facilitate the active process of self-righting and growth.

Figure 21.1.
Higgins' (1994) dynamic conceptualization of the resilient adults.

- remain fiercely committed to reflection and new perspectives
- look at every experience as a source of emotional "mileage"
- grapple actively with personal accountability and self-scrutiny
- absorb information well and take most reasonable suggestions readily
- believe that knowledge is power and that the future can be improved by learning and insight
- negotiate emotionally hazardous experiences proactively rather than reactively, thus solving problems flexibly
- make positive meanings out of their experiences, actively constructing a positive vision
- recruit other peoples "invested regard"
- reduce their discrepant views of themselves and take a measured perspective of what happened.

PARADIGM SHIFT: DEBRIEFING ORIENTATION FROM PATHOGENIC TO SALUTOGENIC

The controversy surrounding debriefing rests on the orientation upon which it is predicated and its efficacy in the prevention or reduction of traumatization. Being based on a pathogenic model, Critical Incident Stress Debriefing has its roots in the theoretical orientations of learned helplessness. An alternative to the pathogenic orientation is a Wellness or Salutogenic approach to serving the mental health needs of trauma survivors.

This paradigm incorporates the constructs of hardiness and resiliency as well as learned resourcefulness (Stuhlmiller & Dunning, in press) and describes the ability of an individual to become inured to fatigue or hardship, to be capable of withstanding austere or horrific conditions (Funk, 1992). It is an individual's resolute courage and fortitude in the face of the overwhelming demands occasioned by the traumatic event (Williams et al., 1992). Hardiness represents the characteristic manner in which a person approaches and interprets an experience and it has a moderating effect on traumatic stress symptoms (Bartone et al., 1989; Funk, 1992). Hardiness is described variously along five dimensions with the attributes of control, challenge and commitment significantly influencing how people process and cope with stressful events (Kobasa et al., 1982).

Resiliency involves the capability to recover after stress or adjust to dramatic changes. Antonovsky (1993) first posited that a salutogenic orientation has far wider implications than simply proving a directive to focus on the health rather than the pathology of traumatized persons. According to Antonovsky (1987, 1990a,b), a "sense of coherence," or way of making sense of the world, is a major factor in determining how well a person manages stress and stays healthy (see also Janoff-Bulman (1992) and Herman (1992)).

While the pathogenic approach focused on the more immediate problem of the individual and on appropriate therapy, the salutogenic orientation is concerned with overall "mental health." It examines strengths within the work group (Antonovsky, 1991). When one realizes that the outcome of a traumatic stressor is not preordained trauma, then one can see that even undesirable traumas can have salutary outcomes. This requires what Antonovsky (1993) called a sense of coherence—comprehensibility, manageability, and meaningfulness. Antonovsky (1993) notes that of the three, it is meaningfulness that is primary. Traumatic stress can be seen as a burden or a challenge. Starting from hopelessness, one can only despair about gaining understanding or mobilizing resources. Starting from the perspective that coping is desirable, whatever the difficulty in being assured of a positive outcome, increasing comprehensibility and meaningfulness make manageability more likely and results in a stronger, more capable officer.

The question is how to achieve comprehension and meaningfulness to facilitate manageability. Readjustment following catastrophic events requires consideration of need for control, a positive sense of self, and an optimistic view of the future (Taylor, 1989). Adjustment after trauma revolves, in her estimation, around themes that include attempts to restore self-esteem, regain a sense of mastery, and require a search for meaning in the experience (Taylor, 1983). Taylor (1989) provides an excellent treatise to understanding how human beings cognitively deceive themselves in order to affirm self-concept, self-esteem, and self-efficacy. It is through self-schemas that individuals selectively impose information through which they construe knowledge about and perceive situations. This affects how they later remember the incident and how they perceive themselves in the incident. Taylor (1989) suggested that these positive illusions involved the self as hero, personal historian, and causal actor; the need and the illusion of control; and unrealistic optimism about the future and illusions of progress.

Cognitive psychologists have shown that people actively strive to overcome negative feelings and cognitions associated with traumatic events. What is surprising about the research is that persons who draw on their own internal resources, or use the social support available to them, successfully resolve conflicts between illusion and reality, thus restoring assumptive illusions (Gurin, Veloff & Feld, 1960). Mental health tended to be sustained as long as there was no disconfirmation of the illusion. This resulted in hesitation on the part of some therapists to intervene to enhance people's feelings of control, however illusionary, in traumatic situations. Taylor (1989) argued that people respond to disconfirmed expectations of control very differently. In this conception, people achieved control in traumatic circumstances by becoming actively involved in cognitively restructuring the event and its meaning. This learned resourcefulness refers to what the individual or group can do when stressful circumstances call for self-direction, a more internally-directed process that reinforces strength (Rosenbaum, 1990).

What is evolving is a debrief protocol that requires a reinterpretation of the circumstances of performance, from failure to success, and identification of new environments in which to exert control. This is easier to accomplish in the group than in the individual. Control in complex environments, such as a workplace, involves multiple goals and means, making it easier to redirect energies of a group toward cognitive restructuring. Even then, individual responses do not occur in isolation. Individuals use social support to help them in this process. It makes sense then to use the group to achieve learned resourcefulness to overcome the deleterious effects of traumatic events. If one goal is thwarted, this does not block the group from moving in another direction in returning to options not selected in the first round. Disconfirmation of a single attempt to address an issue the group is grappling with is not a setback, as the group has already generated many different ideas to which they can turn to recreate their positive illusions.

Taylor (1983) and others (Frankl, 1963; Visotsky et al., 1961) suggested that the process of recreating positive illusions often advances people beyond their trauma and beyond any point they might have reached in their lives without their tragic experience. Taylor defined meaning as a need to understand why the event occurred (causation), its impact (insight), and whether it signifies any value or purpose for the individual (affect). What we are reminded of is that meaning and need for mastery are intertwined. This orientation is similar to Meichenbaum's (1985) Stress Inoculation Training (SIT) which was designed to nurture and develop coping skills or "learned resourcefulness": what one can do to when stressful circumstances call for self-direction. Antonovsky's sense of coherence furthers this conception to include a set of personal beliefs that guide the way in which one copes with stress. A sense of coherence expresses the belief that life, or the situation at hand, is comprehensible, manageable, and meaningful.

Research by Antonovsky and others consistently supported the finding that to emerge psychologically and behaviorally unimpaired from disabling traumatic injury, survivors needed to undertake a course of action that was salutogenic in focus. Further, Antonovsky asserted that to be salutary, the survivor of a trauma must learn to utilize social and occupational resources to pursue a commitment to viewing trauma as a challenge and as a source of positive growth.

THE SALUTOGENIC DEBRIEF

Using a Salutogenic approach to trauma mitigation, the mental health profession would play a different role than counselor or therapist in the acute stage of intervention. Rather than utilizing standard group modalities based on CISD, Crisis Intervention, or talk therapy protocols, the mental health professional facilitates the individual or group toward activities to accomplish manageability, comprehensibility, and meaningfulness. As a consultant, the mental health professional must assess the reaction of those involved to the event, their immediate and previous coping skills, as well as assess their resiliency, sense of coherence, and hardiness as individuals, as a group, and as an organization. Any intervention requires such an assessment to determine an appropriate course of action.

The mental health professional must assess the degree to which any of those affected report depersonalization, derealization, or other forms of dissociation during and subsequent to the event. These serve as important predictors of later PTSD (McFarlane, 1988; van der Kolk, McFarlane, &

Weiseth, 1997). Those individuals would be targeted for immediate assessment and possible individual counseling. The mental health professional functions primarily to facilitate positive growth/sense of coherence that provides salutary effects for stressed or traumatized individuals through group activities.

The Salutogenic Debrief recommends that the mental health professional perceive his/her role as one of facilitator in a debrief process that occurs informally as the professional participates in organizational processes of trauma recovery. In this context, they assess the need for the group to explore activities related to what are being proposed as Salutogenic Cs or concepts, allowing the group to control selection of goal and activity. Research by Kobasa, Maddi, and Cahn (1982) and others has consistently shown the benefits of attending to five functions or tasks by sick or injured individuals seeking to regain health. While even Kobasa expressed dismay at the seemingly simplistic conception afforded hardiness through the mnemonic of using the Cs, Spiegel (1994) found the pattern useful in describing acute interventions for dissociation. Spiegel noted that while dissociative defenses prove effective in helping trauma survivors manage fear, pain, and helplessness, they might result in a failure to work through the experience. He used the principles of the C's to direct the concepts to be addressed in treating dissociation in acute trauma. The C's of Kobasa et al. (1982) are described in Figure 21.2. These have repeatedly been found to be predictive of physical health recovery. The C's of Spiegel (1994) connected to psychotherapeutic intervention for individuals suffering acute traumatic dissociative reaction are described in Figure 21.3.

The Cs provide a framework for the mental health professional to identify and conceptualize issues which trauma survivors need addressed through group activities or tasks. The concepts of wellness facilitates developing a "healing theory" (Figley, 1989) that fosters a sense of coherence—compre-

---

Figure 21.2.
The C's of Kobasa, Maddi, and Cahn (1982).

- CONTROL over one's body.

- COHESION with other individuals or group.

- COMMUNICATION of what is happening and the affect connected.

- CHALLENGE perceived by situation to be overcome.

- COMMITMENT to a course of action to overcome challenge.

Figure 21.3.
Spiegal's C's for psychotherapeutic intervention.

- CONDENSATION in the form of memory.

- CONFESSION of guilt, however inappropriate.

- CONSOLATION in the form of comfort.

- CONSCIOUSNESS in trauma making material restructured into recollection that is not so demoralizing.

- CONCENTRATION to visualize through injury what was done and what they did to protect themselves.

- CONTROL over memories, the ability to change them from negative to positive.

- CONGRUENCE to integrate traumatic memories in such a way that they do not overwhelmingly conflict with previous self-concepts.

hensibility, manageability, and meaningfulness for the individual and the work group. The Salutogenic Approach continues the nmemonics of the C's to assist in the creation of a therapeutic community in the work group, a sanctuary in which members who range from the stressed to the traumatized to begin to process the traumatic incident. The goal of sanctuary (Bloom, 1997, 1998) is to create an environment within which people can maximize their potential for recovery from trauma as well as experience growth with as little reexposure to trauma as possible. This leads to the final C'S, and

Figure 21.4.
The C's of sanctuary.

- CULTURE or ecological environment in which the event and its resolution takes place

- COMMEMORATION to provide validation of the reality of the event and ritualistic closure of its acute phase (Johnson, et al., 1995)

- CLOSURE to provide a demarcation some end for the event, even when normalcy or the previous state may not be yet attained these are described in Figure 21.4.

The work organization and work groups need to be educated in the need for and process of creating sanctuary. Sanctuary should be described as a state-of-being to allow the work group and the individual to continue to function at an acceptable level during the mitigation of the traumatic incident. It is important as well as in the return to regular duty assignments. It is in this context that a formal group meeting might be called. Participants are encouraged to use this group process to explore ways in which negative cognitions and meanings can be reexamined for their positive strength or resolution. Group activities can be selected for their positive or salutary contribution to trauma resolution. The mental health professional does not elicit worst emotion, cognition, or meaning. Instead, the focus is on making the experience a challenge to be mastered, with the group acting as validators and supporters of the process.

The facilitator helps the group to identify the Cs that are the most important and/or problematic about the event and leads them through a process that supports the use of positive language associated with emotion, insight, and causation regarding the event (Murray & Segal, 1994; Pennebaker, 1997). Reduction of stress and resolution of trauma are antecedents to the process (Pennebaker, Mayne, & Francis, in press). The Thirteen C's of Salutogenesis act as an assessment map to allow the facilitator to identify and assess, rather than serving as a therapeutic protocol.

Just as the role of the mental health professional changes in the Salutogenic Approach, so too does that of the peer counselor. Their role is to discern and articulate the problematic area operant in the work group or organization. It is not necessarily to act as counselor per se, but as liaison between the occupational group and the mental health professional. The peer counselor assists in developing an action plan that addresses identified issues, leads its implementation, and evaluates its effect. The role of the mental health professional is to translate the problematic areas that are identified into goals to be targeted and assist in developing the means by which they can be realized by the group. The group states the cognition associated with congruence, its negative effect, and what cognition where congruence would be positive. An example relating to the Oklahoma City bombing is described in Figure 21.5.

To identify issues the group must address to attain a sense of coherence, the mental health professional must informally scan the behaviors and verbal disclosures of those who were exposed to the traumatic event as well as their colleagues, supervisors, and the organization. In recognizing positive and negative feedback that might ensue in relation to perceived beliefs and effects of trauma survivors, the mental health professional must become a part of the trauma mitigation team. Being attached to the organization for as

Figure 21.5. Salutogenic examples from Oklahoma City bombing.		
CONGRUENCE - INCONGRUENCE	DEBRIEF ACTION PLAN	CONGRUENCE IN OUTCOME
1. Police officers thought families of dead must think rescuers incompetent and afraid as they were proceeding slowly through wreckage to recover bodies	1. Three rescuer representatives were sent to meet with families at Compassion Center to explain reasons for length of time and caution in search and to express regret at necessity	1. Families sent word that their expectation was that no one else would be hurt by bombing. Made guardian angel pins to remind rescuers to make safety a priority.
2. Rescuers expressed sense of incompetence at fact that more people were not saved, so operation was a failure	2. Each rescuer was encouraged to visit a survivor at home or hospital to express their happiness for survivor recovery.	2. Rescuers saw happiness and thankfulness of survivors and family, progress toward recovery, the strong support response of community and medical profession, and fostered a sense of recovery and progress, success rather than failure.

long as it takes to determine whether negative consequences have occurred in relation to trauma response is important. Thus, it is not necessary for the consultant to conduct small group sessions as long as they maintain a role as an integral member of the organization in regards to issues related to the traumatic event. Rather, the trauma advisor would use the Salutogenic Approach chart presented below (Figure 21.6) to pinpoint issues to be addressed for coherence by developing action plans to check out negative and modify to positive cognitions concerning trauma response.

Participants are encouraged to use the group to explore ways in which negative cognitions and meanings can be examined for their positive strength or resolution. Group activities are selected for their positive or salutary contribution to trauma resolution. In this approach, the mental health facilitator does not elicit worst emotions, cognitions, or meanings. Instead, the focus is on making the experience a challenge to be mastered, with the group acting as validators and supporters of the process. The facilitator listens and observes the group, scanning for negative emotions, statements of

Figure 21.6.
The Thirteen C's of Salutogenesis.

C's of Salutogenesis	Positive Emotion	Insight	Causation
1. **Control** of external environment, activities.	Development of sense of autonomy, control, and ability to influence destiny	Analysis of personal role and actions in the event and subsequently that were controlled or controllable	Analysis of uncontrollable causes and positive actions taken to mitigate impact during event and in present
2. **Cohesion** with significant others, support systems, and fellow survivors	Foster sense of belonging with concerned others	Assessment of advantages and benefits of social support from colleagues and significant others	Acknowledgement of buffering impact of group and the positive consequences of avoiding withdrawal and isolation
3. **Communication** of verbal and written perceptions and cognitions about event and role	Expression of positive self-discovery and growth	Confiding realization of all factors that influenced event and its aftermath	Discussion of information regarding cause of event and its positive resolution and efforts at prevention of re-occurrence
4. **Challenge** of opportunities for growth and development	Gain confidence in personal strengths to respond to future capabilities	See the hardship as something to be overcome using one's skills, knowledge, and intelligence	Gain sense of ability to proactively change situation
5. **Commitment** to remaining active in the process of resolving sequelae	Find a meaning related to continuing attempts to further resolution or prevention that engenders faith and action	Find a sense of meaning and purpose to improve future to prevent, mitigate, or improve resolution for self or others	Commitment to proactive course of action to forestall repetition of event, decrease its potential impact, or improve ability to mitigate
6. **Connection** with 'healing theory' to trust in others that together healing will occur	Form a bond of trust for healing	Recognize steps to be taken to gain trust	Realize the impact the event has made both positive and negative on level of trust
7. **Clarification** by making the event understandable	Accept that the event and its reasons for occurring go beyond influence of individual	Discover areas of lack of information or ignorance of its import	Gain sufficient informant to process event and seek answers

Figure 21.6.
The Thirteen C's of Salutogenesis.

C's of Salutogenesis	Positive Emotion	Insight	Causation
8. **Coherence** by making the trauma story logical and consistent to personal and professional expectation	Acknowledge the fact that the event needs to have a meaning in relation to past and future performance	Understand the need to make the event manageable and understandable based on need for control of what can be controlled	Make event comprehensible by acknowledging cause and the inability to have prevented its occurrence but, factors could be manageable
9. **Cognition** involving awareness and judgement of event	Accept that every event has an inevitable consequence of feelings of blame, responsibility, and failure	See the event through the eyes of others to reorder, conform, or appreciate consequences, good and bad	Understand that diverse external forces played a part outside of the control of the person
10. **Commemoration** to provide a ritualistic closure to event for memorialization and remembrance	Feel a part of a larger community through the use of societal conventions of assembly and representation	Place the event within the context of history and the future through memorial	Acknowledge the power of forces outside control of man and the individual
11. **Comfort** to develop a feeling of relief or encouragement	Identify feelings of relief, encouragement and need for consolation	Accept consolation that things have changed	Realize that worry about reoccurrence requires consolation
12. **Culture** as the ecological context in which the event and healing take place	Realize that feelings are the reflection of socialization and acculturation	Understand the fact that everyone perceives and evaluates events differently with in the context at their experience and perspective	Separate evaluation of role and reaction from expectation of culture and community
13. **Closure** to achieve a state of feeling that the event has ended, although may never be the same	Define parameters of "before" and "now" to engender an optimistic future	Accept a new definition and expectation about what the future might be	Realize that some things happen but that person is the important consideration, not event

insight, or causation. Salutogenic C strategies are selected to target an action plan to foster a change to a positive affective and cognitive appraisal or perception. The facilitator assists the group in developing the action plan and in facilitating its implementation. Lastly, the facilitator reinforces the outcome and its interpretation in positive terms.

CONCLUSION

While the Salutogenic Debrief paradigm is appropriate for all groups, it is only the work group that will in all probability continue to exist long after the traumatic incident. All other groups, except for continuing communities, tend to be time-limited and have no future unless members ELECT to continue. Police officers have no such option unless they resign. They are in it together for the long haul. So if they have no choice in having their lives "meddled" with by mental health professionals where they have little choice in the matter, at the very least the mental health professional has a responsibility to DO NO HARM. This imposes a grave responsibility to make sure that any modality or protocol that is used in a work setting is based on sound theoretical and empirical grounding. The C's represent the operationalization of the paradigm and are not a comprehensive manual for the protocol. Continued research might highlight new concepts that act to impede the resolution of the traumatic event for the police officer. The C's could be regrouped to fit Antonovsky's Sense of Coherence-meaningfulness, comprehensibility, and manageability to determine which thread needs the greatest attention. What the mental health professional wants to achieve is a reintegration of the police officer to the routine of regular duty assignment, not necessarily to achieve immediate closure of the event. This process embodies a way to step from the high-intensity of the trauma often found in police work to the mundane demands of the job and of life.

One might argue that EMDR, which is now being used in acute situations, achieves essentially the same effect. Without disclosing the horrific and gruesome imagery and experience, survivors are asked to practice the shift from negative to positive cognition in the process of action rather than eye movement. The action plan orientation of the Salutogenic Approach, through its use of exercise of discovery, will be perceived as less gimmicky to police officers and therefore will probably be more culturally acceptable. The fact that it can and should be done in the police organization will allow the to effect permeate the culture and norms of the organization which should sustain its effect. EMDR cannot be used on all emergency responders. Salutogenic consultation can. As Smith (1989) pointed out, it is the sanction, the definition derived by the unit in Vietnam, which if sustained throughout life, acts to protect the veteran from PTSD. It is only when society intervenes and reinforces the negative that PTSD ensues. We've have seemed to have forgotten that reality.

REFERENCES

American Psychiatric Association: *Diagnostic and statistical manual of mental disorders (3rd ed.)*, Washington, DC: American Psychiatric Press, 1980. (4th ed. current, 1994).

Alexander, D. A., & Wells, A.: Reactions of police officers to body handling after a major disaster: A before and after comparison. *British Journal of Psychiatry, 159*: 517-555, 1991.

Antonovsky, A.: *Unraveling the mystery of health: How people manage stress and stay well.* San Francisco, Jossey-Bass, 1987.

Antonovsky, A. Pathways leading to successful coping and health. In Rosenbaum M. (Ed.), *Learned resourcefulness: On coping skills, self-control, and adaptive behavior.* New York, Springer, 1990a.

Antonovsky, A.: Personality and health: Testing the sense of coherence model. In Friedman, H. (Ed.), *Personality and Disease.* New York, John Wiley, 1990b..

Antonovsky, A.: The structural sources of salutogenic strengths. In Cooper, C. & Payne R. (Eds.), *Personality and stress: Individual differences in the stress process.* London, John Wiley, 1991.

Antonovsky, A.: The implications of salutogenesis: An outsider's view. In Turnbull, A., Patterson, J., Behr, S., Murphy, D. et al., (Eds.), *Cognitive coping, families, and disability.* Baltimore, MD, Paul H. Brookes, 1993.

Alexander, D. A., & Wells, A.: Reactions of police officers to body handling after a major disaster: A before and after comparison. *British Journal of Psychiatry, 159*: 517-555, 1991.

Avery, A., & Orner, R.: First report of psychological debriefing abandoned–The end of an era? *Traumatic Stresspoints, 12*: 3-4, Summer, 1998.

Bartone, P.; Ursano, A. R.; Wright, K., & Ingraham, L.: The impact of a military air disaster on the health of assistance workers: A prospective study. *Journal of Nervous and Mental Disease, 177*: 317-328, 1989.

Bisson, J. I., & Deahl, M. P.: Psychological debriefing and prevention of post-traumatic stress: More research is needed. *British Journal of Psychiatry, 165*: 717-720,1994.

Bloom, S.: *Creating Sanctuary: Toward an Evolution of Sane Societies.* New York, Routledge, 1997

Bloom, S.: By the crowd they have been broken, by the crowd they shall be healed: The social transformation of trauma. In R. Tedeschi, C. Park, & L. Calhoun (Eds.), *Posttraumatic growth: Positive change in the aftermath of crisis.* New York, Lawrence Erlbaum, 1998.

Bourne, P.: Military psychiatry and the Vietnam war in perspective. In P. Bourne (Ed.), *The psychology and physiology of stress.* New York, Academic Press, 1969.

Breslau, N. G.; Davis, P.; Andreski, R., & Peterson, E.: Traumatic events and post traumatic stress disorder in an urban population in young adults. *Archives of General Psychiatry, 48*: 216-222, 1991.

Carlier, I. V. E.; Lamberts, R. D.; Van Uchelen, A. J., & Gersons, B. P. R.: Effectiveness of psychological debriefing: A controlled study of traumatized police officers. *The Lancet,* 1997.

Creamer, M.; Buckingham, W. J., & Burgess, P. M.: A community-based mental health response to a multiple shooting. *Australian Psychologist, 26*: 99-102, 1991.

Davidson, A.: Air disaster: Coping with stress-a program that worked. *Police Stress, 1*: 20-22, 1979.

Deahl, M. P.; Gillham, A. B.; Thomas, J.; Searle, M., & Srinivason, M.: Psychological sequelae following the Gulf War: Factors associated with subsequent morbidity and the effectiveness of psychological debriefing. *British Journal of Psychiatry, 165*: 60-65, 1994.

Dunning, C. M.: Intervention strategies for emergency workers. In M. Lystad (Ed.), *Mental health response in mass emergencies*. New York, Brunner/Mazel, 1988.

Dunning, C. M.: Fostering resiliency in rescue workers. In A. S. Kalayjian, *Disaster and mass trauma: Global perspectives on post disaster mental health management*. Long Branch, NJ, Vista Press, 1995.

Dunning, C. M., & Silva, M.: Disaster-induced stress in rescue workers. *Victimology: An International Journal, 5*: 287-297, 1980.

Dynes, R.: *Organized behavior in disasters*. Lexington, KY, Heath-Lexington, 1970.

Elder, G., & Cliff, E.: Combat experience and emotional health: Impairment and resilience in later life. *Journal of Personality, 57*: 311-341, 1989.

Eitenger, L. *Concentration camp survivors in Norway and Israel*. Oslo, Universitetsforlaget, 1964.

Fontana, A., & Rosenheck, R.: Psychological benefits and liabilities of traumatic exposure in the war zone. *Journal of Traumatic Stress, 11*: 485-503, 1998.

Figley, C.: *Helping traumatized families*. San Francisco, Jossey-Bass, 1989.

Frankl, V. E.: *In search of meaning*. New York, Washington Square Press, 1963.

Funk, S. C.: Hardiness: A review of theory and research. *Health Psychology, 11*: 335-345, 1992.

Griffiths, J. A., & Watts, R.: *The Kempsey and Grafton bus crashes: The aftermath*. University of New England, Australia, Instructional Design Solutions, 1992.

Gurin, G.; Veloff, J., & Feld, S.: *Americans view their mental health*. New York, Basic Books, 1960.

Herman, J.: *Trauma and recovery: Aftermath of violence from domestic abuse to political terror*. New York, Basic Books, 1992.

Higgins, G. O.: *Resilient adults: Overcoming a cruel past*. San Francisco, Jossey-Bass, 1994.

Hytten, K., & Hasle, A.: Firefighters: A study of stress and coping. *Acta Psychiatrica Scandinavia, 80, Supplement 355*: 50-55, 1989.

Janoff-Bulman, R.: *Shattered assumptions: Toward a new psychology of trauma*. New York, The Free Press, 1992.

Johnson, D. R.; Feldman, S. C.; Lubin, H., & Southwick, S.: The therapeutic use of ritual and ceremony in the treatment of post-traumatic stress disorder. *Journal of Traumatic Stress, 8*: 283-298, 1995.

Joseph, S.; Williams, R., & Yule, W.: Changes in outlook following disaster: The preliminary development of a measure to assess positive and negative responses. *Journal of Traumatic Stress, 6*: 271-279, 1993.

Kenardy, J. A.; Webster, R. A.; Lewin, J. J.; Carr, V. J.; Hazell, P. I., & Carter, G. I.: Stress debriefing and patterns of recovery following a natural disaster. *Journal of Traumatic Stress, 9*: 37-49, 1996.

Kobasa, S. C.: Stressful life events, personality, and health: An inquiry into hardiness. *Journal of Personality and Social Psychology, 17*: 1-11, 1979.

Kobasa, S.; Maddi, S., & Cahn, S.: Hardiness and health: A prospective study. *Journal of Personality and Social Psychology, 42*: 168-177, 1982.

Krystal, H.: *Massive psychic trauma.* New York, International Universities Press, 1968.

Lyons, J. A.: Strategies for assessing the potential for positive readjustment following trauma. *Journal of Traumatic Stress, 4*: 93-112, 1991.

McFarlane, A. C.: The phenomenology of posttraumatic stress disorders following a natural disaster. *The Journal of Nervous and Mental Disease, 179*: 20-29, 1988.

McFarlane, A. C.: The longitudinal course of posttraumatic morbidity. *Journal of Nervous and Mental Disease, 176*: 30-39, 1988.

Meichenbaum, D.: *Stress Inoculation Training.* New York, Pergamon Press, 1985.

Mitchell, J. T.: When disaster strikes: The critical incident stress debriefing process. *Journal of Emergency Medical Services, 8*: 35-39, 1983.

Mitchell J. T., & Everly, G. S.: *Critical incident stress debriefing: An operations manual for the prevention of traumatic stress among emergency service workers.* Ellicott City, MD: Chevron, 1995.

Murray, E. J., & Segal, D. L: Emotional processing in vocal and written expression of feelings about traumatic experience. *Journal of Traumatic Stress, 7*: 391-404, 1994.

Paton, D., & Stephens, C.: Training and support for emergency responders. In D. Paton, & J. M. Violanti (Eds.), *Traumatic stress in critical occupations: Recognition, consequences, and treatment.* Springfield, IL, Charles C. Thomas, 1996.

Pennebaker, J. W.: *The effects of traumatic disclosure on physical and mental health: The values of writing and talking about upsetting events.* Paper presentation, Fourth World Congress on Stress, Trauma, and Coping, Baltimore, MD, April 1997.

Pennebaker, J. W.; Mayne, T. J., & Francis, M. E.: Linguistic predictors of adaptive bereavement, *Journal of Personality and Social Psychology*, in press.

Raphael, B.: *When disaster strikes.* London, Century Hutchinson, 1986.

Richards, B.: *Thriving after surviving.* Murray, UT, Hartley Communications, 1989

Roberts, M.: *Debriefing and peer counseling of police officers subsequent to shootings and crises.* FBI Training Key, 1975.

Robinson, R. C., & Mitchell, J. T.: Evaluation of psychological debriefings. *Journal of Traumatic Stress, 6*: 367-382, 1993.

Rosenbaum, M.: *Learned resourcefulness: On coping skills, self-control, and adaptive behavior.* New York, Springer, 1990.

Siebert, A.: *The survivor personality.* Portland, OR, Practical Psychology Press, 1993.

Smith, R. S.: Sealing over and integration. Modes of the solution in post-traumatic stress recovery press. In C.R. Figley (Ed.), *Trauma and its wake, Vol. 1.* New York, Brunner/Mazel, 1985.

Spiegel, D.: *Dissociation: Culture, mind, and body.* Washington, DC, American Psychiatric Press, 1994.

Stuhlmiller, C., & Dunning, C. M.: Concerns about debriefing: Challenging the mainstream. In B. Raphael, & J. Wilson (Eds.), *Debriefing.* London, Cambridge University Press, in press.

Taylor, S. E.: Adjustment to threatening life events: A theory of cognitive adaptation. *American Psychologist, 38*:1161-1173, 1983.

Taylor, S. E.: *Positive illusions: Creative deception and the healthy mind.* New York, Basic Books, 1989.

Tedeschi, R., & Calhoun, L: Posttraumatic growth inventory: Measuring the positive legacy of trauma, *Journal of Traumatic Stress, 9*: 455-471, 1996.

Tedeschi, R.; Park, C., & Calhoun, L. (Eds.), *Posttraumatic growth: Positive change in the aftermath of crisis.* New York, Lawrence Erlbaum, 1998.

van der Kolk, B.; McFarlane, A., & Weiseth, L.: *Traumatic stress: The effects of overwhelming experience on mind, body, and society.* New York, Guilford Press, 1996.

Violanti, J. M.: Trauma stress and police work. In D. Paton, & J. M. Violanti (Eds.), *Traumatic stress in critical occupations: Recognition, consequences, and treatment.* Springfield, IL, Charles C. Thomas, 1996.

Visotsky, H. M.; Hamburg, D. A.; Goss, M. E., & Lebovitz, B. Z.: Coping behavior under extreme stress, *Archives of General Psychiatry, 5*, 423-445, 1961.

Wagner, M.: Stress debriefing: Flight 191. *Chicago Police Star, August*: 4-7, 1979.

Wagner, M.: Airline disaster: A stress debrief program for police. *Police Stress Magazine, 2*:16-19, 1981a.

Wagner, M.: Trauma Counselling and Law Enforcement. In R. Thomlinson (Ed.), *Perspectives on industrial social work practice.* Ottawa, Canada, Family Service Canada, 1981b.

Williams, P.; Wiebe, D.,& Smith, T: Coping processes as mediators of the relationship between hardiness and health. *Journal of Behavioral Medicine, 15*: 237-255, 1997.

Woolf, H. B.: (Ed.), *Webster's new collegiate dictionary.* Springfield, MA, G. and C. Merriam, 1977.

Yehuda, R.: *Psychological trauma.* Washington, DC., American Psychiatric Publishing Group, 1998.

Yehuda, R., & McFarlane, A.: *Psychobiology of posttraumatic stress disorder.* New York, The New York Academy of Sciences Publishers, 1997.

CONCLUSION

Chapter 22

TRAUMA STRESS IN POLICING: ISSUES FOR FUTURE CONSIDERATION

Douglas Paton & John M. Violanti

INTRODUCTION

In the course of protecting and serving the public, police officers must contend not only with the kinds of occupational stress that characterize contemporary organizations, but also with violence, abuse, and other events capable of eliciting traumatic stress reactions. The nature of these events, and the frequency with which they occur, led to police work being defined as "civilian combat" (Williams, 1987). It is against this backdrop that the contributors to this volume prepared their chapters.

POLICE WORK AND COMBAT

As Foreman and Eränen, Koppel and Friedman, and Solomon and Mastin, who described the experience of officers serving in Bosnia, South Africa, and at Waco, Texas, respectively, pointed out, the reality of serving in a combat zone can be very real for some officers. In particular, the demand for officers to volunteer for police duties outside their home country will continue into the foreseeable future. The specific demands associated with working in such high-risk contexts makes preparation essential. At present, this is lacking. If national police agencies are going to support UN policing initiatives, then they, and the UN themselves, must adopt the kinds of training and preparatory activities outlined by Foreman and Eränen. A failure to do so not only lessens the effectiveness of the peacekeeping force, but also the well-being and effectiveness of officers on their return home.

MANAGING OCCUPATIONAL AND TRAUMATIC STRESSORS

While police agencies may have little direct control over the kinds demands that police officers encounter on a daily basis, they have the capability to protect their officers and promote their well-being, adaptation, and growth. As the contributions to this volume have demonstrated, police agencies have several highly cost-effective means at their disposal to assist them in realizing this objective.

Although the primary focus of this book was on the traumatic aspects of police work, several chapters highlighted the role of routine occupational stressors as determinants of officers' mental health and as potential precursors to the development of traumatic stress reactions. Alexander discussed how constant exposure to, for example, bureaucratic constraints and autocratic, directive management, can erode commitment to the police role and lead to burnout. Figley developed this idea to illustrate how officers' commitment to their role can be diminished to the point where they experience compassion fatigue. Addressing this issue is important.

Effective policing requires a high level of the commitment from serving officers. If police agencies allow its erosion, or fail to sustain it, the cost to officers, agencies, and the criminal justice system is high. This issue takes on even greater importance in the light of Loo's contention that, if left unchecked, intolerable work and life experiences from which an officer can see no escape can lead to suicide. While often considered at the level of the individual officer, police agencies must accept their role in this context. This issue was reiterated by Patterson and by Violanti in their discussions of coping. As Violanti pointed out, socialization into the profession and the agency can constrict coping efficacy, restricting options to deal with intolerable demands. Yet, as these authors demonstrated, highly cost effective interventions are readily available. Similarly, Carlier offered a therapeutic intervention capable of increasing both understanding and coping flexibility. These interventions must be assimilated into the fabric of police operations to sustain well-being.

ORGANIZATIONAL, SOCIAL AND COMMUNITY ISSUES

An issue common to several contributions concerned the fact that we often fail to examine the impact of traumatic events within the wider organizational and societal context. Their implications must be accommodated in conceptualizing duty-related traumatic stress phenomena. MacLeod and Paton discussed how social cognitive theories can enrich our understanding of the implications of repetitive exposure to primary and secondary victimization. Rothberg and Wright demonstrated the utility of cross-fertilization of intervention from military to police agencies. Paton, Flin, and Violanti described the special needs of incident commanders. In their respective chapters, Danielli, Violanti, and Williams highlighted the need to encompass family issues within the research and intervention agenda. Taken together, these chapters highlight the need there for research to be more holistic in nature, both in terms of the groups studied and the theoretical and applied literatures surveyed. In addition to accommodating environmental factors, greater consideration must be given to temporal factors.

A LIFESPAN PERSPECTIVE

Stephens, Long, and Flett demonstrated how experience of trauma prior to entering police work increases both potential vulnerability following subsequent exposure and the likelihood of early disengagement from police work. Paton, Violanti, and Schmuckler described how repetitive exposure during an officers career increases risk status both during and beyond the tenure of their employment. Clearly, we must expand both the research and intervention focus to encompass these longitudinal factors. However, extending the focus to cover the lifetime of the individual may not be going far enough. Danielli's discussion of the intergenerational transmission of traumatic memories suggests that research and intervention development must extend to include both historical and contemporary perspectives. Pursuing these issues will require using the kinds of methodological techniques canvassed by Paton and Smith.

PATHOLOGY VERSUS RESILIENCE

Another thread which ran through several chapters concerned the assumptions we make regarding the consequences of exposure to high-risk situations and traumatic events. In some cases, misconceptions arise for methodological reasons. Loo described how the short time frame used for several studies of police suicide created an inaccurate picture of its incidence. Only by having an accurate understanding of the nature and incidence of a particular phenomenon can we develop realistic models and interventions. Assumptions regarding the consequences of exposure can also occur for conceptual reasons.

Several contributors (e.g., Carlier, Dunning, Danielli, Foreman &

Eränen, Paton & Smith) drew a distinction between conceptual models based on assumptions of pathology and those that advocate a resilient or saluto-genic perspective. As these authors point out, the automatic assumption of pathology does a disservice to those we are seeking to assist and, in the process, may result in our inadvertently making things worse. A pathologi-cal orientation also tends to encourage the application of a medical-inter-ventionist approach rather than seeking to facilitate personal and group strengths and resilience. As Mitchell pointed out, the high profile nature of traumatic incidents and their consequences for officers and agencies alike may have stimulated the desire to act immediately and, in the process, have precluded developing interventions based on systematic and objective research and evaluation. Mitchell also raised the possibility that, under these circumstances, specific interventions may become enshrined in legal or reg-ulatory frameworks. This is a cause for concern given the lack of clear evi-dence for the efficacy of several popular interventions. As such, there is a risk that regulatory frameworks established to protect officers may have the opposite effect. Moreover, the existence of regulatory frameworks may lessen the perceived need for the systematic evaluation of these interventions and the need to explore of alternatives. This point was picked up in the final chapter.

Dunning emphasized the importance of creating an organizational envi-ronment that facilitates resilience rather than imposing or sustaining depen-dency and learned helplessness. The message is clear. Intervention must be directed towards the organization as much as the individual officer.

Dunning is correct in arguing for a paradigm shift in this context. Duty-related populations differ from the clinical populations upon whom much of our understanding has developed in several ways. While understanding pathology, and developing appropriate interventions to manage its conse-quences, is a legitimate activity, we should not pursue this line to the exclu-sion of others.

While notions such as the "therapeutic community" and " trauma mem-brane" have been in existence for some 15 - 20 years, it is only relatively recently that that those who do well in a traumatic incident, or who do not present pathology, have received the attention they deserve. As Paton and Smith pointed out, officers, in the course of exercising their role, face sever-al potentially traumatic hazards, but this should not be taken to imply a direct causal link with psychopathology. Rather we need to define the indi-vidual, organizational and community factors that interact with these hazards to facilitate resiliency and sustain it in the face of adversity. We also need to pay closer attention to differentiating those who do well from those who develop the kind of behavioral addiction to high-risk situations described by Paton, Violanti, and Schmuckler. Developing this capability should thus be added to the assessment agenda.

CONCLUSION

Overall, the contents of this book suggest a need for several practical, conceptual, and methodological shifts. First, we need to adopt a more holistic approach, and one which embraces individual, family, agency, and community characteristics. We need to explore diverse theoretical bases (e.g., social cognitive, public health) for their relevance for understanding and managing stress and traumatic stress in police officers. Conceptually, we must adopt an interpretative framework that focuses on resilience, adaptation, and positive resolution while acknowledging the need to develop appropriate assessment instruments and support and therapeutic interventions that are theoretically and ecologically rigorous in their orientation. Methodologically, the fact that these factors, and the relationships between them, develop and change and exercise their influence over time necessitates that we adopt a longitudinal framework for research, intervention planning, and evaluation.

Collectively, the contributions to this text not only defined the implications of "civilian combat" for police officers, they also described what can be done, and what needs to be done, to minimize and contain these problems. It is up to police agencies to embrace these concepts and interventions and adopt the measures suggested to ensure that they protect those who serve at the front line. The women and men who serve in law enforcement worldwide deserve no less.

REFERENCES

Williams, C.: Peacetime combat: Treating and preventing delayed stress reactions in police officers. In T. Williams (Ed.), *Post-traumatic stress disorders: A handbook for clinicians.* Cincinnati, OH, Disabled American Veterans, 1987.

APPENDIX

Compassion Satisfaction/Fatigue Self-Test for Helpers

Helping others puts you in direct contact with other people's lives. As you probably have experienced, your compassion for those you help has both positive and negative aspects. This self-test helps you estimate your compassion status: How much at risk you are of burnout and compassion fatigue and also the degree of satisfaction with your helping others. Consider each of the following characteristics about you and your current situation. Write in the number that honestly reflects how frequently you experienced these characteristics in the last week. Then follow the scoring directions at the end of the self-test.

0=Never	1=Rarely	2=A Few Times	3=Somewhat Often	4=Often	5=Very Often

Items About You

_____ 1. I am happy.

_____ 2. I find my life satisfying.

_____ 3. I have beliefs that sustain me.

_____ 4. I feel estranged from others.

_____ 5. I find that I learn new things from those I care for.

_____ 6. I force myself to avoid certain thoughts or feelings that remind me of a frightening experience.

_____ 7. I find myself avoiding certain activities or situations because they remind me of a frightening experience.

_____ 8. I have gaps in my memory about frightening events.

_____ 9. I feel connected to others.

_____ 10. I feel calm.

_____ 11. I believe that I have a good balance between my work and my free time.

_____ 12. I have difficulty falling or staying asleep.

_____ 13. I have outburst of anger or irritability with little provocation

_____ 14. I am the person I always wanted to be.

_____ 15. I startle easily.

_____ 16. While working with a victim, I thought about violence against the perpetrator.

_____ 17. I am a sensitive person.

_____ 18. I have flashbacks connected to those I help.

_____ 19. I have good peer support when I need to work through a highly stressful experience.

_____ 20. I have had first-hand experience with traumatic events in my adult life.

_____ 21. I have had first-hand experience with traumatic events in my childhood.

_____ 22. I think that I need to "work through" a traumatic experience in my life.

_____ 23. I think that I need more close friends.

_____ 24. I think that there is no one to talk with about highly stressful experiences.

_____ 25. I have concluded that I work too hard for my own good.

_____ 26. Working with those I help brings me a great deal of satisfaction.

_____ 27. I feel invigorated after working with those I help.

_____ 28. I am frightened of things a person I helped has said or done to me.

_____ 29. I experience troubling dreams similar to those I help.

_____ 30. I have happy thoughts about those I help and how I could help them.

_____ 31. I have experienced intrusive thoughts of times with especially difficult people I helped.

_____ 32. I have suddenly and involuntarily recalled a frightening experience while working with a person I helped.

_____ 33. I am pre-occupied with more than one person I help.

_____ 34. I am losing sleep over a person I help's traumatic experiences.

_____ 35. I have joyful feelings about how I can help the victims I work with.

_____ 36. I think that I might have been "infected" by the traumatic stress of those I help.

_____ 37. I think that I might be positively "inoculated" by the traumatic stress of those I help.

_____ 38. I remind myself to be less concerned about the well being of those I help.

_____ 39. I have felt trapped by my work as a helper.

_____ 40. I have a sense of hopelessness associated with working with those I help.

_____ 41. I have felt "on edge" about various things and I attribute this to working with certain people I help.

_____ 42. I wish that I could avoid working with some people I help.

_____ 43. Some people I help are particularly enjoyable to work with.

_____ 44. I have been in danger working with people I help.

_____ 45. I feel that some people I help dislike me personally.

Items About Being a Helper and Your Helping Environment

_____ 46. I like my work as a helper.

_____ 47. I feel like I have the tools and resources that I need to do my work as a helper.

_____ 48. I have felt weak, tired, run down as a result of my work as helper.

_____ 49. I have felt depressed as a result of my work as a helper.

_____ 50. I have thoughts that I am a "success" as a helper.

_____ 51. I am unsuccessful at separating helping from personal life.

_____ 52. I enjoy my co-workers.

_____ 53. I depend on my co-workers to help me when I need it.

_____ 54. My co-workers can depend on me for help when they need it.

_____ 55. I trust my co-workers.

_____ 56. I feel little compassion toward most of my co-workers

_____ 57. I am pleased with how I am able to keep up with helping technology.

_____ 58. I feel I am working more for the money/prestige than for personal fulfillment.

_____ 59. Although I have to do paperwork that I don't like, I still have time to work with those I help.

_____ 60. I find it difficult separating my personal life from my helper life.

_____ 61. I am pleased with how I am able to keep up with helping techniques and protocols.

_____ 62. I have a sense of worthlessness/disillusionment/resentment associated with my role as a helper.

_____ 63. I have thoughts that I am a "failure" as a helper.

_____ 64. I have thoughts that I am not succeeding at achieving my life goals.

_____ 65. I have to deal with bureaucratic, unimportant tasks in my work as a helper.

_____ 66. I plan to be a helper for a long time.

Scoring Instructions

Please note that research is ongoing on this scale and the following scores should be used as a guide, not confirmatory information.

1. Be certain you respond to all items.
2. Mark the items for scoring:
   a. Put an x by the following 26 items: 1-3, 5, 9-11, 14, 19, 26-27, 30, 35, 37, 43, 46-47, 50, 52-55, 57, 59, 61, 66.
   b. Put a check by the following 16 items: 17, 23-25, 41, 42, 45, 48, 49, 51, 56, 58, 60, 62-65.
   c. Circle the following 23 items: 4, 6-8, 12, 13, 15, 16, 18, 20-22, 28, 29, 31-34, 36, 38-40, 44.
3. Add the numbers you wrote next to the items for each set of items and note:
   a. *Your potential for Compassion Satisfaction (x):* 118 and above=extremely high potential; 100-117=high potential; 82-99=good potential; 64-81=modest potential; below 63=low potential.
   b. *Your risk for Burnout (check):* 36 or less=extremely low risk; 37-50=moderate risk; 51-75=high risk; 76-85=extremely high risk.
   c. *Your risk for Compassion Fatigue (circle):* 26 or less=extremely low risk, 27-30=low risk; 31-35=moderate risk; 36-40=high risk; 41 or more=extremely high risk.

Professional Resource Information

NOTE: URLs are given beside references rather than linked to the document name so that they can be read from print copy. While online, if you would like to link to a particular resource, click on the URL.

The Compassion Fatigue Scale has been established, presented, and published in several articles/chapters including, among others, the following:

Figley, C.R. (1995). Compassion Fatigue: Coping with Secondary Traumatic Stress Disorder in Those Who Treat the Traumatized. New York: Brunner Mazel. http://www.opengroup.com/open/dfbooks/087/0876307594.shtml.

Figley, C.R. (1995). Compassion Fatigue. In Figley, C.R. (1995). In B. H. Stamm, (Ed.) Secondary traumatic stress: Self-care issues for clinicians, researchers and educators. Lutherville, MD: Sidran Press. http://www.sidran.org/digicart/products/stss.html.

Stamm, B.H. (April 1997). Mental Health Research in Telehealth. Invited address at From Research to Practice: A Conference on Rural Mental Health Research, National Institute of Mental Health. Oxford MS.

Rudolph, J.M, Stamm, B.H., & Stamm, H.E. (November, 1997). Compassion Fatigue: A Concern for Mental Health Policy, Providers and Administration. Poster presented at the 13th Annual Conference of the International Society for Traumatic Stress Studies, Montreal, ON, CA. http://www.dartmouth.edu/~bhstamm/ISTSS97cf.PDF.

There is a psychometric review in:

Figley, C.R. & Stamm, B.H. (1996). Psychometric Review of Compassion Fatigue Self Test. In B.H. Stamm (Ed), Measurement of Stress, Trauma and Adaptation. Lutherville, MD: Sidran Press http://www.sidran.org/dicart/products/stss/html.

For general information on Secondary Traumatic Stress/Vicarious Traumatization/Compassion Fatigue:

Pearlman, L. et al. (1998). Traumatic Stress Institute & Center for Adult & Adolescent Psychotherapy, LLC Web Site http://www.tsicaap.com.

Pearlman, L. Saakvitne, K. (1995). Trauma and the Therapist: Countertransference and Vicarious Traumatization in Psychotherapy with Incest Survivors. New York: WW Norton. http://web.wwnorton.com/catnos/tl070183.htm.

Figley, C.R. (1998). Traumatology E-Journal Web Site. http://psy.uq.edu.au/PTSD/trauma/j1.html.

Stamm, B.H. & Pearce, F.W. (1995). Creating virtual community: Telemedicine applications for self-care. In B.H. Stamm. (Ed.), Secondary Traumatic Stress: Self-Care Issues for Clinicians, Researchers and Educators. Lutherville, MD: Sidran Press. http://www.dartmouth.edu/~bhstamm/vircom.htm.

Stamm, B.H. (1997). Work-related Secondary Traumatic Stress. PTSD Research Quarterly,(8) 2, Spring. http://www.dartmouth.edu/dms/ptsd/RQ_Spring_1997.html.

Stamm, B.H. (1997). Work-related Secondary Traumatic Stress (reprint). Anxiety Disorders Association of America Reporter Summer/Fall.

Stamm, B. H. (1998). Rural-Care: Crossroads of Health Care, Culture, Traumatic Stress & Technology Web Site http://www.dartmouth.edu/~bhstamm/index.htm.

Stamm, B. H. (1998). Traumatic Stress Secondary Traumatic Stress Web Site. http://www.dartmouth.edu/~bhstamm/ts.

The psychometric information reported here is based on a pooled sample of 370 people. Multivariate analysis of variance did not provide evidence of differences based on country of origin, type of work, or sex when age was used as a control variable.

Age	Sex	Type of Work	Country of Origin
Mean 35.4	Males n=121 (33%)	Trauma Professional n=58 (16%)	USA Rural-Urban mix n=160 (43%)
Median 36	Females n=207 (56%)	Business volunteer n=130 (35%)	Canada-Urban n=30 (8%)
SD 12.16	Unknown n=42 (11%)	Red Cross n=30 (8%)	South Africa-Urban n=130 (35%)
		Caregivers in training n=102 (27%)	Internet (unknown origin) n=50 (13%)

Scale	Alpha	Mean	Standard Deviation	Interpretation
Compassion Satisfaction	.87	92.10	16.04	higher is better satisfaction with ability to caregiver (e.g. pleasure to help, like colleagues, feel good about ability to help, make contribution, etc.)
Burnout	.90	24.18	10.78	higher is higher risk for burnout (feel hopeless and unwilling to deal with work, onset gradual as a result of feeling one's efforts make no difference or very high workload)
Compassion Fatigue	.87	28.78	13.15	higher is higher risk for Compassion Fatigue (symptoms of work-related PTSD, onset rapid as a result of exposure to highly stressful caregiving)

Additional Information: Lay Mental Health Caregivers in Rural Africa (n=16) (note, compassion satisfaction subscale was not given).

First assessment   (min 3 months work)   CF Mean 45 (SD 14.4)   BO Mean 32   (SD 11.3)
Second assessment (3 months later)   CF Mean 44 (SD 13.6) BO Mean 28.86 (SD 9.6)

Here is the SPSS Scoring Code

COMPUTE Comsat=SUM(1, 2, 3, 5, 9, 10, 11, 14, 19, 26, 27, 30, 35, 37, 43, 46, 47, 50, 52, 53, 54, 55, 57, 59, 61, 66)
COMPUTE Brnout=SUM(17, 23,24, 25, 41, 42, 45, 48, 49, 51, 56, 58, 60, 62, 63, 64, 65)
COMPUTE ComFat=SUM(4, 6, 7, 8, 12, 13, 15, 16, 18, 20, 21, 22, 28, 29, 31, 32, 33, 34, 36, 38, 39, 40, 44)

AUTHOR INDEX

A

Abramson, L. Y., 27
Adams, J., 16
Adlam, K. R., 215
Adshead, G., 263
Affleck, G., 26, 27
Ainsworth, P. B., 255
Aldwin, 214
Alexander, D. A., 18, 28, 124, 135, 216, 255, 266, 271
Alexander, R. J., 171
Amick-McMullen, A., 26
Andreasen, N. J. C., 238
Andreski, P., 71, 101, 228
Andrews, B., 31
Anshel, M. H., 255, 264
Anson, R. H., 66
Antonovsky, A., 117, 276
Aron, F., 56, 101, 103, 181
Aronson, E., 55, 57, 61
Asgard, U., 250
Astin, M. C., 68
Auf der Heide, E., 130, 133
Avery, A., 271
Ayalon, O., 162, 167
Ayers, R., 57

B

Backer, P., 132
Baechler, J., 244
Barber, S., 99
Barret, T. W., 145
Bartone, P., 273, 276
Baumeister, R. F., 244
Bechtle, A. E., 67
Beckman, R., 162
Bedian, A. G., 241
Bergman, L. R., 14, 19
Bergman, M. S., 179
Bernstein, J., 117

Bertman, S., 170
Berton, M. W., 68
Beskow, J. 250
Bickman, L., 151
Billingsley, K., 14
Bisson, J. I., 263, 271
Blau, T. H., 56, 88, 93
Blazer, D. G., 68
Bloom, M. E., 66
Bloom, S., 280
Boman, B., 92
Bonifacio, P., 18, 216
Boninger, D. S., 30
Bootzin, R., 58
Borrill, C. S., 255
Borum, R., 41–43
Boscarino, J. A., 39
Boudewyn, A. C., 68
Bourne, P., 269
Bowman, M., 160
Braham, R. L., 179
Brannick, M., 129
Brent, D. A., 250
Brent, S. B., 161
Breslau, N. G., 68, 71, 100, 101, 228, 274
Brett, E. ,101, 105, 108
Britton, N. R., 67, 68
Bromet, E., 71
Brown, J., 255, 264, 266
Buchanan, A., 182
Buchanan, G., 69, 73
Bullman, T. A., 5
Burke, R. J., 59
Burnett, P., 150
Burr, J., 19
Burrows, G. D., 265
Byrne, B. M., 15

C

Cacioppe, R., 14
Calhoun, L., 17, 273, 274

307

Campbell, D. T., 19
Campbell, E., 255, 264, 266
Cantor, C. H., 243
Card, J., 237
Carlier, I. V. E., 88, 227–31, 271
Carmelly, F., 184
Carson, L., 26, 28
Carver, C. S., 29, 265
Catherall, D. R., 162, 163, 168, 171
Chamberlain, K., 66, 67
Childers, J., 266
Clarke, K. M., 236
Cliff, E., 274
Cobb, S., 57
Cohen, J. 19
Cohen, P., 19, 20
Cohen, S., 57, 83
Coleman, E., 68
Colless, E., 16
Collins, L. M., 14, 19, 20
Coman, G. J., 215, 216, 265
Condon-Rall, M. E., 207, 208, 211, 212
Cook, J. D., 151
Cook, T. D., 19
Cooper, C. L., 216
Corr, C. A., 160
Couta, M., 128
Cox, A., 100
Coyne, J. C., 27
Creamer, M., 271
Crego, J., 134
Curran, S. F., 103

D

Dahl, B. B., 43
Danieli, Y., 176–80, 184
Danto, B. L., 140
Dantzker, M. L., 255, 256
Dash, J., 242
Davidson, A., 269, 270
Davidson, J., 165, 179
Davidson, J. R., 68, 228
Davidson, M. J., 58, 59, 216
Davis, C. G., 28, 30
Davis, G. C., 68, 71, 100, 101, 228
Deahl, M. P., 263, 271
Decker, S., 238
Denkers, A., 26
Diamond, A., 215

Dishlacoff, L., 216
Doepal, D., 18
Draucker, C. B., 237
Driskell, J., 133
Duckworth, D., 28, 31, 32, 79, 127, 135
Dunning, C. M., 270, 272, 276
Dynes, R., 272
Dyregrov, A., 257

E

Eberly, R. E., 178
Edward, K. E., 25, 27, 28
Egendorf, A., 237
Eisenberg, T., 56, 59
Eitenger, L., 274
Elder, G., 274
Ellard, J. H., 27
Elliott, J., 43
Ellis, A., 126
Ellis, B., 43
Ellis, T. E., 250
Ellison, K. W., 101
Engdahl, B. E., 178
Eränen, L., 26, 190
Erickson, C. A., 83
Erikson, E., H., 43, 160, 161
Eustace, K. L., 71
Evans, B. J., 215, 216
Evans, D. J., 265
Everly, G. S., 117–19, 271

F

Fairbank, J. A., 101
Farber, B. A., 55, 56
Farberow, N. L., 5
Feld, S., 277
Fell, R. D., 242
Felner, R. D., 245, 246
Figley, C. R., 43–45, 82, 100, 151, 279
Fisher, C. R., 180
Flett, R., 71
Flin, R., 124, 126, 128, 132–34
Foa, E. B., 228
Fogarty, J. A., 165
Folkman, S., 146, 215, 218, 219
Follette, V. M., 67
Fontana, A., 108, 274
Fouwels, A. J., 229

Fox, S., 168, 170
Foy, D. W., 68
France, K., 169
Francis, D. J., 19
Francis, M. E., 281
Frank, R. G., 66
Frankl, V. E., 274, 278
Frazier, P. A., 25–28
Freudenberger, H. J., 56
Frey-Wouters, E., 5
Freyberg, J. T., 44
Fried, B., 179
Friedman, P., 242, 244
Funk, S. C., 273, 276

G

Gaines-Lane, P., 169
Gallagher, B., 259, 261
Gallops, M. S., 5, 101, 105
Geates, J., 260
Gecas, V., 91
Gelinas, D. J., 237
George, L. K., 68
Gerson, E. M., 92
Gerson, R., 183
Gersons, B. P. 88, ,103, 107, 109, 191, 227–31
Giaconia, R. M., 71
Gilmartin, K. M., 80, 81, 83
Gleicher, F., 30
Godofredo, D. D., 215
Goenjian, A. K., 67
Gold, D. B., 32
Gold, D. N., 153
Golembiewski, R. T., 14
Goodman, J. S., 184
Gould, 57
Grace, M. C., 82, 91, 190
Green, B. L., 15, 18, 68, 82, 83, 91, 101, 108, 165, 190
Green, S. G., 20
Gregorich, S., 127
Griffiths, J. A., 271
Gross, E., 89
Gudjonsson, G. H., 215
Guerin, P. J., Jr., 183
Gump, B. B., 33
Gurin, G., 277

H

Haas, A. P., 237
Habenicht, M., 82
Hagenaars, J. A., 19, 20
Haines, V. A., 249
Hammond, J. M., 171
Hannaford, M. J., 171
Harel, Z., 177
Hargrave, G., 93
Harkness, A. R., 178
Harkness, L. L., 179
Harris, C. J., 171
Harris, R. N., 88, 90
Hart, P. M., 18, 66
Hartog, S. B., 14
Hartsough, D. M., 15, 79, 179
Hasle, A., 271
Hayman, P. M., 84
Headey, B., 18, 66
Heegaard, M., 166, 169, 171
Heiman, M. F., 243
Helmreich, R., 127
Helmreich, W. B., 177
Helzer, J. E., 69
Hendin, H., 237
Henry, V. E., 248
Herman, J., 271
Hiatt, D. P., 93
Higgins, G. O., 272, 273, 275
Hightower, H. C., 128
Hilberman, E., 82
Hindman, J., 163
Hoath, D. R., 249
Hobbs, M., 263
Hobfoll, S., 117, 118
Hodgekinson, E., 129
Hogg, I., 257
Hogg, M. A., 130
Horn, J. L., 14, 19
Horn, J. M., 101, 117, 120
Horowitz, K., 67
Horowitz, M., 26, 105, 197
Horvitz, L. A., 183
Houghton, B., 128
Hovanitz, C., 68
Howe, B., 88, 91, 216
Hughes, D., 68
Hughes, M., 71
Hunter-King, E. J., 181

Hurlbert, J. S., 249
Hurrell, J. J., Jr., 58, 59, 101
Hyatt, D., 93
Hyatt-Williams, A., 103, 107, 181
Hytten, K. 271

J

Jackson, S. E., 180
Janik, J., 18, 183, 250
Janoff-Bulman, R., 15, 25–27, 238, 257
Jekel, J., 67
Johnson, C., 37, 182
Johnson, D. R., 176
Johnston, D., 128
Jones, F. D., 204
Jordan, B. K., 101, 179
Joseph, P., 31
Joseph, S., 266, 274
Josephson, R. L., 242, 244, 251
Jucovy, M. E., 179

K

Kachur, S. P., 246
Kafry, D., 55, 61
Kahana, B., 177
Kahana, E., 177
Kahler, A. S., 26
Kamerman, J., 183
Kaminer, H., 177
Kang, H. K., 5
Kastenbaum, R., 162
Kazak, A. E., 91
Kearney, R., 189
Keilson, H., 176
Kelling, G. E., 92
Kelso, B. A., 84
Kemp, A., 68, 101
Kenardy, J. A., 271
Kessler, R. C., 66, 71, 228
Kilpatrick, D. G., 26
Kirmeyer, S. L., 215
Kleber, 44
Klein, G., 132
Klein-Parker, F., 177
Kliesmet, R., 59
Kobasa, S. C., 274, 276
Kolb, L. C., 80, 81

Kotler, M., 178
Krauss, G. E., 101, 105, 109
Kravitz, D. O., 183
Kravitz, H. M., 250
Krischman, E., 90
Kroes, W. H., 56–59, 216
Kroll, J., 82
Krystal, H., 184, 274
Kubler-Ross, E., 163
Kudler, H., 179
Kulik, J. A., 33
Kulka, R. A., 44, 68, 101
Kurke, M., 124

L

Lagorio, J., 161–63, 171
Lamberts, R. D., 88, 227–29
Landy, L., 171
Laufer, R. S., 5, 101, 102, 105, 108
Lauterbach, D., 67, 71
Lavie, P., 177
Law, F., 68
Lazarus, J., 100
Lazarus, R. S., 146, 215, 218, 219
Lee, M. D., 69
Leenars, A. A., 243, 251
Lehman, D. R., 28
Leiter, M. P., 39, 46
Leon, G., 178
Lester, D., 242–44, 251
Lester, G. R., 43
Liebert, J., 182
Liebkind, K., 26, 190
Liem, J. H., 68
Lifton, R. J., 237
Light, S. C., 83, 92
Lin, N., 83, 92
Lindemann, E., 150
Lindy, J. D., 15, 82, 91, 107, 190
Linville, P. W., 91
Lofland, J., 189
Lofland, L. H., 189
Long, N., 66, 67, 69, 71
Loo, R., 243, 244, 246–51
Loutzenhiser, L. A., 249
Lundin, T., 191
Lyons, J. A., 17, 18, 237, 273, 274

M

Mackenzie, T., 82
MacLeod, M. D., 25–28
Madamba, H. J., 41, 91
Maghan, J. L., 182
Magnusson, D., 14, 19
Maloney, L. J., 44
Mann, J. P., 32, 66
Manning, P. K., 93
Manolias, M. B., 103, 107, 181, 255
Margolis, B., 57–59
Marks, S. R., 92
Marmar, C. R., 228
Maroda, K., 43
Marris, R. W., 245
Marshall, J. R., 88, 91, 216, 241, 242
Martin, R. A., 20
Maslach, C., 39, 46, 54, 55, 180
Matsakis, A., 179
Matthews, K. A., 92
Matussek, P., 176
Mayne, T. J., 281
McCafferty, E. A., 215
McCafferty, F. L., 102, 215
McCann, I. L., 43, 44, 167
McCreery, J. M., 154
McCubbin, H. I., 43
McDonald, C., 71
McDonald, V. N., 60
McDowell, E. E., 248
McEvoy, L., 69
McFarlane, A. C., 101, 106, 108, , 263, 271, 278
McGinnis, J. H., 60
McGoldrich, M., 159, 183
McKay, G., 83
Meichenbaum, D., 278
Meldrum, L., 263
Menaghan, 214
Meredith, N., 93
Meyer, C. B., 25, 27
Mikulincer, M., 178
Milgram, N., 117, 118
Miller, I., 66, 67, 69, 73
Miller, K., 43
Millsap, R. E., 14
Mirowsky, J., 219
Mitchell, J. T., 117–19, 140, 270, 271
Mitchell, M., 255–57, 263

Monahon, C., 168
Moosa, F., 102
Moran, C., 16, 67, 68
Mordock, J. B., 163
Moscovici, S., 192
Murray, E. J., 281
Myers, D. G., 15, 79

N

Nader K., 162, 166
Nathan, P., 44, 179, 180
Naugle, A. E., 67
Neal, B., 93
Neece, J., 32, 66
Neiderhoffer, A., 40, 90, 140, 216
Nelson, C. B., 71
Nelson, Z., 242
Nesselroade, J. R., 19
Niederhoffer, E., 140
Niederland, W. G., 184
Norris, A. S., 238
Norris, F. H., 67, 70, 71, 228
Northcroft, G. B., 130

O

O'Carroll, P. W., 242
Ochberg, F. M., 151
Ogland-Hand, S. M., 68
Oliver, J. E., 182
Orasanu, J., 132
Orner, R. J., 189, 271
Ottenberg, D. J., 83
Otto, U., 191

P

Park, C., 273, 274
Parker, D. A., 103
Parkes, C. M., 153
Pate, A., 59
Pate, T., 92
Paton, D., 14, 15, 17, 19, 26, 69, 8O, 82, 84, 88, 89, 127, 128, 130, 133, 134, 151, 190, 191, 272, 273
Patterson, G. T., 88, 216
Pearlin, L. I., 146
Pearlman, L. A., 43, 44, 167
Pendagast, E. G., 183

Penn, P., 58
Pennebaker, J. W., 32, 281
Peterson, E., 71, 228
Peterson, K. C., 15, 18
Petralia, S., 242
Philpot, C., 41–43
Pickett, G., 109
Pines, A., 55, 57, 61
Pitts, S. C., 20
Pogrebin, M. R., 32
Polusny, M. A., 67
Poole, E., 32, 90
Popkin, M., 171
Potter, L. B., 246
Powell, K. E., 246
Powell, T. C., 128
Powers, L., 167
Prescott, R. G. W., 26
Prince, C., 129
Prout, M. F., 15, 18
Purchy, M. K., 170
Putter, A. M., 167
Pynoos, R., 159, 162, 164–66, 171

Q

Quinn, R., 59

R

Radloff, L. S., 219
Raphael, B., 78, 150, 263, 272
Rawlings, E. I., 68, 101
Reese, J. T., 56
Regoli, R., 90
Reiser, M., 59, 65, 91, 242, 244, 251
Reiss, A. J., 40
Remer, R., 43
Repetti, R. L., 92
Resnick, H. S., 26, 228
Richard, W. C., 242
Richards, B., 275
Richelson, G., 56
Ricoeur, P., 189
Roberts, M., 269, 270
Robins, N., 69
Robinson, P., 216
Robinson, R. C., 271
Rodney, D., 100, 103
Rollins, J. C., 43

Rosenbaum, M., 277
Rosenheck, R., 43, 44, 107, 179, 180, 274
Rosenthal, P. A., 179
Rosenthal, S., 179
Ross, B., 43
Ross, C. E., 219
Roszell, P., 91
Rubenstein, I., 179
Runeson, B., 250
Ryan, D. A., 43, 179
Rynearson, E. K., 154

S

Salas, E., 129, 133
Scaturo, D. J., 84
Schauben, L., 28
Schaubroeck, J., 20
Scheier, M. F., 29, 265
Schlenger, W. E., 101
Schneidman, E. S., 90
Schooler, C., 146
Schulz, R., 238
Schwarz, R. A., 15, 18
Scott, M., 256
Scott, S. T., 67, 68
Scott, T. B., 145
Scotti, J. R., 17, 18
Scrivner, E., 124
Scurfield, R. M., 229, 237
Seeley, M. F., 249
Seff, M. A., 91
Segal, D. L., 281
Seligman, M. E. P., 27
Selman, R., 161
Serpe, R. T., 91
Sewell, J. D., 101, 215, 216
Shalev, A. Y., 27, 33
Shapiro, F., 119
Shaw, J. H., 140
Shaw, R., 128
Shirk, S. R., 160
Short, P., 31
Siebert, A., 273, 275
Sigal, J. J., 179
Silberg, J. R., 166
Silva, M., 270
Silver, R., 27, 238
Silverman, M. M., 245, 246
Simon, R. L., 182

Skolnick, J., 90
Skriver, J., 126
Slater, H. R., 65
Slater, P. J., 243
Smith, A. B., 181
Smith, D. A. F., 27
Smith, L. M., 14, 15, 17, 19
Smith, R., 165, 179
Smith, R. S., 273, 285
Smith, W., 242
Snibbe, J. R., 103
Solomon, R. M., 101, 117, 120
Solomon, S. D., 18
Solomon, Z., 44, 82, 178, 189
Sonnega, A., 71
Sorenson, G., 237
Speece, M. W., 161
Spiegel, D., 279
Spinks, T., 134
Stabb, S. D., 68
Stallard, P., 68
Stanley, R. O., 265
Staub, E., 192
Staudacher, C., 160, 161, 163, 164, 168, 169
Stephens, C., 66, 67, 69, 73, 190, 272, 273
Stewart, E., 128
Stewart, M., 129
Stiff, J., 43
Stillion, J. M., 248
Stillman, F. A., 139–41, 151, 155
Stradling, S., 256
Straker, G., 102
Strathman, A., 30
Stratton, J. G., 90, 103
Strawbridge, D., 93
Strawbridge, P., 93
Stryker, S., 91
Stuhlmiller, C., 272, 276

T

Taylor, S. E., 25, 27, 238, 274, 277
Teasdale, J. D., 27
Tedeschi, R., 17, 273, 274
Tehrani, N., 18
Tein, J. U., 20
Tennen, I. I., 26, 27
Terry, W. C., 57
Thoits, P. A. 88, 91, 93
Thom, A., 100

Thompson, J., 18
Thomson, J., 43
Tierney, R. J., 246
Timko, C., 26
Traisman, E. S., 169
Turner, R. J., 91
Turvey, B., 92
Tyman, R., 243

V

van der Kolk, B. A., 80, 81, 151, 278
van Eye, A., 19
van Ornum, W., 163
Van Si, L., 167
Velicer, W. F., 20
Veloff, J., 277
Vena, J. E., 241, 242
Veno, A., 58, 59, 216
Verbosky, S. J., 43, 179
Verbugge, L. M., 93
Viet, C. T., 15
Vincent, C., 66, 67
Violanti, J. M., 5, 6, 25, 28, 56, 66, 80, 82, 88, 89, 91, 101, 103, 135, 140, 151, 155, 181, 216, 217, 241–43, 246, 247, 249, 251, 269
Visotsky, H. M., 278
Vondra, J. I., 162
Vrana, S., 67, 71
Vrij, 26

W

Wachtel, E. F., 184
Wachtel, P. L., 184
Wagner, M., 269, 270
Waldron, I., 92
Walker, L. G., 124, 216
Walsh, F., 159
Walsh, M., 129
Ware, J. E., 15
Wass, H., 160
Watts, R., 271
Waysman, J., 44
Wearning, A. J., 18, 66
Webb, N. B., 172
Wegner, D. M., 32
Weine, S., 67
Weinfeld, M., 179

Weintraub, J. K., 265
Weisaeth, L., 191
Weiss, D. S., 105
Wells, A., 18, 28, 135, 271
West, S. G., 20
Whisenand, P., 89
White, P. N., 43
Whitehead, J. T., 60
Whiteman, D. B., 177
Whiting, N., 249
Wilhem, J., 127
Williams, C., 5, 80, 83, 102, 107, 179, 181, 293
Williams, G., 167
Williams, M. B., 169, 171
Williams, P., 276
Williams, R., 31, 266
Williams, T., 68, 189, 197
Willis, T. A., 57
Wilson, J. P., 31, 80, 101, 105, 109
Winkel, F. W., 26, 29

Woelfel, M. W., 83, 92
Woolf, H. B., 270
Worden, J. W., 154, 162–64
Wortman, C. B., 27, 238
Wosner, Y., 179
Wraith, R., 84
Wynn, V., 126

Y

Yeager, S., 14
Yehuda, R., 178, 271
Young, M. B., 83
Yule, W., 31, 266

Z

Zilberg, N. J., 105
Zimmer, C., 249

SUBJECT INDEX

A

Action junkies, 80
Amnesia, 100
Analytical decision making, 132
Army's response to Green Ramp disaster, 206–13
Avoidance, 32–33, 100, 103–9

B

Behavioral addiction and police work, 80–85
    action addiction, 80–81
    family issues, 84–85
    physical readiness, 80–82
    psychological arousal, 80–82
    risk takers, 80
    traumatic exposures review, 81
Boarding, 99
Branch Davidian Compound, Waco, TX
    BATF raid, 113–23
Bureau of Alcohol, Tobacco, and Firearms
    Branch Davidian Compound, Waco, TX raid, 113–23
Burnout, 6, 37, 39, 43–46, 54–61
    compassion fatigue, 39–51
    definition, symptoms, characteristics, 54–56
    depersonalization, 54
    emotional exhaustion, 54
    personal accomplishment, 54
    physical demands, 55
    psychological stress, 54
    societal attitudes, 61–62
    trauma exposure, 62–63, 101

C

Center for Epidemiological Studies' Depression Scale, 219
Childhood trauma, 67–69
Childhood trauma, death, 160–72

five central concepts of death, 160–61
    elementary age, 162–63
    preschool child, 161–62
    preteen and adolescent, 163–64
healing strategies, 167–71
    death presentation, 168
    grief workbooks, 169
    group support, 170–71
    immediate intervention, 168
    PTSD counseling principles, 171
    resumption of normalcy, 168
    rituals, 167–68
    saying good-bye, 169
psychological distress and developmental stages, 171–72
reactions and symptomatology, 164–70
    preschool child, 164–65
    elementary age, 165–66
    preteen and adolescent, 166–67
PTSD development, 160
CIVPOL (see also UN), 189–99
    catastrophe planning, 195
    corruption, 195
    criminal activity, 196
    cross-cultural issues, 193
    driving skills, 194
    human rights abuses, 196
    language skills, 193
    living accommodations, 194
    multinational policing units, 192–99
    UN peacekeeping duties in Yugoslavia, 189–99
        psychological reactions, 197–99
    snipers and landmines, 194
    weapons prohibition, 193
Coherence, 276
Communication and information, 131
Community-oriented policing, 38–39
    critical incident response recovery, 135–36
    incidence of PTSD, 39
    public perceptions 39

unwarranted use of force, 39
Compassion fatigue, 37–51
    burnout v. STS, 43–44
    community policing, 38–39
    incidence of PTSD, 39
    individual attitudes and action plans,
        49–50
    institutional policies and procedures,
        46–51
    police compassion fatigue model, 45
    self-test, 301–2
    table 4.1, compassion fatigue burnout
        symptoms, 41
    table, 12.2, PTSD symptoms, 144
    work group attitudes and action plans,
        47–48
Compassionate Friends, 153
Compassion Satisfaction/Fatigue Self-Test for
        Helpers, 301–2
Concentration, loss of, 132
Concerns of Police Survivors (COPS), 151,
        153
Coordination and team work
    Crew Resource Management, 127, 129
    group membership and interaction, 130
    management of police team, 129–30
    multiagency management, 129–30
    social identity, 130
    Tactical Decision Making Under Stress
        (TADMUS), 129–30
    trauma membrane, 189–190
Coping, 8, 214–24
    duty-related officer death, 101, 139–56,
        159–72
        children, 159–72
    emotion-focused strategies, 216, 220–24
    occupational stress and coping effective-
        ness, 214–24
    posttraumatic stress disorder, 88–93
    problem-focused strategies, 216, 220–24
    reappraising events, 28, 215, 218–19
    reexposure to traumas, 65–69, 101
    self-blame, other-blame, 26–28
    strategies and reactivity, 17–18, 146–47,
        214–24
        risk takers, 80–81
    table 12.3, line-of-duty death survivors,
        146
    transactional model, 214–24
Counterfactual thinking, 6, 25, 29, 30

Countertransference, 38, 43
Counseling phases for traumatized families,
        50–51
    goals of treatment, 50
    telling the story, 50
    reconsidering the story, 50
    healing theory, 51
Counterdisaster phenomenon, 79
Crew resource management, 127, 129
Criminal violence (*see* Violence, exposure to)
Critical incident response
    CIDB model, 258–59
        facts, 258
        feelings, 258
        future, 259
    response and recovery management,
        124–36
    stress debriefing, 48, 114–18, 255–67
    Waco, TX, raid, 113–23
Critical incident response recovery, 135–36
Critical incident stress debriefing, 269–85 (*see
        also* Psychological debriefing)
    dynamic conceptualization of resilient
        adults, 275, 277
    resiliency, 275, 276, 295
    salutogenic debrief, 278–85
        depersonalization, 278–79
        derealization, 278–79
        dissociation, 278–79
        salutogenic Cs/concepts, 279–81, 283
    salutogenic v. pathogenic approach,
        276–85
        Oklahoma City bombing, 282
        overall mental health, 276
        13 Cs of salutogenesis, 283–84
    sanctuary, 280–81
    stress inoculation training, 278
    trauma and coherence, 276–85
        comprehensibility, 276–78
        manageability, 276–78
        meaningfulness, 276–78

D

Danger
    and incident response stress, 126
    sense of, 5, 54, 88–93, 102, 126
Death
    criminal victimization, 7
    line-of-duty, 7, 101, 139–56

departmental impact, 150–55
spouse, 139–48
surviving children, 159–72
protect and serve, 102
witness to criminal suspect's death, 101
witness of officer's death, 101
Death, child's view, 160–72
five central concepts of death, 160–61
elementary age, 162–63
preschool child, 161–62
preteen and adolescent, 163–64
healing strategies, 167–71
death presentation, 168
immediate intervention, 168
grief workbooks, 169
group support, 170–71
PTSD counseling principles, 171
resumption of normalcy, 168
rituals, 167–68
saying good-bye, 169
psychological distress and developmental
stages, 171–72
reactions and symptomatology, 164–70
preschool child, 164–65
elementary age, 165–66
preteen and adolescent, 166–67
PTSD development, 160
Death notification, 148–50
procedures, 149
support and follow-up, 149–50
Debriefing (*see* Psychological debriefing)
Decision making and rapid response (*see also*
Critical incident response)
acute stress, 124–36
and decision making, 131–32
command decision making, 124–36
communication and information, 131
coordination and team work, 129–30
emergency and disaster planning,
128–130
operational systems and structures,
128–29
police liaison, 129
team building, 129–30
police incident command stress, 124–36
stressors
communications, 126
environmental conditions, 126
fatigue, 126
limitations recognition, 127

managing resources, 126
media, 126
personality differences, 127
physical fitness, 126
psychological fitness, 126
responsibility for unit, 126
risk of danger 126
sight of casualties, 126
time, 126
thinking and decision-making styles, 132
Decision making, officer involvement, 6, 59
Denial, 107
Depersonalization of emotion, 5, 55
Duty-related death, 101, 139–56, 159–72
Duty-related psychological trauma, 14–21;
65–74, 215
accidents, 215
action addiction behaviors, 78–85
coping strategies, 214–24
officer death, 101, 139–56, 159–72, 215
protect and serve, 102
psychosocial model, 88–93
recovery, 25–34, 135–36, 214–24
Duty-related risks (*see also* Burnout)
assault, 16
communication problems, 16
equipment failure, 16
exposure to noxious stimuli, 16
exposure to violence and death, 101,
139–56, 227
duty-related death of officer, 101,
139–56
leadership issues, 16, 18
police role in safeguarding public, 16, 21,
102
witness to violence and death, 5, 21, 25,
99–109
avoidance, 32–33, 100, 103–9
criminal suspect killed, 101
line-of-duty risk, 102, 139
officer killed, 101, 139–56
PTSD, 99–109
survivor guilt, 139–56
Duty-related stressors (*see also* Burnout;
Familial stressors)
critical incident response, 135–36
Compassion Satisfaction/Fatigue Self-Test
for Helpers, 301–2
police compassion fatigue, 37–51
police role in safeguarding public, 16, 21,

102, 227
protect and serve, 102, 214–15
psychological burnout, 54–61
training and expectations of risks, 16, 21,
    29, 31
vulnerability to trauma, 65–74
witness to violence and death, 5, 21, 25,
    101, 215
Duty-related traumatic reactions (*see also*
    Traumatic stress)
avoidance, 32–33, 103–9
critical incident response recovery,
    135–36
dispositional and organizational factors,
    16, 21
leadership issues, 16, 18
overview, 13–21
police compassion fatigue, 37–51
PTSD, 216, 227–39
vulnerability to reexposure, 67–74

E

Emergency and disaster planning, 128–30
    (*see also* Critical incident response)
Emotional contagion, 43–46
Emotional numbing, 100, 107
Environmental conditions and incident
    response stress, 126
Exhaustion and fatigue, 54–56, 126
Expectations
    performance expectations, 31
    recurrence of traumatic events, 16, 21,
        28–29
Eye Movement Desensitization and Repro-
    cessing, 40

F

Failure to prioritize, 132
False personalization, 90 (*see also* Police role)
Familial stressors
    agency requirements, 41
    boredom, 40
    confidentiality, 40
    danger, 40
    hostility, 40
    isolation, 40
    peer socialization and comradeship,
        41–42, 88–93

police role, 41, 42, 88–93
public apathy, 40
shift work, 40, 58
Family burnout, 44 (*see also* Secondary
    Traumatic Stress)
Family issues and action addiction, 84–85
    induced effects, 84
    repercussion effects, 84
    transmission effects, 84
Fatigue and exhaustion, 54–56, 126
Federal Bureau of Investigation
    Branch Davidian Compound, Waco, TX
        raid, 113–23
Freezing, 132

G

Gender and job burnout, 60–61
Guilt, 120–21

H

Hazard-risk management model, 13–21
    CDIB model overview, 255–67
    critical incident response recovery,
        135–36
    dispositional and organizational factors,
        16, 21
    line-of-duty death management, 150–56
        family notification and support,
            148–59
    risk homeostasis, 16
Helplessness, 27, 43, 55
Helper stereotype, 31–32
    Compassion Satisfaction/Fatigue Self-Test
        for Helpers, 301–2
    group cohesion and identity, 32, 117–18,
        122, 189–90
    survivor groups, 190
Hopelessness, 55
Humor, 48
Hypervigilence, 100

I

Incident response and recovery (*see also*
    Critical incident response)
    acute stress, 124–36
        and decision making, 131–32
        critical incident decision-making

styles, 132
command decision making, 124–36
  communication and information, 131
  coordination and team work, 129–30
  emergency and disaster planning, 128–130
  emergency response simulation training, 132–36
  operational systems and structures, 128–29
  police liaison, 129
  team building, 129–30
  thinking and decision-making processes, 132
police incident command stress, 124–36
  recovery, 135–36
stressors
  communications, 126
  duty-related death, 139–56
  environmental conditions, 126
  fatigue, 126
  limitations recognition, 127
  managing resources, 126
  media, 126
  personality differences, 127
  physical fitness, 126
  psychological fitness, 126
  responsibility for unit, 126
  risk of danger 126
  sight of casualties, 126 (*see also* Death, duty-related)
  time, 126
Incident response command training, 132–36
  program elements, 133–36
  simulation, 133–35
  training needs analysis, 133
Individual actions v. PCF, 49–50
Intuition and decision making, 132
Intrusive thoughts, 6, 32, 100, 103–9
  avoidance, 6, 32, 100, 103–9
  hyperaccessibility, 32
  hypervigilence, 100
  nightmares, 100
Isolation, 83

J

Job burnout (*see* Burnout)

L

Learned defensiveness, 80
Learned helplessness, 27, 276 (*see also* Self-esteem)
Letdown phenomenon, 79
Line-of-duty death, 7, 101, 136–59, 159–72, 215
  survivors
    children, 159–72
    police officers, 139, 148–56, 215
    spouse, 139–56
Longitudinal analysis of duty-related traumatic stress, 19–21

M

Media and incident response stress, 126, 206
  exposure of traumatic events beyond immediate area, 205–6
Mediating factors, 126, 127
Methodology and cluster analysis
  groups and traumatic stress, 14–15
MINERVA, 134

N

National Police Survivor Study, 141–48
Nightmares, 100

O

Occupational hazards
  assault, 16
  communication problems, 16, 18
  equipment failure, 16
  exposure to noxious stimuli, 16
  leadership issues, 16, 18
  lengthy proceedings for blame assignment, 31
Occupational stress, 5, 6, 65–74, 214–24, 270–71 (*see also* Traumatic stress)
  acute exposure, 78–79
  childhood trauma, 67–69
  chronic exposure and behavior addiction, 80–85
  critical incident response recovery, 135–36
  coping strategies, 214–24
  duty related, 6, 17, 78–85, 214–24

duty-related death, 101, 139–56
  child view, 159–72
event reappraisal, 28, 215, 218–19
future issues overview, 293–97
prior civilian life incidents, 6, 65–74
PTSD, 227–39 (*see* PTSD)
survivor guilt, 101, 139–56
witness to violence and death, 5, 21, 25,
  101, 227
Occupational stressors, 6, 56–60, 220
administrative support, 5, 6, 18, 57,
  114–18
career development, 59–60
CDIB overview, 255–67
decision-making involvement, 6, 59
lengthy proceedings for blame assignment, 31
management practices, 56–57
postvention strategies, 269–85
prevention strategies, 255–67
race and gender, 60–61
rotating shifts, 40, 58
Occupational support
CDIB overview, 255–67
critical incident program, 7, 18, 114–18,
  124–36
leadership, 7, 18
line-of-duty death, departmental management, 150–56
peer support, 7, 18

P

Peacekeeping duties of world policing,
  189–99
Peacetime combat, 5
Penn Inventory, 114
Perceived avoidability, 29, 30
Perceived control, 6, 25–34
expectations of recurrence, 16, 21, 28–29
low-, high-control events, 27–29
outcome severity, 29
past, present, future events, 28
self-esteem and ascription of blame,
  26–28
Perceived likelihood of recurrence, 6, 21, 25,
  28–29
Physical health predictors, 279–81
Police burnout, 37, 54–61
Police compassion fatigue, 6, 37–51

community policing, 38–39
family involvement and stress, 40–43
incidence of PTSD, 39
institutional policies and procedures,
  46–51
PCF model, 45
public perceptions, 39
self-test, 301–2
spousal disclosures, 39
table 4.1, compassion fatigue burnout
  symptoms, 41
table 12.2, PTSD symptoms, 144
institutional procedures to deter, 46–48
applicant screening for resilience 47
awareness of police risks and familial
  involvement, 46
commitment to lower risks, 47
compassionate fatigue education 47
critical incident stress education, 47
police family burnout education, 47
psychological risk factors education, 47
Police civilian combat, 5, 203, 293
Police, duty-related death, 7, 101, 139–56
child view, 159–72 (*see also* Posttraumatic
  stress disorder)
departmental management, 150–56
  death notification, 152
  family support, 152–54
  intervention, group level, 150–52,
    269–85
  legal issues, 154
grief responses, 145–46
spousal reactions, 140–48
  death notification and support, 148
survivor guilt, 139–56
Police officers and criminal victimization,
  25–34
counterfactual thinking, 6, 25, 29, 30
likelihood of event recurrence, 6, 21, 25,
  28–29
perceived avoidability, 25, 26
perceived control, 6, 25–34
PTSD, 101 (*see also* Posttraumatic stress
  disorder)
self- other-blame, 26–34
Police organizations
cohesive communities, 13, 117–18, 122
separation and identity, 78–85
support groups and identity, 32–33
survivor groups, 189–90

Police recruits and traumatic experiences, 69–74
Police role
   assimilation: individual and social, 88–90
      false personalization, 90
      solidarity, 90
   coping efficacy, 90
      constrictive inflexibility, 90
      diminished use of other social roles, 91
      interpersonal relationships, 91–92
      salience hierarchy, 91
Police stress (*see* Occupational stress)
Police Stress and Coping Questionnaire, 218
Police suicide, 5, 108, 183, 241–51
   postvention program elements, 250–51
      intervention evaluation, 251
      psychological autopsies, 250
      survivor supports, 251
   prevention program elements, 245–46
      critical incidents, 248
      drug abuse and life-styles, 249
      high-risk identification, 248
      peer support programs, 249
      preretirement counseling, 250
      psychological assessment for special duties, 248
      psychological services, 248
      recruit selection criteria, 247
      spousal support program, 250
      stress inoculation training, 247
      stress management training, 247
      suicide hotlines, 249
      supervisor training, 247
   ready access to firearms, 246
   women and minorities, 243–44
Police survivor study, 141–48
   posttraumatic stress disorder, 144–45
   spousal survivors, 140–48
      death notification and support, 148
      grief responses, 145–46
Post traumatic growth, 272–75
   dynamic conception of resilient adult, 275
Post Traumatic Growth Inventory, 274
Posttraumatic stress disorder, 5, 39, 65–74, 92–93, 144–45, 216, 227–39
   duty-related police death, 101, 139–56
   duty-related death, childhood trauma, 160–72
      five central concepts of death, 160–61
      elementary age, 162–63

preschool child, 161–62
preteen and adolescent, 163–64
   healing strategies, 167–71
      death presentation, 168
      grief workbooks, 169
      group support, 170–71
      immediate intervention, 168
      PTSD counseling principles, 171
      resumption of normalcy, 168
      rituals, 167–68
      saying good-bye, 169
   psychological distress and developmental stages, 171–72
   reactions and symptomatology, 164–70
      preschool child, 164–65
      elementary age, 165–66
      preteen and adolescent, 166–67
   PTSD development, 160
early retirement, 65–66
incidence in police officers, 39, 88–93, 216
police psychosocial model, 88–93
   coping strategies, 214–24, 255–67
previous trauma vulnerability, 65–74
recruit screening and selection, 65–74
special police units
   BATF, Waco, TX raid, 113–23
   South African police, 99–109
survivor guilt, 101, 139–56
symptoms
   amnesia, 101
   anger, 101
   avoidance, 6, 32, 100, 103–9
   depression, 101
   emotional numbing, 101, 107
   flashbacks, 101
   hyperaccessibility, 32
   hypervigilence, 100
   intrusive thoughts, 6, 32, 100, 103–9
   isolation, 83
   nightmares, 100
   sleep difficulties, 101
table 12.2, survivor PTSD symptoms, 144
therapeutic treatment, 230–39
witness to violence and death, 5, 21, 25, 101, 215, 227
   constructing meaning, 230–39
   criminal suspect killed, 101
   officer killed, 101, 215

Prioritizing, 132
Psychological autopsies, 250
   descriptive dimension, 250
   psychological/behavioral dimension, 251
   situational dimension, 250
   teleological dimension, 251
Psychological burnout, 6, 37, 39, 43–46,
   54–61
Psychological constructs, 14–15
Psychological contradictions
   combat ready but socially adaptive, 5, 203
Psychological debriefings
   CIDB model, 258–59
      facts, 258
      feelings, 258
      future, 259
   critical incident stress debriefing
      coherence, 276
         comprehensibility, 276
         manageability, 276
         meaningfulness, 276
      hardiness, 276
         challenge, 276
         commitment, 276
         control, 276
      resiliency, 275, 276
      salutogenic v. pathogenic approach,
         276–
   group cohesion and identity, 32–33,
      117–18, 122, 189–90
   postvention strategies, 269–85
   perceived control, 26–34
   recovery management, 26–34, 135–36,
      255–67
   traumatic reactivity, 6, 21, 25, 28–29, 34,
      81
   United Kingdom CDIB model overview,
      255–67
Psychological trauma, 6, 65–74 (*see also*
   Posttraumatic stress disorder)
   constructing meaning, 230–39
   coping, 6, 17–18, 26–28
   coping mechanism's breakdown, 65–68
   police, duty-related death, 139–56
   police, duty-related death, childhood trau-
      ma, 160–72
      five central concepts of death, 160–61
         elementary age, 162–63
         preschool child, 161–62
         preteen and adolescent, 163–64

healing strategies, 167–71
   death presentation, 168
   grief workbooks, 169
   group support, 170–71
   immediate intervention, 168
   PTSD counseling principles, 171
   resumption of normalcy, 168
   rituals, 167–68
   saying good-bye, 169
postvention strategies, 269–85
prevention strategies, 26–34, 135–36,
   255–67
psychological distress and developmental
   stages, 171–72
   reactions and symptomatology,
      164–70
      preschool child, 164–65
      elementary age, 165–66
      preteen and adolescent, 166–67
PTSD development, 160, 270–71
police role, 6
Thirteen Cs of Salutogenesis, 279–81,
   283–84
trauma sequence for construction of
   meaning, 230–39
   frame of reference for symptoms,
      231–32
   working through avoided, emotions,
      232–33
   existential questions and insight, 234
   personal growth, 234–35
   acceptance and farewell ritual, 235–36
traumatic event, 6
Psychotherapeutic intervention, 279–81
PTSD (Posttraumatic Stress Disorder) (*see also*
   Trauma; Trauma recovery)
   construction of meaning to trauma
      sequence, 230–39
   frame of reference for symptoms,
      231–32
   working through avoided, emotions,
      232–33
   existential questions and insight, 234
   personal growth, 234–35
   acceptance and farewell ritual, 235–36
   duty-related police death, 101, 139–56,
      215
      child view, 159–72
   early retirement, 65–66
   incidence in police officers, 5, 39, 65–74,

88–93, 216
previous trauma vulnerability, 65–74
recruit screening and selection, 65–74
special police units
    BATF, Waco, TX raid, 113–23
    South African police, 99–109
survivor guilt, 101, 139–56
symptoms
    amnesia, 101
    anger, 101
    avoidance, 6, 32, 100, 103–9
    depression, 101
    emotional numbing, 101, 107
    flashbacks, 101
    hyperaccessibility, 32
    hypervigilence, 100
    intrusive thoughts, 6, 32, 100, 103–9
    isolation, 83
    nightmares, 100
    sleep difficulties, 101
table 12.2, survivor PTSD symptoms, 144
table 18.1, treatment plan for PTSD
trauma exposure and posttraumatic growth, 272–75
treatment, 227–39
witness to violence and death, 5, 21, 25, 101, 227
    criminal suspect killed, 101
    line-of-duty death, 101, 139–56
    grief responses, 145
Public Health Model, 246–51

R

Race and job burnout, 60–61
Reactivity
    individual determinants, 17–18
    organizational determinants, 18
    risk takers and behavior addictions, 80–82
Recovery interventions or debriefings
    critical incident debriefing, 255–67
    group cohesion and identity, 32–33, 117–18, 122
    postvention strategies, 269–85
    receiving/seeking help re abilities, 27, 107, 116
    survivor groups, 190
    threat to perceived control, 27
Residual stress hypothesis, 82–83
Resilience, 273, 275, 276, 293

police applicant screening for resilience 47
    vulnerability and/or resilience, 177–78
Response and recovery management issues, 7, 8, 27, 135–36
Responsibility guilt, 120–21
Rest and relaxation strategies, 50 (*see also* Coping strategies)
Retirement
    early retirement, 65
    organizational stressors, 66
    planning to facilitate civilian life, 83
    retirement counseling, 250
    traumatic job stressors, 65–68
    vulnerability to trauma, 67–74
Risk homeostasis, 16
Risk status evaluation, 13–21
Rotating shifts, 40, 58

S

Safety, generalized notions, 16
Salience hierarchy of relationships, 91
Salutogenesis, 276–85
    critical incident stress debriefing, 269–85
    dynamic conceptualization of resilient adults, 275, 277
    resiliency, 275, 276
    salutogenic debrief, 278–85
        depersonalization, 278–79
        derealization, 278–79
        dissociation, 278–79
        salutogenic Cs/concepts, 279–81, 283
    salutogenic v. pathogenic approach, 276–85
        Oklahoma City bombing, 282
        overall mental health, 276
        13 Cs of salutogenesis, 283–84
    sanctuary, 280–81
    stress inoculation training, 278
    trauma and coherence, 276–85
        comprehensibility, 276–78
        manageability, 276–78
        meaningfulness, 276–78
Secondary Traumatic Stress (STS), 39, 43–46
also known as:
    countertransference, 43
    emotional contagion, 43
    proximity trauma, 43
    secondary survivor, 43

toxification of family, 43
vicarious traumatization, 43
burnout v. STS, 43–44
    helplessness and confusion, 43, 55
    isolation, 43
cost of caring, 43
familial involvement, 43–44
family burnout, 44
stress of helping traumatized person, 44
Secondary Traumatic Stress Disorder
    (STSD), 39
Self-blame, other-blame 26–28, 31
    attribution and recovery, 26–28
    perceived avoidability, 29, 30
    perceived control, 6, 25–34
    performance expectations, 31
    helper stereotype, 31–32
    withdrawal from police work, 31
Self-esteem
    burnout symptoms, 54–56
    perceived control, 6, 25–34
    receiving/seeking help re abilities, 27,
        107, 116
    self-blame, other-blame, 26–28
    survivor guilt, 146–47
    vulnerability, 27
Sense of achievement, strategies, 49
Sexual abuse and revictimization, 67–69
Simulations, training, 133–34
Social cognitive theories
    attributions and recovery, 26–34
        low/high control events, 27–28
        self-blame, other-blame, 26–28
    Compassion Satisfaction/Fatigue Self-Test
        for Helpers, 301–2
    counterfactual thinking, 6, 25, 29, 30
    childhood line-of-duty death of parent,
        159–72
    group support and identity, 32–33
    helper stereotype, 31–32
    learned helplessness, 27, 276
    performance expectations, 31, 33
    perceived avoidability, 29, 30
    perceived control, 6, 25–34
    survivor groups, 190
    trauma membrane, 189–90
    victimization and recovery, 25–34,
        135–36
        coping strategies, 6, 17, 26–28
        counterfactual thinking, 6, 25, 29, 30

event-related ideation and memories,
    26
outcome severity, 29
perceived avoidability, 29, 20
perceived control, 25–34
reconciliation and assimilation of emo-
    tion, 26
South African police
    boarding (medical retirement), 99–100
    duty-related trauma, 99, 105
    Internal Stability Unit, 99, 103–9
    PTSD, 100–9
        avoidance, 100, 103–9
        intrusive thoughts, 100, 103–9
        methodology of study, 103–9
    survivor guilt, 139–56
    stigma of seeking psychological help, 100,
        107, 116
    stress-related psychological disorders,
        99–100
    suicide rate, 100, 108
    trauma exposures, 99–101
    violent attacks on, 99
Special police populations
    South Africa, 99–109
Stress, baseline levels, 17
Stress, command level, 124–36 (*see also*
    Critical incident response)
Stress reduction methods, 47–50, 214–24 (*see
    also* Coping strategies)
Stress reactions and job separation, 82–85
    absence of support and stress reaction vul-
        nerability, 82
    detrimental pattern of residual trauma, 82
    loss of support resources, 82
    inability to form new relationships, 83
    residual stress hypothesis, 82–83
    trauma membrane, 82
STS (Secondary Traumatic Stress), 39
STSD (Secondary Traumatic Stress Dis-
    order), 39
Substance abuse, 5
Substance abuse intolerance, 48
Suicide, 5, 108, 183, 241–51 (*see also* Police
    suicide)
Suicide Trajectory model, 248
Survivors, line-of-duty death, 101, 139–56,
    159–72
    children, 159–72
Survivors of Homicide Victims, 153

T

Tactical Decision Making Under Stress (TADMUS), 129–30
Team work, coordination, 129–30 (*see also* Critical incident response)
Thirteen Cs of Salutogenesis, 279–81, 283–84
3:1 ratio rule, 47
Time and incident response stress, 126
Training and critical incident response, 133–35
Training needs analysis, 133–34
Trauma (*see also* PTSD)
   acute exposure, 78–79
   avoidance of emotional reactions, 32–33, 100, 103–9
   dependence reactions, 79
   childhood view of line-of-duty death, 159–72
   chronic exposure and behavioral addiction, 80–85
   continuity of self, 175–76
   intergenerational context, 176–77
     family legacies, 179–83
   predisposition to retraumatization, 67–69
   police, duty-related death, 139–56
     intergenerational legacies, 175–84
   posttraumatic growth, 272–75
   PTSD treatment, 227–39
   suicide, 183
   time span stages, 205–6
     impact period, 205
     warning period, 205
     recoil period, 205
     postimpact period, 205
   victimization and recovery, 25–34, 135–36
     coping strategies, 6, 17, 26–28
     counterfactual thinking, 6, 25, 29, 30
     event-related ideation and memories, 26
     outcome severity, 29
     perceived avoidability, 29, 20
     perceived control, 25–34
     reconciliation and assimilation of emotion, 26
   vulnerability and/or resilience, 177–78
   witness to violence and death, 5, 21, 25, 101, 227
Trauma membrane, 82, 189–90

Trauma, prevention of duty-related, 203–13
   case study of Pope AFB Green Ramp disaster, 206–13
   disasters, mass casualties, psychiatric support, 205–6
     primary prevention training, 207–8
     command consultation, 208
     secondary prevention, 209–12
       critical incident stress debriefing, 209, 255–67
       outreach to on-scene participants, 209–11
       outreach to families, community, 211–12
     tertiary prevention, 212
     after-action report, 212
   exposure differences/similarities between military and police, 203–6
   military training for trauma response, 204–6
     field training exercises, 205
     military medicine's mental health outreach, 204–5
   PTSD treatment, 227–39
Trauma Reaction Index, 140
Trauma recovery
   attributions and recovery, 26–34
     low/high control events, 27–28
     self-blame, other-blame, 26–28
   counterfactual thinking, 6, 25, 29, 30
   critical incident response, 135–36 (*see also* Traumatic stress)
   learned helplessness, 27, 276
   management styles, 135–36
   perceived avoidability, 29, 30
   perceived control, 6, 25–34
   survivor guilt, 139–56
   victimization and recovery, 25–34, 135–36
     coping strategies, 6, 17, 26–28
     counterfactual thinking, 6, 25, 29, 30
     event-related ideation and memories, 26
     outcome severity, 29
     perceived avoidability, 29, 30
     perceived control, 25–34
     reconciliation and assimilation of emotion, 26
Traumatic stress, 5, 6, 65–74 (*see also* Duty-related traumatic stress)

acute exposure, 78–79
childhood trauma, 67–69
chronic exposure and behavior addiction,
    80–85
critical incident response recovery,
    135–36
coping strategies, 214–24
duty related, 6, 17, 78–85
duty-related death, 101, 139–56
    child view, 159–72
policing stress, future issues, 293–97
prior civilian life incidents, 6, 65–74
survivor guilt, 101, 139–56
witness to violence and death, 5, 21, 25,
    101, 227
Traumatic stressors, 15–17
    childhood line-of-duty death of parent,
        159–72
    events transcending operational schema-
        ta, 15–16
    longitudinal analysis methodology, 19–21
    nature and intensity, 16
    recovery factors, 25–34, 135–36
Traumatology, 43–46
Tunnel vision, 132
21st century cop, 182–83

                    U

United Kingdom
    CIDB model, 258–59
        facts, 258
        feelings, 258
        future, 259
    Critical Incident Debriefing (CIDB)
        overview, 255–67
United Nations (*see also* CIVPOL)
    CIVPOL, 189, 191–99
    interpersonal violence, 192
    peacekeeping duties, 189, 191–99
    peacekeeping duty stressors
        alcohol use, 191
        inability to intervene in hostile actions,
            191
        military training, response suppres-
            sion, 191–92
        passive role, 191
        repatriation, 191
        suppressed aggressiveness, 191
        vulnerability, 191

                    V

Vicarious traumatization, 42
Victimization processes, 6, 13–21, 25–34
    avoidance of emotional reactions, 32–33,
        100, 103–9
    perceived intention, 28
    perceived likelihood of recurrence, 6, 21,
        25, 28–29
    predisposition to traumatization, 67–69
    survivor guilt, 101, 139–56
Vietnam Era Stress Inventory, 104
Vietnam veterans
    family trauma, 179–82
    exposure to war trauma, 101
    PTSD, 101
    witness to violence and trauma, 101
Violence and death, witness (*see* Witness to)
Violence, exposure to, 6, 21, 25, 99–109, 227
    line-of-duty death of parent, 159–72
Violence, support of victims, 5, 25, 102

                    W

Waco, TX
    Branch Davidian Compound and BATF
        raid, 113–23
Ways of Coping Questionnaire, 219
Witness to violence and death, 5, 21, 25,
    99–109, 227
    avoidance, 32–33, 100, 103–9
    criminal suspect killed, 101
    line-of-duty risk, 102, 139
    officer killed, 101, 139–56
    PTSD, 99–109
        treatment strategy, 227–39
    survivor guilt, 139–56
Work group attitudes v. PCF, 47–48
    coworker health and self care, 48
    critical incident stress debriefing plans, 48
    humor, 48
    substance abuse intolerance, 48
    3:1 ratio rule, 47
Work, letting go of, 49
Work, return to, 135–36
World policing, 8, 189–99
    Civilian Police Unit of the UN
        (CIVPOL), 180–99, 293
        Yugoslavian war zone, 189–99
    peacekeeping duties, 189–99

Y

Yugoslavia
    UN peacekeeping in war zone, 189–99, 293
        catastrophe planning, 195
        corruption, 195
        criminal activity, 196
        cross-cultural issues, 193

        driving skills, 194
        human rights abuses, 196
        language skills, 193
        living accommodations, 194
        multinational policing units, 192–99
        psychological reactions, 197–99
        snipers and landmines, 194
        weapons prohibition, 193